Being Measured

SUNY series in Ancient Greek Philosophy

Anthony Preus, editor

Being Measured

Truth and Falsehood
in Aristotle's *Metaphysics*

Mark R. Wheeler

Cover painting by Ana Guerra

Published by State University of New York Press, Albany

© 2019 State University of New York

All rights reserved

No part of this book may be used or reproduced in any manner whatsoever without written permission. No part of this book may be stored in a retrieval system or transmitted in any form or by any means including electronic, electrostatic, magnetic tape, mechanical, photocopying, recording, or otherwise without the prior permission in writing of the publisher.

For information, contact State University of New York Press, Albany, NY
www.sunypress.edu

Library of Congress Cataloging-in-Publication Data

Names: Wheeler, Mark Richard, 1966– author.
Title: Being measured : truth and falsehood in Aristotle's Metaphysics / Mark R. Wheeler.
Description: Albany, NY : State University of New York Press, [2019] | Series: SUNY series in ancient Greek philosophy | Includes bibliographical references and index.
Identifiers: LCCN 2018058255 | ISBN 9781438476858 (hardcover : alk. paper) | ISBN 9781438476841 (pbk. : alk. paper) | ISBN 9781438476865 (ebook)
Subjects: LCSH: Aristotle. Metaphysics. | Truth.
Classification: LCC B434 .W44 2019 | DDC 110—dc23
LC record available at https://lccn.loc.gov/2018058255

10 9 8 7 6 5 4 3 2 1

For Alix and Betsy

Contents

Acknowledgments   xi

Introduction: Stating the Puzzles   1
    The Knots   4
    My Approach to the *Metaphysics*   8

PART I
PHILOSOPHICAL WISDOM AND TRUTH

Chapter 1
The Demands of Philosophical Wisdom   17
    The Divine Science   23
    Hitting the Barn Door   26
    Being, Truth, and Causality   30
    The Beta Test   36
    Conclusion   39

PART II
TRUTH AND THE LOGICAL AXIOMS

Chapter 2
What "Truth" and "Falsehood" Signify   43
    The Canonical Definition of Truth in Context   45
    Kinds of Definition   52
    Arguing for the Axioms   57
    Aristotle's Fundamental Philosophical Semantics   60
    Aristotle's Opponents   68

The Nominal Definition of "Truth"	71
What the Nominal Definitions Entail	80
Conclusion	83

Chapter 3
The Nominal Definition of "Truth" and the Axioms	85
Truth and the Law of the Excluded Middle	86
Simple Assertions and Contradictory Pairs	88
Intermediate Assertions and LNC	94
The Elenctic Argument at 1011b23–29 and the Nominal Definitions	103
Conclusion	111

PART III
TRUTH AND BEING

Chapter 4
The Being of Truth	115
Truth is a Kind of Being	117
Being True is not Being a Kind of Object	124
Matthen's Proposal	139
Being a True Assertion	142
Truth and the Other Kinds of Being	148
Conclusion	152

Chapter 5
Aristotle's Homonymous Truth Bearers	153
The Homonymous Kinds of Truth and Falsehood	154
True and False Assertions	154
True and False Things	158
Aristotle's Core Kind of Truth and Falsehood	160
Conclusion	172

Chapter 6
The Genus of Truth	173
Identifying the Genus	173
The Category of the Genus of Truth	178
An Outstanding Problem: True Definitions of Essences	183
Conclusion	188

Chapter 7
The Activity of Truth — 191
   True Assertions about Simples — 191
   The Core Kind of Truth *Redux* — 201
   The Power and Activity of Truth — 208
   Conclusion — 221

Part IV
Truth and Measurement

Chapter 8
Truth, Oneness, and Measurement — 225
   The Extension of the Term "One" — 226
   The Intension of the Term "One" — 231
   Metaphysics Δ 6 on Oneness and Measure — 237
   Conclusion — 242

Chapter 9
The Ground of Truth — 245
   The Measure and the Measured — 245
   Aristotle's Measure Doctrine — 248
   Aristotle's Metrical Account of the Correspondence Relation — 250
   Aristotle's Asymmetrical Measurement Relation — 258
   Conclusion — 273

Conclusion: The Subsequent Free Play of Thought — 279

Notes — 287

Bibliography — 323

Index — 335

Index Locorum — 347

Acknowledgments

Many colleagues helped me to think through the ideas and arguments in this book. My chief debts are to Anne Ashbaugh (who first introduced me to Aristotle at Colgate) and to Deborah Modrak (who has been my vigilant Virgil since I began studying with her at Rochester).

The NEH funded two summer seminars for professors (FS-23299-02 and FS-50235-09), both of which I co-directed with Deborah Modrak, and both of which were focused on Aristotle's semantic theory. These seminars were ideal contexts for philosophical dialogue and research. I reaped more from, than I sowed among, the two groups of seminarians.

My colleagues at SDSU have offered support and inspiration. A sabbatical leave in 2003 helped me to begin the project. The members of my CAL writing group—Michael Borgstrom, Joanna Brooks, Victoria Gonzalez-Rivera, David Kamper, Irene Lara, and Kate Swanson—helped me to finish it.

Over the years I have presented parts of the book to various audiences. I am particularly grateful to Devin Henry, Blake Hestir, John Mourecade, and Rusty Jones for inviting me to participate in collegial workshops they hosted. The participants in those workshops graciously suffered very rough formulations of my arguments. Their feedback was invaluable.

I could not have written this book without the help offered by the following people: Prasanta Bandyopadhyay, John Bennett, Elizabeth Burbank, David Charles, Maudemarie Clark, Earl Connee, Randall Curren, Scot Danforth, Scott DeVito, Jeff Downard, Rolf Eberle, David Ebrey, Richard Feldman, Al Floyd, Rob Francescotti, Kelly Garneau, Devin Henry, Hud Hudson, Jonathan Jacobs, Kelly Jolley, Kimberly Kennelly, Richard Landsdowne, Steve Martin, Mike Mathias, Catherine McKeen, Keith McPartland, Ralf Meerbote, Fred Miller, Stan Miller, Darrel Moellendorf,

John Mourecade, Vince Ney, Art Pena, Jeffrey Poland, Jonathan Saville, Bill Schneider, Ravi Sharma, Clerk Shaw, Joe Smith, Nick Smith, Christine Thomas, John Thorp, Don Tittle, Pierre Vaughn, and Frank Willey.

I owe an extra debt of gratitude to Steve Barbone, J. C. Boyle, Travis Butler, Keitel Del Rosario, Michael Ferejohn, Dwight Furrow, Blake Hestir, Rusty Jones, Jordan Schummer, Joe Smith, Sean Tracy, Tom Weston, and three anonymous referees for SUNY Press, all of whom read and made comments on penultimate, antepenultimate, or somewhere-near-ultimate drafts of the manuscript.

It took a while to write the book. I wish my teachers Jerry Balmuth, Lewis White Beck, Henry E. Kyburg, Jr., and Huntington Terrell had lived to see it.

Some of the arguments developed in chapter 2 were published in "A Deflationary Reading of Aristotle's Definitions of Truth and Falsehood at *Metaphysics* 1011b26–27," *Apeiron*, vol. 44, June 2011, pp. 67–90 and "Aristotle's Canonical Definition of Truth is not a Real Definition of Truth," *History of Philosophy Quarterly*, Vol. 35, issue 1, Spring 2018. A version of chapter 4 is published as "Aristotle on Being True in *Metaphysics* v 7," *Ancient Philosophy*, vol. 39, Spring 2019, pp. 1–17. Some of the ideas in chapter 6 are related to the arguments in "The Parts of Definitions, Unity, and Sameness in Aristotle's Metaphysics: A Resolution of an Outstanding Problem for Aristotle's Theory of Definition," *The Journal of Neoplatonic Studies*, Volume II, Number II, 1994. I am grateful to these journals for permission to reproduce some of the material contained in these articles.

And a most enthusiastic thanks to Alix, Chris, Mom, and Dad!

Introduction

Stating the Puzzles

> For those who wish to get clear of the puzzles it is advantageous to state the puzzles well; for the subsequent free play of thought is attained by solving the puzzles raised in advance, and it is not possible to untie a knot which one does not know.
>
> —*Metaphysics* A 1.995a27–36
> (trans., mine, following Ross and Reeve)

No definitions of truth and falsehood are more well-known or more important to Western thought than those offered by Aristotle in *Metaphysics* book Γ 7 at 1011b26–27:

> δῆλον δὲ πρῶτον μὲν ὁρισαμένοις τί τὸ ἀληθὲς καὶ ψεῦδος. τὸ μὲν γὰρ λέγειν τὸ ὂν μὴ εἶναι ἢ τὸ μὴ ὂν εἶναι ψεῦδος, τὸ δὲ τὸ ὂν εἶναι καὶ τὸ μὴ ὂν μὴ εἶναι ἀληθές.
>
> This will be clear if we first define what truth is and what falsehood is. For to say of what is that it is not, or of what is not that it is, is false, whereas to say of what is that it is, and of what is not that it is not, is true. (trans., Reeve)

In this book, I argue that Aristotle presents these canonical definitions as part of a sustained and comprehensive account of the essence of truth in the *Metaphysics*. I take it this is not a humdrum assertion. No other commentator seems to agree with it—neither Aquinas nor Brentano do, both of whom think the being of truth is an important topic in the

Metaphysics; neither Crivelli nor Long do, whose books are the most comprehensive studies yet of Aristotle's theory of truth; nor do any of the leading contemporary commentators who attempt to assess the treatise taken as a unified whole—neither Aubenque, Halper, Jaeger, Mansion, Menn, Owens, Reale, Reeve, Ross, nor Wedin.

Aristotle not only explains carefully the nature of truth in the *Metaphysics*, he does so in a rigorously methodical fashion. Or so I think. When I say that Aristotle *methodically* develops his account of the essence of truth and falsehood in the *Metaphysics* I mean that the different parts of his account track the different phases of inquiry he thinks are involved in establishing the definition of an essence of a given object of study. Aristotle explains these phases of inquiry in *Posterior Analytics* B 10, in terms of what Charles has called "the three-stage view" of inquiry:[1]

[Stage 1] Knowing an account of what a term *t* signifies.

[Stage 2] Knowing that what *t* signifies exists.

[Stage 3] Knowing the essence of the kind signified by *t*.

I argue that in the *Metaphysics* Aristotle establishes what the term "truth" signifies, demonstrates that what it signifies exists, and explicates the essence of the kind signified by "truth."

It goes without saying that for Aristotle truth (ἀλήθεια) is important—fundamentally so.[2] Acquiring and retaining truth are the natural functions of the various modes of human cognition; truth is the final end of all human cognitive activity, practical and theoretical; it is the recognized lodestone for Aristotle's logical, natural scientific, mathematical, rhetorical, and poetic methods. Aristotle's understanding of truth drives his epistemology and informs his ethical theory both with regard to practical wisdom (which he thinks is essential for the virtues of character) and with regard to philosophical wisdom (which he thinks is essential for human flourishing). Perhaps these are commonplaces, but they imply that Aristotle's account of the nature of truth is crucial for comprehending his philosophical system.

Yet no one thinks that Aristotle systematically explained the nature of truth in any of the surviving works. Even Crivelli—who attributes to Aristotle a complex Neo-Fregean theory of truth—thinks all of Aristotle's claims about truth and falsehood in all of the treatises are no more than "asides":

> Aristotle speaks about truth and falsehood in passages from several works [. . .] Truth and falsehood are not the main topic of these works: their discussions of truth and falsehood are asides. Reconstructing an Aristotelian theory of truth and falsehood on the basis of such asides poses complicated problems of various sorts.[3] (Crivelli 2004, 1)

Modrak, who has offered a careful reconstruction of Aristotle's account of truth, agrees with Crivelli. She views the various claims Aristotle makes about truth and falsehood as an "array of remarks," and goes so far as to say that Aristotle leaves the notion of truth undefined in the treatises:

> In short, Aristotle has many things to say about truth but leaves the notion of truth undefined. Faced with this array of remarks, an interpreter might despair of finding a core conception of truth here at all. This would be a mistake, I believe, for Aristotle's various remarks on the topic of truth give expression to a coherent and interesting, underlying conception of truth. (Modrak 2001, 55)

Crivelli and Modrak represent the received view: Aristotle nowhere explains his account of truth in a methodical fashion.

As the quotes from Crivelli and Modrak also indicate, however, commentators nevertheless believe Aristotle said enough about truth and falsehood in the various treatises to give us reasonable grounds for thinking we can reconstruct his theory. As proof of this, in the last twenty years a number of commentators have developed sophisticated reconstructions of Aristotle's theory of truth and falsehood.[4] Crivelli's *Aristotle on Truth* (2004) is surely the most impressive and extensive of these efforts. Crivelli offers a comprehensive reconstruction of Aristotle's theory of truth and falsehood using the methods and concepts of analytic philosophy, methods and concepts rooted ultimately in the semantic theories developed by Frege and Russell. Long's *Aristotle on the Nature of Truth* (2011) is similarly comprehensive in its scope. Long adopts what I can only describe as a rhapsodic approach to Aristotle's account of truth, using a heterogeneous mix of concepts and methods derived from both the phenomenological tradition (grounded in the works of Husserl and Heidegger) and the pragmatist tradition in America (emphasizing the ideas of John Dewey, John Herman Randall, George Santayana, and

Frederick Woodbridge). In her *Aristotle's Theory of Meaning and Language* (2001), Modrak develops her interpretation of Aristotle's theory of truth in the light of his account of language, his general semantic theory, and his general ontology. In her earlier book, *The Power of Perception* (1987), she had established the groundwork for the cognitive dimension of her interpretation of Aristotle's semantic theory. Charles, in *Aristotle on Meaning and Essence* (2000), attributes to Aristotle a theory of meaning that has obvious bearing on his account of truth. Recently, Charles and Peramatzis, in "Aristotle on Truth Bearers" (2016), have offered a careful reading of most of the crucial passages concerning truth in Aristotle's *Metaphysics*, defending *contra* Crivelli an interpretation of Aristotle's account of truth bearers. Hestir has produced a series of excellent articles on Plato's and Aristotle's conceptions of truth. His recent book on Plato's theory of meaning, *Plato on the Metaphysical Foundations of Meaning and Truth* (2016), offers a chapter on Aristotle's account of truth. In various articles, Pritzl has drawn on Aquinas's account of truth in order to make sense of Aristotle's conception, at the same time remaining alert to both analytic and phenomenological concerns.[5] In his two-volume work, *Aristotle: Semantics and Ontology* (2002), De Rijk includes some discussion of Aristotle's claims about truth and falsehood. All of these recent perspectives offer valuable insights, and I have benefitted enormously from the careful work done by these colleagues.

The Knots

In making my case I need to untie some tight knots. The first is the tangle created by the different kinds of truth and falsehood Aristotle recognizes in the *Metaphysics*. Aristotle works with more than one conception of truth in the treatise. None of these notions are straightforward, nor is it clear how they are related. The second knot is the skein binding Aristotle's account of truth to the main lines of thought in the *Metaphysics*. Aristotle's defense of philosophical wisdom, his vindication of the logical axioms, and his theory of being are among the major achievements of the treatise. It is not evident how, or even *that*, his account of truth is related to these accomplishments. The third knot is the twist of problems that arise when we attempt to relate Aristotle's conceptions of truth to the various ways in which we now conceive of truth. My aim in this work is to untie the first knot, to loosen the second, and to suggest how to approach the third.

What, then, are the different kinds of truth in the *Metaphysics*? How are they related? How do the different kinds of truth inform the main lines of thought in the *Metaphysics*? What, in the end, is Aristotle's considered account of truth? And is his account still relevant?

The answers I offer to these questions differ from existing proposals in various ways. Contrary to the received view, I argue that Aristotle presents and systematically explicates his *definition* of the essence of the truth in the *Metaphysics*. He states the nominal definitions of the terms "truth" and "falsehood" in *Metaphysics* book Γ as part of his elenctic arguments in defense of the logical axioms. These nominal definitions express conceptions of truth and falsehood his philosophical opponents would have recognized and accepted in the context of dialectical argument. On the basis of these nominal definitions, in *Metaphysics* books E–I Aristotle develops his definitions of the essences of truth and falsehood—his real definitions of truth and falsehood—and in so doing he relies upon the various philosophical distinctions he makes in books E–I. Aristotle's methodical exposition of his essential definitions of truth and falsehood in the *Metaphysics* serve as a well-developed example of how his philosophical inquiry starts with nominal definitions and ends with real definitions.

Recognizing that Aristotle explicitly acknowledges different kinds of truth and falsehood in the *Metaphysics*, I argue that in each case the different kinds are so-called "homonyms"—i.e., the kinds that share the same name, but not the same essence. Moreover, the different kinds of truth are "core-dependent" homonyms (adopting Shields's way of putting it in Shields 1999): the different kinds of truth share the same name because there is one kind, the "core" kind of truth, on which all the others depend. Likewise with the different kinds of falsehood. *Pace* Crivelli, I argue that for Aristotle the sort of truth and falsehood that belongs to linguistic and mental assertions is the core kind of truth and falsehood. Although Aristotle acknowledges a sort of truth and falsehood that properly belongs to beings in the world—a kind of objectual truth—he does not think this sort of truth and falsehood is fundamental.

Having identified Aristotle's core kind of truth, I argue that he *defines* the most fundamental kind of truth in terms of accurate measurement. So far as I know, this is a novel interpretive claim. Aristotle's metrical conception of truth serves as the theoretical basis for specifying the truth conditions of various assertions (the primary sort of truth bearers), for identifying the sorts of beings implicated in these truth conditions (the various sorts of truth-makers), and for explaining the nature of approximate truth and falsehood. Thus, *pace* Long, it turns out that the chief value of truth, for Aristotle, is theoretical and not practical.

Owens warned us that "to approach Aristotle with a thesis is a sure way of courting disaster." (Owens 1978, 11) When I began this project I did not think the *Metaphysics* contained Aristotle's methodical explanation of the essence of truth. I was mainly interested in understanding his account of linguistic truth, mining passages in the *Metaphysics* to this end. I assumed that, once I understood Aristotle's account of linguistic truth, it would be fairly straightforward to explain his account of doxastic truth in terms of it, and easier still to make sense of (and explain away) his talk of objectual truth. This was the thesis with which I initially approached Aristotle's treatise. I placed weight on the canonical definitions of truth and falsehood presented by Aristotle in *Metaphysics* Γ 7, 1011b26–27, but I thought these were presented in passing as part of his defense of the logical axioms and *not* as an integral part of a methodical discussion of the nature of truth that stretched through the treatise. I also discounted the relationship among the other passages in the *Metaphysics* having to do with truth—Δ 7, Δ 29, E 4, and Θ 10—all of which initially appeared to me to be mere amplifications of Aristotle's theory of linguistic and doxastic truth. I ignored altogether what Aristotle had to say about oneness and measurement in the treatise. Having courted disaster, I have abandoned my intial approach.

If we consider synoptically Aristotle's claims about truth in the *Metaphysics*, we can discern the following outline. In books A, α, B, Γ 1–3 (and the corresponding chapters in book K), he explains why truth is fundamental to his inquiry in the *Metaphysics*. Then, in Γ 3–8 and the corresponding chapters in K, he presents (so-called "nominal") definitions of what the terms "truth" and "falsehood" signify, arguing that truth and falsehood so understood exist, and using these nominal definitions to demolish arguments that might be brought against the logical axioms that serve as the starting points for all rational inquiry. Next, in book Δ, chapters 7 and 29, Aristotle differentiates among a number of different kinds of truth and falsehood. He demonstrates that the terms "truth" and "falsehood" denoting these different kinds are *pros hen* equivocal, or alternatively, that the terms are related in virtue of sharing a focal meaning, or—as I will prefer to say, following Shields 1999 and Ward 2008—that the different kinds of truth and falsehood themselves constitute a core-dependent field of homonyms. Lastly, Aristotle explicates his account of the essence of the core kind of truth, the kind of truth that belongs to acts of assertion.⁶ In books E, Z, H, and Θ, he relates the being of true assertion to the other kinds of being, articulating the relationship between his account of the essence of truth and his account of οὐσία, and he explicates his full account of the essence of truth in terms of his accounts of substance, potentiality, and actuality. In so doing, he presents his "real" definition of the essence of truth, using it to distinguish among various kinds of truth and explaining how these different kinds of truth are related to each other. In books I, M, and N, he completes his account of the essence of truth by explaining the relationship between acts of assertion and acts of measurement.

In chapter 1, I examine the relationship between Aristotle's understanding of philosophical wisdom and his account of truth. I argue that in *Metaphysics* book A he defines philosophical wisdom and the purpose of philosophical inquiry in terms of true assertions about the most important principles and causes. Then I explain how, in books α, B, and Γ 1–3, he summarizes the main problems concerning truth that must be solved in order to acquire philosophical wisdom.

In chapters 2 and 3, I argue that the definitions of the terms "truth" and "falsehood" presented in Γ 7.1011b26–27 are nominal definitions (not "real" definitions). Everyone agrees that Aristotle defines the notion of truth at *Metaphysics* Γ 7.1011b26–27. This much at least, but perhaps at most, is uncontroversial. What is controversial is the status of the definition. Does Aristotle present it as his considered account of the essence of truth—his real definition of truth? Or does he offer it as an account of the meaning of the term "truth"—a nominal definition of the term—an account his philosophical opponents might be willing to grant in the context of dialectical debate?

In the subsequent chapters, I argue that Aristotle methodically presents his definition of the essence of truth as an important part of his theory of being. I begin with *Metaphysics* book Δ, chapter 7, where Aristotle distinguishes among various kinds of being, and I argue that he identifies truth as a kind of being, one he compares with coincidental being, categorial being, and the being of potentiality and actuality. I turn next to book Δ, chapter 29, where Aristotle differentiates among various kinds of truth and falsehood, and I argue that these homonymous kinds of truth depend upon one another and that the kind of truth that belongs to assertions, the kind identified in Δ 7, is the most fundamental or core kind of truth.

My assessment of Δ 7 and Δ 29 leads naturally to Aristotle's discussion of truth in *Metaphysics* book E, chapter 4, where, I argue, he identifies the genus of his core conception of truth, explaining the potential for truth in terms of the capacity for psychological acts of affirmation and denial. He also differentiates the being of truth from coincidental being and shows that the being of truth depends upon, and is posterior to, categorial being.

Having identified the genus of his core conception of truth, Aristotle carefully articulates its differential characterstics in *Metaphysics* books Z, H, and Θ, establishing along the way the importance of truth for his theory of substance. Although it is well known that in books Z and H Aristotle solves various problems for his account of the definitions of essences, I argue that these semantic problems are best understood in terms of the requirements imposed by his understanding of truth. I go on to defend a reading of book Θ according to which Aristotle is concerned to use the concepts of power and activity in order to explain the nature of rational activity and, hence, truth. In book Θ, chapter 10, Aristotle completes his definition of the essence of truth and provides the basis for his subsequent claim in book Λ that the complete activity of truth is the most fundamental and important activity there is.

Lastly, on the basis of the distinctions Aristotle has made in books Γ–Θ, I argue that in *Metaphysics* book I Aristotle completes the exposition of his real definition of truth in terms of oneness and accurate measurement. This discussion of truth and measurement removes the veil of ignorance that shrouds our understanding of how he conceived of the intrinsic relation between acts of assertion and the beings in the world in virtue of which such assertions are true or false. The discussion of truth in book I also informs a proper reading of *Metaphysics* books M and N, where Aristotle extends his accounts of being, truth, and measurement to the question of mathematical substances.

My Approach to the *Metaphysics*

I will defend the view that Aristotle's account of the essence of truth is one of the philosophical ligaments that binds his thought in the *Metaphysics*. I approach each part of the *Metaphysics* as an autonomous whole first. Then I compare each part with those already considered. In the end, I assess the coherence of all the parts taken together. I do not assume that Aristotle himself or any of the editors of the treatise *intended* the various parts of the treatise to be read together. Rather, I look to see whether or not they can be read together profitably, and I argue that they can be—at least with regard to his theory of truth.

It might be thought that there are no "main projects" in the *Metaphysics*. This could mean there is no single project that unifies all of the different books of the *Metaphysics*, or that there is no project that unifies many, some, or even one of the books of the *Metaphysics*. I am not moved by any of these hypotheses. Alternatively, one might think that there is at least one project (maybe more) that unifies all or some of the different parts of the *Metaphysics*. I follow a number of recent commentators—and the majority of commentators in the ancient and medieval periods—who think that we ought to read the *Metaphysics* as a unified philosophical work. But even if the *Metaphysics* is best understood as a unified philosophical work, it may be that Aristotle's account of the essence of truth is not a part (or is not an important part) of the project. The majority of commentators maintain some version of this hypothesis, and I reject it.

Some readers may think my approach to the *Metaphysics* is naïve; others may think it hopeless. It might be judged naïve because it presupposes an illegitimate hermeneutic, namely, reading the *Metaphysics* as a unified whole. It might be considered hopeless because of the (seeming) conspicuous lack of evidence for one of my main contentions: Is it not as clear as day that truth is at best a minor topic in the *Metaphysics*? Let me address both charges, beginning with the allegation that it is jejune to read the *Metaphysics* as a unified philosophical work.

Although my reading does assume that the *Metaphysics* can be read as a unified whole, I do not presuppose that Aristotle intended it to be read as such, or that the editor(s) of the treatise—if other than Aristotle—intended this. The books that constitute the *Metaphysics* are a set of manuscripts the authenticity, unity, and title of which have been challenged.[7] If we assume that all of the parts of the *Metaphysics* were written by or at least edited by Aristotle himself, and I do, then it is likely that he wrote the different parts at times between 368/7 BCE (when he is thought to have entered Plato's Academy) and 323 BCE (when he died in Chalcis). This puts roughly two thousand three hundred years between us and the time when Aristotle may have written the various parts of the *Metaphysics*. I doubt we will ever know the ultimate origins of the various parts of the *Metaphysics*, or who authored them and with what intentions, or how and why they were organized as they are in the extant manuscripts. No one thinks Aristotle fashioned the title.[8] As noted above, some challenge the philosophical unity of the treatise.[9] To explain the putative lack of unity, some have challenged the authenticity of various parts of the treatise, while others have argued that different parts of the treatise—while properly attributed to Aristotle—represent different and conflicting phases of his philosophical development.[10] These are important worries, but we shouldn't let these mysteries impede our efforts to make sense of the ideas and arguments in the treatise as we have received it.

At least since Jaeger's 1912 *Entstehungsgeschichte der Metaphysik des Aristoteles*, scholars have been far less likely to approach the treatise as a unified work.[11] According to Jaeger:

> It is totally inadmissible to treat the elements combined in the *corpus metaphysicum* as if they were a unity, and to set up, for purposes of comparison, the average result of these entirely heterogeneous materials. As I have shown in another place [*Entstehungsgeschichte der Metaphysik des Aristoteles*], internal analysis leads to the view that various periods are represented, and this is confirmed by the tradition that the collection known as the *Metaphysics* was not put together until after its author's death. (Jaeger 1934, 168)

Jaeger's admonition had considerable force on the philosophical community, but enthusiasm for his approach had begun to wane already by the middle of the last century. Nevertheless, many contemporary commentators still interpret the different parts of the treatise as independent contributions to Aristotle's philosophy, often dismissing or ignoring either the relationship between the various parts of the treatise or the relationship between these parts and the whole.[12]

Following Reale, we can distinguish between the literary unity of the treatise and its philosophical unity. I am interested here only in the latter. I do not attempt to show that the different sections of the treatise, as they are now arranged, constitute a unified literary work.[13] Although cognizant of the textual difficulties Jaeger and others have identified, I follow Ross in thinking that *Metaphysics* books A, B, Γ, E, Z, H, Θ, I, M, and N constitute a more or less continuous work, and accept his reasoning with respect to the "outlying" books α, Δ, K, and Λ. To be clear, however, I take very seriously Jaeger's point that:

> On no account must we, by assuming that it [the *Metaphysics*] is philosophically homogeneous, cover up the problems which its content as well as its form presents at every step. We must reject all attempts to make a literary whole out of the remaining materials by rearranging or removing some of the

books, and we must condemn the assumption which overhastily postulates their philosophical unity at the expense of their individual peculiarities. (Jaeger 1934, 170)

The arguments I present aim to advance our understanding of how Aristotle's investigation of truth in the *Metaphysics* informs the various sections of the treatise taken separately, taken in relation to each other, and taken as parts of a unified whole. My chief concern is to show that the various parts of the treatise concerned with truth constitute a carefully executed and systematic account of the nature of truth. I don't claim that my proposed reading is the only way to read the treatise. The treatise has been read profitably with an eye to Aristotle's theory of being (Owens), his theory of substance (Wedin), of first philosophy (Reale), of first principles (Menn), of the one and the many (Halper), et cetera. I do think, however, that my proposed reading is viable. Even Jaeger would condone the effort I undertake here. My goals are consonant with his proviso about the strength of his own conclusions:

> I have shown in my *Ent Metaph Artst* (pp. 15.ff) that Aristotle's treatises arose by the combination of isolated and self-contained monographs . . . This does not mean that there is never an idea uniting a large group of such monographs, or that their relationship is one of loose juxtaposition in thought as well as in expression. It is simply an aid to the understanding of the way in which Aristotle's 'works' were composed and it enables us to explain their incoherences and apparent irrelevancies by recalling the philosopher's manner of working and teaching. (Jaeger 1934, n3)

I turn now to the charge that my approach to the treatise is hopeless because there is no evidence that truth is an important topic in the *Metaphysics*. I have already outlined above my main reasons for rejecting this accusation, but let me offer some additional reasons to diminish despair.

First, some explanation of the nature of truth is essential to Aristotle's main purpose in the *Metaphysics*. One of the goals of his investigation in the *Metaphysics* is to specify fully, and to secure, philosophical wisdom. Philosophical wisdom, as he conceives of it in the *Metaphysics* and elsewhere, is a special sort of knowledge. He defines it in terms of truth: philosophical wisdom is the comprehension of *true* first principles combined with the capacity to demonstrate *true* conclusions from these first principles. Aristotle explicitly makes this point about philosophical wisdom. It is also entailed by what he says about comprehension and demonstrative understanding.[14] He defines all these forms of cognition in terms of truth. As a consequence, he must tell us what truth is if he is to have a reasonable hope of persuading us that he has specified fully, and has secured, philosophical wisdom. But when we look to what Aristotle says about truth in treatises other than the *Metaphysics* it becomes clear that, while he does provide us with important insights into the nature of truth in some of these, he has not undertaken to explain the nature of truth in any treatise other than the *Metaphysics*. Therefore, unless we wish to conclude that we simply do not have his account of the essence of truth, we should expect to find it in the *Metaphysics*. I think we do.

A second reason why we should expect Aristotle to explain the nature of truth in the *Metaphysics* is that his defense of the logical axioms in book Γ (and again in book K) crucially depends upon the definitions of truth and falsehood presented in Γ 7. I will make the case for the latter claim in part II. Given that Aristotle has not explained the nature of truth outside of the *Metaphysics*, he needs to explain it in the *Metaphysics* if he hopes to adequately vindicate the logical axioms.[15]

A third reason to expect that Aristotle will explain the nature of truth in the *Metaphysics* is that truth is among the basic kinds of being he takes seriously in the treatise.[16] His theory of being is one of the major achievements of the *Metaphysics*. The central claims of this theory explain the being in-itself of the categorial schemata, the nature of coincidental being, the being of potentiality and actuality, and the being of truth. The most widely discussed part of the theory of being is Aristotle's account of substance [οὐσία]—and the related concepts of essence [τὸ τί ἦν εἶναι], definition [ὁρίσμος], and the formula of the essence [λόγος τοῦ τί ἦν εἶναι]. Yet, in order to provide a complete account of being, he needs to explain the nature of the other kinds of being, the being of truth included. He does. I make the case for this in part III.

A fourth and final reason why we should expect Aristotle to explain the nature of truth in the *Metaphysics* is that his unmovable first mover—his God [ὁ θεός]—always actualizes, by virtue of its very nature, truth. This point may not be obvious. It is prima facie plausible that in the *Metaphysics* Aristotle considers his God to be the most important first principle and substance, and that his God is thus the proper object of philosophical wisdom. He is quite emphatic about these points in *Metaphysics* A 2. Subsequently, in book Λ, Aristotle defines the essence of his God as the perfect actuality of thought thinking thought. While this idea is hardly transparent, no one doubts that Aristotle's God is the perfect realization of contemplative activity [θεωρία] or that this contemplative activity essentially involves truth. Given this way of understanding God's nature, and assuming that Aristotle has not explained the nature of truth in any treatise other than the *Metaphysics*, he needs to explain the nature of truth in the treatise in order to satisfactorily account for the proper *object* of philosophical wisdom. He does not disappoint us on this score, or so I will maintain.

Taken together these reasons constitute good evidence for thinking that Aristotle will explain the nature of truth in the *Metaphysics*. Of course, the *Metaphysics* is not devoted exclusively to the topic of truth—other major topics include Aristotle's criticisms of his predecessor's views on causality, his conception of the science of being, his defense of the logical axioms, his exploration of the homonymous nature of being, his theory of substance, his theology, and the status of mathematical objects. But this should not obscure the fact that truth is an important topic in the treatise. If my reading accurately tracks Aristotle's reasoning about truth in the *Metaphysics*, then to that extent the various parts of the treatise present a well-integrated set of arguments concerning truth. My reading also entails that truth is among the more important topics in the *Metaphysics*.

Part I

Philosophical Wisdom and Truth

Chapter 1

The Demands of Philosophical Wisdom

In books A, α, and B, Aristotle announces his principal purpose in the *Metaphysics*—to investigate philosophical wisdom—and he prepares us for this investigation. Truth emerges early on as an important element in the investigation. In all three books, Aristotle identifies difficulties that can only be resolved through an understanding of the nature of truth.

Aristotle begins *Metaphysics* A with a summary overview of his own previously expressed views about philosophical wisdom. He reviews and refines common opinions and his predecessor's views about philosophical wisdom. He details the difficulties involved in discerning philosophical wisdom, and he identifies the two main parts of his investigation into it in the *Metaphysics*: a defense of the first principles of argument and an inquiry into the first principles and causes of being insofar as it is being. The rest of the *Metaphysics* is devoted to these two efforts.

Aristotle's first statement in the *Metaphysics*—that all human beings by nature yearn to know [πάντες ἄνθρωποι τοῦ εἰδέναι ὀρέγονται φύσει]—identifies a principal theme of the treatise: knowledge. In the first chapter of book A, Aristotle digests the genetic relations among (and the comparative cognitive worth of) sensory perceptions, memories, experience, art, demonstrative understanding, and philosophical wisdom. By the end of the first chapter of book A, at 982a1–3, Aristotle has focused our attention on the species of knowledge he hopes to investigate in the treatise: philosophical wisdom.

Aristotle's lead assertion in the *Metaphysics* is not a throwaway line. Our love of wisdom is a species of our natural yearning to know: we could not love wisdom if we lacked the natural capacity to desire knowledge. As Aristotle would put it, we are by our very nature moved to know. But for what purpose do we yearn [ὀρέγονται] to know? Aristotle has a ready answer—we yearn to know because we crave truth.

Someone might think that human beings seek truth in order to acquire knowledge and that we pursue knowledge—not truth—for its own sake. Philosophers, on this view, are first and foremost lovers of knowledge and not lovers of truth. This is not Aristotle's view. Aristotle does grant the unexceptionable point that truth is a constitutive part of the essence of knowledge: no truth, no knowledge. And he would not wish to deny that we desire to know *only if* we desire truth.[1] But Aristotle does not think we pursue truth because it is a means to knowledge. He reverses the order of this explanation: according to Aristotle, we desire knowledge *for the sake of* possessing truth. Truth is the final cause—the τέλος—of knowledge. Knowledge is prized because it is a stable way of having truth. Philosophical wisdom is a particularly valuable kind of knowledge because it is the most secure way to possess truth and because it involves truth about the most important things.

Let me provide some justification for these claims. In distinguishing the modes of human cognition in *Metaphysics* A 1, Aristotle refers us to the more elaborate taxonomy he articulates in book VI of the *Nicomachean Ethics*. There, at 1139b15–17, Aristotle lists philosophical wisdom among the five ways the psyche possesses truth by means of affirmation and denial: technical knowledge [τέχνη], demonstrative knowledge [ἐπιστήμη], practical wisdom [φρόνησις], philosophical wisdom [σοφία], and noetic comprehension [νοῦς]. Each of these modes of cognition, according to Aristotle, essentially involves the psyche possessing truth by means of acts of assertion. Two consequences of this fact are fundamentally important to our discussion of truth in the *Metaphysics*.

First, Arisotle understands all of the modes of knowledge in terms of psychological acts of true assertion. In the passage from the *Nicomachen Ethics*, Aristotle explicitly specifies the genus of knowledge. Knowledge is, generically, the activity of the psyche by means of which it possesses truth by way of affirmation and denial. Each of the five kinds of knowledge listed at *NE* VI.1139b15–17 and subsequently defined in *NE* VI are species of this genus—each is a different way that the psyche possesses truth by means of acts of assertion. Therefore, understanding the nature of the kind of truth that belongs to assertions is essential to understanding the nature of the various species of knowledge.

Second, it is important that *philosophical wisdom* is one of the ways the psyche possesses truth by means of acts of assertion. Aristotle distinguishes the various species of knowledge in *Nicomachean Ethics* book VI by differentiating among the acts of assertion they involve (acts of definition, acts of demonstration, etc.) and among the kinds of objects these acts of assertion are about (necessary beings, non-necessary beings, etc.). He defines philosophical wisdom in *NE* VI 7, first at 1141a18–20 and then again at 1141b2–3. He tells us that it is "demonstrative knowledge combined with noetic comprehension, of the things that are highest by nature." He explains demonstrative knowledge in *NE* VI 3. Demonstrative knowledge is a psychological capacity to demonstrate, from first principles, true assertions about necessary beings. Demonstration itself is the activity of the psyche asserting affirmations or denials (the conclusions of demonstrations) on the basis of other affirmations or denials it has asserted (the premises of the demonstrations) all of which demonstrative activity involves the psyche possessing truth by means of acts of assertion. Aristotle defines noetic comprehension in *NE* VI 6. Noetic comprehension as a state in which the psyche grasps [λείπεται] the first principles of demonstrative knowledge. A first principle of demonstrative knowledge is a definition that expresses the essence of the subject matter known. These definitions are a kind of assertion. When the psyche grasps the first principles of demonstrative knowledge, it does not grasp them on the basis of other assertions—its grasp of first principles is not mediated by other acts of assertion. In cases of noetic comprehension, the psyche immediately grasps the nature of essences by means of acts of true assertion. When the psyche grasps principles in this way, Aristotle tells us, it possesses truth [ἀληθεύομεν] and it never has falsehood [διαψευδόμεθα].

These relatively terse accounts of philosophical wisdom, demonstrative knowledge, and noetic comprehension in book VI of the *Nicomachean Ethics* recapitulate the gist of the extended discussions of these sorts of knowledge in the *De Anima* and the *Analytics*, to which latter work Aristotle explicitly refers us at *Nicomachean Ethics* VI.1139b31ff. The *Posterior Analytics* confirms that true assertion is essential to Aristotle's accounts of demonstrative knowledge and noetic comprehension and, hence, his conception of philosophical wisdom. That true assertion is essential to all forms of knowledge is also evident from Aristotle's account of sensory perception and thinking in *De Anima* III. There Aristotle tells us that when the psyche perceives and thinks—which latter activity includes all of the species of knowing—it discriminates by means of assertions which are either true or false.

Aristotle also develops his logical methods in order to secure truth. We have just seen how Aristotle's methods of demonstration and definition employ and aim at true assertions. Aristotle defines both demonstration and definition in terms of affirmative and negative assertions (see *APr.* I 1.24a10–b17; *APo.* I 1.71b17–26; *Top.* I.1.100a27–30) which he in turn defines in terms of truth and falsehood (see *Int.* 4.17a2–3 and 6.17a25–6). Aristotle defines dialectic as a method for reasoning without contradiction about generally accepted beliefs (see *Top.* I.1.100a18–21). Since Aristotle defines contradiction in terms of affirmative and negative assertions and, hence, in terms of truth and falsehood (see *Int.* 17a31–35), he understands the method of dialectic in terms of truth and falsehood, and one of the chief aims of dialectic—as specified in the *Topics*—is to secure true first principles. Aristotle also defines rhetoric (at least insofar as it is concerned with enthymemes made up of affirmative and negative assertions) in terms of true and false assertion and, hence, in terms of truth.

Aristotle thus conceives of philosophical wisdom, demonstrative knowledge, and noetic comprehension in terms of psychological acts of true assertion. True assertion is also constitutive of the remaining modes of knowledge, the sensory modalities, memory, and experience.[2] We need to understand the nature of true assertion, then, if we wish to understand the nature of philosophical wisdom.

In summary, from what Aristotle tells us in the *Metaphysics* and other treatises, he conceives of philosophical wisdom as follows:

> Philosophical wisdom is a state of the psyche wherein, by means of affirmation or denial, (1) it noetically comprehends, and is never deceived about, the first principles and causes of the necessary beings that are by nature highest and (2) it has the capacity to demonstrate on the basis of these first principles.

Philosophical wisdom, therefore, is essentially a complex state of the psyche in which noetic comprehension of true definitions about things that are highest by nature is combined with the power to demonstrate from these other true assertions about those same things. The noetic acts of assertion partly constitutive of philosophical wisdom are acts by means of which the psyche immediately possesses truth about the essences of the things that are highest by nature. These are the first principles or the immediate definitions of essence that the psyche noetically comprehends. The power to demonstrate other true assertions about the things highest by nature—which power is constitutive of the remaining part of philosophical wisdom—is the psyche's potential to possess true assertions, mediated by means of inferential acts of assertion, about those same things.

Aristotle is thus quite explicit about the relationship between philosophical wisdom and truth in the various treatises where he has already discussed the cognitive powers constitutive of philosophical wisdom—noetic comprehension and demonstrative knowledge. In the first chapter of *Metaphysics* book A he harks us back to those other discussions before undertaking the difficult work of explaining what was left unexplained by those earlier discussion: What are the things highest by nature, i.e., what is substance, and which are the first principles and causes of substance that are the proper objects of philosophical wisdom? And how is noetic comprehension of the true definitions about these highest things, and how is demonstration from these true definitions, possible, i.e., how are the true assertions about the essences of the proper objects of philosophical wisdom possible?

Even this much reveals the importance of truth for Aristotle's account of philosophical wisdom. But he gives truth a more exalted status than merely being a part of the essence of philosophical wisdom. Truth, he tells us, is the natural purpose and the ultimate good of philosophical wisdom—truth is the final cause of philosophical wisdom.

In the *Nicomachean Ethics* VI 1, at 1139a27–31, after summarizing his discussions of the differences between the excellences of character and the excellences of the intellect—in *Nicomachean Ethics* I 13 and II 1—Aristotle lays out his view that truth is the proper function and the good of the intellect:

> τῆς δὲ θεωρητικῆς διανοίας καὶ μὴ πρακτικῆς μηδὲ ποιητικῆς τὸ εὖ καὶ κακῶς τἀληθές ἐστι καὶ ψεῦδος (τοῦτο γάρ ἐστι παντὸς διανοητικοῦ ἔργον)· τοῦ δὲ πρακτικοῦ καὶ διανοητικοῦ ἀλήθεια ὁμολόγως ἔχουσα τῇ ὀρέξει τῇ ὀρθῇ.

> Of the theoretical intellect, and not the practical nor the productive intellect, the good and the bad state are truth and falsehood (for this [truth and falsehood] is the function of everything intellectual); while of the practical and intellectual the good state is truth in agreement with right desire. (trans., mine, following Ross)

Here Aristotle emphasizes that the function of everything intellectual is to secure the truth. As a consequence, the function (or work) of the contemplative intellect is truth, and the good state of the theoretical intellect is truth. Then, on the basis of these claims, he explains at *NE* 1139b12–13 why a given state of the intellect is an excellence: it is an excellence of the intellect *because* it enables the intellect to realize truth:

> ἀμφοτέρων δὴ τῶν νοητικῶν μορίων ἀλήθεια τὸ ἔργον. καθ' ἃς οὖν μάλιστα ἕξεις ἀληθεύσει ἑκάτερον, αὗται ἀρεταὶ ἀμφοῖν.

> The function, then, of both parts of the intellect is truth. Therefore, the states that best enable each part to secure the truth are the excellences of both parts. (trans., mine, following Ross)

Aristotle here repeats that the function (or work) of the intellect—whether theoretical or practical—is truth. He infers that those states (or habits[3]) that "secure truth" [ἀληθεύσει] are the excellences of the intellect. In other words, the virtues of the intellect aim at truth.

He makes the same point in the *Eudemian Ethics*. First, at 1215a35–b5, he notes that the philosopher is concerned with the contemplation of truth:

> τρεῖς ὁρῶμεν καὶ βίους ὄντας, οὓς οἱ ἐπ' ἐξουσίας τυγχάνοντες προαιροῦνται ζῆν ἅπαντες, πολιτικὸν φιλόσοφον ἀπολαυστικόν. τούτων γὰρ ὁ μὲν φιλόσοφος βούλεται περὶ φρόνησιν εἶναι καὶ τὴν θεωρίαν τὴν περὶ τὴν ἀλήθειαν, ὁ δὲ πολιτικὸς περὶ τὰς πράξεις τὰς καλάς (αὗται δ' εἰσὶν αἱ ἀπὸ τῆς ἀρετῆς), ὁ δ' ἀπολαυστικὸς περὶ τὰς ἡδονὰς τὰς σωματικάς.

> We see there are three lives, which all those who have power happen to choose: the political, the philosophical, the pleasurable. Of these, then, the philosopher chooses to concern himself with practical wisdom and the contemplation of the truth, the political man with what is practical and noble (i.e., those actions that relate to the virtues), the epicure with bodily pleasures. (trans., mine)

Then he emphasizes, at 1221b27–30, that truth is the function of all intellectual activity:

εἰλημμένων δὲ τούτων, μετὰ ταῦτα λεκτέον ὅτι ἐπειδὴ δύο μέρη τῆς ψυχῆς, καὶ αἱ ἀρεταὶ κατὰ ταῦτα διῄρηνται, καὶ αἱ μὲν τοῦ λόγον ἔχοντος διανοητικαί, ὧν ἔργον ἀλήθεια, ἢ περὶ τοῦ πῶς ἔχει ἢ περὶ γενέσεως.

Having grasped these things, after this one should say that since there are two parts of the soul, and the virtues of these are divided, those of the rational part are the intellectual virtues, whose function is truth, whether about a thing's nature or genesis. (trans., mine)

In the ethical works, therefore, where Aristotle endeavors to prove that the essence of human flourishing is the activity of philosophical wisdom or—depending on how we interpret Aristotle's account of human flourishing—the activity of philosophical wisdom combined with the activity of practical wisdom, he asserts that truth is the function and ultimate good of *all* intellectual activity. By implication, truth is the function and ultimate good of philosophical wisdom and, hence, of the activity that defines human flourishing. The important point here is that Aristotle thinks truth is the function and ultimate good of the most perfect contemplative intellectual activity—philosophical wisdom.[4]

The Divine Science

Up to this point I have argued that, by the end of *Metaphysics* A 1, Aristotle has focused his investigation on philosophical wisdom and has reminded us, by way of his reference to the *Nicomachean Ethics*, that truth is the proper function and the ultimate good of all forms of knowledge and, hence, of philosophical wisdom. I have also offered reasons for thinking that truth, for Aristotle, is the proper function and final cause of all intellectual activity, that it is the work and purpose of philosophical wisdom in particular, and that insofar as the activity of philosophical wisdom is the essence of human flourishing, truth is also our proper work and final cause.

Thus, by the end of *Metaphysics* A 1, Aristotle has prepared us for his assessment of the various topics that need to be covered in his investigation of philosophical wisdom. This is the thrust of the second chapter of book A.[5] Aristotle begins the second chapter at 982a4–6 with the most important of these subsidiary topics:

> Ἐπεὶ δὲ ταύτην τὴν ἐπιστήμην ζητοῦμεν, τοῦτ' ἂν εἴη σκεπτέον,
> ἡ περὶ ποίας αἰτίας καὶ περὶ ποίας ἀρχὰς ἐπιστήμη σοφία ἐστίν.
>
> Since we seek this knowledge, we must look into the causes and the principles the knowledge of which is philosophical wisdom. (trans., mine, following Ross)

Aristotle will devote considerable energy to this part of his inquiry, explaining his account of substance and refuting alternative proposals about the causes and principles grasped by philosophical wisdom. Having announced this most important subtopic, he then specifies the various characteristics of philosophical wisdom and surveys the common opinions about who the wise man is and what philosophical wisdom is. He identifies in this way additional subtopics for his investigation.[6] He also describes the salient characteristics of philosophical wisdom in a subsequent passage in A 2, at 982a19–982b8: philosophical wisdom is knowledge of the most universal things, of what is most difficult to know and furthest from the senses, and of all things; it is knowledge that is by nature most able to be known and most teachable, that is pursued for its own sake and, hence, that is theoretical and not practical; and it is knowledge of the end, i.e., the good, for which each thing must be done. Aristotle, in surveying these salient characteristics of philosophical wisdom in A 2, differentiates philosophical wisdom from the productive sciences (982b11–28). He argues that philosophical wisdom exists for its own sake and not for some other end (983a4–11). It is at the very least inclusive of theology, if not identical with it. As such, he suggests, it seems the province of God alone (982b28–30, but also 1026a19 and 1064b3).

In the light of this last possibility, Aristotle considers briefly whether or not it would be impious for us to pursue philosophical wisdom (982b30–983a3). He rejects the idea that it would be impious, demonstrating that philosophical wisdom is divine in two ways—God itself would pursue it, and it is knowledge of God (983a5–11).[7] He concludes that philosophical wisdom is worthy of our pursuit.[8]

Aristotle's digression about philosophical wisdom and God in the second chapter of book A indicates a basic reason he needs to define truth in the *Metaphysics*—he needs to explain the nature of God. Philosophical wisdom is, as we have seen above, noetic comprehension of, and an ability to demonstrate from, true first principles and causes of what is by nature highest. Philosophical wisdom is thus a special way for a psyche to possess truth by way of affirmation and denial, combining noetic comprehension with demonstrative capacity. But philosophical wisdom is also special because it involves possessing true assertions about what is by nature most important. Since in *Metaphysics* book A and elsewhere Aristotle explicitly claims that nothing surpasses God in worth, philosophical wisdom is special because it involves true assertions about God.[9] And according to Aristotle, moreover, God's own essential activity either involves or is identical with philosophical wisdom: understanding true assertion is thus essential to understanding the nature of the proper object of philosophical wisdom—God.

I will elaborate on this a bit. In *Metaphysics* book Λ, Aristotle explains God's essence. He tells us there that God is the unmovable prime mover, the purely actual essence of which is thought thinking thought. God's essential activity is, therefore, an intellectual activity and, more specifically, an activity of intellectual contemplation. As such, and as we saw above, since the proper work and the final cause of all intellectual activity is true assertion, true assertion is God's proper function and final cause. And if God essentially involves and fully realizes true assertion, and if this is the basis of God's unsurpassed worth, Aristotle had better help us understand the nature of the kind of truth that belongs to assertions and its presumed inherent worth. This is so, indeed, independently of our interest in theology because, according to Aristotle, human beings themselves are able to engage in the very same activity—or one very much like it—that God realizes always and perfectly: philosophical wisdom. That is to say, Aristotle explains the worthiness of philosophical wisdom *for us* by pointing out that it is the ultimate good for God, and it is the ultimate good for God because it is the final end and ultimate purpose of thought.

The main claim I would need to establish to vindicate the preceding interpretation of how truth is involved in Aristotle's theology is that true assertion belongs to the essential actuality of God. The argument involves two steps. I would need to show that when God thinks, and therefore *is* essentially thought thinking thought, God's activity involves the prefect realization of Aristotle's definition of truth. And I would need to explain how true assertion informs God's essential activity. Does it belong to God's essential activity but only coincidentally, does it belong to it as a *proprium*, or as I think, does it exhaustively constitute God's essential activity? I cannot present the full argument here but I will return to the topic in the final chapter after I have presented my reconstruction of Aristotle's real definitions of truth and falsehood in the *Metaphysics*.

By the end of *Metaphysics* A 2, at 983a21–23, Aristotle tells us he has stated "the nature of the science we are searching for, and what is the target which our search and our whole investigation must reach" (trans., Ross). He devotes the remainder of book A to summarizing and criticizing his predecessors's views about the first principles and causes of all things.

Book A, then, introduces the central themes of the *Metaphysics*. Aristotle announces that one of his purposes in the treatise is to explain and acquire philosophical wisdom. He defines philosophical wisdom in terms of true assertion about the most important principles and causes, and he explicitly states that God, by its very nature—which, again, is the perfect activity of thought thinking thought—is the most important principle and cause of all and, hence, a proper object of philosophical wisdom. Moreover, he insists that only God possesses philosophical wisdom or that God has it to a greater extent than anything else. Truth looms large in all of these themes.

Hitting the Barn Door

Each of the main themes in *Metaphysics* book A generates important questions about truth. Aristotle articulates and addresses these questions in books α and B, where he summarizes the main problems that must be solved in order to acquire philosophical wisdom. That he addresses these themes and questions about truth in *Metaphysics* A, α, and B should diminish our doubts that he is concerned with truth in these early books and should augment our expectation that truth will be one of the topics addressed subsequently in the treatise.

The relevance of truth to Aristotle's project in the *Metaphysics* becomes quite apparent in the opening chapter of α, where he explicitly broaches the subject of truth. The entire chapter is about truth. He establishes two main points. Both bear on the broader importance of truth in the *Metaphysics*. First, at 993a30–993b19, Aristotle describes the general difficulty philosophers face in attempting to acquire the kind of truth needed for philosophical wisdom. This is about as close as Aristotle ever comes to acknowledging and responding to skeptical worries. Second, he explains at 993b19–31 why, properly speaking, the goal of philosophical wisdom is not action, but knowledge of truth about principles of eternal things.

With regard to the first of these points—that it is hard to acquire the sort of truth constituting philosophical wisdom—Aristotle is principally concerned in the opening chapter of book α with whether or not philosophers *can* comprehend the truth about the nature of things. More specifically, he considers whether philosophers can reasonably hope to intellectually comprehend the objects of philosophical wisdom, which he characterizes as the things that are *by nature* most evident. He begins by specifying at 993a30–b7 the relevant sort of things he has in mind:

> Ἡ περὶ τῆς ἀληθείας θεωρία τῇ μὲν χαλεπὴ τῇ δὲ ῥαδία. σημεῖον δὲ τὸ μήτ' ἀξίως μηδένα δύνασθαι θιγεῖν αὐτῆς μήτε πάντας ἀποτυγχάνειν, ἀλλ' ἕκαστον λέγειν τι περὶ τῆς φύσεως, καὶ καθ' ἕνα μὲν ἢ μηθὲν ἢ μικρὸν ἐπιβάλλειν αὐτῇ, ἐκ πάντων δὲ συναθροιζομένων γίγνεσθαί τι μέγεθος· ὥστ' εἴπερ ἔοικεν ἔχειν καθάπερ τυγχάνομεν παροιμιαζόμενοι, τίς ἂν θύρας ἁμάρτοι; ταύτῃ μὲν ἂν εἴη ῥᾳδία, τὸ δ' ὅλον τι ἔχειν καὶ μέρος μὴ δύνασθαι δηλοῖ τὸ χαλεπὸν αὐτῆς.

> Theoretical knowledge concerning the truth is in one way difficult to get and in another way easy. An indication of this is that while none is capable hitting upon it in the way it deserves, neither do all completely fail to hit it, but rather each has something to say about the nature of things, and whereas taken individually they contribute little or nothing to it, a gathering together of all results is a contribution of some magnitude. So if indeed the truth is like the proverbial barn door that none can miss, in this way it would be easy, but the fact that we can have some grasp on the whole while being incapable of grasping the part makes clear how difficult it is. (trans., Reeve)

The truth that philosophers fail to grasp adequately, but can say something about, is the truth about the *nature* of things [περὶ τῆς φύσεως]. It is unlikely that Aristotle uses the technical term "nature" [φύσεως] loosely in this passage. More plausibly, he is using it in its technical sense to denote the basic causes of things, a sense robustly considered already in the survey of his predecessors's views in *Metaphysics* book A.[10] This supposition is confirmed when he goes on to explain at 993b7–11 why no philosopher is able to adequately attain truth about the nature of things:

> ἴσως δὲ καὶ τῆς χαλεπότητος οὔσης κατὰ δύο τρόπους, οὐκ ἐν τοῖς πράγμασιν ἀλλ' ἐν ἡμῖν τὸ αἴτιον αὐτῆς· ὥσπερ γὰρ

τὰ τῶν νυκτερίδων ὄμματα πρὸς τὸ φέγγος ἔχει τὸ μεθ' ἡμέραν, οὕτω καὶ τῆς ἡμετέρας ψυχῆς ὁ νοῦς πρὸς τὰ τῇ φύσει φανερώτατα πάντων.

Presumably too, since difficulties occur in two ways, it is not in the things but in us that the cause of this one lies. For as the eyes of bats are to the light of day so is the understanding in our souls to the things that are by nature most evident of all. (trans., Reeve)

Our capacity for rational comprehension—i.e., νοῦς—is somehow inadequate for the task of grasping the natures of things, which are the things *by their very nature* most evident. Aristotle employs this distinction between what is knowable by nature and what is knowable to us in various treatises. What is most knowable to us but imperfectly intelligible (perceptual truths about particulars) is farthest from what is most knowable by its very nature (truths about what is most universal, necessary, and important). As a consequence, what is most evident by nature is not most evident to us, and we have trouble grasping the truth about these things.

In asking whether or not philosophers can comprehend the truth about what is by nature most evident, Aristotle is not wondering whether we can acquire perceptual truths, or true memories, or the truths of common sense, or those of experience, or those of practical wisdom. He is not focused on the aims of these cognitive capacities. He is focused on the possibility of pursuing philosophical wisdom. Comprehending the truth about what is by nature most evident is the same as comprehending true assertions about the first principles and causes of the necessary beings that are by nature highest. (It should be noted here that the Greek word here for "most evident" is φανερώτατα and not μάλιστα ἐπιστητὰ, which latter phrase Aristotle uses to describe philosophical wisdom in *Metaphysics* book A.)

In book α 1, then, he is directly confronting the question of whether or not philosophical wisdom is possible for us. The metaphor of our reason being blinded by the things that are by nature most evident—even though they are the proper objects to be grasped by our reason—is a familiar trope from Plato's Cave analogy. It is one way of putting Aristotle's distinction between what is most knowable to us as opposed to what is most knowable by nature, a distinction he employs in the *Metaphysics*, as for example in the following passage from book Z, at 1029b3ff:

πρὸ ἔργου γὰρ τὸ μεταβαίνειν εἰς τὸ γνωριμώτερον. ἡ γὰρ μάθησις οὕτω γίγνεται πᾶσι διὰ τῶν ἧττον γνωρίμων φύσει εἰς τὰ γνώριμα μᾶλλον· καὶ τοῦτο ἔργον ἐστίν, ὥσπερ ἐν ταῖς πράξεσι τὸ ποιῆσαι ἐκ τῶν ἑκάστῳ ἀγαθῶν τὰ ὅλως ἀγαθὰ ἑκάστῳ ἀγαθά, οὕτως ἐκ τῶν αὐτῷ γνωριμωτέρων τὰ τῇ φύσει γνώριμα αὐτῷ γνώριμα. τὰ δ' ἑκάστοις γνώριμα καὶ πρῶτα πολλάκις ἠρέμα ἐστὶ γνώριμα, καὶ μικρὸν ἢ οὐθὲν ἔχει τοῦ ὄντος· ἀλλ' ὅμως ἐκ τῶν φαύλως μὲν γνωστῶν αὐτῷ δὲ γνωστῶν τὰ ὅλως γνωστὰ γνῶναι πειρατέον, μεταβαίνοντας, ὥσπερ εἴρηται, διὰ τούτων αὐτῶν.

For it advances the work to proceed toward what is more knowable. For learning comes about for all in this way—through things by nature less knowable toward ones that are more knowable. And just as with things in the sphere of action the work is to begin from things that are good for each particular person and make things that are wholly good, good for each person, so too the work here is to begin from things more knowable to oneself and make the ones that are by nature knowable, knowable to oneself. But the things that are knowable and primary for particular groups of people are often only slightly knowable and have little or nothing of the being in them. Nonetheless, beginning from things that are poorly known but known to ourselves, we must try to know the ones that are wholly knowable, proceeding, as has just been said, through the former. (trans., Reeve)

In pursuing philosophical wisdom, philosophers are pursuing truth about the things that are by nature most evident of all. When, therefore, in the first line of book α 1, Aristotle states that "the contemplation of the truth [ἡ περὶ τῆς ἀληθείας θεωρία] is in one way hard, in another easy" (993a30–31) he is making a point about our human ability to theorize or comprehend truths about the things that are by nature most evident. His subsequent quip that "truth seems to be like the proverbial barn door, which no one can fail to hit" (993b4–6) is thus a remark about the considerable distance between our *ability* to contemplate philosophical truth and our *actually* contemplating what is perfectly intelligible. We can all hope to hit the barn door, but very few will be able to pitch a perfect game.

Philosophers have made it their business to acquire the truth about what is by nature most evident. Philosophers are the ones most likely to be blinded by the blaze of these things, and not because philosophers have particularly weak "eyes," but because philosophers are the ones earnestly looking at such things. It is the rare bat (presumably a very hungry bat) that emerges from its cave into the light of day to fly and hunt; it is the rare person (presumably a person yearning for wisdom) who emerges from the relative ignorance of sense perception and common sense to theorize and comprehend truths about the most fundamental principles and causes of being.

Aristotle notes that, taken individually, even philosophers contribute little or nothing to the contemplation of this rarefied sort of truth. However, he remains optimistic. One can see, he thinks, that over time our capacity to contemplate truths about what is by nature most evident has increased. Having gathered together what all the philosophers have contributed—"both the better thinkers and the more superficial"—he tells us that they have thus far acquired a fair amount of such truth. He then admonishes the reader that "philosophy should be called knowledge of the truth."

One major problem about the sort of truth involved in philosophical wisdom, then, is whether or not one can acquire it. In the subsequent parts of the *Metaphysics*, Aristotle makes his case for thinking we can. In book Γ he explains why we are justified in using the logical axioms to pursue the kind of truth involved in philosophical wisdom. In books Z, H, and Θ, he claims it is possible to formulate true definitions of the essences of substance, the noetic comprehension of which is presupposed by philosophical wisdom. In books I, Λ, M, and N, he asks how such truths are possible with regard to divine and mathematical substances.

Being, Truth, and Causality

In thinking about *Metaphysics* book A we saw that, for Aristotle, understanding truth is important for understanding philosophical wisdom and the nature of God. This provides him with compelling reasons to explain the nature of truth in the *Metaphysics*, given that he has not yet done so elsewhere. We have just seen that in *Metaphysics* book α Aristotle explicitly confronts the question of whether or not we can acquire the kind of truth involved in philosophical wisdom, and we will look to see if he offers us a positive answer to this question. I turn now to the second point about truth addressed by Aristotle in *Metaphysics* book α 1—that the goal of philosophical wisdom is not action, but true assertions about the first principles and causes of eternal things that are by nature most important and most evident. As with the other points just noted, the fact that the goal of philosophical wisdom involves the kind of truth that belongs to assertions, and the fact that philosophical wisdom principally involves *true* assertions about the first principles and causes of those eternal things that are most important and most evident, reveals yet again how crucial truth is to Aristotle's project in the *Metaphysics*. In addition, in the course of explaining these ideas, Aristotle also introduces two basic questions about truth: Does truth come in degrees and, if it does, how so? Are some truths more fundamental than others and, if some are, how so?

Aristotle begins by asserting that the goal of philosophical wisdom is not action, but true assertions about the first principles and causes of eternal things that are by nature most important and most evident. Aristotle notes that philosophical wisdom "should be called knowledge of truth" [ἐπιστήμην τῆς ἀληθείας] (993b19–20). This claim may well be expected. Aristotle has made it clear already in *Metaphysics* book Α that philosophical wisdom is a kind of theoretical knowledge. However, there seems to be no reason for him to emphasize in book α that it is theoretical knowledge of *truth* except that he wants to highlight the importance of truth as the goal of philosophical wisdom in contrast to the importance of action as the goal of practical wisdom. He emphasizes the importance of truth in this context because, he says, the aim of theoretical knowledge is truth [θεωρητικῆς μὲν γὰρ τέλος ἀλήθεια] while the aim of practical wisdom is action [πρακτικῆς δ' ἔργον].

Having noted these facts, Aristotle presents an argument for the existence of a hierarchy of truths some of which are "most true." The argument is worth considering in some detail. The passage in which the argument is found reads as follows:

> οὐκ ἴσμεν δὲ τὸ ἀληθὲς ἄνευ τῆς αἰτίας· ἕκαστον δὲ μάλιστα αὐτὸ τῶν ἄλλων καθ' ὃ καὶ τοῖς ἄλλοις ὑπάρχει τὸ συνώ-νυμον (οἷον τὸ πῦρ θερμότατον· καὶ γὰρ τοῖς ἄλλοις τὸ αἴτιον τοῦτο τῆς θερμότητος)· ὥστε καὶ ἀληθέστατον τὸ τοῖς ὑστέροις αἴτιον τοῦ ἀληθέσιν εἶναι. διὸ τὰς τῶν ἀεὶ ὄντων ἀρχὰς ἀναγκαῖον ἀεὶ εἶναι ἀληθεστάτας (οὐ γάρ ποτε ἀληθεῖς, οὐδ' ἐκείναις αἴτιόν τί ἐστι τοῦ εἶναι, ἀλλ' ἐκεῖναι τοῖς ἄλλοις), ὥσθ' ἕκαστον ὡς ἔχει τοῦ εἶναι, οὕτω καὶ τῆς ἀληθείας.

> Now we do not know the truth without [knowing] its cause; and a thing is thus-and-so most of all in relation to other things if in virtue of it the other things are thus-and-so (e.g., fire is the hottest of things; for it is the cause of the heat of all other things); so that which causes derivative truths to be true is most true. Therefore, the first principles of eternal things must always be most true; (for they are not merely sometimes true, nor is there any cause of their what-is, but they themselves are the cause of the others), so of each as it is of being, so also of truth. (993b23–31, trans. mine, following Ross)

Here Aristotle appears to distinguish among degrees of truth where all of the assertions in question are true as opposed to being merely approximately true. Although Aristotle allows that some assertions are approximately true and that there are degrees of approximate truth, at 993b23–31 he is not concerned with the degrees of truth in this sense. Rather, he is attempting to make sense of the idea that some true assertions are *more true* than other true assertions.

As I understand the passage, Aristotle's argument has two stages. The first stage of the argument establishes the fact that there is a hierarchy of true assertions within which the truth of some assertions is greater than the truth of others. In the second stage, Aristotle argues that, of all true assertions, true assertions about the first principles and causes of eternal things have the highest degree of truth.

According to the conclusion of the first stage of the argument, there is a hierarchy among truths: some truths are truer than others because the former cause the truth of the latter. This assertion may sound odd to us for at least two reasons. On the one hand, aside from theorists investigating the nature of approximate truth, few contemporary philosophers think that truth and falsehood admit of degrees. Yet Aristotle clearly seems committed to this view in the passage. On the other hand, Aristotle apparently describes the inferential relationship among truths in terms of causality, whereas nowadays philosophers tend to strongly dissociate logical and causal relations. Let me help to diminish these apparent oddities.

Aristotle's first premise in the passage, at 993b23–24, is that one does not know a truth without knowing its cause. This premise is familiar from Aristotle's discussion of theoretical knowledge in the *Posterior Analytics*. According to that discussion, one does not know a truth without knowing the cause of that truth, where by "cause" in the *Analytics* Aristotle literally means the premises that explain the truth in question. More precisely, Aristotle asserts the middle term is the cause that relates the major and the minor terms in the premises and thereby causally explains the truth which is the conclusion of the syllogism.

In book B of the *Posterior Analytics* Aristotle discusses at length how the middle term in a syllogism is the cause of the truth of the conclusion, and how even the indemonstrable first premises of demonstrations are caused to be true by the middle term. For example, one does not know that Socrates is mortal unless one knows that Socrates is a human being and one knows that all human beings are mortal. Here the middle term "human being" is the cause of the truth of the assertion that Socrates is mortal. The middle term, as we might say, explains the connection between Socrates and his being mortal.

Now it may be that the first part of our passage from *Metaphysics* book α 1, from 993b23–31, deals only with demonstrable truths and the latter part only with indemonstrable first principles. In which case, and perhaps contrary to what Aristotle says in the *Analytics*, one might think that we can know the first principles of demonstrations without knowing the cause. Alternatively, consonant with the view in the *Analytics*, and therefore more plausibly, it may be that the first part of the passage deals with both demonstrable and indemonstrable truths. On this reading, when one knows the indemonstrable truths one *ipso facto* knows their causes. As Aristotle puts it at *Posterior Analytics* 94a20–24:

Ἐπεὶ δὲ ἐπίστασθαι οἰόμεθα ὅταν εἰδῶμεν τὴν αἰτίαν, αἰτίαι δὲ τέτταρες, μία μὲν τὸ τί ἦν εἶναι, μία δὲ τὸ τίνων ὄντων ἀνάγκη τοῦτ' εἶναι, ἑτέρα δὲ ἡ τί πρῶτον ἐκίνησε, τετάρτη δὲ τὸ τίνος ἕνεκα, πᾶσαι αὗται διὰ τοῦ μέσου δείκνυνται.

We think we know when we know the cause, and there are four causes, one is what it is to be a thing, one is that this is necessary if these others obtain, one is that which produced the change, and one is the aim, all of which are proved through the middle term. (trans., Ross)

I am inclined to think that at 993b23–31 Aristotle is committing himself to the idea that we know an assertion is true, whether the assertion is indemonstrable or demonstrable, only if we know the cause of the truth of that premise.

Aristotle next asserts a general principle according to which something has an attribute "most of all" [μάλιστα] in comparison with other things, if the attribute belongs to the other things because the attribute belongs to it (993b24–25). Hence, for example, a truth A is true "most of all" [μάλιστα] in comparison with other truths B and C, if truth belongs to B and C because truth belongs to A. Put another way, if truth belongs to derivative assertions because truth belongs to the assertion from which the other assertions are derived, then the assertion from which the others are derived is true most of all in comparison with the others (see 993b26–27).

This creates a hierarchy of truths. One truth is higher than another in this hierarchy if the latter is derived from the former, and those truths from which all other derivative truths are derived are true "most of all." This may seem odd since, again, inferential relations are no longer thought of in terms of causality, but it made perfect sense to Aristotle: the truth of the premises in a demonstration explains the truth of the conclusion derived from them, and to explain why a given assertion is true, for him, is to explain that the given assertion is derived from others.[11] How we explain the truth of indemonstrable assertions, which in fact are the most true assertions on Aristotle's view, is a question that remains outstanding.

In the passage from Metaphysics book α, Aristotle is concerned exclusively with causal explanations. He places severe restrictions on the kind of inference that counts as a causal explanation. We know from the *Analytics* that a causal explanation is an "epistemonic deduction" [συλλογισμὸς ἐπιστημονικός] by means of which one comes to understand something simpliciter [ἁπλῶς], as opposed to knowing it by virtue of its accidental features. (See APo. 71b9–17.) That is to say, the formal cause or the essence of a thing is understood by means of an epistemonic deduction. Understanding something in this way involves, according to Aristotle in the *Analytics*, (i) knowing the cause [αἰτία] of the thing understood, (ii) knowing of this cause that it is, in fact, the cause of the thing understood, and (iii) knowing that the cause of the thing understood must be its cause. (See APo. 71b10–12.) In order to secure this sort of understanding, Aristotle tells us we need to base it on assertions that are true [ἀληθῶν], primitive [πρώτων], immediate [ἀμέσων], more familiar than [γνωριμωτέρων], prior to [προτέρων], and the cause of [αἰτίων] the understanding of the conclusion. (See APo. 71b19–22.)

Very few inferences will meet this rigorous standard. All such arguments are, of course, about the real causes of things in the world and are, thus, arguments about causes. But the crucial point to acknowledge here is that all such arguments are causal in a different sense: they involve true premises that cause the truth of the conclusions. The ultimate premises of these arguments are themselves the first causes of the truth of what comes to be known.

Returning to our main passage in book α, it is not obvious that either of the main claims Aristotle has made thus far—the general principle that generates the hierarchy of truths and the claim inferred from it about first principles—is true. Much depends on how we understand the locution "most of all" [μάλιστα] in the general principle. To use Aristotle's example in the passage, suppose that heat belongs to fire and that this fact causes heat to belong to everything else. It follows that heat belongs to fire most of all. If one takes this to mean that fire is the hottest thing of all, then one ought to have doubts. Why could not fire cause heat to belong to everything else and for everything else to be just as hot as fire? But if, more charitably, one takes "heat belongs to fire most of all" to mean that heat belongs to fire most fundamentally, one ought to have fewer doubts, if any. If heat belongs to fire and this fact—that heat belongs to fire—explains why heat belongs to everything else, then there is a clear sense in which heat belongs to fire most fundamentally: heat belonging to fire is the ultimate cause of heat belonging to everything else. What is most fundamentally hot need not be hotter than everything else.

Similarly, if one takes "most true" (ἀληθέστερον at 993b27) to mean "is truer than everything else," one quite naturally boggles. But if one takes "most true" to mean "the assertion the truth of which causes truth to belong to all other assertions" then, at least apparently, one is dealing with a fairly familiar claim about explanatory priority. The idea that some truths are more fundamental than others is related to Aristotle's distinction between things that are knowable to us most of all and things that are knowable by nature most of all (APo. 71b33–72a6 and Met. 1029b3ff). The truths knowable by nature most of all are the most fundamental truths on the basis of which we argue demonstratively. The truths knowable by us most of all are the perceptions of particulars on the basis of which we argue inductively.

In the first stage of the argument, then, Aristotle establishes that some truths are most true because they are explanatorily fundamental. In the second stage of the argument, he identifies the fundamental truths. He argues that the first principles of eternal things are the most fundamental truths of all. The second stage of the argument may be reconstructed as follows: The first principles that are true of eternal things are always true (993b29). Now if nothing is the cause of the being of eternal things, and the being of eternal things is always the cause of the being of everything else, then the being of eternal things is always greater than the being of everything else. But, as a matter of fact, nothing is the cause of the being of eternal things, and the being of eternal things is always the cause of the being of everything else. (993b29–30) Thus, the being of eternal things is greater than the being of everything else. In addition, as each being is with respect to being, so also each being is with respect to the truth about it (993b30–31). Therefore, the truth about eternal things is always greater than the truth about everything else and, hence, the first principles of eternal things must always be most true, in the sense of being most fundamental (993b28–29).

The crucial premise in the preceding argument—at least as concerns truth and falsehood—is the claim that as each being is with respect to being so also each being is with respect to the truth about it. Without attempting to explain here how it is that Aristotle ultimately understands the relationship about being and truth, it is sufficient to note that it is a major problem in the *Metaphysics*.

In book α 1, then, Aristotle asks us to consider how some truths are most fundamental and in what way they might be said to be the causes of other truths. In doing so Aristotle raises some difficult questions about truth insofar as it is related to the goals of philosophical wisdom. Philosophical wisdom, again, is noetic comprehension of the first principles and causes of what is most important and most evident and a capacity to demonstrate what follows from these first principles and causes. By the end of the book, I hope to have made significant progress toward clarifying how Aristotle understood the relationship between truth and being.

The Beta Test

Aristotle does not explicitly mention truth or falsehood in his review of the difficulties [ἀπορίαι] noted in *Metaphysics* book B—those difficulties that must be resolved in order to provide a complete and satisfactory account of philosophical wisdom. The catalogue of problems in book B fairly well exhausts what he goes on to discuss in the treatise. Thus, the lack of any explicit mention of truth or falsehood constitutes evidence that truth may not be among the topics dealt with in the remainder of the *Metaphysics*.[12]

That the problems canvassed in *Metaphysics* book B are related to philosophical wisdom, on the other hand, is evident from the first sentence of the book, at 995a24–25: "We must, with a view to the science which we are seeking [i.e., philosophical wisdom], first recount the subjects that should be first discussed" (trans., Ross). Immediately after prefacing the problems in this way, at 995b5ff, Aristotle differentiates between the main subjects of philosophical wisdom: the first principles of substance and the principles on which all men base their proofs [περὶ τῶν ἀρχῶν ἐξ ὧν δεικνύουσι πάντες].

That truth is important for an investigation of the principles on which all proofs are based is almost immediately apparent in *Metaphysics* book B. For example, in the first chapter of book B, Aristotle offers as an instance of a such a principle the Law of Non-Contradiction (LNC)—as he formulates it there: whether it is possible at the same time to assert and deny one and the same thing or not. (995b7–8) Then again, in the second chapter of book B, he considers whether or not the principles on which all proofs are based are proper objects of philosophical wisdom:

ἀλλὰ μὴν καὶ περὶ τῶν ἀποδεικτικῶν ἀρχῶν, πότερον μιᾶς ἐστὶν ἐπιστήμης ἢ πλειόνων, ἀμφισβητήσιμόν ἐστιν (λέγω δὲ ἀποδεικτικὰς τὰς κοινὰς δόξας ἐξ ὧν ἅπαντες δεικνύουσιν) οἷον ὅτι πᾶν ἀναγκαῖον ἢ φάναι ἢ ἀποφάναι, καὶ ἀδύνατον ἅμα εἶναι καὶ μὴ εἶναι, καὶ ὅσαι ἄλλαι τοιαῦται προτάσεις, πότερον μία τούτων ἐπιστήμη καὶ τῆς οὐσίας ἢ ἑτέρα, κἂν εἰ μὴ μία, ποτέραν χρὴ προσαγορεύειν τὴν ζητουμένην νῦν.

But then about the starting-points of demonstration too, and whether there is one science of them or more than one, there is dispute (by the starting-points of demonstration I mean the common beliefs on the basis of which we all prove things, such as that in every case it is necessary either to affirm or to deny, and that it is impossible for something at the same time to both be and not be, and any other propositions like that), namely, about whether there is one science of these and of substance or distinct ones, and, if it is not one science, which of the two should be identified with what we are now inquiring into? (996b26–33, trans., Reeve)

Aristotle uses "principles of demonstration" in the passage to refer to the principles on which everyone bases their proofs. He raises the question as to whether the philosopher pursuing philosophical wisdom ought to investigate these logical principles, and he concludes:

καθόλου γὰρ μάλιστα καὶ πάντων ἀρχαὶ τὰ ἀξιώματά ἐστιν, εἴ τ' ἐστὶ μὴ τοῦ φιλοσόφου, τίνος ἔσται περὶ αὐτῶν ἄλλου τὸ θεωρῆσαι τὸ ἀληθὲς καὶ ψεῦδος;

> For it is the axioms that are most universal and the starting-points of all things, and if not the philosopher, then to whom does it belong to get a theoretical grasp on what is true and what is false about them? (997a12–15, trans., Reeve)

It is the business, then, of the philosopher to inquire about what is true and untrue about the logical axioms. In the second chapter of *Metaphysics* book B Aristotle offers as another example of such an axiom of the Law of the Excluded Middle (LEM), which he formulates as "that everything must be either affirmed or denied" (996b29). It is sufficient to note here that Aristotle defines assertions and denials in terms of truth and falsehood. As a consequence, in order to investigate the logical axioms, the philosopher must investigate truth and falsehood. In part II of this book, I address how Aristotle's account of truth informs his arguments for the logical axioms.

The majority of the problems in *Metaphysics* book B pertain to the investigation into the first principles of substance. It is admittedly unclear when we are first reading book B how the topic of truth fits into this investigation, and were *Metaphysics* book B a digest of the *results* of his investigation of philosophical wisdom, this might be thought to damage the hypothesis that his account of truth is an important part of the investigation. Book B however is not at all a summary of Aristotle's conclusions about philosophical wisdom. Quite to the contrary. Book B is a survey of the *outstanding problems* Aristotle thinks he must solve in order to give an adequate account of philosophical wisdom. As such, *Metaphysics* book B need not explicitly identify the concepts that he believes are crucial for the solution of the problems. If he uses his account of truth to solve some of the main problems raised in book B, then that diminishes the weight of the fact that truth itself is not listed among these problems.

Conclusion

In this chapter I have argued that Aristotle needs to explain the nature of truth if he hopes to solve the two main problems that arise for his account of philosophical wisdom: What are the first principles of substance, and how are we to vindicate the logical axioms on which all men base their proofs? I hope to have made it clear not only that Aristotle himself was aware of this need in books A, α, and B but that he also explicitly announces these problems in advance of his investigation proper into the logical axioms and the first principles of substances.

Part II

Truth and the Logical Axioms

Chapter 2

What "Truth" and "Falsehood" Signify

We have seen that for Aristotle philosophical wisdom is a state of the psyche in which, by means of affirmation or denial, the psyche (1) comprehends and is never deceived about the first principles and causes of the necessary beings that are by nature highest and (2) has the capacity to demonstrate on the basis of these first principles. This is his explicit definition of philosophical wisdom in *Nicomachean Ethics* book VI, and he confirms it in his remarks about philosophical wisdom in *Metaphysics* A.

I argued in the last chapter that philosophical wisdom—as Aristotle conceives it—essentially involves truth, ultimately aims at truth, and has for its proper object truth about the things highest by nature. If Aristotle is interested in explaining the nature of philosophical wisdom in the *Metaphysics*, he is *ipso facto* concerned with the nature of truth.

If one had read all of Aristotle's other works before reading the *Metaphysics*, one would already understand most of the ideas involved in his conception of philosophical wisdom. But not all. He discusses linguistic and mental assertion, comprehension, demonstration, definition, first principles, and indemonstrability in the *Organon*, in the *De Anima*, and in the *Nicomachean Ethics*. He examines the concepts of nature and necessity in the *Physics* and addresses the distinctions to be made among different kinds of priority in the *Categories*.[1] He relies upon these discussions in the *Metaphysics* as he develops his account of philosophical wisdom.

In treatises other than the *Metaphysics*, however, Aristotle leaves undefined and largely unexplained two concepts essential to his account of philosophical wisdom—the concepts of being and truth. As we saw in chapter 1, he needs to elucidate both concepts in order to explain philosophical wisdom. Of course, no one doubts that Aristotle expounds the nature of being in the *Metaphysics*. Yet no one thinks he expounds the essence of truth in the treatise.

Aristotle has not presented his account of the essence of truth in any treatise other than the *Metaphysics*. He offers no definitions of truth outside the *Metaphysics*, and there is no record of a missing treatise in which Aristotle explained the nature of truth.² Since Aristotle has not explained the nature of truth in any of the other treatises, either he explained it in the *Metaphysics*, or he left it unexplained. The good news, I think, is that that he did not leave it unexplained.

We saw in the last chapter that according to Aristotle the pursuit of philosophical wisdom involves investigating the first principles of argument. He makes this plain, for example, at *Metaphysics* book Γ 3.1005b5–8:

ὅτι μὲν οὖν τοῦ φιλοσόφου, καὶ τοῦ περὶ πάσης τῆς οὐσίας θεωροῦντος ᾗ πέφυκεν, καὶ περὶ τῶν συλλογιστικῶν ἀρχῶν ἐστὶν ἐπισκέψασθαι, δῆλον.

That, therefore, the philosopher, who theorizes about the nature of all substance, is also the one who inquires into the starting-points of arguments, is clear. (trans., mine)

The philosopher—and no one else—must study the first principles of argument, not only because nobody else will, not just because they are the axioms of all rational inquiry, but also because defending them is necessary in order to vindicate the very possibility of philosophical wisdom. As Aristotle develops this point later in the same chapter—*Metaphysics* book Γ 3.1005a33–b8—he differentiates natural philosophy and first philosophy, and argues that the first principles of argument fall within the purview of first philosophy. The axioms are the first principles of all reasoning and therefore must already be comprehended and defended prior to specific rational inquiry of the sort natural philosophers undertake. All philosophers must examine and justify their methods before employing them, but that work is a part of first philosophy (i.e., part of the investigation of philosophical wisdom).

Before he presents his theory of being insofar as it is being in *Metaphysics* books Δ–N Aristotle prepares the way by vindicating the possibility of such theorizing—he establishes the general terms on which truths should be accepted. He vindicates thereby the basic logical methods the philosopher should employ in pursuing philosophical wisdom. Part of this preparatory work is defensive. Before he can legitimately employ the first principles of argument, he needs to justify them. This last purpose—justifying the use of the logical axioms—is a crucial step in proving that the investigation of philosophical wisdom is at least possible.[3] The other part of this preparatory work is conceptual. He needs to present and make sense of the logical concepts involved in or presupposed by the first principles of argument themselves. Chief among these are the concepts of contradiction, assertion, and truth.

In this chapter and the next I argue that Aristotle articulates and makes use of nominal yet philosophically sophisticated definitions of the terms "truth" and "falsehood" in his defense of the first principles of argument. More specifically, I defend the view that in book Γ, chapters 3–8, Aristotle's elenctic arguments for the axioms of demonstration presuppose nominal definitions of the terms "truth" and "falsehood," definitions presented by Aristotle in book Γ 7.1011b26–27—the canonical definitions of truth and falsehood usually attributed to Aristotle.

The Canonical Definition of Truth in Context

Aristotle not only recognizes different kinds of definition, he requires different kinds for different sorts of argument. "Real" definitions expressing indemonstrable first principles function as basic premises in demonstrative syllogisms; "nominal" definitions of what terms serve as agreed upon premises in certain kinds of destructive dialectical arguments. Prima facie, given that Aristotle deploys the canonical definitions of truth and falsehood in *Metaphysics* book Γ 7.1011b26–27 as premises in a destructive elenctic argument for the Law of the Excluded Middle (LEM), it would seem the definitions should be interpreted as nominal definitions of what the terms "truth" and "falsehood" signify, definitions that might be accepted by Aristotle's presumed dialectical opponents.

I will make the case that this first impression is accurate. The definitions at 1011b26–27 are best understood as nominal definitions expressing concepts of truth and falsehood that are anodyne but adequate for Aristotle's dialectical purposes in book Γ. The definitions capture what the terms "truth" and "falsehood" signify prior to sustained philosophical investigation into the nature of what they signify. In particular, the definientia of these nominal definitions do not express developed philosophical conceptions that presuppose the full machinery of Aristotle's—or any other—philosophical system. They are not intended to express Aristotle's real definitions of the essence of truth and falsehood. These come later.[4]

Rather, the definitions at 1011b26–27 express concepts Aristotle assumes his opponents will grant in the context of his dialectical demonstrations about the first principles of argument. Understood in this dialectically neutral way the definitions nevertheless commit Aristotle's opponents to various semantic presuppositions—the nominal definitions provide the general semantic framework within to pursue truth and falsehood, the framework within which Aristotle expects his philosophical opponents (and us) to judge his elenctic arguments for the logical axioms and all of his subsequent claims in the *Metaphysics*.

Aristotle defines "ἀληθὲς" (or "truth") and "ψεῦδος" (or "falsehood") in *Metaphysics* Γ 7.1011b26–27.[5] This much at least—and perhaps at most—is uncontroversial. How should we understand these definitions? There are various textual and exegetical issues to consider first.

Aristotle offers his definitions as premises in an argument for the Law of the Excluded Middle from 1011b23–29. The following Greek text for b23–29 has been adopted by Bekker, Jaeger, Ross, and Tredennick:[6]

> b23 Ἀλλὰ μὴν οὐδὲ μεταξὺ ἀντιφάσεως[7] ἐνδέχεται εἶναι
> b24 οὐθέν, ἀλλ' ἀνάγκη ἢ φάναι ἢ ἀποφάναι ἓν[8] καθ' ἑνὸς ὁτιοῦν.
> b25 δῆλον δὲ πρῶτον μὲν ὁρισαμένοις τί[9] τὸ ἀληθὲς καὶ ψεῦδος.
> b26 τὸ μὲν γὰρ λέγειν τὸ ὂν μὴ εἶναι ἢ τὸ μὴ ὂν[10] εἶναι ψεῦ—
> b27 δος, τὸ δὲ τὸ ὂν[11] εἶναι καὶ τὸ[12] μὴ ὂν μὴ εἶναι ἀληθές, ὥστε
> b28 καὶ ὁ λέγων[13] εἶναι ἢ μὴ[14] ἀληθεύσει ἢ ψεύσεται· ἀλλ'
> b29 οὔτε τὸ ὂν λέγεται[15] μὴ εἶναι ἢ εἶναι οὔτε τὸ μὴ ὄν.

> But then neither is it possible for there to be anything in the middle between contradictories, but it is necessary either to affirm or to deny one thing, whatever it may be, of one thing. This will be clear if we first define what truth is and what falsehood is. For to say of what is that it is not, or of what is not that it is, is false, whereas to say of what is that it is, or of what is not that it is not, is true. So he who says of anything that it is, or that it is not, will say either what is true or what is false. But it is said that neither what is nor what is not either is not or is. (trans., Reeve)

First, with regard to 1011b23–25, the manuscripts differ on three points. Whereas E, A[b], Al[1], Asc[1] have 'ἀντιφάσεως' at 1011b23, J records 'ἀποφάσεως.' Bekker, Bonitz, Cassin and Narcy, Ross, and Jaeger retain "ἀντιφασις"; Cassin and Narcy and Ross note the alternative in J. In the context of Aristotle's writings, "ἀντίφασις" is used to denote a contradiction or a contradictory assertion, whereas "ἀποφάσις" can be used either as a cognate of "ἀποφαίνω" or as a cognate of "ἀπόφημι." In the first case, "ἀποφάσις" can mean the same as "statement," "assertion," "judgment," or "an affirmative or negative predication." The second use of "ἀποφάσις" is defined by Aristotle in *De Interpretatione* as "an assertion of one thing away from another" and is opposed to the related use of "κατάφασις," meaning "an assertion of one thing with another." Given the immediate context (a claim at 1011b23 about intermediate assertions [μεταξὺ] as part of an argument for LEM), the broader context (an elenctic defense of the logical axioms in Γ 4–8), and Aristotle's account of contradictory assertions and intermediate assertions in the *Organon* and in the *Metaphysics* (in particular, in book I), the sense of the phrase "Ἀλλὰ μὴν οὐδὲ μεταξὺ ἀντιφάσεως ἐνδέχεται εἶναι" at 1011b23 will be the same whether we choose "ἀντιφάσεως" at 1011b23 or "ἀποφάσεως": "But on the other hand there cannot be an intermediate between contradictories" (Ross).

Second, at 1011b24 E, J, Γ, Al^c, and Asc^p have 'ἕν'; it is omitted in A^b. Bekker and Bonitz retain "ἕν," noting the alternative in A^b. Cassin and Narcy, Jaeger, and Ross retain it. Given how Aristotle understands affirmative and negative assertions, the sense of "ἀνάγκη ἢ φάναι ἢ ἀποφάναι ἓν καθ' ἑνός" ("it is necessary either to affirm or to deny one of one") is basically the same as that of "ἀνάγκη ἢ φάναι ἢ ἀποφάναι καθ' ἑνός" ("it is necessary either to affirm or deny of one").

Third, "τί" at 1011b25 is omitted in A^b and Asc^l, but found in E, J, Al^p, and Asc^c. Bekker, Bonitz, Cassin and Narcy, Jaeger, and Ross all retain "τί." Bekker and Bonitz record "ὁρισαμένοις τί" without noting alternatives and without comment (see Bonitz 1960, 212). Cassin and Narcy, Jaeger, and Ross note that "τί" is omitted in Al^b but ignore this alternative in their commentaries. The difference at 1011b25 between "δῆλον δὲ πρῶτον μὲν ὁρισαμένοις τί τὸ ἀληθὲς καὶ ψεῦδος" ("This is clear first if we give a definition of the true and the false") and "ὁρισαμένοις τὸ ἀληθὲς καὶ ψεῦδος" ("This is clear first if we define the true and the false") is negligible.

None of these lexical variations entail important exegetical differences, but Aristotle's statement at 1011b25 ("δῆλον δὲ πρῶτον μὲν ὁρισαμένοις τί τὸ ἀληθὲς καὶ ψεῦδος") is problematic. It can be taken to mean "it is clear first of all if we define [what is] the true and [what is] the false," but it can also mean "it is clear first of all if we lay down criteria for [what] the true and the false [are]" or "it is clear first of all if we differentiate

[what] the true [is] and [what] the false [is]." "ὁρισαμένοις" is the dative plural masculine/neuter aorist participial form of "ὁρίζω" the root meaning of which is to divide, in the sense of establishing boundaries between two or more things. Perhaps, then, Aristotle isn't *defining* truth and falsehood at 1011b26–27. Perhaps, more modestly, he is offering distinguishing (but not defining) marks of truth and falsehood. This is a serious issue. To determine which of these uses of 'ὁρισαμένοις' Aristotle had in mind at 1011b25, we will need to consider below the context of its use.

With regard to 1011b26–27, the manuscripts differ on two points. On the one hand, at 1011b26, E, J, Al^c have "τοῦτο" where A^b has "τὸ μὴ ὄν"; on the other hand, at 1011b27, E and A^b have "καὶ τὸ μὴ ὄν μὴ εἶναι" where J and Al^c have "τὸ δὲ μὴ ὄν μὴ εἶναι." I will deal with the variations at 1011b27 first, since they are easy to reconcile.

At 1011b27, E and A^b have "καὶ τὸ μὴ ὄν μὴ εἶναι" where J and Al^c have "τὸ δὲ μὴ ὄν μὴ εἶναι." Bekker, Bonitz, Jaeger, and Ross follow E and A^b. Ross does not address his decision in his commentary, nor does Kirwan (who accepts Jaeger's text) in his. Cassin and Narcy follow J an Al^c but also add a comma before "τὸ δὲ μὴ ὄν μὴ εἶναι." Given the context of 1011b26–27, the force of the copulative "καὶ" at 1011b27 would be the same as the force of an adversative "δὲ." "Both would continue the contrast begun earlier in 1011b27 by the adversative "δὲ," which relates back to the antithetical "μὲν" at the beginning of 1011b26.

With regard to the variations at 1011b26, Bekker, Bonitz, Cassin and Narcy, Jaeger, and Ross follow A^b in choosing "τὸ μὴ ὄν" instead of "τοῦτο." Smyth (sec. 1253) tells us that "τοῦτο" may take up a substantive idea not expressed by a preceding neuter word. "τοῦτο" seems to refer backwards to a prior part of 1011b26 as opposed to some part of 1011b23–25. For example, it is hard to make sense of it referring back to the substantive idea of a definition associated with (although not expressed by) "ὁρισαμένοις τί" at 1011b25 or to either "τὸ ἀληθὲς" or "τὸ ψεῦδος" at 1011b25, and harder still to see how it might refer back to "οὐθέν" at 1011b24.

If we take "τοῦτο" to refer to a prior part of 1011b26, we have two choices. The grammatically obvious alternative is to assume that "τοῦτο" refers back to "τὸ ὄν" at 1011b26. Our other alternative is to assume that "τοῦτο" refers back to the immediately preceding neuter phrase "μὴ εἶναι."

If we assume "τοῦτο" refers back to "τὸ ὄν" at 1011b26, the consequences are intolerable. For, on this reading, Aristotle would define (or distinguish)[16] falsehood at 1011b26 in terms of asserting of what is (τὸ ὄν) that it is not (μὴ εἶναι) or asserting of what is (τὸ ὄν) that it is (εἶναι), and he would define truth at 1011b27 as asserting of what is (τὸ ὄν) that it is (εἶναι) and asserting of what is not (τὸ μὴ ὄν) that it is not (μὴ εἶναι).

I will focus first on how this proposed reading of "τοῦτο" at 1011b26 would affect the account of falsehood at b26. We would expect Aristotle to say that it is false to assert of what is (τὸ ὄν) that it is not (μὴ εἶναι). But the idea that it is false to assert of what is (τὸ ὄν) that it is (εἶναι) flies in the face of everything Aristotle, his predecessors, and everyone else says about falsehood—to wit: a true assertion either is or involves asserting of what is (τὸ ὄν) that it is (εἶναι), and a false assertion is the opposite of a true one.[17] So far as I know, nobody denies these assumptions—not even contemporary dialetheists. Thus, assuming "τοῦτο" refers back to "τὸ ὄν" at 1011b26 yields an account of falsehood that would be repugnant to anyone familiar with the topic. This is especially problematic given the immediate argumentative context: Aristotle is in the midst of presenting an elenctic argument for LEM partly on the basis of his claims about falsehood at 1011b26, and Aristotle needs to offer accounts of truth and falsehood that his opponents are likely to have accepted. Who among his opponents would go along with an account of falsehood according to which it is false to assert of what is that it is?

Moreover, insofar as the accounts of truth and falsehood at 1011b26–27 function as premises in the argument for LEM at 1011b23–29, the proposed reading of "τοῦτο" at 1011b26 would complicate Aristotle's case in a peculiar manner.[18] On the standard reconstructions of Aristotle's argument, he aims to show that an assertion intermediate between a pair of contradictory assertions is neither true nor false and, therefore, is no assertion at all. Given any pair of contradictory assertions, he assumes that one of the assertions involves predicating "is" of some subject—either "that which is" or "that which is not"—and that the other assertion involves predicating "is not" of that subject. The subject of these contradictory assertions is either "that which is" or "that which is not." Were there to be an intermediate assertion between the contradictory pair, Aristotle assumes that neither "is" nor "is not" would be predicated of either "what is" or "what is not." Since on the standard reconstructions, truth and falsehood are defined in terms of predicating either "is" or "is not" of either "what is" or "what is not," the supposed intermediate assertion would neither be true nor false. Hence, given that assertions are defined as accounts that are either true or false, the supposed intermediate assertion would not be an assertion. If, however, we assume the account of falsehood that emerges when we take "τοῦτο" to refer back to "τὸ ὄν" at 1011b26, then in order to prove that the supposed intermediate assertion is no assertion at all, Aristotle would have to show that it is neither true nor false but also that is not *both* true *and* false.

While Aristotle could show this, it is utterly implausible that he should have to. For, if we assume that at 1011b26 "τοῦτο" refers back to "τὸ ὄν," then the proposed accounts of truth and falsehood at 1011b26–27 would jointly entail that (i) to assert of what is that it is not is false, (ii) to assert of what is not that it is not is true, and (iii) to assert of what is that it is, is both true and false. (i) and (ii) are standard. (iii) is offensive, and not just because asserting of what is that it is would be false. On the proposed reading, the accounts of truth and falsehood at 1011b26–27 would entail the denial of the very axioms Aristotle is defending in book Γ. The law of the excluded middle would be violated whenever we assert of what is that it is, since every such assertion would be both true and false, and being true and false is one candidate for the intermediate state between being true and being false. We would also violate the law of non-contradiction with such assertions, since each would be true and false at the same time, in the same respect, et cetera. All of this goes beyond the pale.

We also have to wonder why Aristotle would limit falsehood to assertions about what is while allowing true assertions to range over both what is and what is not. Given his Parmenidean and Platonic precursors, we would expect him to go in the opposite direction—that true assertions are only about what is whereas false assertions are either logically impossible or are about both what is and what is not.

Thus, all things considered, I agree with Cassin and Narcy (1989, 259) that the first option—assuming "τοῦτο" refers back to "τὸ ὄν" at 1011b26—«ne donne pas le sens»: it does not make sense. Turning now to the second option, "τοῦτο" at 1011b26 may take up from the preceding neuter phrase "μὴ εἶναι" the idea of that which is not, a substantive idea which is not expressed by the phrase "μὴ εἶναι" itself but is expressed by the phrase "τὸ μὴ ὄν" commonly used by Aristotle and others in discussing falsehood and truth. Adopting this interpretation of "τοῦτο" at 1011b26, we reconcile the apparent difference between A[b] and E, J, and Al[c].

All of the manuscripts agree with regard to 1011b29. E and J agree with respect to 1011b28; Cassin and Narcy place a comma after "ψεύσεται" instead of a colon, otherwise agreeing with E and J; Al[c] has "τοῦτο" after "καὶ ὁ λέγων"; A[b] replaces "καὶ ὁ λέγων" with "ἐκεῖνο λέγων." These variations yield different reconstructions of the argument at 1011b23–29.

What "Truth" and "Falsehood" Signify   51

There are two remaining exegetical issues to resolve: are the formulae presented at 1011b26–27 intended to express definitions of truth and falsehood, or were they intended to express distinguishing but not essential characteristics of truth and falsehood? Contemporary commentators generally accept that Aristotle is explicitly defining truth and falsehood in the passage. The textual evidence supporting the claim that the formulae express definitions is weighty. First, Aristotle explicitly states at 1011b25 that he will define [ὁρισαμένοις] "truth" [τὸ ἀληθὲς] and "falsehood" [τὸ ψεῦδος].[19] Second, at 1012a3 Aristotle refers back to the formulae at 1011b26–27, describing them as definitions [ἐξ ὁρισμοῦ]. Third, at 1012a21–24 Aristotle describes the general argumentative tactic he is employing against those who deny LEM, positing an intermediate between contradictories:

ἀρχὴ δὲ πρὸς ἅπαντας τούτους ἐξ ὁρισμοῦ. ὁρισμὸς δὲ γίγνεται ἐκ τοῦ σημαίνειν τι ἀναγκαῖον εἶναι αὐτούς· ὁ γὰρ λόγος οὗ τὸ ὄνομα σημεῖον ὁρισμὸς ἔσται.

In response to all these people the original [step] is from a definition. Definition arises from the necessity that they should themselves signify something, for the formula of [the thing of] which the name is a sign will be a definition [. . .]. (trans., Ross)

Aristotle's basic tactic in arguing against those who deny a logical axiom is to get them to signify something. In book Γ Aristotle repeatedly and explicitly stresses the relationship between agreeing upon definitions of terms and establishing that each of those terms signifies at least one thing. In the preceding quote, he is claiming that the definition of "truth" at b26–27 is a formula of the one thing signified by the term "truth." It is plausible, then, that Aristotle is employing his preferred tactic at 1011b26–27, defining "truth" and "falsehood" and thus establishing the formulae of each one of the things signified by the terms "truth" and "falsehood." Given, therefore, the kind of argument in which the formulae at 1011b26–27 function as premises, it makes sense to interpret them as definitions. Fourth, at 1012b7 Aristotle again explicitly refers to the formulae as definitions—"ἐξ ὁρισμοῦ διαλεκτέον λαβόντας τί σημαίνει τὸ ψεῦδος ἢ τὸ ἀληθές"—and relies upon them as such in the subsequent argument at 1012b8–11. It is of course possible that all of these uses of "ὁρισαμένοις" and its cognates are intended to signify something other than a definition, but it seems implausible.

The immediate argumentative context also supports the claim that the formulae express definitions. There are four competing reconstructions of Aristotle's argument in the secondary literature. Two of these are based on traditional readings of the Greek text. These two versions reflect different readings of 1011b27–28. The first reading is defended by Alexander and Bonitz, with an epanalectic "τοῦτο" at 1011b26 referring to what is putatively in the middle of a contradictory pair. The second reading is defended by Asclepius, Ross and Kirwan. A third is a recent proposal by Cassin and Narcy (1989) based on their novel reading of the Greek. A fourth is a proposal by Cavini (1998) that attempts a rapprochement between the traditional readings and that of Cassin and Narcy. This is not the place to ask whether or not these proposed reconstructions of the argument are sound. Nor is this the place to ask whether or not all of Aristotle's philosophical contemporaries would have embraced all of the premises in the various reconstructions. What is crucial here is to recognize that *definitions* of "truth" and "falsehood" are seen as essential to the success of the argument on all of the leading interpretations. Each reading is presented as valid only if the formulae at 1011b26–27 are understood as definitions. The different analyses reflect different editorial decisions about punctuation in 1011b26–29. While commentators disagree over the proper reconstruction of the argument from 1011b23–28, all agree that Aristotle is arguing on the basis of the definitions presented at 1011b26–27. If these interpreters are correct and if we respect the principle of charity, then we have a compelling reason for thinking the formulae express definitions.

Kinds of Definition

We may suppose, then, that Aristotle presents definitions at 1011b26–27, and we can go on to ask what precisely Aristotle is defining, and what kind of definition he is giving. The textual evidence just reviewed points to *what* is being defined: the definitions at 1011b26–27 are formulae of what the terms "τὸ ψεῦδος" and "τὸ ἀληθὲς" signify. It is clear from both 1011b25 and 1011b26–27 that the explicit definienda are "τὸ ἀληθὲς" and "τὸ ψεῦδος," which are most naturally taken as substantive expressions well translated by "truth" or "the true" and "falsehood" or "the false." Thus, we can imagine Aristotle posing the dialectical question to his opponent in Γ 7: "What do you signify by the terms 'truth' and 'falsehood'?" To which question Aristotle replies, on behalf of his opponents: "By 'truth' I signify the same as 'to assert of what is that it is, or of what is not that it is not' and by 'falsehood' I signify the same as 'to assert of what is that it is not, or of what is not that it is.'"

It is not so clear how to interpret the defining phrases proposed for these terms. The surface grammar of the definientia is well tracked by Ross's formulation "to say of what is that it is not, and of what is not that it is, is falsehood, while to say of what is that it is, and of what is not that it is not, is truth." Yet genuine textual and philosophical difficulties arise when we attempt to interpret the mains terms: "τὸ λέγειν," "τὸ ὄν," "εἶναι," and "μή." And how we interpret these terms in part depends on whether or not we think they express ordinary language concepts, common philosophical concepts, or technical concepts from one philosophical school or another. In order to make this latter determination, we first need to know the kind of definition Aristotle is presenting given the different kinds of definitions he recognizes.

In *Topics* book A 4, at 101b19ff., Aristotle introduces the notion of a definition [ὅρος] as one of the two kinds of phrases that signify the part of a thing that is peculiar to it—the kind of phrase that signifies the essence of the thing as opposed to the kind that signifies one of its propria. In *Topics* book A 5, he elaborates on this basic idea:

ἔστι δ' ὅρος μὲν λόγος ὁ τὸ τί ἦν εἶναι σημαίνων, ἀποδίδοται δὲ ἢ λόγος ἀντ' ὀνόματος ἢ λόγος ἀντὶ λόγου.

A definition is an account signifying the essence of something, rendered either as a phrase instead of a name or a phrase instead of a phrase. (trans., mine)

Every definition, according to this passage, is an account that is given in place of some name or some phrase, and every definition signifies the essence of something. A little further on in the same passage, at 101b36, Aristotle claims that a definition is a λόγος signifying the essence of something, asserted as a phrase used in place of a term or as a phrase used in place of a phrase.[20] Again, in *Topics* book E 1, at 130b25–26, Aristotle claims that "it is necessary that nothing be involved in a definition apart from the account which reveals the being of something" (trans., mine). In his fuller discussion of definitions in *Topics* book Z, Aristotle claims that a definition is a phrase involving a term that signifies some genus and a term that signifies some differentia of that genus. Throughout *Topics* Z Aristotle discusses the construction and destruction of a definition with reference to what is signified by the definiendum and what is signified by the definiens, clearly assuming that the correct definiens signifies the essence of the thing signified by the definiendum. Thus, according to Aristotle in the *Topics*, every definition is an assertion involving a definiendum that signifies some thing and a definiens that signifies the essence of that thing.[21]

As in the *Topics*, in the *Posterior Analytics* Aristotle explicates the nature of a definition [ὁρισμός] in terms of what something is. He distinguishes among four kinds of definitions in the *Posterior Analytics*,[22] introducing the first kind in book B, chapter 10, at 93b29–37:

Ὁρισμὸς δ' ἐπειδὴ λέγεται εἶναι λόγος τοῦ τί ἐστι, φανερὸν ὅτι ὁ μέν τις ἔσται λόγος τοῦ τί σημαίνει τὸ ὄνομα ἢ λόγος ἕτερος ὀνοματώδης, οἷον τί σημαίνει [τί ἐστι] τρίγωνον. ὅπερ ἔχοντες ὅτι ἔστι, ζητοῦμεν διὰ τί ἔστιν.

Since a definition is said to be an account of what something is, it is apparent that some will be accounts of what some name, or some other name-like account, signifies—e.g., what 'triangle' signifies. When we know that this very thing [triangle] is, then we seek for why it exists. (trans., mine)

Aristotle describes the first kind of definition as an account of what some name or name-like phrase signifies. As an example of this kind of definition, Aristotle says that the name "thunder" signifies a noise of fire being extinguished in the clouds. This kind of definition—the definition of what a name or phrase signifies—is traditionally called a "nominal definition."

At *Apo.* 93b39–40 Aristotle introduces a second kind of definition, describing it as an account that reveals why something is; at *Apo.* 94a7–9 he introduces a third kind of definition, describing it as the conclusion of a demonstration of the essence of something. He describes the fourth and last kind of definition as an indemonstrable account of the essence of something. The latter three kinds of definition involve definientia that signify the essence of what is signified by the definienda. Each is a kind of "real" definition, as this phrase is traditionally understood.[23]

Aristotle explicitly asserts—*Apo.* B 10, 93b29–30—that some definitions are accounts of what some name or name-like phrase signifies. What a given name signifies and what the nominal definition corresponding to that name signifies may be such that it does not exist. This explains Aristotle's subsequent assertion at 93b32 that before we can seek to know *why* that which is signified by the name exists we need to know *that* what is signified by the name exists. We can possess a nominal definition of a name—and thus we can complete Stage 1 of our inquiry into the nature of something—before we know that what is signified by that name exists.

At *Apo.* B 1, 89b24–25, Aristotle asserts that we always seek to understand one of four kinds of things: *that* it is, *why* it is, *if* it is, and *what* it is. Aristotle explicitly identifies seeking to understand *why* it is with seeking to understand *what* it is in *Apo.* B 2, at 90a14–15. Similarly, Aristotle's assertions and examples in *Apo.* B 1 and 2 imply that seeking to understand *that* something is, is identical with seeking to understand *if* something is. Aristotle's fourfold distinction thus reduces to a twofold distinction between seeking to understand *that* something is and seeking to understand *why* something is.

This twofold distinction corresponds with the distinction between nominal definitions and definitions that signify the essence of something. At the outset, all we have is a nominal definition, and this is an account of what some name signifies but not an account of the essence of something. At this stage, we do not know except accidentally whether or not what is signified by the name or phrase and its corresponding nominal definition exists. Determining whether or not what is signified by a nominal definition exists is a difficult task, as Aristotle notes at *Apo.* B 10, 93b32–34. At the stage where all we know is what a name and its corresponding nominal definition signify, the only grasp we have of the thing signified is accidental knowledge. (Aristotle discusses the nature of this accidental knowledge that something exists in *Apo.* B 8.) According to Aristotle in *Apo.* B 10, at 93b32, the first thing we need to do in such a situation is determine *that* what is signified by the nominal definition is or is not. This implies that it is possible for a nominal definition to be an account of what a name or phrase signifies and for that which the name or phrase signifies either to exist or not. If it were always necessary for nominal definitions to signify what exists, or if it were always impossible for them to signify what exists, then we would not need to determine whether or not *that* what is signified exists.

The definiens of a nominal definition, therefore, need not signify the essence of what is signified by the definiendum. In extreme cases this is because what is signified by the definiendum doesn't exist and, hence, cannot have an essence. In other, more ordinary cases the definiens fails to signify the essence is because the nominal definitions of the terms we use rarely capture the essences of the things signified by our terms. In Aristotle's example at 93b29–37 the definiens of the nominal definition of "thunder"—i.e., the phrase "a noise of fire being extinguished in the clouds"—need not and likely will not signify the essence of what is signified by the definiendum "thunder." As Aristotle might put it, the nominal definition of a term is a definiens that signifies what is signified by the definiendum as that thing is better known by us and not as it is better known by nature. We know thunder better as the noise that accompanies lightning; thunder is better known by nature as the sound of the compression wave caused by the rapid expansion and contraction of air super-heated by a bolt of lightning. Put another way, the defining phrase "a noise that accompanies lightning" may well signify the noise signified by the term "thunder," but it need not—and does not—signify the essence of that noise, since the fact of mere accompaniment is not what is essential to the noise of thunder being what it is. Aristotle's example makes the point even more strongly: the defining phrase "a noise of fire being extinguished in the clouds" is serviceable enough as a definition of what "thunder" signifies as long as we allow that lightning can be seen as a kind of "fire" and we allow the supposition that the clouds through which lightning arcs are moist and can extinguish such fire. Though serviceable, the phrase "a noise of fire being extinguished in the clouds" fails to signify the essence of thunder—the noise of thunder in fact has nothing to do with clouds or with fire being extinguished. The essence of what is signified by "thunder" is expressed by a quite different phrase that accurately describes and signifies the essence of that kind of noise: "the sound of the compression wave caused by the rapid expansion and contraction of air super-heated by a bolt of lightning."[24]

Once we know *that* what is signified by a nominal definition and its corresponding name (or phrase) exists—thus completing Stage 2 of our inquiry—we can seek to understand *why* that thing is as it is.[25] Given what Aristotle claims in *Apo.* B 8–10, this investigation into why something is as it is involves proceeding through middle terms until we have an indemonstrable definition that makes this clear. Since, according to Aristotle, the essence of something makes clear why it is as it is, the definition of *why* something is as it is, is a definition of its essence. Such definitions are real definitions.

Arguing for the Axioms

The definitions at 1011b26–27 are presented as premises in an argument for LEM at 1011b23–28. This argument is the first in a set of arguments supporting LEM, a set that immediately follows an elaborate series of elenctic demonstrations in support of the Law of Non-Contradiction (LNC). We gain further insight into how we should interpret the definitions at 1011b26–27 by understanding how they function within this larger argumentative context. To this end we first need to grasp how Aristotle understands the axioms of demonstration in general and how he imagines he might defend them.

The axioms of demonstration—Aristotle also calls them "common axioms" [τὰ κοινὰ ἀξιώματα]—occupy his attention in the *Analytics*. An axiom [ἀξίομα] is an immediate proposition that one must grasp if one is to learn anything. An axiom is a proposition [πρότασις]; a proposition is either an affirmative or a negative assertion (see, e.g., *Apo*. 72a8–9). Hence every axiom is either an affirmative or a negative assertion. In *De Interpretatione* Aristotle defined an assertion as an account [λόγος] that is either true or false. It follows that an axiom is essentially an affirmative or negative account that is either true or false. He has also established in *De Interpretatione* that an affirmative or negative assertion is either part of a contradiction. The part of a contradiction asserting that one thing belongs to another is called an affirmation [κατάφασις]. The other part of a contradiction asserts that one thing does not belong to another and is called a denial [ἀπόφασις]. A contradiction, by definition, is an opposition of assertions that excludes of itself any intermediate assertion. Aristotle reiterates these points in the *Posterior Analytics* at 72a11–13.

On the basis of these distinctions we can see that an axiom of demonstration is an immediate affirmative or negative assertion that one must grasp if one is to learn anything. Aristotle distinguishes such axioms from posits. A posit [θέσαν] is an immediate proposition that is *not* a necessary condition for learning in general. (Aee *Apo*. 72a14–16.) There are two kinds of posits: hypotheses and definitions. An hypothesis [ὑπόθεσις] is a posit that asserts either that something is or that something is not is. (See *Apo*. 72a18–20.) A definition [ὁρισμός] is a posit that does not assert *that* something is or is not. (See *Apo*. 72a20.) Rather, as we just saw above at *Apo*. 72a21–24, a definition asserts *what* something is, not *that* it is.

The logical axioms are among the three kinds of primitive claims involved in demonstration. The other two are, on the one hand, the supposition of the genus of study and, on the other hand, the posits concerning the attributes of the supposed genus. According to Aristotle, at *Apo.* 71b25–26, all such primitive [πρῶτον] claims are true [ἀληθῆ]. From these three kinds of primitive claims all demonstration proceeds. (See *Apo.* 76b14–15.)

Aristotle claims at *Apo.* 72a7 that a principle of demonstration is an immediate proposition [πρότασις ἄμεσος]. An immediate proposition is a proposition to which no other is prior. This means that the axioms of demonstration cannot be inferred from other premises. (See *Apo.* 72a8.) They are the first principles of arguments.[26] To argue for them requires a kind of argument that respects these facts.

When assessing the elenctic demonstrations in book Γ in support of the logical axioms, perhaps the most important fact to keep in mind is that Aristotle assumes his elenctic demonstrations presuppose the norms governing philosophical inquiry. The opponents he has in mind are *philosophical* opponents willing to engage in logical argument. He is not concerned with ordinary conversation. It is important, therefore, to be clear about what he thinks such philosophical inquiry can and cannot achieve.[27]

His elenctic defense of the logical axioms is constrained by the norms of dialectical inquiry. Dialectic was a common form of logical inquiry by the time Aristotle wrote his treatises on dialectic. The *Topics* and the *Sophistical Refutations* proceed on the assumption that dialectic is part of the normal philosophical curriculum.[28] In defense of axioms, according to Aristotle, there can be neither demonstration [ἀπόδειξις] of the sort defined in the *Posterior Analytics* nor reasoning [συλλογισμός] of the sort defined in the *Topics*. To defend a logical axiom, one must refute the claims of those who oppose it. He calls this type of refutation an elenctic demonstration [τὸ ἐλεγκτικῶς ἀποδεῖξαι].[29] He explicitly distinguishes elenctic demonstration from demonstration proper [ἀπόδειξις] in Γ.4, at 1006a15ff.

Aristotle differentiates elenctic demonstration and reasoning [συλλογισμός] at *Sophistical Refutations* 164b25ff. Reasoning, on the one hand, involves positing certain assertions in such a way as "necessarily to cause the assertions other than those assertions and as a result of those assertions" (trans., mine). In an elenctic demonstration, on the other hand, one employs reasoning of the same sort but in order to contradict a conclusion offered by an opponent as opposed to positing something oneself (for which claim see *Sophistical Refutations* 170a39ff., 171a1ff., 174b19ff., and 174b36ff.).

Demonstration proper [ἀπόδειξις] is a kind of reasoning [συλλογισμός]. If anything is obvious, it is that one cannot demonstrate the truth of an *indemonstrable* logical axiom. Aristotle argues in *Metaphysics* book Γ that one *cannot* provide a demonstration of an axiom. For one's opponent might think that one assumes the very axiom one aims to prove: demonstration of a logical axiom might be thought to presuppose the axiom in question. In an *elenctic* demonstration, on the other hand, the opponent is responsible for everything that is assumed.

In arguing for the logical axioms, then, Aristotle cannot assume them. He is fully aware of this fact in book Γ. He is quite clear that there can be no "epistemonic" demonstration of the logical axioms. Hence, there can be no constructive philosophical proof of a logical axiom. He does, however, promise an elenctic demonstration [τὸ ἐλεγτικῶς ἀποδεῖξαι] in Γ 4, at 1006a11ff. In making this promise, Aristotle has in mind the distinctions noted above concerning dialectic in the *Topics* and *Sophistical Refutations*. This is evident at 1006a11–27:

ἔστι δ' ἀποδεῖξαι ἐλεγκτικῶς καὶ περὶ τούτου ὅτι ἀδύνατον, ἂν μόνον τι λέγῃ ὁ ἀμφισβητῶν· ἂν δὲ μηθέν, γελοῖον τὸ ζητεῖν λόγον πρὸς τὸν μηθενὸς ἔχοντα λόγον, ᾗ μὴ ἔχει· ὅμοιος γὰρ φυτῷ ὁ τοιοῦτος ᾗ τοιοῦτος ἤδη. τὸ δ' ἐλεγκτικῶς ἀποδεῖξαι λέγω διαφέρειν καὶ τὸ ἀποδεῖξαι, ὅτι ἀποδεικνύων μὲν ἂν δόξειεν αἰτεῖσθαι τὸ ἐν ἀρχῇ, ἄλλου δὲ τοῦ τοιούτου αἰτίου ὄντος ἔλεγχος ἂν εἴη καὶ οὐκ ἀπόδειξις. ἀρχὴ δὲ πρὸς ἅπαντα τὰ τοιαῦτα οὐ τὸ ἀξιοῦν ἢ εἶναί τι λέγειν ἢ μὴ εἶναι (τοῦτο μὲν γὰρ τάχ' ἄν τις ὑπολάβοι τὸ ἐξ ἀρχῆς αἰτεῖν), ἀλλὰ σημαίνειν γέ τι καὶ αὑτῷ καὶ ἄλλῳ· τοῦτο γὰρ ἀνάγκη, εἴπερ λέγοι τι. εἰ γὰρ μή, οὐκ ἂν εἴη τῷ τοιούτῳ λόγος, οὔτ' αὐτῷ πρὸς αὑτὸν οὔτε πρὸς ἄλλον. ἂν δέ τις τοῦτο διδῷ, ἔσται ἀπόδειξις· ἤδη γάρ τι ἔσται ὡρισμένον. ἀλλ' αἴτιος οὐχ ὁ ἀποδεικνὺς ἀλλ' ὁ ὑπομένων· ἀναιρῶν γὰρ λόγον ὑπομένει λόγον. ἔτι δὲ ὁ τοῦτο συγχωρήσας συγκεχώρηκέ τι ἀληθὲς εἶναι χωρὶς ἀποδείξεως [ὥστε οὐκ ἂν πᾶν οὕτως καὶ οὐχ οὕτως ἔχοι].

There is, however, a demonstration by refutation even that his view [that we started with] is impossible, if only the disputant says something. But if he says nothing, it is ridiculous to look for an argument against someone who has an argument for nothing, insofar as he has none. For such a person, insofar as he is such, is like a vegetable. And by "demonstrating by refutation" I mean something different from demonstrating, because in demonstrating we might seem to be assuming the starting-point at issue, but if the other person is responsible for an assumption of this sort, it would be refutation not demonstration. The starting-point for all such arguments is to ask the disputant not to *state* something to be or not to be (since someone might take this to be assuming the starting-point at issue), but rather to *signify* something both to himself and to another person, either with himself or with another. But if he does grant it, demonstration will be possible, since there will already be something definite. The one responsible for it, however, is not the one who gives the demonstration but the one who submits to it, since in doing away with argument, he submits to argument. Further, anyone who agrees to this has agreed that something is true without a demonstration, so that not everything will be so-and-so and not so-and-so. (trans., Reeve)

In this passage Aristotle recognizes the need to avoid begging the question in defending the logical axioms. The passage also indicates that, in presenting his elenctic arguments, he plans to work with a small subset of the concepts governing dialectical inquiry, a set disjoint from that containing the logical axioms. In particular, he demands we accept two basic semantic assumptions in arguing elenctically for the logical axioms. These basic semantic assumptions inform the sort of definitions Aristotle has in mind in *Metaphysics* book Γ 7.1011b26–27 and will help us to decide on the kind of definition he has in mind there.

Aristotle's Fundamental Philosophical Semantics

Aristotle's first semantic assumption in *Metaphysics* book Γ 4 is that a dialectical opponent must say something that is significant both for himself and for another. According to Aristotle, the key to the sort of elenctic demonstration needed to defend the logical axioms is that the opponent "signify something that is significant for himself and for another" [σημαίνειν γέ τι καὶ αὐτῷ]. (See 1006a18–21.)

Part of what this involves is, strictly speaking, exogenous to the *Metaphysics*. Aristotle here relies upon very general claims derived from his account of linguistic signification and thought in the *Organon* and the psychological treatises. According to Aristotle's considered view, the linguistic terms and assertions of written and spoken language are conventional symbols of the intensional contents of thoughts in the psyches of language users and, by means of these intensional contents, these linguistic terms and assertions also signify the real correlates of the intensional contents.[30] For his purposes in book Γ he need only assume the much weaker assumption that either (i) the linguistic terms and assertions of written and spoken language signify the intensional contents of thoughts of both the opponent and her interlocutor or (ii) they signify things in the world available to both the opponent and her interlocutor.

But in signifying something significant to both herself and her interlocutor, the opponent need not commit herself to one side or another of a contradiction (see 1006a18–20), since this might again be seen as begging the question about the axiom in question.[31] But if the opponent need not posit a hypothesis, she must signify something both for herself and for another. (See 1006a21.) Aristotle claims at 1006a21–22 that this is necessary if the opponent is to say anything and if she is to reason with herself or with another.

In the context of dialectical and philosophical debate, Aristotle tells us that signifying something amounts to demanding that an opponent define the term or terms she is using. If the opponent signifies something both for herself and for another, then something will have been defined [τι ὡρισμένον, at 1006a24–25]. In *Met.* Γ 7, at 1012a21–24, in reference to those who "demand a reason for everything," he recommends that:

ἀρχὴ δὲ πρὸς ἅπαντας τούτους ἐξ ὁρισμοῦ. ὁρισμὸς δὲ γίγνεται ἐκ τοῦ σημαίνειν τι ἀναγκαῖον εἶναι αὐτούς· ὁ γὰρ λόγος οὗ τὸ ὄνομα σημεῖον ὁρισμὸς ἔσται.

The starting-point in dealing with all such people is definition. Now the definition rests on the necessity of their signifying something; for the formula of that which the word signifies will be its definition. (trans., mine, following Ross 1924)

Following this at 1012b5–8, he urges that:

> ἀλλὰ πρὸς πάντας τοὺς τοιούτους λόγους αἰτεῖσθαι δεῖ, καθάπερ ἐλέχθη καὶ ἐν τοῖς ἐπάνω λόγοις, οὐχὶ εἶναί τι ἢ μὴ εἶναι ἀλλὰ σημαίνειν τι, ὥστε ἐξ ὁρισμοῦ διαλεκτέον λαβόντας τί σημαίνει τὸ ψεῦδος ἢ τὸ ἀληθές.

> Against all such arguments [i.e., arguments that either nothing is true, everything is true, or both nothing and everything is true] we must postulate, as we said above, not that something is or is not, but that people signify something, we must argue from a definition, having got what falsity or truth signifies. (trans., mine, following Ross)

There are two ways to interpret this last passage.[32] On the first interpretation, Aristotle is asserting that every elenctic argument involves, as an explicit step, getting the opponent to accept the proposed definitions of truth and falsehood. If this is Aristotle's claim, then the proposed definitions may be seen as explicit premises in *every* elenctic argument for the logical axioms. On the second interpretation, Aristotle is asserting (i) that every elenctic argument presupposes but does not make explicit some definition of truth and falsehood or other and (ii) that every elenctic argument involves some definition or other—perhaps even the definitions of truth and falsehood themselves—as an explicit premise in the argument. If the latter interpretation is correct, then the definitions of truth and falsehood in the various elenctic arguments need not be explicit premises, but would be implicit premises. Either way, according to the passage, some definition or other of truth and falsehood are crucial to every elenctic demonstration. And either way, every elenctic demonstration involves some definition or other of some term. Although I cannot make the case here, for reasons of space, it can be shown that each elenctic argument in book Γ involves the definitions of truth and falsehood presented at 1011b26–27 as either explicit or tacit premises.

According to Aristotle, a definition is the starting point in arguing against opponents who demand a reason for everything. At the very least, a nominal definition is an account of what the name or names used by an opponent signify. In such a case, the opponent need not postulate that what the name signifies exists, or that it does not exist, only that the name signify some one thing. She could, say, postulate that the name "Vulcan" signifies some one planet in the solar system. In establishing the signification of "Vulcan," our opponent need not commit herself to the claim that the planet exists. The opponent could also offer a definition—a real definition—that is supposed to actually signify one and only one essence in the world. Diogenes, for example, might suggest that the term "human being" actually signifies the species of featherless bipeds, which might be thought to be the essence of what is signified by "human being." In such a case, the opponent may offer a real definition that is supposed to be an indemonstrable first principle, or she may offer an instance of one of the two kinds of definitions mentioned in the *Posterior Analytics* that involve demonstrating the essence in question. In either case, given how Aristotle understands such posits, it follows that elenctic demonstration begins with some sort of definition.

Every definition is itself an assertion and, as such, is either true or false. Thus, if the opponent signifies something both for himself and for another, he thereby admits that something is true [συγκεχώρηκέ τι ἀληθές] independently of whatever else might be shown by means of the elenctic demonstration.[33] Thus, if an opponent offers a term d as the definiens of a definiendum n, then the opponent asserts that the definition "$n =_{df.} D$" is true. There are two principal factors here, neither of which is incidental. First, the opponent must signify something. Second, he must signify something *both for himself and for another*. Signifying even this much, according to Aristotle, entails definition and truth.

If the opponent is to say something, then he must signify at least one thing with the name he uses. (1006b12–13) Thus, if d is the *definiens* of the definition of a name n, then d signifies one and only one thing. Aristotle is explicit in book Γ about how to go about ensuring that this constraint is respected. His explanation involves assertion about what it is to be one, an argument about the presuppositions of thinking, and an argument about the conditions for name giving. The claim about what it is to be one comes at 1006b25–28. According to Aristotle, to be one thing signifies that the definition [λόγος] of the thing is one. Aristotle insists, and argues, that being and oneness are coextensive. Where there is being, there you find some sort of oneness, and vice versa. In signifying one thing by means of a name, one is signifying a being. In the case where this is all the opponent offers—the admission that name signifies some one thing—the assertion he makes has the logical form of a definition, which entails that it does not involve assertorically combining or separating two distinct beings. Rather, a definition asserts, of some being, what it is to be that being. In other words, a definition asserts that a being is itself. With regard to all other sorts of assertions, he presupposes that all of these, regardless of their complexity and insofar as they are genuine assertions, will succumb to an analysis that reduces them to simple assertions involving one thing being combined or separated from another.

Aristotle explains having a definite signification in terms of signifying one thing [σημαίνει ἕν].[34] By "signifying one thing" he means: if y is x, then if anything is x, y will be what being x is. (See 1006a32–34, where he uses the example of being human.) Here y is what is signified by the formula d expressing the *definiens* of x, which is what is signified by the *definiendum n*. If a *definiens d* of the definition of a name n signifies one and only one thing b, then if anything a is signified by n, being b is what it is to be a. Thus, following Aristotle's example, if the term "human" is univocal and is defined by the univocal definiens "being a two-footed animal," then if h is signified by "human," what is signified by the phrase "being a two-footed animal" will be what h is. When we discuss Aristotle's account of measurement and number, we will consider with care Aristotle's account of what it is for something to be one thing and how this informs his real definition of truth.

The argument about the conditions for thought comes at 1006b10–11: It is not possible for our opponent to think of anything unless our opponent thinks of one thing. It is possible to think of something. Hence, it is possible to think of one thing (1006b10). To this account of thinking, at 1006b11–13, Aristotle adds an account of name giving: It is possible for the opponent to assign one name to the one thing about which he is thinking (1006b11). Suppose the opponent assigns a name, n, to the single thing o about which he is thinking. If so, then n signifies something and signifies one thing for the opponent. Presumably this is not enough, for Aristotle insists that the opponent must say something that is significant for both himself and for us. This is why he adds, to the requirement that each name signifies only one thing, that two names signify one and the same thing just in case they signify "synonyms," i.e., the *things* they signify have the same definition [λόγος]. Two terms signify one and the same thing if what they signify is synonymous. (See 1006b1–4 and 1006b11–18.) Thus, suppose n_1 signifies one thing o_1 and n_2 signifies one thing o_2. If so, then n_1 is associated with an account (a definition) d_1 that signifies the being of o_1. Moreover, n_2 is associated with an account (a definition) d_2 that signifies the being of o_2. o_1 and o_2 are synonyms, for Aristotle, just in case $d_1 = d_2$. If so, then n_1 and n_2 are synonymous names in the sense that they have the same signification. This account of signifying one thing in terms of Aristotelian synonymy makes it clear that signifying one thing [τὸ ἓν σημαίνειν] is not the same as being said of one thing [τὸ καθ' ἑνός].

Aristotle is, therefore, rather laconic in claiming that, for an elenctic demonstration, the opponent needs only say something. It is not as if anything goes. The opponent needs to say something that conforms to the rules of dialectical exchange. Minimally, the opponent must define his terms and, in so doing, not only stake a claim to truth but assume (at least implicitly) some definition or other of truth and falsehood. In addition, he requires that the opponent, in saying something, uses at least one word that signifies only one thing, the oneness of the signification being a function of having only one definition.[35]

What if the opponent refuses to provide appropriate premises with which to work? Aristotle dismisses such opponents as being no better than plants, his point being that such opponents forego rational discourse and, hence, are no better than vegetables in the context of dialectic.[36] Indeed, they may be worse than plants, since such opponents are nonsensical and noisy. In refusing to say something definite, the opponent lacks argument [λόγος] and is not capable of arguing either with himself or with another.

According to Aristotle, elenctic demonstrations are the only sort of arguments that can be given in support of the logical axioms. We have just seen that the terms involved in the elenctic demonstration must be univocal. The second semantic assumption noted in 1006a11–27 (see the passage above) is that the dialectical opponent is responsible for the assumptions involved in the elenctic proof. That is to say, the opponent is the one who asserts that some term or other has a definite signification and "he who admits this has admitted that something is true" (trans., Ross). Therefore, for an elenctic argument to proceed, the opponent must assert that some claim or other is true.[37] This is not to say that the opponent must assert one or another side of an opposed pair of assertions. That this is not required is clear from 1006a19–20. The opponent is not required to affirm or deny that one thing belongs to another. Rather, the opponent is simply required to assume that a given term signifies one and only one thing, which assumption takes the form of a definition. The asserted definition is assumed to be true for the sake of the elenctic argument. In providing the assumption, the opponent admits that something is true independently of the logical axioms governing demonstration,

LNC and LEM, because these axioms not only presuppose that the terms involved signify something definite, but also that there are opposed pairs of assertions. Thus, the assumed definition is made in a way relevantly "apart from demonstration."

One can imagine philosophical opponents who might balk at this latter constraint.[38] Aristotle evinces no worry over this practical problem. Why is he optimistic in the face of this threat to rational inquiry?

First, engaging in argument essentially involves making assertions, and assertions, by definition, are truth claims.[39] If the opponent refuses to make this initial move, if he refuses to make an assertion, then he opts out of rational inquiry altogether. As Aristotle sees it, the opponent chooses the life of a plant. Why a plant as opposed to a slug? Perhaps this is because every animal at least has some capacity for sensation. There may be some sense in which the capacity for sensation presupposes a capacity for assertion (although, and quite obviously, not the capacity for the sort of assertion involved in higher cognitive functions). This speculation cannot be defended here. However, if it is at all plausible to think that sensory perception involves some degenerate form of assertion, plants lack even this. Plants, then, are like those opponents who refuse to assert anything. Aristotle, therefore, is not engaged in wanton ad hominem argument. He is pointing out that his opponent has resigned, altogether, his status as a being capable of discriminating one thing from another. Of course, the opponent remains capable of discrimination, and as a consequence mischaracterizes his cognitive abilities in resigning his status. In much the same way, the person who claims to be able to believe both sides of a contradiction mischaracterizes his cognitive state.

If, however, the opponent is willing to make an assertion, and commit to some account being true or false, then Aristotle presses his case. By the definition of an assertion, in asserting that some claim is true, the opponent is saying something the significance of which is agreed upon. She also commits herself to some conception of truth or other. Having elicited this much, Aristotle then proceeds to explain why the opponent is, ipso facto, committed to the logical axiom she has denied.

In an elenctic demonstration, our opponent does not remain "indifferent" to the truth or falsehood of the logical axiom in question. The opponent emphatically denies the axiom is true. This makes it clear that elenctic demonstrations differ from merely dialectical exercises, since dialectical training involves entertaining dialectical premises without committing oneself to its truth or falsehood. Hence, unlike dialectical arguments pursued simply for the sake of training, the arguments in book Γ for the logical axioms begin with an assertion that one or another axiom is false. They are pursued in earnest in order to secure the first principles of philosophical inquiry.[40]

Suppose, then, that someone denies one of the logical axioms. What are we supposed to do next? First, we get the opponent to define her terms, or at least one of them. Apparently, any definition of any term will do. This is an innocuous demand because this sort of posit, as explained above, does not commit our opponent to the assertion that something is or is not. Rather, such a posit is a definition and commits the opponent only to an assertion that some term signifies some one thing. Second, we ensure that all of the terms in the *definiens* of the opponent's definition are univocal. This involves establishing that each term in the *definiens* signifies one and only one thing in the context of the assertion. Having secured these points, we proceed to demonstrate that the opponent's definition is true only if the logical axiom she denies is also true. Thus, the opponent is refuted.[41]

The general form of such an elenctic demonstration involves three basic steps: First, a philosophical opponent denies the truth of some logical axiom. Second, the opponent grants that some definition is true. Third, Aristotle demonstrates that the definition assumed by his opponent is true only if the logical axiom denied by his opponent is true. The first and second steps require that the opponent commit himself to the truth or falsehood of some assertion or other. (See Dancy 1975, 30.) The first step requires that the opponent deny the truth of this or that logical axiom. The second step ensures that the opponent grants that some definition or other of some term is true. The final step describes the basic tactic Aristotle employs once his opponent has taken the first two steps. When combined with explicit statements of the semantic constraints placed upon elenctic demonstrations, the general form of an elenctic demonstration can be reconstructed as follows:

E1: A philosophical opponent o denies the truth of some logical axiom λ.

E2: o asserts that a definition $n =_{df.} d$ is true, where d is the *definiens* of the *definiendum* n.

E3: If d is the *definiens* of the definition of a name n, then d and n signify one and only one thing b.

E4: If a *definiens* d of the definition of a name n signifies one and only one thing b, then if anything a is signified by N, being b is what it is to be a.

E5: Demonstrate that $n =_{df.} d$ is true only if λ is true.

Aristotle's Opponents

We now understand the general form of Aristotle's elenctic demonstrations in book Γ 3–8 and how definitions of truth and falsehood are involved at this general level. He is attempting to vindicate first principles which, given their logical priority, cannot be justified by means of demonstrative argument. If someone opposes this sort of principle, and we wish to engage them in rational discussion, he tells us we need to argue using premises provided by the opponent. The fundamental move is to get the opponent to say something significant, which entails that they use a term that has a definite signification (i.e., is explicitly defined for the sake of the argument). This is the kind of argument he undertakes in Γ 3–6, considering various premises an opponent might give for doubting this principle.

Importantly, in denying that a logical axiom is true and in granting that some definition is true, our opponent at least implicitly acknowledges and works with some conception of truth or other. Given what is known about their divergent views, it is unlikely that Aristotle's philosophical opponents shared a common account of the essence of truth and falsehood. It is plausible, for example, that Antisthenes, Plato, and Aristotle differed about the exact nature of linguistic and mental assertion. It is also known that none of Aristotle's opponents maintained the same account of being.[42] Thus, if a real definition of truth and falsehood presupposes philosophically sophisticated accounts of assertion and being, and if philosophical and dialectical debate requires agreement on a real definition of truth and falsehood, then it looks like such debate is practically impossible. Since Aristotle clearly thinks such debate is possible—he is engaging in it—it seems best to assume that such debate relies on nominal definitions of truth and falsehood as opposed to real definitions. Is this assumption correct?

Returning to the immediate context in which Aristotle presents his definition of 'truth' at 1011b23–29—the argument for LEM at 1011b23–28—we can ask first of all to whom does Aristotle direct the argument? The argument is part of the continuous series of arguments developed in book

Γ in support of the logical axioms. He has established that a reasonable opponent may well submit to the proposed premises. The subsequent arguments in book Γ 7 and 8 make it clear that he continues to think of his tactics in terms of the sort of destructive elenctic arguments that can be employed in defense of the logical axioms. In addition, in arguing for LNC in Γ 1–6, he presupposes the definitions of truth and falsehood in Γ 7. Thus, it seems that at 1011b23–29 Aristotle is engaging philosophical opponents in an elenctic argument for LEM.

Quite generally in *Metaphysics* book Γ Aristotle is addressing philosophical opponents as diverse as those accepting Anaxagorean, Democritean, Empedoclean, Heraclitean, Homeric, Parmenidean, and Protagorean frameworks. At 1011b23–28 he does not indicate that he is limiting his attention to any particular opponent among these likely opponents. It would seem that he offers his argument at 1011b23–29 to all comers. What sort of argument could he propose to such motley opponents with a shred of optimism that he might persuade even a minority of them?

The argument at 1011b23–29 conforms to the type of argument Aristotle refers to as "τὸ δ'ἐλεγκτικῶς ἀποδεῖξαι" earlier in book Γ at 1006a11 and 1006a15–16. The key to all such argument, again, is that our partner in dialectic signify something both for herself and for another [σημαίνειν γέ τι καὶ αὑτῷ καὶ ἄλλῳ]. As noted above, at 1012a21–24, in reference to those who "demand a reason for everything," Aristotle recommends that the starting point in arguing against all such comers is a definition [ἀρχὴ δὲ πρὸς ἅπαντας τούτους ἐξ ὁρισμοῦ]. And just after this, at 1012b5–8, with respect to all arguments that either nothing is true, everything is true, or both nothing and everything is true, Aristotle urges that we argue from the definition, having established what "true" and "false" signify [. . . ἐξ ὁρισμοῦ διαλεκτέον λαβόντας τί σημαίνει τὸ ψεῦδος ἢ τὸ ἀληθές]. We should expect, then, that the argument at 1011b23–29—a proof by refutation based on what "true" and "false" signify—would begin with nominal definitions of truth and falsehood.

Given the kind of destructive elenctic argument Aristotle explicitly claims can be wielded in defense of the principles at stake in book Γ, he must be exploiting premises his opponents accept since they themselves provide them. That Aristotle thinks his opponents *might* offer the premises with which he works does not commit him to the claim that in fact they will. He leaves it open that his opponents might reject the particular premises he considers. However, he insists that they must admit some such premises, premises that are relevant to the truth or falsehood of the principles and that are consonant with the opponent's philosophical perspective, or they are not reasonable.

For these reasons, insofar as the definitions at 1011b26–27 play a role in the arguments in book Γ, they are best understood as expressing nominal definitions of the terms "truth" and "falsehood." In particular, we ought not to think they express Aristotle's real definitions of the terms. For, were we to do so, we would have to charge him with repeatedly committing *petitio principii*.

Perhaps, though, the argument in Γ 7 in which the definitions of truth and falsehood are deployed is a properly Aristotelian argument, and not an argument of the destructive sort just discussed? There is no good reason for thinking so. It is of course possible that Aristotle develops his arguments in book Γ without concern for whether or not his opponents would be persuaded by them. He often develops arguments marshalling premises his opponents would reject. There is, however, textual evidence that strongly suggests that in book Γ he directs the arguments to his opponents.[43] If we assume, as seems reasonable, that a Protagorean, a Platonist, a Heraclitean, and a member of the Lyceum would differ over the exact signification of the philosophical terms "assertion," "being," and "negation," then it ought not be difficult to see that they would disagree over the precise signification of the *definientia* of the definitions of "truth" and "falsehood" presented by Aristotle at 1011b26–27.[44] Yet all might be willing to grant that the *definientia* are the correct linguistic accounts of what the terms "truth" and "falsehood" signify.[45]

Though the definitions presented at 1011b26–27 are best understood as nominal definitions, they nevertheless merit careful scrutiny. For, first, they circumscribe the terms of the investigation into the real definitions of the terms "truth" and "falsehood." As it turns out, the definitions are crucial for Aristotle's considered account of truth and falsehood. But even if the definitions were largely irrelevant to his subsequent theorizing about truth and falsehood, they would still be important since they play an important role in one of the few arguments Aristotle provides in support of LEM. Second, the arguments in which they serve as premises are among the most important philosophical arguments ever developed in support of the most fundamental philosophical principles. Aristotle offers the definitions of truth and falsehood at 1011b26–27 as premises in an argument for LEM from 1011b23–29. The relation among the definitions, LEM, and LNC, however, also illuminates Aristotle's understanding of the Principle of Bivalence, which in turn is critical to his rejection of Fatalism. There is, thus, a lot at stake in securing a proper interpretation of the definitions in the local argumentative context at 1011b23–29. Third, even if they are nominal definitions, they generate entailments we may presume were shared by Aristotle and his philosophical contemporaries.

Supposing, then, that the argument at 1011b23–29 is a proof by negation beginning with nominal definitions Aristotle's opponents accept, and given that Aristotle's opponents are such a varied lot, what sense can be made of the definitions?

The Nominal Definition of "Truth"

Aristotle's formulae have a Platonic pedigree, and Plato's use of these concepts in the *Cratylus* and the *Sophist* suggests that they are generally accepted and applicable. There is also a striking resemblance between the proposed definitions at 1011b26–27 and Protagoras's famous dictum, as preserved by Plato:

Πάντων χρημάτων μέτρον ἐστὶν ἄνθρωπος, τῶν μὲν ὄντων ὡς ἔστιν, τῶν δὲ οὐκ ὄντων ὡς οὐκ ἔστιν. (DK 80 B1)

The human being is the measure of all things, of things that are that they are, and of things that are not that they are not. (trans., mine)

Plato's character claims that this is a direct quote from Protagoras's book "Truth." Plato himself presents concepts of truth and falsehood in the *Cratylus* (385b2–11). Socrates and Hermogenes agree that to say what is true is to say of what is that it is, and that to say what is false is to say of what is that it is not, which captures at least part of Aristotle's formulae at 1011b26–27. Plato also discusses false beliefs and false statements in the *Sophist* (240d1–241a1). Here the analysis of falsehood presented in the *Cratylus* is ramified, so that to say what is false is either to say of what is that it is not or to say of what is not that it is, which exactly corresponds with Aristotle's formulation of the concept of falsehood at 1011b26–27. And, again in the *Sophist*, Plato considers the nature of true and false speech at 263a11–16. In this passage, Plato's point seems to be that a true statement says something about Theaetetus which captures the way Theaetetus is, and that a false statement says something about Theaetetus which is different from the way Theaetetus is. Generalizing from the case of Theaetetus, it is plausible that Plato intends us to understand that to say what is true is to say of what is the case that it is the case, and that to say what is false is to say of what is the case something different from what is the case.⁴⁶ Apparently, then, it is likely that the ordinary ancient Greek philosopher would recognize Aristotle's formulae as standard definitions of the terms "truth" and "falsehood." How would they have understood the proposed formulae?

Although common, it is somewhat misleading to translate "λέγειν" at 1011b26 by "to say" and to characterize truth and falsehood in terms of "what is said."⁴⁷ I think the best choice is to translate "λέγειν" here with the English verb "to assert." First, it is clear from 1012a2–5 that Aristotle intends the definitions at 1011b26–27 to apply to mental acts as well as speech acts. And in the *Metaphysics*, in book Γ but also quite generally, he is chiefly—if not exclusively—concerned with true and false mental activity as opposed to true and false linguistic activity. This will become evident in subsequent chapters. We need to translate "λέγειν" at 1011b26 with a term that includes, and even privileges, the mental activity of affirmation and denial as well as the analogous linguistic activities. Aristotle himself uses the term "ἀπόφανσις" to denote this kind of mental and linguistic activity. We might simply transliterate the term and talk about apophantic activity had Husserl and Heidegger not secured already this locution for their own purposes. Using "to assert" is a safer choice.

Second, "to say" and "what is said" are problematically ambiguous between acts of saying themselves and what they express. Someone might say, in German, "Gott is tot." If someone asks what was said, I might answer "He said 'Gott ist tot'" or I might answer "She said that God is dead." Or, in an ironical moment, I might say of a dullard "He's a real wit." I say these words, but what I am saying (in the sense of what I express) is that the man is a peabrain. Although similar concerns arise in the case of assertion with respect to the act and content distinction, at least we are less likely—although we will still be prone—to restrict our attention to linguistic activity in using "to assert" to translate "λέγειν."

Cases of irony point to another reason for avoiding "to say" and "what is said" in translating "λέγειν" and its cognates: What is said, in the sense of what is expressed by a speech act, is ambiguous between the pragmatic content and the semantic content of a speech act. To say something is to perform a speech act. From the point of view of pragmatics, what is said in a given speech act may be highly context dependent. From the point of view of semantics, however, what is said is a function of the conventional semantic rules governing the expressions involved in the speech act. Kahn, following Mourelatos, has argued that to interpret "λέγειν" pragmatically is to misconstrue ancient Greek usage.[48] More specifically, in the context of Aristotle's treatises, translating "λέγειν" by "to say" may suggest that he is concerned primarily with pragmatics in defining "truth" and "falsehood" in book Γ, whereas in fact he seems more interested in what is expressed by linguistic symbols given the conventional rules of signification that govern them.[49]

I will press these concerns further later, merely noting them here, and will turn now to the grammatical construction "λέγειν" + "τὸ ὄν" + "εἶναι." There is nothing unusual about this grammatical construction *per se*. It is an instance of indirect discourse: the verb "λέγειν" takes the infinitive "εἶναι" for its object, and the supplementary participle "τὸ ὄν" completes the idea expressed by "εἶναι."[50]

More serious difficulties arise with proposed interpretations of "τὸ ὄν" and "εἶναι." It will help to consider two recent and plausible analyses to get a sense for the general problems. As a first example, Kahn proposed the following interpretation of the definitions:

> To say of what is (so) that it is not or of what is not (so) that it is, is falsehood; to say of what is (so) that it is and of what is not (so) that it is not, is truth. (Kahn 1971, 336n7)

Kahn explains the introduction of the parenthetical "so":

> I have introduced the "(so)" to indicate the more strictly veridical or semantic use of the verb, which occurs in Aristotle's text as the participle οἴη. The infinitive εἶναι, on the other hand, in indirect discourse after λέγειν, represents the descriptive content of what is said, precisely that repeated occurrence of the verb which is usually zeroed even in the most explicit colloquial examples [. . .]. (Kahn 1971, 336n7)

Thus, for Kahn:

> Aristotle defines truth as saying of what-is that it is and of what-is-not that it is not, and falsehood conversely: Here the participial forms ("what is" and "what-is-not") refer to states

of affairs in the world, to positive and negative facts as it were, while the infinitival clauses ("that it is," "that it is not") represent the propositional content asserted: what is said to be the case. (Kahn 1981, 106)

Kahn notes here the two main semantical difficulties: First, with regard to the infinitive "εἶναι," given that it is used in indirect discourse after "λέγειν" to represent the intentional content of the assertion, how should we understand the intentional content of assertions in this context? Kahn talks about the intentional content of assertions in terms of "descriptive" or "propositional" content, but it is an open question, given only the grammatical construction at 1011b26–27, how Aristotle understood the intentional content of assertions. Second, with respect to the participial phrase "τὸ ὄν," given that it is used in such constructions to represent the real correlates of the intentional contents of assertions, what real correlates does Aristotle posit? Kahn discusses these real correlates in terms of "states of affairs" and "facts," but again it is an open question given only the grammatical construction at 1011b26–27, how Aristotle understood the real correlates.

Matthen proposed the following interpretation of the definition of truth at 1011b27: for all propositions, p, there is an x such that p is true if and only if x is (Matthen 1983, 16). Reconstruing this in terms of assertion, we can get: for all assertions, p, there is an x such that p is true if and only if x is. Here, by means of the quantifiers, Matthen too makes explicit the two semantical concerns addressed by Kahn. First, the universal quantifier ranges over propositions, which (whatever else they might be) are, among contemporary semantic theorists, the paradigmatic intentional contents of assertions. Although we may not wish to interpret Aristotelian intentional contents in terms of propositions, Matthen is surely right that some sort of intentional content is called for by the construction. Again, it is an open question, given only the grammatical construction at 1011b26–27, what these are for Aristotle. Second, the existential quantifier ranges over objects in Aristotle's ontology. Matthen argues—persuasively, I think—that we should include among these objects what he calls "predicative complexes," but his arguments for these go beyond the grammatical construction at 1011b26–27. The definitions themselves do not restrict the admissible real correlates, again leaving it an open question what these are for Aristotle.

What can plausibly be inferred from the grammatical construction "λέγειν" + "τὸ ὄν" + "εἶναι" is (1) that "εἶναι" is used to signify the intentional content (however this is understood) of the act of assertion signified by "λέγειν," and (2) that "τὸ ὄν" is used to signify the real correlate (however this is understood) of the intentional content signified by "εἶναι." That is to say, as we might put it, truth and falsehood involve asserting *of* some real correlate *that* it either is or is not. To go further than this, we must attend to the likely meanings of the infinitive εἶναι and its supplementary participle τὸ ὄν.

The proper interpretation of the cognates "εἶναι" ("to be") and "τὸ ὄν" ("being")—as used by ancient Greek philosophers—has exercised commentators. Vis-à-vis Aristotle we may ask:[51] First, how many different senses of the verb "to be" does Aristotle recognize? This is a question about the syntax and semantics of the verb in his treatises. Second, given that Aristotle recognizes at least one objectual sense of the verb, expressed by means of the participle "τὸ ὄν," does he distinguish among different sorts of being? This is a question about Aristotle's ontology. We confront both questions interpreting the definitions at 1011b26–27, since he employs the infinitive of the verb "to be" ("εἶναι"), and its participle "being" ("τὸ ὄν").

Commentators argue over whether Aristotle distinguished among the following senses of the infinitive "to be": (v1) the existential sense: "to be" means the same as "to exist," (v2) the copulative sense: "to be" means the same as "to be F" (where F is a predicate variable),[52] and (v3) the veridical sense: "to be" means the same as "to be true." It is less controversial that he distinguished among the following senses of the participle "τὸ ὄν" ("being"): (n1) being in-itself, (n2) being as potentiality and actuality, (n3) accidental being, and (n4) being as truth.[53]

Now whatever else we might wish to claim about n1–n3, on the one hand, and v1–v2, on the other hand, it is clear that all express objectual senses of the verb. It is less obvious how to understand the sense(s) expressed by n4 and v3, both of which are forms of the veridical sense of being, a sense common among ancient Greek philosophers, which itself has both an objectual and a semantic interpretation.[54] Aristotle, thus, may have employed either the three straightforwardly objectual senses, one of the two veridical senses, or some combination of all of these in formulating his definitions. I will argue that he does not have either of the veridical senses in mind, and that he is most plausibly interpreted as working with a quite general objectual sense of the verb.

The argument that we cannot make sense of the definitions using the veridical sense has two stages because, as Kahn has shown, the veridical sense is ambiguous between a "worldly" sense that expresses, of some being described in a particular way, that it is as it is described to be (e.g., it is true that Homer wrote the poem) and a less common "linguistic" sense that expresses, of some statement, that it is true (e.g., his statement "Homer wrote the poem" is true). These variant senses, if used to interpret the definitions, yield very different results.

Interpreting the definitions in terms of the linguistic veridical sense of the infinitive and participle is, I think, hopeless. The linguistic variation of the veridical sense expresses an attribute of statements: Statements can be true. Were we to reformulate the definitions at 1011b26–27 in terms of the linguistic variation of the veridical sense, we would get something like the following:[55]

> To assert of a true statement that it is not true, or of a statement that is not true that it is true, is false, while to assert of a true statement that it is true, and of a statement that is not true that it is not true, is true.[56]

The formulations have the air of redundancy about them: Truth just is to assert of a true statement that is true. They seem to capture a concept of truth some contemporary theorists have in mind. For example, Horwich defends a concept of truth exhausted by the fact that:

> ... for any declarative sentence '*p*' we are provided with an equivalent sentence 'the proposition that *p* is true,' where the original sentence has been converted into a noun phrase, 'The proposition *that p*,' occupying a position open to object variables, and where the truth predicate serves merely to restore the structure of a sentence: it acts simply as a denominalizer. (Horwich 1998, 4–5)

On such a view, Aristotle would conceive of truth and falsehood at 1011b26–27 as a kind of transformation relation for statements: Take any statement you like, nominalize it somehow, and you may predicate "is true" or "is not true" of it. Suppose the nominalized statement is true. If you predicate "is true" of it, then the statement you generate is true, and if you predicate "is not true" of it, the statement you generate is false. Suppose the nominalized statement is not true. If you predicate "is true" of it, then the statement you generate is false, and if you predicate "is not true" of it, the statement you generate is true.

This may be a coherent reading of Aristotle's definitions, but I don't think it is the intended reading. In the first place, nothing in book Γ thus far prepares us to interpret "εἶναι" and "τὸ ὄν" veridically. Aristotle has established unequivocally at the beginning of Γ 2, 1003a33ff, that the primary sense of "being" ("τὸ ὄν") is substance (οὐσία), and in Γ 5, 1009a32–35, closer to where he presents his definitions, he notes that "being" is spoken of in two ways, as potentiality and as actuality. We have every reason to expect he has an objectual sense of the terms in mind in Γ 7, here echoing Matthen (1983, 120). So, in particular, it would be very surprising were Aristotle to formulate his definitions of truth and falsehood in terms of the linguistic veridical sense of being.

Second, the argument exploiting the definitions at 1011b23–29—difficult on any reading—becomes nearly incomprehensible when interpreted in terms of the linguistic veridical sense. On this interpretation of the definitions, the argument would appear to go something like this, modifying Ross's version: (i) to assert of a true statement that it is not true, or of a statement that isn't true that it is, is false; (ii) to assert of a true statement that it is true, or of a statement that isn't true that it isn't, is false; (iii) therefore, to assert of any statement that it is true or that it is not true is either true or false; (iv) the opponent, in asserting that the intermediate of a contradictory is true, is not asserting either of a true statement or of a statement that is not true that it is true or is not true; (v) therefore, the opponent's statement is neither true nor false. (vi) therefore, the opponent's statement is not a statement, which is absurd. (iv) is false. Given the interpretation we are considering, if Aristotle has the opponent asserting that the intermediate of a contradictory is true, then he must mean that the opponent is asserting of a statement that it is true. But that is what (iv) denies. To avoid this problem, we might say that the opponent asserts, of a statement that is itself neither true nor not true, that it is true. But (iii) follows only if we assume the principle of bivalence, otherwise there may be statements that are neither true nor not true to which the definitions in (i) and (ii) don't apply. So, the opponent's statement must itself be either true or false. The argument makes much more sense if we interpret the terms objectually.

Third, on the linguistic veridical interpretation, the definitions appear viciously circular: we would have Aristotle defining truth in terms of truth, which would either be a sophomoric error or sophistry. An unlikely error. But suppose it is not an error—the sense of "is true" being defined must differ from the sense of "is true" in the definiens. But they don't appear to differ: By hypothesis, the linguistic veridical sense of "to be" expresses an attribute of statements, i.e., being true; Aristotle uses this linguistic veridical sense of "to be" to define truth at 1011b26–27; so defined, truth would appear to be the very attribute of statements by means of which it is defined. I see no reason for thinking that he uses the linguistic veridical sense of "to be"—instead of simply using "is true"—in order to mask the fact that the definitions are circular.

Fourth, if the definitions aren't circular, and the linguistic veridical sense of "to be" differs from the sense of "is true" introduced at 1011b26–27,[57] we are totally at a loss as to the nature of the attribute expressed by the linguistic veridical sense. We cannot explain why statements are true or false, and must treat the concept of truth as an undefined primitive.[58]

Lastly, all of these difficulties vanish, and we can make ready sense of the definitions and related passages, when we reverse the order of explanation and explicate the veridical sense of "to be" in terms of the definition of truth at 1011b26–27. So, we can rule out the linguistic veridical sense.

Kahn has argued that Aristotle's definitions "make explicit what was given in the idiomatic form of the veridical construction," where the idiomatic form for this is "things are just as you say they are."[59] According to Kahn, then, Aristotle's definitions are explicit definitions of the worldly veridical sense of the verb "to be." In other words, they are explicit definitions of the ordinary philosophical concepts of truth and falsehood, presupposing a longstanding philosophical usage and making it explicit. If Kahn is right about this (and I think he is), then we can't interpret the verb "to be" in the definitions at 1011b26–27 using the worldly veridical sense itself—such a reading *would* be viciously circular.

Turning now to the various objectual senses of the verbs, it would be uncharitable to interpret the definitions at 1011b26–27 in any of the peculiarly Aristotelian senses of v1 and v2 that might be captured by n1–3. As noted above, given the argumentative context, Aristotle cannot beg too many questions in arguing for the Law of the Excluded Middle. A narrow technical objectual sense of the verb would restrict the application of the definitions and unhappily diminish their argumentative force. We ought to expect that Aristotle is using senses of the infinitive and the participle that have the broadest scope possible, preferably senses that allow for any common philosophical usages that makes sense and for any proposed ontology that distinguishes between being and not being.

So, he needs a generic objectual sense of "being" if he has an objectual sense in mind.

Scholarly consensus has more or less emerged that the ancient Greek philosophers, and Aristotle in particular, used the verb "to be" to express a sense involving both senses captured by v1 and v2. As Kahn puts it, for the ancient Greek philosopher, an apparently existential use of the verb "to be" implicitly entails a copulative complement, and an apparently copulative use of the verb entails existential commitment.[60] Thus, for the ancient Greek philosopher, "to be" means the same as "to exist as something or other" or "to exist as a y."[61] For example, were Aristotle to assert "Man is a rational animal" this would mean the same as "Man exists as a rational animal."

It seems plausible, then, that this inclusive sense captures the general objectual notion appropriate for the argument in Γ 7. So, the most plausible choice is to interpret the definitions in terms of the inclusive sense of the infinitive and participle. Ross—translating the infinitive with "that it is" and the participle with "of what is"—made the most elegantly unassuming choice, and we needn't balk at it. Given the inclusive sense of "is," Ross's phrase "of what is" (i.e., in the Greek, the participle "τὸ ὄν") in the definitions would mean the same as "of what exists as a y." It is worth repeating that "what exists as a y" (τὸ ὄν) doesn't presuppose a particular metaphysical framework. If the ancient Greek philosophers generally expressed their metaphysical views by means of the inclusive sense of the verb "to be," then we should expect Atomists and Parmenideans as well as Platonists and Peripatetics to paraphrase "τὸ ὄν" in their own terms. Similarly, given the comprehensive sense of "is," Ross's phrase "that it is" (i.e., in the Greek, the infinitive εἶναι) means the same as "that it (i.e., what exists as a y) exists as a y," where the nature of the intentional content is left undefined and open to various specifications.

On the basis of these considerations, and taking into account the fact that dialectical assertions conform to the fundamental semantic assumptions discussed above, we can reformulate Aristotle's definitions as follows:

> For one and only one thing x and one and only one thing y, *falsehood* is (ia) to assert of x, which is a y, that x is not a y, or (ib) to assert of x, which is not a y, that x is a y, while *truth* is (iia) to assert of x, which is a y, that x is a y, and (iib) to assert of x, which is not a y, that x is not a y.[62]

What the Nominal Definitions Entail

What do these nominal definitions entail? It is often claimed that Aristotle has a correspondence conception of truth,[63] yet a number of distinguished contemporary philosophers have noted the deflationary character of his definitions at 1011b26–27.[64] And do his nominal definitions express Realist conceptions?[65] How much can we hope to squeeze from the nominal definitions themselves?

I will now argue that the definitions impose relatively weak philosophical commitments. I will argue that Aristotle's nominal definitions presuppose that there are assertions, intentional contents of assertions, correlates in the real world of these, and a very weak relation of what Pitcher has called "correspondence-as-correlation," but they do not presuppose philosophical conceptions or theories of any of these. Thus, construed as nominal definitions of truth and falsehood, the definitions do not presuppose robust philosophical commitments and are neither Realist nor Nonrealist, but they do express a kind of correspondence conception of truth and falsehood—they do presuppose a correlation among assertions, the intensional contents of assertions, and the real correlates of these.

We saw above that Aristotle's nominal definitions aren't deflationary in Horwich's sense—Aristotle uses the infinitive and participle of "to be" with their objectual senses in the nominal definitions, not their veridical senses.[66] Hence, the nominal definitions of "truth" and "falsehood" denote attributes that intrinsically involve metaphysical commitments. On the other hand, Aristotle's conceptions are deflationary if we follow Wright (1992, 21n15) in thinking that the root idea of deflationary conceptions is "that truth is not *intrinsically* a metaphysically substantial notion." For, even though the nominal definitions presuppose some sort of real correlate to the intentional contents of assertions, we have seen that no particular ontology is presupposed. Again, robust metaphysical commitments would unduly restrict the application of the definitions in general and would undermine the argumentative role the definitions play in the passage in which they appear. Interpreting the metaphysical commitments weakly, the nominal definitions are consistent with any proposed ontology that acknowledges a distinction between what is and what is not—that is to say, any ontology worthy of the name. Indeed, the ontology associated with the conceptions is minimally constrained, allowing anything whatsoever to count as an instance of what exists as an F, and in this sense the conceptions are deflationary.

The metaphysical presuppositions of Aristotle's nominal definitions are too weak to be either Realist or Nonrealist conceptions. According to a Realist:

> A concept of truth, *T*, is a Realist concept if and only if, according to *T*, an assertion is true only if the very same state of affairs that the assertion expresses exists independently of any mind or with only derivative dependence.[67]

If a concept of truth isn't a Realist concept, it's a Nonrealist concept. I leave aside for the moment whether or not it makes sense to talk about the nominal definitions in terms of states of affairs. Crucial here is that they are silent about whether or not the real correlates of the intentional contents of assertions are mind-independent. It may be that Aristotle develops a Realist *theory* of truth and falsehood, but his concepts leave this undetermined.

Are his nominal definitions correspondence conceptions of truth and falsehood? It is obvious that they make no explicit mention of a correspondence relation. However, they do presuppose a relation of some sort between the intentional contents of assertions and their real correlates, but the nature of this relation (if, indeed, Aristotle assumed there is only one such relation) is left unspecified. Following Pitcher (1964, 9–11), we may distinguish between *correspondence-as-correlation* and *correspondence-as-congruence*. A relation of correspondence-as-correlation is any correlation of the members of two or more groups of things.[68] This is the weakest requirement we might place on a correspondence relation—any correlation among the members of the groups will suffice. A relation of correspondence-as-congruence is any correlation of the members of two or more groups where the correlation is governed by an isomorphism between or among the members of these groups. Isomorphism is a fairly stringent condition to place upon a correspondence relation, requiring some sort of structural identity among the correlated members. Pitcher (1964, 10) develops his notion of correspondence-as-congruence is terms of agreement. I follow Kirkham (1995) in developing the notion in terms of isomorphism.

Aristotle's nominal definitions do not suggest anything like an isomorphism. Perhaps a fuller account of the relation between Aristotelian truth-bearers and Aristotelian truth-makers would reveal that the intentional contents of assertions and their correlates in the real world are related isomorphically, but this would import materials extrinsic to the definitions at 1011b26–27. I argue below that his theory of truth is best understood as a correspondence-as-congruence theory, agreeing on this general point with Crivelli (2004, 129ff) although differing with him in respect to the details. So, Aristotle's nominal definitions do not entail a correspondence-as-congruence relation.

They do entail a correspondence-as-correlation relation, agreeing with Kirkham (1995, 119). They presuppose that the intentional content of an assertion is correlated either with what exists as an *F* or what does not exist as an *F*.[69] How this correlation is determined is left open by the nominal definitions, but the correlation is essential—truth and falsehood so conceived are "seriously dyadic" relations. But, supposing the nominal definitions do entail a correspondence-as-correlation relation, is this enough to claim that they are correspondence conceptions?

Davidson (1996, 266 and 268) has claimed that Aristotle's definitions do not presuppose an ontology of states of affairs or facts or any other special sort of real correlate to which assertions and their intentional contents must correspond. Davidson does not consider whether or not the definitions at 1011b26–27 are nominal definitions, and it seems he interprets them as expressions of Aristotle's real definitions. If states of affairs or facts or the like must be presupposed by a correspondence conception of truth—and it does seem that states of affairs, at least, play an essential role in almost every contemporary correspondence account of truth—and if Aristotle's nominal definitions do not presuppose these (or rule them out), then they are not correspondence conceptions.

Whether or not we agree with Davidson's claim depends on what is meant by "states of affairs." If, for example, we adopt David Armstrong's (1997, 20 and 122) conception, according to which a state of affairs is a unit composed (non-mereologically) either of a particular and an attribute or of two or more particulars and a relation, then Davidson is surely right that Aristotle's nominal definitions don't presuppose anything of the sort. (Strictly speaking, this is how Armstrong understands atomic states of affairs, but since molecular states of affairs are conjunctions of atomic states of affairs, if Aristotle's definitions don't presuppose the latter, the latter are moot.) More generally: If states of affairs are cashed out in terms of a specific metaphysical theory, then the nominal definitions don't presuppose them. However, following Kirkham (1995), if we define "states of affairs" to mean all and only those things the existence of which can be asserted, Davidson is incorrect—the nominal definitions obviously presuppose things the existence of which can be asserted.

Conclusion

To recapitulate the course of my reasoning in this chapter, I have argued that the definitions presented at *Metaphysics* book Γ 7.1011b26–27 are best understood as nominal definitions of the terms "truth" and "falsehood." So understood, the *definientia* express concepts Aristotle expects his philosophical contemporaries will accept. They entail minimal metaphysical commitments and are in that sense deflationary; they are not Realist definitions, but neither are they Nonrealist; and if we claim they express correspondence conceptions, we must make it clear that they presuppose the weakest sort of correspondence relation (i.e., that of correspondence-as-correlation) and a thoroughly anodyne notion of states of affairs (i.e., anything the existence of which can be asserted).

In subsequent chapters I will explain how Aristotle analyzes the nominal definitions presented at 1011b26–27 in terms of his own philosophical system in order to establish his real definitions of truth and falsehood. I will also explain how the concepts defined at 1011b26–27 relate to the other concepts of truth and falsehood recognized by Aristotle in the *Metaphysics*. In the next chapter I inspect how the nominal definitions function inferentially in the elenctic arguments in order to reveal additional and important semantic assumptions bearing on the contexts in which he thinks it makes sense to apply concepts of truth and falsehood.

Chapter 3

The Nominal Definition of "Truth" and the Axioms

The conceptions constitutive of the definiens of the nominal definitions of "truth" are among the basic ideas driving the elenctic arguments for the logical axioms in *Metaphysics* book Γ. They are also the ideas driving the development of Aristotle's account of the essence of truth. When we combine these ideas with the additional notions involved in the logical axioms themselves—the conception of a simple assertion, the conception of a contradictory pair of simple assertions, and the conception of an intermediate assertion between opposed simple assertions—we exhaust the ideas Aristotle uses to explain the essence of truth. In books Δ–N Aristotle develops his analyses of these conceptions on the basis of his own philosophical system, differentiating his account of the essence of truth from alternatives.

In the preceding chapter I discussed Aristotle's understanding of the common axioms and the general semantic constraints he places on elenctic demonstrations. I argued that every elenctic demonstration involves the following basic premises:

E1: A philosophical opponent o denies the truth of some logical axiom λ.

E2: o asserts that a definition $n =_{df.} d$ is true, where d is the *definiens* of the *definiendum* n.

E3: If d is the *definiens* of the definition of a name n, then d and n signify one and only one thing b.

E4: If a *definiens* d of the definition of a name n signifies one and only one thing b, then if anything a is signified by N, being b is what it is to be a.

E5: Demonstrate that $n =_{df.} d$ is true only if λ is true.

I also argued that the definition of truth presented by Aristotle in Γ 7.1011b26–27—the canonical definition which, as Künne (2005) has noted, is "almost obsessively quoted" in philosophical discussions of truth—is best understood as a nominal definition expressing a conception of truth that Aristotle thought his dialectical opponents would have accepted.

I will now focus on the arguments Aristotle presents in support of the logical axioms in book Γ. These arguments are interesting for their own sake, of course. They aim to prove important conclusions. They are, however, particularly important for understanding Aristotle's nominal definitions of truth and falsehood in book Γ. In part this is because, as we have seen, Aristotle explicitly defines the terms "truth" and "falsehood" in the midst of these arguments. But more to the point, because the nominal definitions *are* made explicit in these arguments, they provide us with contextual clues about how best to understand the conceptions expressed by the definientia of the nominal definitions.[1] Understanding the nominal definitions as well as we can is germane, since in subsequent chapters it will become clear that Aristotle's real definitions are particular ways of elaborating each of the concepts in the field picked out by the nominal definitions.

Truth and the Law of the Excluded Middle

Aristotle includes the Law of Non-Contradiction (LNC), the Law of the Excluded Middle (LEM), and the Law of Identity (LI) among the logical axioms.[2] He conceives of these axioms as assertions that are either true or false. In *Metaphysics* book Γ he argues that the axioms are true if any assertion is true. To this end, he offers first a constructive demonstration that LNC is the most certain of all assertions, and then he presents a series of elenctic arguments in support of LNC and LEM. Each kind of argument presupposes concepts of truth and falsehood. Given that all of the arguments are elenctic arguments, none succeeds if the concepts of truth and falsehood involved beg questions from Aristotle's opponents.

It is plausible, therefore, for the reasons given in the preceding chapter, that Aristotle has in mind the nominal definitions of truth and falsehood presented at 1011b26–27 in presenting his elenctic arguments for LNC and LEM.

The elenctic demonstrations in book Γ can be grouped as follows: (1) those from 1006a18–1007b18 based on the semantics of definitions; (2) those from 1007b18–1008b2 based on the semantics of affirmations and denials; (3) those from 1008b2–31 based on the relationship between what an opponent says and what he does; (4) those from 1008b31–1009a5 based on claims about degrees of truth and falsehood; (5) those from 1009a5–1009a16 based on the semantics of true and false assertions;[3] (6) those from 1011a13–1011b12 based on the claim that not all things are relative; (7) one from 1011b12–22, based on LNC itself, which Aristotle has established already, for the claim that contraries cannot belong at the same time to the same thing; (8) those from 1011b23–1012a17 based on explicit definitions of truth and falsehood and on the nature of intermediates; and (9) those from 1012a17–1012b31 based on explicit definitions of truth and falsehood and marshaled against the claims that (i) all things are true and (ii) all things are false.[4] Even this outline of the arguments reveals that definitions of truth and falsehood are at least implicitly involved in many of Aristotle's elenctic demonstrations.

Aristotle presents eight elenctic demonstrations in support of LEM in book Γ. Each is an elenctic demonstration conforming to the general pattern described above. In each case, it is assumed that the philosophical opponent denies LEM. The first elenctic demonstration of LEM is presented at 1011b23–29. Analyzing it leads us to discuss all of the conceptions relevant to the nominal definitions of truth and falsehood at 1011b26–27. The passage, again, in which the argument appears follows:

> Ἀλλὰ μὴν οὐδὲ μεταξὺ ἀντιφάσεως ἐνδέχεται εἶναι οὐθέν, ἀλλ' ἀνάγκη ἢ φάναι ἢ ἀποφάναι ἓν καθ' ἑνὸς ὁτιοῦν. δῆλον δὲ πρῶτον μὲν ὁρισαμένοις τί τὸ ἀληθὲς καὶ ψεῦδος. τὸ μὲν γὰρ λέγειν τὸ ὂν μὴ εἶναι ἢ τὸ μὴ ὂν εἶναι ψεῦδος, τὸ δὲ τὸ ὂν εἶναι καὶ τὸ μὴ ὂν μὴ εἶναι ἀληθές, ὥστε καὶ ὁ λέγων εἶναι ἢ μὴ ἀληθεύσει ἢ ψεύσεται· ἀλλ' οὔτε τὸ ὂν λέγεται μὴ εἶναι ἢ εἶναι οὔτε τὸ μὴ ὄν.

> But then neither is it possible for there to be anything in the middle between contradictories, but it is necessary either to

affirm or to deny one thing, whatever it may be, of one thing. This will be clear if we first define what truth is and what falsehood is. For to say of what is that it is not, or of what is not that it is, is false, whereas to say of what is that it is, or of what is not that it is not, is true. So he who says of anything that it is, or that it is not, will say either what is true or what is false. But it is said that neither what is nor what is not either is not or is. (trans., Reeve)

The conclusion—asserted at 1011b23–24, with respect to which lines the manuscripts largely agree—is an explicit statement of LEM.[5] There are two claims, each of which is an expression of LEM. The first can be translated by:

[LEM$_1$] It is not possible that there is an intermediate between contradictories,

and the second by:

[LEM$_2$] But of one subject we must either affirm or deny one predicate.

Although Aristotle typically formulates LEM along the lines of [LEM$_2$], [LEM$_2$] and [LEM$_1$] make the same claim.[6]

Simple Assertions and Contradictory Pairs

LEM$_1$ at 1011b23 squarely situates Aristotle's elenctic argument in the context of contradictory pairs of assertions. This is no surprise, as all of his elenctic arguments for LNC in Γ concern contradictory pairs and assume that his philosophical opponents are familiar with the rules of dialectical arguments. Aristotle's understanding of contradictory pairs and the rules dialectical argument are conceptually tied to the nominal definitions of "truth" and "falsehood" offered at Γ 7.1011b26–27. Reminding ourselves of the basic rules of dialectical argument and analyzing Aristotle's concept of a contradictory pair will give us insight into the nominal definitions.

According to Aristotle's account of dialectic in the *Topics* and his account of contradictory pairs in *De Interpretatione*, in the context of dialectical inquiry we aim to secure the truth or falsehood of one of the simple assertions constituting a contradictory pair of simple assertions.[7] Aristotle articulates his account of simple assertions and contradictory pairs in De Interpretatione. Every assertion, for Aristotle, is either a linguistic or a mental assertion, and every simple assertion is either an affirmation or a denial. Aristotle develops his account of assertion in terms of linguistic and mental assertions. Although he never severs the two dimensions of his theory, he is primarily concerned with linguistic assertion in De Interpretatione and with mental assertion in De Anima III 3–8.

An affirmation asserts of one and only one thing y that it is combined with (or belongs to) another thing x that is one and only one thing. A denial asserts of one and only thing y that it is separated from (or does not belong to) another thing x that is one and only one thing.[8] A linguistic affirmation immediately signifies a mental assertion and purports to mediately signify some real correlate. Similarly, a linguistic denial immediately signifies a mental denial and purports to mediately signify some real correlate.[9] Given these ditsintctions, we can reformulate [LEM$_1$] and [LEM$_2$] in terms of linguistic assertions as follows:

[LEM$_{1L}$] For every subject expression n that signifies one and only one thing x, for every predicate expression p that signifies one and only one thing y, for every linguistic predicative relation + that denotes the real predicative relation of belonging, for every linguistic predicative relation − that denotes the real predicative relation of not-belonging, and for any linguistic predicative relation *, it is not possible that there is a linguistic assertion n * p that is intermediate between $n + p$ and $n - p$.

[LEM$_{2L}$] For every subject expression n that signifies one and only one thing x, for every predicate expression p that signifies one and only one thing y, for every linguistic predicative relation + that denotes the real predicative relation of belonging, and for every linguistic predicative relation − that denotes the real predicative relation of not-belonging, it is necessary to assert either $n + p$ and $n - p$.

Alternatively, [LEM$_1$] and [LEM$_2$] can be reformulated in terms of mental assertions as follows:

[LEM$_{1M}$] For every subject concept *c* that signifies one and only one thing *x*, for every predicate concept *p* that signifies one and only one thing *y*, for every conceptual predicative relation + that denotes the real predicative relation of belonging, for every conceptual predicative relation − that denotes the real predicative relation of not-belonging, and for any conceptual predicative relation *, it is not possible that there is a mental assertion *c* * *p* that is intermediate between *c* + *p* and *c* − *p*.

[LEM$_{2M}$] For every subject concept *c* that signifies one and only one thing *x*, for every predicate concept *p* that signifies one and only one thing *y*, for every conceptual predicative relation + that denotes the real predicative relation of belonging, and for every conceptual predicative relation − that denotes the real predicative relation of not-belonging, it is necessary to mentally assert either *c* + *p* or *c* −*p*.

To see that these are proper interpretations of Aristotle's claims at 1011b23–24, and that they are equivalent formulations of LEM, it will help to clarify the constituent notions of a contradictory pair of assertions, an intermediate assertion, and a single simple assertion. Aristotle introduces the notion of a contradictory pair of assertions in *De Interpretatione*, at 17a31–37:

ὥστε δῆλον ὅτι πάσῃ καταφάσει ἐστὶν ἀπόφασις ἀντικειμένη καὶ πάσῃ ἀποφάσει κατάφασις. καὶ ἔστω ἀντίφασις τοῦτο, κατάφασις καὶ ἀπόφασις αἱ ἀντικείμεναι· λέγω δὲ ἀντικεῖσθαι τὴν τοῦ αὐτοῦ κατὰ τοῦ αὐτοῦ,—μὴ ὁμωνύμως δέ, καὶ ὅσα ἄλλα τῶν τοιούτων προσδιοριζόμεθα πρὸς τὰς σοφιστικὰς ἐνοχλήσεις.

Thus it is clear that for every affirmation there is an opposite denial, and for every denial an opposite affirmation. Let us call an affirmation and a denial which are opposite a contradiction. I speak of assertions as opposite when they affirm and deny the same thing of the same thing—not homonymously, together with all other such conditions that we add to counter the troublesome objections of sophists. (trans., mine, following Ackrill)

The Nominal Definition of "Truth" and the Axioms

Thus, a contradictory pair of assertions is constituted by two assertions. One of these affirms that one thing y belongs to one thing x. The other denies that the very same thing y belongs to the very same thing x.

In the *Prior Analytics*, at 24a17, Aristotle relates his conception of a contradictory pair to his theory of deductive inference: "A premise, then, is an account affirming or denying something of something" [πρότασις μὲν οὖν ἐστὶ λόγος καταφατικὸς ἢ ἀποφατικός τινος κατά τινος]. This is a claim about premises—the proper parts of Aristotelian syllogisms—according to which a premise either affirms something of something or denies something of something.[10] Taken by itself, the claim at *Apr.* 24a17 isn't equivalent to LEM, nor does it entail LEM.[11] However, if the opponent of LEM were to assert that he expresses a premise but neither affirms something of something nor denies something of something, *Apr.* 24a17 is the basis for an argument against him. Given Aristotle's definition of premises in terms of affirmations and denials, it makes no sense to say that—as it is assumed the opponent of LEM does say—a premise neither affirms something of something nor denies something of something.

If we consider *Apr.* 24a17 in light of the immediately subsequent discussion in the *Prior Analytics* and another passage from the *Posterior Analytics*, it becomes clear that Aristotle understands premises in terms of contradictory pairs of assertions. The passage from the *Posterior Analytics* comes at 72a8–14:

> πρότασις δ' ἐστὶν ἀποφάνσεως τὸ ἕτερον μόριον, ἓν καθ' ἑνός, διαλεκτικὴ μὲν ἡ ὁμοίως λαμβάνουσα ὁποτερονοῦν, ἀποδεικτικὴ δὲ ἡ ὡρισμένως θάτερον, ὅτι ἀληθές. ἀπόφανσις δὲ ἀντιφάσεως ὁποτερονοῦν μόριον, ἀντίφασις δὲ ἀντίθεσις ἧς οὐκ ἔστι μεταξὺ καθ' αὑτήν, μόριον δ' ἀντιφάσεως τὸ μὲν τὶ κατὰ τινὸς κατάφασις, τὸ δὲ τὶ ἀπὸ τινὸς ἀπόφασις.

> A premise is one part of a contradiction, one thing said of one; it is dialectical if it assumes indifferently either part, demonstrative if it determinately assumes the one that is true. An assertion is either part of a contradiction. A contradiction is an opposition which of itself excludes any intermediate; and the part of a contradiction saying something *of* something is an affirmation, the one saying something *from* something is a denial. (trans., Barnes)

Perhaps the most important thing to note here is that Aristotle defines a contradiction in terms that bear directly on LEM: a contradiction is "an opposition which of itself excludes any intermediate."

According to this passage, a contradictory pair has two parts, each of which is a premise. For Aristotle, a premise is an assertion. In the context of the passage, an assertion may be understood as a kind of linguistic entity, but it also may be interpreted as a kind of mental entity. Whether linguistic or mental, every assertion involves either one thing being asserted of another. One thing may be asserted to belong to another, in which case it is an affirmation, or one thing may be asserted not to belong to another, in which case it is a denial. A contradiction, then, is defined as a pair of assertions p and q such that, with respect to one thing x and another y, [1] p asserts y belongs to x, [2] q asserts y does not belong to x, and [3] p and q are opposed such that there can be no assertion r intermediate between them. Using Aristotle's technical notions of predicative combination and separation, an equivalent formulation is to say that p and q constitute a contradictory pair of assertions just in case there is one thing y and another thing x such that (1) p asserts that y is combined with x, (2) q asserts that y is separated from x, and (3) p and q are opposed such that there can be no assertion r intermediate between them. It is assumed here that (i) y does not belong to x iff y is separated from x, and (ii) y belongs to x iff y is combined with x. Thus, Aristotle's definition of a contradictory pair may be provisionally interpreted as follows:

> p contradicts q just in case [1] p = (y belongs to x), [2] q = (y does not belong to x), and [3] it is not possible that there is an assertion r that is intermediate between (y belongs to x) and (y does not belong to x).

Clause [3] here is another way of asserting [LEM_1], and Aristotle appears to be quite careful in formulating LEM at 1011b23–24.[12] Aristotle argues for LEM from within the dialectical context of making simple assertions, where the live options are either affirmation or denial. When Aristotle claims that "Everything is affirmed or denied," he means that, in the context of philosophical dialectic, and given any one subject and any one predicate, either one says that the predicate belongs to the subject (in which case one affirms something of it) or one says that the predicate does not belong to it (in which case one denies something of it). Therefore, LEM precludes saying of one thing that some other thing either (1) belongs and does not belong to it or (2) neither belongs nor does not belong to it. These middle "possibilities" are excluded. Thus:

> [LEM$_{1*}$.] In the dialectical context of making simple assertions, it is necessary that there is no intermediate between contradictory assertions, and

> [LEM$_{2*}$.] In the dialectical context of making simple assertions, of one subject it is necessary that we either affirm or deny any one predicate.

[LEM$_{1*}$.] is an explicit denial of the possibility of an intermediate assertion between two contradictory assertions.

Given the larger context of book Γ, and Aristotle's general account of assertion, Aristotle is concerned with contradictory assertions at 1011b23–24. It follows that an intermediate between contradictory assertions would itself be an assertion, were it to exist.[13] Thus, [LEM$_{1*}$.] claims that it is impossible that there is an intermediate assertion between contradictory assertions. On the basis of the distinctions just made, we can restate [LEM$_{1*}$.] as follows:

> [LEM$_{1**}$.] For all simple assertions p and q, if p and q are contradictories, then it is not possible that there is a single simple assertion r such that r is intermediate between p and q.

[LEM$_{1**}$.], then, is a claim about the impossibility of a certain kind of assertion—assertions intermediate between contradictory assertions. While [LEM$_{1**}$.] makes no overt reference to assertions intermediate between contradictory assertions, it makes the same claim.

Aristotle claims that "a contradiction is an opposition which of itself excludes any intermediate." Given the preceding, this means that there is no intermediate assertion r between a contradictory pair of assertion p and q. Aristotle thinks that such intermediate assertions are impossible. As a consequence, it is unreasonable to expect an actual example of one, at least from Aristotle. What would such an intermediate assertion r be like if—as the opponent of LEM urges—it were to exist?

Intermediate Assertions and LNC

First and foremost, one should look to Aristotle's various formulations of LNC, since in effect he specifies what an intermediate between a contradictory pair would be, were it possible. As Lukasiewicz has noted, Aristotle expresses LNC in various ways. At 1005b19–20, he formulates LNC metaphysically as follows:

> The Metaphysical Formulation of LNC: The same real predicate cannot both belong and not belong to the same real subject at the same time, in the same respect, et cetera.[14]

Here the claim is that "the same real predicate" (which is one thing, y) cannot both belong to and not belong to "the same real subject" (also one thing, x). Following Lukasiewicz (1971), this version of LNC is formulated in terms of one thing belonging or not belonging to another thing. Ignoring the complications introduced to meet sophistical objections, it can be stated as follows:

> Metaphysical LNC: For every real subject x and every real predicate y, it is not possible that [y belongs to $x \wedge y$ does not belong to x].

Assuming standard transformation rules—which, of course, are in question in book Γ—this is logically equivalent to a metaphysical version of LEM: It is necessary either for y not to belong to x or for y to belong to x. This can be put more formally as follows:

> Metaphysical LEM: For every real subject x and every real predicate y, it is necessary that [y does not belong to $x \vee y$ belongs to x].

At 1007b18 Aristotle claims that "... contradictories cannot be predicated at the same time," [ἀδύνατον ἅμα κατηγορεῖσθαι τὰς ἀντιφάσεις] and at 1006a3–4 he states another metaphysical version of LNC:

> It is impossible for anything at the same time to be and not to be. [ἀδυνάτον ὄντος ἅμα εἶναι καὶ μὴ εἶναι]

This claim may be interpreted narrowly as the assertion that one and the same subject cannot both be and not be, where being is treated as an attribute and, as LNC specifies, cannot both belong and not belong to the same subject at the same time. This would be to interpret the claim as an instance of the more general formulations of LNC already considered. Or, if being should not be treated as an attribute in Aristotle's system, one could interpret the verb "to be" aspectually and as implicitly involving some predicative adjective "to be an F," yielding the assertion that, for any real subject x and any real attribute y, it is impossible for x at the same time to be y and not to be y. For Aristotle, this is equivalent to saying that, for any real subject x and any real attribute y, it is impossible at the same time for y to belong to x and for y not to belong to x. That is to say: for every real subject x and every real attribute y, it is not possible that (y belongs to x) ∧ (y does not belong to x). Either interpretation conforms to what Aristotle claims at 1006b18–22:

> καὶ οὐκ ἔσται εἶναι καὶ μὴ εἶναι τὸ αὐτὸ ἀλλ' ἢ καθ' ὁμωνυμίαν, ὥσπερ ἂν εἰ ὃν ἡμεῖς ἄνθρωπον καλοῦμεν, ἄλλοι μὴ ἄνθρωπον καλοῖεν· τὸ δ' ἀπορούμενον οὐ τοῦτό ἐστιν, εἰ ἐνδέχεται τὸ αὐτὸ ἅμα εἶναι καὶ μὴ εἶναι ἄνθρωπον τὸ ὄνομα, ἀλλὰ τὸ πρᾶγμα.

> And it will not be possible for the same thing to be and not to be, except in virtue of an ambiguity, just as one whom we call 'man,' others might call 'not-man'; but the point in question is not this, whether the same thing can at the same time be and not be man in name, but whether it can in fact. (trans., Ross)

From the sequel to this claim, it is clear that an attribute and its negation are contradictories. As a consequence, Aristotle asserts here that, given a real subject x and a real attribute y, it is not possible at the same time to predicate y of x and not-y of x. In other words, it is not possible at the same time that y belongs to x and not-y belongs to x. If we assume that not-y belongs to x just in case y does not belong to x, which seems to be his point in the passage, then again he is claiming that it is not possible at the same time that both (y belongs to x) and (y does not belong to x).

Aristotle also expresses doxastic and logical formulations of LNC. At 1005b23–24, he states the doxastic version: no one can believe that the same thing can (at the same time) be and not be. Lukasiewicz (1971) expresses the doxastic version as follows: "Two acts of believing which correspond to two contradictory propositions cannot obtain in the same consciousness." This should be revised to reflect the fact that he is principally concerned with the sorts of simple mental assertions appropriate to dialectic, as follows:

> Doxastic LNC: It is not possible for someone to assert mentally that y belongs to x and, at the same time, to assert mentally that y does not belong to x.

Then, at 1011b13–14, Aristotle expresses the logical version: the most certain of all basic principles is that contradictory assertions are not true simultaneously. Lukasiewicz (1971) expresses the logical version as follows: "Two conflicting (contradictory) propositions cannot be true at the same time." Again, this should be crafted in terms of simple linguistic assertions: It is not possible for someone to assert linguistically that one thing y belongs to another x and, at the same time, to assert linguistically that y does not belong to x:

> Logical LNC: It is not possible for someone to assert linguistically that y belongs to x and, at the same time, to assert linguistically that y does not belong to x.

The metaphysical version of LNC is obviously different from the doxastic and logical formulations. The former is about things in the world, whereas the latter two are about mental and linguistic assertions about things in the world.[15]

At 1011b13–22, Aristotle concludes his extended argument for LNC. He then uses LNC to defend the claim that contrary predicates cannot belong at the same time to the same thing. The argument not only provides insight into the distinction between the logical and metaphysical formulations of LNC, but also illustrates how the nominal definitions of "truth" and "falsehood" are employed in the context of arguing for the axioms. The argument is worth quoting in full:

> Ὅτι μὲν οὖν βεβαιοτάτη δόξα πασῶν τὸ μὴ εἶναι ἀληθεῖς ἅμα τὰς ἀντικειμένας φάσεις, καὶ τί συμβαίνει τοῖς οὕτω λέγουσι, καὶ διὰ τί οὕτω λέγουσι, τοσαῦτα εἰρήσθω· ἐπεὶ δ' ἀδύνατον

τὴν ἀντίφασιν ἅμα ἀληθεύεσθαι κατὰ τοῦ αὐτοῦ, φανερὸν ὅτι οὐδὲ τἀναντία ἅμα ὑπάρχειν ἐνδέχεται τῷ αὐτῷ· τῶν μὲν γὰρ ἐναντίων θάτερον στέρησίς ἐστιν οὐχ ἧττον, οὐσίας δὲ στέρησις· ἡ δὲ στέρησις ἀπόφασίς ἐστιν ἀπό τινος ὡρισμένου γένους· εἰ οὖν ἀδύνατον ἅμα καταφάναι καὶ ἀποφάναι ἀληθῶς, ἀδύνατον καὶ τἀναντία ὑπάρχειν ἅμα, ἀλλ' ἢ πῇ ἄμφω ἢ θάτερον μὲν πῇ θάτερον δὲ ἁπλῶς.

The fact that the most secure belief of all is that opposite affirmations are not true at the same time, what the consequences are for those who say that they are, and why it is that they say this, may now be regarded as adequately discussed. But since it is impossible for contradictories to be true of the same thing at the same time, it is evident that contraries cannot belong to the same thing at the same time either. For one of a pair of contraries is a lack no less [than a contrary], or a lack of substance, and a lack is the denial [of a predicate] to some definite kinds (*genos*). So if it is impossible at the same time to affirm and to deny truly, it is also impossible for contraries to belong at the same time, unless either both belong in a certain way or one in a certain way and the other unconditionally. (trans., Reeve)

Here the concepts of truth and falsehood expressed at 1011b26–27 are presupposed by the shift between premises about contradictory and contrary assertions and premises about the real correlates of these. The following reconstruction of the argument makes this clear:

P1: Assume, for a linguistic subject term n, a linguistic predicate term p, and a time t, that it is impossible that "p belongs to s" is true at t and that "p does not belong to s" is true at t.

P2: Hence, given the definition of assertoric truth at 1011b26–27, for a linguistic subject term n, a linguistic predicate term p, a time t, and real subject x and a real predicate y, if (1) n signifies x and p signifies y and "belongs to" and "does not belong to" signify respectively the real relations of belonging and not belonging, then it is impossible that y belongs to x at t and that y does not belong to x at t.

P3: Given the definition of contraries at 1005b26–27, for real subject x, real predicates y and z, and time t, if y and z are contraries, then (i) y belongs to x at t iff z does not belong to x at t and (ii) y does not belong to x at t iff z belongs to x at t.

P4: Therefore, given the definition of contraries at 1005b26–27, for real subject x, real predicates y and z, and time t, if y and z are contraries, then if y belongs to x at t and z belongs to x at t, then (1) y belongs to x at t and y does not belongs to x at t and (2) z belongs to x at t and z does not belong to x at t.

P5: P4 is impossible, given P1 and P2.

P6: Therefore, it is impossible that y belongs to x at t and z belongs to x at t.

It is instructive to reconstruct the argument solely in terms of linguistic assertions and the logical version of LNC:

PL1: Assume, for a linguistic subject term n, a linguistic predicate term p, and a time t, that it is impossible that the linguistic assertion "p belongs to n" is true at t and that the linguistic assertion "p does not belong to n" is true at t.

PL2: Given the definition of contraries, for a linguistic subject term n, linguistic predicate terms p and k, and time t, if p and k are contraries, then (i) "p belongs to n" is true at t iff "k does not belong to n" is true at t and (ii) "p does not belong to n" is true at t iff "k belongs to n" is true at t.

PL3: Therefore, given the definition of contraries, for a linguistic subject term n, linguistic predicate terms p and k, and time t, if p and k are contraries, then if "belongs to n" is true at t and "k belongs to n" is true at t, then (1) "p belongs to n" is true at t and "p does not belong to n" is true at t and (2) "k belongs to n" is true at t and "k does not belong to n" is true at t.

PL4: The consequent of PL3 is impossible, given PL1.

The Nominal Definition of "Truth" and the Axioms

PL5: Therefore, it is impossible that "p belongs to n" is true at t and "belongs to n" is true at t.

This reconstruction should be compared with a reconstruction developed solely in terms of real complexes and the metaphysical version of LNC:

PO1: Assume, for a real subject x, and a real predicate y, and time t, it is impossible that y belongs to x at t and that y does not belong to x at t.

PO2: Given the definition of contraries, for real subject x, real predicates y and z, and time t, if y and z are contraries, then (i) y belongs to x at t iff z does not belong x at t and (ii) y does not belong to x at t iff z belongs to x at t.

PO3: Therefore, given the definition of contraries, for real subject x, real predicates y and z, and time t, if y and z are contraries, then if y belongs to x at t and z belongs to x at t, then (1) y belongs to x at t and y does not belong to x at t and (2) z belongs to x at t and z does not belong to x at t.

PO4: The consequent of PO3 is impossible, given PO1.

PO5: Therefore, it is impossible that y belongs to x at t and z belongs to x at t.

The symmetry of reasoning between the logical and the metaphysical reconstructions is evident. The conceptions of truth and falsehood expressed at 1011b26–27 bridge the gap in the original formulation of the argument, which clearly differentiates the logical and metaphysical formulations of LNC. Given that the doxastic and the linguistic formulations are respectively about mental and linguistic assertions, it is not clear that they are importantly different: they are only as different as are linguistic and mental assertions.[16]

Aristotle claims that there is no intermediate assertion r between a contradictory pair of assertions p and q. Having investigated Aristotle's understanding of a contradictory pair, we are gaining insight into what such an intermediate assertion might look like—it will look like a simple assertion about a real subject x and a real predicate y. An intermediate assertion, were it to exist, would assert that y is related to x by means of a real predicative relation that is intermediate between the real predicative relation of belonging and the real predicative relation of not belonging.

Aristotle rejects the possibility of the latter real predicative relation. He thinks that the real predicative relation of belonging is opposed to the real predicative relation of not belonging such that there can be no intermediate relation between them.[17] If one takes the relations of belonging and not belonging as primitive binary relations, then one can conceive of the relations as complements: for every x and y, either (y belongs to x) or (y does not belong to x). Surely this is conceivable.

One might think that Aristotle defines the relations of belonging and not belonging in terms of more primitive binary relations—the obvious choices being either [1] the relations of *being-said-of* and *being-present-in*, particularly as these are used in the *Categories*, [2] the relations of essential and accidental predication as these are used in the *Analytics*, the *Metaphysics*, and elsewhere, or [3] the relations of definitional, essential, proper, and accidental predication as these are used in the *Topics*. It still seems clear that Aristotle can conceive of the derived binary relations of belonging and not-belonging as complementary. For example, define the relation of belonging so that: y belongs to x just in case either y is essentially predicated of x or y is accidentally predicated of x. Define the relation of not belonging so that: y does not belong to x just in case neither y is essentially predicated of x nor y is accidentally predicated of x. So defined, it is logically possible that the relations of belonging and not belonging are complements.

Return, now, to the putative intermediate assertion r.[18] It is most plausible to assume that r would assert that some relation or other obtains between x, the subject of the contradictory assertions p and q, and y, the predicate of both p and q. Presumably, r would not be intermediate between p and q were any of the following to obtain:

1. r is about things wholly other than x and y,
2. r is only about x or only about y,
3. r is about a relation between x and something other than y, or
4. r is about a relation between y and something other than x.

The Nominal Definition of "Truth" and the Axioms 101

Moreover, it seems clear that p and q are not opposed insofar as they are both about x and y. p and q are clearly opposed in virtue of the different relation each asserts obtains between x and y. The linguistic assertions "p" = the linguistic assertion "y belongs to x" and asserts that the real predicate signified by "y" belongs to the real subject signified by "x." The linguistic assertion "q" = the linguistic assertion "y does not belong to x" and asserts that the real predicate signified by "y" does not belong to the real subject signified by "x." The real predicative relation of belonging, signified by the linguistic predicative relation "belongs to," is obviously different from its contradictory opposite the real predicative relation of not belonging, signified by the linguistic predicative relation "does not belong to."

As a consequence, for r to be intermediate between p and q, it would have to posit a real predicative relationship * between x and y that is intermediate between the real predicative relations of belonging and not belonging. That is to say, using another way of characterizing the situation, it would have to assert a real predicative relationship * between x and y that is intermediate between y belonging to x and y not belonging to x.

Aristotle thinks such an intermediate relationship is impossible. Why? Because that is the way things are, given the nature of the predicative relation of belonging. For any two real single things x and y, it is necessary either that y belongs to x or that y does not belong to x. Could Aristotle be wrong about this? On the one hand, perhaps his conception of these binary predicative relations is incoherent. In short, not only might he be mistaken about the relation of belonging, he may not be making sense. Surely, however, he is at least making sense in thinking that, for any two real single things x and y, it is necessary either that y belongs to x or that y does not belong to x. On the other hand, making sense differs from getting it right about the world. Perhaps Aristotle's conceptions are coherent but nevertheless mischaracterize the real predicative relations of belonging and not belonging. The opponent of LEM might press *this* objection. He might argue that his concept of predicative belonging does not apply accurately to things in the world. I cannot vindicate here Aristotle's account of the real predicative relations of belonging and not belonging, but suffice it to say that he thinks they are real and complementary opposite relations.

The discussion, thus far, has focused on LEM insofar as it presupposes Aristotle's account of assertions. Given the preceding, we can restate [LEM_{2^*}] as follows:

[LEM$_{2**}$] For any two linguistic terms n and p, if n signifies one and only one being x, and if p signifies one and only one being y, then it is necessary either to assert "p belongs to n" or "p does not belong to n."

To complete our discussion of LEM and LNC, it remains to address the modal status of LEM.

From the modal point of view, [LEM$_{1**}$] and [LEM$_{2**}$] are claims about what is not possible and what is necessary.[19] What type of necessity is this? In *Met.* Γ 4, at 1006b32–35, Aristotle claims:

τοῦτο γὰρ σημαίνει τὸ ἀνάγκη εἶναι, τὸ ἀδύνατον εἶναι μὴ εἶναι [ἄνθρωπον)· οὐκ ἄρα ἐνδέχεται ἅμα ἀληθὲς εἶναι εἰπεῖν τὸ αὐτὸ ἄνθρωπον εἶναι καὶ μὴ εἶναι ἄνθρωπον.

[. . .] for 'to be necessary' signifies this: to be incapable of not being. Consequently, it is not possible that it should be simultaneously true to say that the same thing is a man and is not a man [. . .]. (trans., Ross)

This account of necessity mirrors that given in Δ 5, at 1015a33–36:

ἔτι τὸ μὴ ἐνδεχόμενον ἄλλως ἔχειν ἀναγκαῖόν φαμεν οὕτως ἔχειν· καὶ κατὰ τοῦτο τὸ ἀναγκαῖον καὶ τἆλλα λέγεταί πως ἅπαντα ἀναγκαῖα·

[. . .] when it is not possible for a thing to be otherwise, we assert that it is necessary for it to be so. Indeed the others are all in some way called necessary by virtue of this [. . .]. (trans., Ross)

Thus, it is necessary that p, just in case and because, it is not possible for p to be otherwise.[20] As a consequence, it is possible to reformulate and combine [LEM$_{1**}$] and [LEM$_{2**}$] as follows, privileging the case of mental assertions:

[LEM] For every thought c that represents one and only one thing x, for every thought i that represents one and only one

thing y, and every thought r that represents a real relation *
between the real relations of belonging and not belonging:

i: It is not possible that there is a mental assertion $i*c$ that is intermediate between the mental assertions i belongs to c and i does not belong to c, and

ii: It is not possible for it to be otherwise than to assert either (i belongs to c) or (i does not belong to c).[21]

The various contexts in which LEM is presented by Aristotle make it plain that, on the one hand, the universal quantifier "every" is unrestricted—all things are affirmed or denied—but that, on the other hand, LEM is employed in the context of philosophical inquiry. Therefore, Aristotle is not issuing the howler that everything is actually either affirmed or denied. Rather, with respect to whatever one considers in the context of philosophical inquiry, either one affirms it or one denies it. Thus, for example, at *Posterior Analytics* 71a14, Aristotle notes that in order to teach or learn, a person must believe LEM. That is to say, teachers and students must believe that everything taught or learned is either asserted or denied truly.[22]

The Elenctic Argument at 1011b23–29 and the Nominal Definitions

Given how Aristotle formulates LEM, and given how he understands the opponent's proposal that there is an intermediate assertion between contradictorily opposed simple assertions, it may be assumed safely that the elenctic demonstrations in defense of LEM are meant to apply to linguistic and mental assertions of two types: (1) to definitions of terms having the logical form "$n =_{df.} d$," where n and d each signify or represent one and only one thing and where "$=_{df.}$" is the linguistic or mental predicate signifying or representing the real relation of numerical sameness, or (2) to simple assertions having the logical form "d belongs to n" or the conceptual form <d belongs to n> or the logical form "d does not belong to n" or the conceptual form <d does not belong to n>, where "n" or <n> and "d" or <d> are univocal terms or concepts and "belongs to" or <belongs to> and "does not belong to" or <does not belong to> are the linguistic and conceptual predicates signifying or representing, respectively, the real relations of belonging to and not belonging to. As a consequence, the elenctic demonstrations are not meant to vindicate LEM for all contexts. Aristotle's arguments are limited to cases of simple assertions having the form of a definition, an affirmation, or a denial as these are defined in *De Interpretatione*. He thinks that this is enough for dialectical purposes.

We can glean from the foregoing that Aristotle expects his philosophical opponents to respect the norms of philosophical dialectic in arguing about the logical axioms. He assumes that all of the terms involved in an elenctic demonstration are, or at least ought to be, univocal. He may have equivocated in presenting one or another of his arguments, but it would be uncharitable to assume that he intended to equivocate. We may also assume that in presenting the elenctic demonstrations, at each step in the argument he aims always to assert only one of the simple assertions constituting a contradictory pair of assertions. And he expects his philosophical opponents similarly to respect this dialectical requirement.

It is within these dialectical constraints that he deploys the nominal definitions of "truth" and "falsehood" explicitly presented at *Met*. Γ 7.1011b26–27 but implicitly involved in all of the elenctic arguments. This is not to say that the nominal definitions themselves are limited in application only to definitions and simple assertions. That is a separate question to be addressed later. Rather, in the context of the elenctic demonstrations of LEM, the terms are employed only with respect to definitions and simple assertions.

Let us now instantiate the nominal definitions of "truth" and "falsehood" to the cases of simple affirmations and denials. Similar considerations apply to definitions, but I will set aside these considerations until we discuss Aristotle's claims about definitions in the middle books of the *Metaphysics*, in particular book Θ. The linguistic affirmation "Being rational belongs to Socrates" signifies the mental assertion <Being rational belongs to Socrates>. Likewise, the linguistic denial "Being rational does not belong to Socrates" signifies the mental assertion <Being rational does not belong to Socrates>.

Suppose Diotima mentally asserts <Being rational does not belong to Socrates>. If so, and if in fact the real predicate represented by the concept <being rational> does not belong to the real subject represented by the concept <Socrates>, then what Diotima asserts is true. She makes an assertion about the real subject Socrates, the real predicate being-rational,

The Nominal Definition of "Truth" and the Axioms 105

and the real relation of not belonging to. She asserts that they constitute the real complex being-rational-belonging-to-Socrates, and in fact, Socrates + rational obtains. If, alternatively, Diotima mentally asserts <Being rational belongs to Socrates> and in fact the real predicate represented by the concept <being rational> does belong to the real subject represented by the concept <Socrates> does not obtain, then what Diotima asserts is false. She makes an assertion about the real subject Socrates, the real predicate being-rational, and the real relation of belonging. She asserts that they constitute the real complex being-rational-belonging-to-Socrates, but in fact this real complex does not obtain. However, if it is not the case that the real predicate being-rational belongs to the real subject Socrates, then according to Aristotle being-rational belongs to Socrates.

Generalizing, one can instantiate the nominal definitions in the cases of mental affirmations and denials as follows:

> For every conceptual subject expression n that represents one and only one real subject x, for every conceptual predicate d that represents one and only one real predicate y, for every conceptual relation + that represents the real predicative relation of belonging to, and for every conceptual relation − that represents the real predicative relation of not belonging to:
>
> [F] Falsehood in the case of a simple assertion, is either (a) to mentally assert that $d + n$ and y does not belong to x or (b) to mentally assert $d - n$ and y belongs to x.
>
> [T] Truth, in the case of a simple assertion, is either (a) to mentally assert that $d + n$ and y belongs to x or (b) to mentally assert that $d - n$ and y does not belong to x.

And one can instantiate the nominal definitions in the cases of linguistic affirmations and denials as follows:

> For every linguistic subject expression n that signifies one and only one real subject x, for every linguistic predicate d that signifies one and only one real predicate y, for every linguistic relation + that signifies the real predicative relation of belonging to, and for every linguistic relation − that signifies the the real predicative relation of not belonging to:

[F] Falsehood, in the case of a simple assertion, is either (a) to linguistically assert that $d + n$ and y does not belong to x or (b) to linguistically assert that $d - n$ and y belongs to x.

[T] Truth, in the case of a simple assertion, is either (a) to linguistically assert that $d + n$ and y belongs to x or (b) to linguistically assert that $d - n$ and y does not belong to x.

Synthesizing these, we get:

For every linguistic or conceptual subject n that signifies or represents one and only one real subject x, for every linguistic or conceptual predicate d that signifies or represents one and only one real predicate y, for every linguistic or conceptual relation + that signifies or represents the real predicative relation of belonging to, and for every linguistic or conceptual relation − that signifies or represents the real predicative relation of not belonging to:

[F] Falsehood, in the case of a simple assertion, is either (a) to linguistically or mentally assert that $d + n$ and y does not belong to x or (b) to linguistically or mentally assert that $d - n$ and y belongs to x.

[T] Truth, in the case of a simple assertion, is either (a) to linguistically or mentally assert that $d + n$ and y belongs to x or (b) to linguistically or mentally assert that $d - n$ and y does not belong to x.

On the basis of these analyses and taking the liberty of adding implicit lemmata, the first elenctic demonstration can be restated rigorously as follows:

LEM0: A dialectical assertion is a simple linguistic or mental assertion.

LEM1: Suppose the opponent of LEM asserts an affirmation or denial; i.e., for some linguistic or conceptual subject n that signifies or represents a real subject x, for some linguistic or conceptual predicate m that signifies a real predicate y, for some linguistic or conceptual relation + that signifies or represents the real predicative relation of belonging to, and for some linguistic or conceptual relation – that signifies or represents the real predicative relation of not belonging to, our opponent linguistically or mentally asserts the simple assertion $m + n$ or she linguistically or mentally asserts the simple assertion $m - n$.

LEM2: Suppose the following nominal definitions of truth and falsehood:

[F] Falsehood, in the case of a simple assertion, is either (a) to assert that $m + n$ and y does not belong to x or (b) to assert $m - n$ and y belongs to x.

[T] Truth, in the case of a simple assertion, is either (a) to assert that $m + n$ and y belongs to x or (b) to assert $m - n$ and y does not belong to x.

LEM3: In fact, either y belongs to x or y does not belong to x.

LEM4: Hence, our opponent—in linguistically or mentally asserting the simple assertion $m + n$ or in linguistically or mentally asserting the simple assertion $m - n$—asserts either what is true or what is false.

LEM5: It follows that someone linguistically or mentally asserts $m + n$ or $m - n$ if, and only if, she asserts what is true or false.

LEM6: In the putative case where our opponent linguistically or mentally asserts what is intermediate between the contradictory pair of simple assertions $m + n$ and $m - n$, neither [1] our opponent asserts $m + n$ and y belongs to x, nor [2] our opponent asserts $m + n$ and y does not belong to x, nor [3] our opponent asserts $m - n$ and y belongs to x, nor [4] our opponent asserts $m - n$ and y does not belong to x.

LEM7: Suppose that $m + n$ and $m - n$ are a contradictory pair of assertions.

LEM8: If LEM7, then [1] either $m + n$ or $m - n$ and [2] there is no real predicative relation between the real predicative relations belonging to and not belonging to.

LEM9: Hence, there is no linguistic or conceptual predicative relation * that signifies or represents a real predicative relation between the real predicative relations of belonging to and not belonging to.

LEM10: Thus, it is not possible to define a linguistic or conceptual predicative relation * that signifies a real predicative relation between the real relations of belonging to or not belonging to.

LEM11: So, our opponent asserts nothing when she utters $m * n$.

LEM12: Therefore, neither [1] our opponent asserts $m + n$ and y belongs to x, nor [2] our opponent asserts $m + n$ and y does not belong to x, nor [3] our opponent asserts $m - n$ and y belongs to x, nor [4] our opponent asserts $m - n$ and y does not belong to x, nor [5] our opponent asserts $m * n$.

LEM13: Therefore, someone who asserts what is intermediate between a contradictory pair of simple assertions asserts neither what is true nor what is false.

LEM14: However, a simple assertion, by definition, is either true or false.

LEM15: Hence, our opponent asserts nothing at all.

LEM16: Thus, the putative case in LEM6 is absurd.

LEMC: Therefore:

[LEM] For every linguistic or conceptual subject n that signifies one and only one thing x, for every predicate term m that signifies one and only one thing y, and every assertoric predicative relation * that signifies a real relation between the real relations belonging to and not belonging to:

i: It is not possible that there is an assertion $m * n$ that is intermediate between $m + n$ and $m - n$, and

ii: It is not possible for it to be otherwise than to assert either $m + n$ or $m - n$.

With regard to the premises, the assumption LEM0 is basic to the practice of dialectic. LEM1 relies upon Aristotle's definition of a simple assertion in *De Interpretatione*. It may be that the opponent of LEM denies Aristotle's way of understanding simple assertions. It is unclear to what extent his account of assertion differs from Plato's account. It is unknown whether or not Aristotle's account differed from those defended by his other philosophical contemporaries.

LEM3 is a basic metaphysical claim driving all of Aristotle's reasoning in book Γ. As was noted above in the discussion of the relations of belonging and not-belonging, he can make sense of the idea that there are binary real predicative relations that are complements. Moreover, he can, and does, insist that proper dialectical reasoning involves only simple assertions about things related by means of these complementary binary predicative relations. If the philosophical opponent refuses to engage in dialectic reasoning so understood, then he holds them in contempt.

Given the definition of a simple assertion and the common philosophical conceptions of assertoric truth and falsehood, LEM6 analyzes the opponent's proposed intermediate simple assertion. LEM8 follows from the concept of a contradictory pair of assertions. LEM9 captures the fact that the binary real predicative relations of belonging and not-belonging are complements. LEM10–15 reflect the facts that every term in a dialectical argument must signify only one thing and that every term must be significant for all the interlocutors involved in the argument.

This reconstruction of the argument reflects the insights of the two most longstanding interpretations of Aristotle's argument at 1011b23–29,[23] and it depends upon the following assumptions:

1. The definitions of truth and falsehood at 1011b26–27,

2. The semantic assumption that every term in a dialectical argument is univocal,

3. The semantic assumption that every simple assertion asserts either that one and only one thing y belongs to one and only one thing x or that y does not belong to x,

4. The metaphysical assumption that there is no real predicative relation between those of belonging and not belonging, and

5. The metaphysical assumption that there is no intermediate metaphysical status between being nothing at all and being one thing.

My reconstruction—sensitive to the interpretive difficulties posed by the Greek texts—leaves it open that the opponent is making an assertion about an intermediate between contradictories while denying LEM or is making an assertion about some one thing or other while denying LEM.

This is not the place to ask whether or not the argument is sound. Nor is this the place to ask whether or not all of Aristotle's philosophical contemporaries would have embraced all of the premises in the argument and all of the assumptions just noted. What is crucial here is to recognize that the nominal definitions of "truth" and "falsehood" are essential to the success of the argument: *The definitions are doing all the heavy inferential lifting in the elenctic argument.* The definitions are not only necessary, they are crucial. Although I cannot make the case here, for reasons of space, similar considerations apply to the other elenctic arguments presented by Aristotle in support of LEM in book Γ.

And now, before concluding this chapter, let me briefly consider Aristotle's strategy for defending LNC in book Γ, which differs slightly from his strategy for vindicating LEM.[24] Aristotle's arguments for LEM immediately follow his extended defense of LNC. Before marshaling elenctic arguments in support of LNC, Aristotle first argues that LNC is "the most indisputable of all principles" at 1006a3. He had just described LNC as "an ultimate belief" [ἐσχάτην δόξαν] and "the starting point for all other axioms" [ἀρχὴ τῶν ἄλλων ἀξιωμάτων] at 1005b32–34. The conclusion of the argument, then, is not the bald assertion of LNC but, rather, the claim that LNC is the most indisputable of all principles. Aristotle stresses that he has posited [εἰλήφαμεν] LNC—not argued for it—and shown [ἐδείξαμεν] that it is the most indisputable of all principles, at 1006a3ff. He infers this from premises showing that various epistemic predicates—most certain, free from the possibility of error, and best known—are properly predicated of LNC. For my purposes here, it is important to stress the fact that Aristotle describes LNC in terms of these epistemic characteristics, and that he understands each of these in terms of truth and falsehood. In demonstrating that each belongs to LNC, he is presupposing concepts of truth and falsehood.[25]

Aristotle does not think he has argued for LNC in demonstrating that it is the most indisputable of all principles. He has posited it and argued that it is the most indisputable posit anyone might make. Aristotle notes at 1005b35–1006a2 that some think they can both say [φάσι] and suppose [ὑπολαμβάνειν] that it is possible for the same thing to be and not to be, and that some even demand that LNC be demonstrated. He presents two constructive arguments against this demand, both of which rely upon the concept of demonstration and, hence, presuppose the concept of truth.

Some conceptions of truth and falsehood are, thus, presupposed by Aristotle's constructive arguments concerning the attributes possessed by LNC. Unless he presupposes concepts his dialectical opponents are likely to accept his opponents are unlikely to be persuaded by these constructive arguments. It seems plausible that he presupposes the concepts expressed by the nominal definitions presented at *Met.* book Γ 7.1011b26–27. Since I have already argued that Aristotle employs the nominal definitions, at least implicitly, in all of his elenctic arguments for the logical axioms, it follows that he relies upon the nominal defintions in all of his arguments for LNC in Γ.

Conclusion

In this chapter I have evaluated how the conceptions constitutive of the definiens of the nominal definition of "truth" (the conceptions of assertion, being, and non-being) relate to the notions involved in the axioms of demonstration themselves (the conception of a simple assertion, the conception of a contradictory pair of simple assertions, the conception of an intermediate assertion between opposed simple assertions) in the context of Aristotle's elenctic arguments for the axioms in *Metaphysics* book Γ. I have argued that these conceptions are tightly linked. In book Γ, Aristotle expects that the nominal definitions of "truth" and "falsehood" are being applied in the context of dialectical inquiry, which inquiry requires that the opponent always asserts one and only one of the simple assertions involved in a contradictory pair of assertions. Aristotle precisely specifies what counts in dialectic as a simple assertion, a contradictory pair of simple assertions, and an intermediate assertion between a contradictory pair of simple assertions. He seems to think that his philosophical opponents will grant these dialectical assumptions. He places very weak constraints on the signification of "being" and "oneness" in the elenctic arguments in book Γ, constraints he thinks are essential for all thought and communication.

Before presenting his own accounts of the essence of truth, being, and oneness in the *Metaphysics*, Aristotle defends the basic philosophical principles he will employ in such theorizing. To this end he argues for the logical axioms in book Γ. The nominal definitions of "truth" and "falsehood" presented at 1011b26–27 are crucial premises in all of Aristotle's arguments for the logical axioms. In the next part of this book I present Aristotle's account of the essence of truth and falsehood—his real definitions of truth and falsehood—as he develops these on the basis of the nominal definitions presented in Γ and as part of his theory of being in books Δ–N of the *Metaphysics*.

Part III

Truth and Being

Chapter 4

The Being of Truth

In the previous two chapters I have argued that—contrary to what is ordinarily thought—Aristotle's definition of truth at *Met.* Γ 7.1011b26–27 is a nominal definition of the term "truth," one his philosophical opponents would grant. He deploys it in the context of arguing elenctically for the logical axioms. We ought not think it expresses Aristotle's considered account of the essence of truth.

We have analyzed the nominal definitions of "truth" and "falsehood," assessed their inferential roles in the elenctic arguments in book Γ, and explored how the concepts in their definiens relate to the concepts essential to the Law of Non-Contradiction and the Law of the Excluded Middle. So conceived, truth and falsehood are characteristics that belong to linguistic and mental assertions. Specifying more fully what this kind of truth involves consumes Aristotle's attention throughout the rest of the *Metaphysics*: what is being, what is non-being, what is it to assert about one and only one being that it is or it is not, what is it to assert about non-being that it is or it is not. Among other concerns, books Δ–N focus on the various problems that must be solved in order to answer these questions.

Aristotle's account of the essence of truth in the *Metaphysics* relates in four principal ways to his theory of philosophical wisdom and his investigation into the first principles and causes of substance. First, truth is fundamental to the ontology in the *Metaphysics*. He recognizes it as one of the four basic kinds of being. I will make the case for this claim in this chapter. Second, in explaining the first principles and causes of substance, Aristotle systematically presents his account of the essence of truth. He articulates his account of the first principles and causes of substance in the brightening light of his developing real definition of truth. His real definition of truth informs and is informed by his accounts of definition, activity, and oneness presented as part of his theory of being insofar as it is being in the *Metaphysics*. I defend this reading of the text in chapters 7, 8, and 9. Third, Aristotle explains the proper object of philosophical wisdom—God—in terms that require us to comprehend his account of the essence of truth. I return to this topic in the concluding chapter of the book.

In chapter 1 I said that Aristotle systematically defines the essence of truth in the *Metaphysics*, defining "systematic definition" in terms of what David Charles (2000, 24ff.) has called "the three-stage view" of inquiry:

[Stage 1] Knowing an account of what a term *t* signifies.

[Stage 2] Knowing that what *t* signifies exists.

[Stage 3] Knowing the essence of the kind signified by *t*.

Given the arguments in the preceding chapters of this book, Aristotle has established Stages 1 and 2 of his systematic inquiry into the nature of truth in *Metaphysics* book Γ. He has explicitly stated an account of what the term "truth" signifies, and he has established *that* what is signified by the nominal definition of "truth" *exists* for anyone willing to say something significant in the context of philosophical dialectic and, thereby, to satisfy the minimal semantic requirements of dialectical and philosophical inquiry. Those who have rejected the existence of truth as described by the nominal definitions in book Γ have thereby rejected the very possibility of rational inquiry and have resigned their status as beings capable of discriminating one thing from another.

What remains to be shown, then, is that Aristotle completes Stage 3 of his inquiry into the nature of truth in the *Metaphysics*—knowing the essence of the kind signified by "truth." In this chapter, I argue that Aristotle identifies truth as a kind of being in *Met.* book Δ, chapter 7. More specifically, I argue that he identifies the kind of truth that belongs to assertions as one of the four kinds of being he takes seriously in his mature ontology.[1] A number of contemporary commentators disagree. They claim that Aristotle posits an objectual kind of truth among the four kinds of being in his ontology. On their view, therefore, when Aristotle includes truth among the four kinds of being under investigation in the *Metaphysics* he is concerned with a kind of truth other than the kind introduced by him in *Metaphysics* book Γ, chapter 7.

Truth is a Kind of Being

Having vindicated the first principles of argument in book Γ, Aristotle begins his investigation into the principles and causes of being insofar as it is being. He pursues this investigation throughout the rest of the treatise. He recognizes different kinds of being [τὸ ὄν] in the *Metaphysics*: coincidental being, being in-itself (which coordinates with the various categories of beings), being true, and potential and actual being. He explicitly addresses these different kinds of being for the first time in Δ 7.[2]

In *Metaphysics* Δ 7, at 1017a31–35, Aristotle claims that truth is a kind of being and that falsehood is a kind of non-being:

> ἔτι τὸ εἶναι σημαίνει καὶ τὸ ἔστιν ὅτι ἀληθές, τὸ δὲ μὴ εἶναι ὅτι οὐκ ἀληθὲς ἀλλὰ ψεῦδος, ὁμοίως ἐπὶ καταφάσεως καὶ ἀποφάσεως, οἷον ὅτι ἔστι Σωκράτης μουσικός, ὅτι ἀληθὲς τοῦτο, ἢ ὅτι ἔστι Σωκράτης οὐ λευκός, ὅτι ἀληθές· τὸ δ' οὐκ ἔστιν ἡ διάμετρος σύμμετρος, ὅτι ψεῦδος.

> "To be" and "is" signify that [something] is true, "not to be" that it is not true but false,—and this alike in affirmation and negation; e.g., that cultured Socrates *is* [signifies] that this is true, or that Socrates not white *is* [signifies] that this is true; on the other hand the commensurate diagonal *is not* [signifies] that it is false. (trans., mine, following Ross)

According to some commentators—Halper, Whitaker, and Crivelli—the use of "τὸ ὄν" considered at 1017a31–35 by means of its cognates "τὸ εἶναι" and "τὸ ἔστιν" is equivalent to a use of "ἀληθές" that signifies an attribute of mind and language independent objects ("real" objects), an attribute Aristotle discusses in *Metaphysics* Δ 29 and Θ 10.[3] Call this "the objectual reading."[4] According to other commentators—Alexander, Aquinas, Ross, Kirwan, De Rijk, and Charles and Peramatzis—1017a31–35 is about a use of "being" equivalent to a use of "truth" that denotes an attribute of linguistic and mental affirmations and denials.[5] Call this "the assertoric reading." I will defend a version of the assertoric reading against the objectual reading. (As a reminder, I use "assertion" to denote the sorts of items Aristotle includes among the things denoted by his technical terms "ἀπόφασις," "κατάφασις," "ἀπόφανσις," and "λόγος." Aristotle's terms denote mental and linguistic truth-bearers, including: uttered and written statements, perceptions, imaginations, opinions, beliefs, and thoughts.[6] In contemporary parlance, we would describe some or all of these as "propositional items."[7])

The arguments considered in this chapter are important for various reasons. First, agreeing with Charles and Peramatzis (2016) and with Menn (n.d.), we should take seriously Aristotle's remarks about "being" and "truth" in *Met.* Δ 7. Yet there has been little discussion of 1017a31–35 in the literature on Aristotle's theory of truth, and no intensive analysis.[8] Second, on the reading defended here, attributes of assertions—*not* attributes of objects, as posited by the objectual reading—are among the things denoted by "being" and "non-being" in Δ 7. This suggests that Aristotle included the attributes of assertoric truth and falsehood among the kinds of being posited in his mature ontology, a suggestion borne out by his claims in E 4 and Θ 10. Third, on the assertoric reading of 1017a31–35, Aristotle's veridical use of "being" in Δ 7 is similar to the existential use of "is" developed by Kant and Frege, according to which "exists" denotes a second-order attribute of thoughts or judgments and not an attribute of things.[9] In the context of understanding the importance of true assertions in the *Metaphysics*, this veridical sense of "being" serves to focus metaphysical inquiry by making explicit the putative ontological commitments posited in the first-order simple assertions of which the veridical sense of "being" is predicated. Fourth, the assertoric reading of 1017a31–35 promises to square the veridical use of "being" in Δ.7 with other important passages on truth in the *Metaphysics*: Γ 7, Δ 29, E 4, and Θ 10.

Aristotle recognizes different kinds of being [τὸ ὄν] in the *Metaphysics*: coincidental being, being in-itself, being true, and potential and actual being. He explicitly addresses these different kinds of being for the first time in *Met.* Δ 7. At the outset of Δ 7, Aristotle notes that "being" is said in one way about the coincidental—the use he dilates at 1017a8–22—and in another way about the in-itself, which use he discusses at 1017a22–30. He considers another use of "being" at 1017a31–35 that signifies that something is true. Finally, at 1017a35–b9, he explores a use of "being" that signifies potentiality and actuality. As the argument in the *Metaphysics* develops Aristotle defines each kind of being, indicating which is the more fundamental. He considers coincidental being in E 2–3, considers various dimensions of being-in-itself—chief among them substance–in Z, H, Θ, I, Λ, M, and N, and defines the being of truth (and relates his other concepts of truth to this kind of truth) in Δ 29, E 2 and 4, Θ 10, and I 1–2. Θ1–9 deals with potential and actual being. Aristotle thus includes truth among the others sorts of being relevant to the study of being insofar as it is being, i.e., his general ontology.[10]

There is no reason to doubt that Aristotle is identifying and attempting to elucidate a use of "being" when, in Δ 7, he considers a use of "being" that signifies that something is true. Throughout *Met.* Δ he distinguishes among various ways in which key philosophical terms are used.[11] Although he need not be committed to every use of every term he considers, it is reasonable to assume that he *is* committed to the different uses of "being" and "not-being" in Δ 7. The concepts distinguished in Δ are plausibly interpreted in terms of his philosophical system which, barring strong reasons to the contrary, are best understood as concepts he embraced. He begins the chapter at 1017a7 by claiming that "being" is said with respect to the accidental and with respect to the in-itself [τὸ ὂν λέγεται τὸ μὲν κατὰ συμβεβηκὸς τὸ δὲ καθ' αὑτό]. It is typical, especially in Δ, for Aristotle to use "is said" to signify that he is distinguishing among different uses of a term.[12]

It is reasonable to assume, then, that at 1017a31–35 Aristotle is concerned with a use of "being" that signifies that something is true and a use of "not-being" that signifies that something is false.[13] The passage is widely recognized as among the more important concerning truth in the treatises. It apparently establishes some kind of equivalence between "being" and "true" and between "not-being" and "false." One can discern the following two claims:

1. "To be$_T$" and "that which is$_T$" signify that something is true.

2. "Not to be$_F$" signifies that something is not true but false.[14]

If one assumes that "to be" [τὸ εἶναι] and "that which is" [τὸ ἔστιν] are used in apposition at 1017a31, and likewise with regard to "not true" [οὐκ ἀληθές] and "false" [ψεῦδος] at 1017a32, then one gets:

D1: "To be$_T$" signifies that something is true.

D2: "Not to be$_F$" signifies that something is false.

There are two leading interpretations of D1 and D2. On the one hand, they can be interpreted in terms of logical equivalence. On this approach, Aristotle is claiming that there is a use of "being$_T$" that is logically equivalent with a use of "being true" and that there is a use of "not to be$_F$" that is logically equivalent with a use of "being false." This is the common way of interpreting the passage, and the objectual and assertoric readings represent two ways of developing this interpretation. On the other hand, the clauses can be understood in terms of a material equivalence. On this approach, defended recently by Matthen, Aristotle is expressing the fact that the semantic predicate "is true" holds of a sentence or judgment just in case (and because) the predicate "is$_T$" holds of what is signified by that sentence or judgment, and similarly that the semantic predicate "is false" holds of a sentence or judgment whenever (and because) the predicate "is not$_F$" holds of what is signified by that sentence or judgment. Call this the "explanatory reading."

Without deciding yet among the objectual, assertoric, and explanatory alternatives, we can assume that the first two clauses at 1017a31–32 establish the following two claims:

D1*: "To be$_T$" is equivalent to "to be true."

D2*: "Not to be$_F$" is equivalent to "to be false."

That Aristotle recognizes such a use of "to be$_T$" and "not to be$_F$" in *Met.* Δ.7, may not be surprising.[15] In the *Prior Analytics* I 36, at 48b1–3, in the midst of a discussion of how the middle terms of a deduction are predicatively related to the extreme terms, he notes:

ἀλλ' ὁσαχῶς τὸ εἶναι λέγεται καὶ τὸ ἀληθὲς εἰπεῖν αὐτὸ τοῦτο, τοσαυταχῶς οἴεσθαι χρὴ σημαίνειν καὶ τὸ ὑπάρχειν.

But we must suppose that "to belong" has as many meanings as the ways in which "to be" and "it is true to say this is that" are used. (trans., Jenkinson)

Aristotle establishes here some sort of equivalence among the predicates "τὸ ὑπάρχειν" ["to belong"], "τὸ εἶναι" ["to be"], and "τὸ ἀληθὲς εἰπεῖν" ["it is true to say"], such that the verb "to be" is said in as many ways as the verb "it is true to say,"[16] Also, in *Apr.* I 37, at 49a6–10, he relates his technical notion of predicative belonging to the concept of truth and the divisions among predications:

Τὸ δ' ὑπάρχειν τόδε τῷδε καὶ τὸ ἀληθεύεσθαι τόδε κατὰ τοῦδε τοσαυταχῶς ληπτέον ὁσαχῶς αἱ κατηγορίαι διῄρηνται, καὶ ταύτας ἢ πῇ ἢ ἁπλῶς, ἔτι ἢ ἁπλᾶς ἢ συμπεπλεγμένας· ὁμοίως δὲ καὶ τὸ μὴ ὑπάρχειν. ἐπισκεπτέον δὲ ταῦτα καὶ διοριστέον βέλτιον.

That this belongs to that or that this is true of that must be taken in as many ways as the predications have been divided, and these either in some respect or without qualification, and furthermore either simple or complex. The same holds for not belonging as well. But these things must be better investigated and determined. (trans., Striker)

In this passage, Aristotle reasserts the equivalence claim at *Apr.* 48b1–3 and extends it to include the logical complements of the relevant predicates: the predicates "τὸ μὴ ὑπάρχειν" ["not to belong"], "τὸ μὴ εἶναι" ["not to be"], and "τὸ μὴ ἀληθεύεσθαι" ["it is not true to say"] are asserted to be equivalent. Again, in *Apr.* I 46, at 52a24–38, while discussing differences in how to prove affirmations and negations, he suggests that there is a use of "to be" that is equivalent to a use of "it is true to say that."[17] Thus, although one might balk at the idea that Aristotle is concerned with the same concepts in the *Prior Analytics* and *Metaphysics* Δ 7, there is clearly precedent for his claim in Δ 7, that "to be" is equivalent to "truth."

Focusing on the claims at 1017a31–35, it is worth noting that the third clause (ὁμοίως ἐπὶ καταφάσεως καὶ ἀποφάσεως) allows for translations compatible with all of the proposed readings. One may translate the third clause either by:

[a] [. . .] equally in the case of affirmation and denial [. . .],

or

[b] [. . .] alike in the manner of affirmation and denial [. . .]

On either reading, Aristotle is somehow qualifying the scope of D1* and D2* in terms of affirmations and denials.

In the case of [a], the idea is that D1* and D2* are about affirmations and denials themselves. On this interpretation, 1017a31–32 is to be understood as follows:

[. . .] Again "to be$_T$" and "that which is$_T$" signify that an affirmation or a denial is true, "not to be$_F$," that an affirmation or a denial is not true but false, [. . .]

D1* and D2*, in turn, may be understood along the lines of the assertoric reading as follows:

D1A: "To be$_T$" is logically equivalent to "to be true," where both terms denote an attribute of simple assertions.

D2A: "Not to be$_F$" is logically equivalent to "o be false," where both terms denote an attribute of simple assertions.

Case [a] also allows us to interpret D1* and D2* in terms of the explanatory reading:

D1Exp: "To be$_T$" is coextensive with "to be true," where "to be$_T$" denotes an attribute of real things and "to be true" denotes an attribute of assertions.

D2Exp: "Not to be$_F$" is coextensive with "to be false," where "not to be$_F$" denotes an attribute of real things and "to be false" denotes an attribute of assertions.

Alternatively, one may interpret the dependent clause at 1017a32–33 along the lines suggested by an objectual reading, which is the purport of case [b]. D1* and D2*, adopting an objectual reading, are not about affirmations and denials themselves but, rather, are about *things in the world conceived in terms of affirmations and denials*. There is clear precedent for this approach. In *Categories* 10, Aristotle discusses four kinds of opposition, one of which is the opposition between an affirmation and a negation. At *Cat.* 11b23, he gives as examples the opposition between "He is sitting" and "He is not sitting," and at *Cat.* 12b5–16, he makes the following claims:

οὐκ ἔστι δὲ οὐδὲ τὸ ὑπὸ τὴν κατάφασιν καὶ ἀπόφασιν κατάφασις καὶ ἀπόφασις· ἡ μὲν γὰρ κατάφασις λόγος ἐστὶ καταφατικὸς καὶ ἡ ἀπόφασις λόγος ἀποφατικός, τῶν δὲ ὑπὸ τὴν κατάφασιν ἢ ἀπόφασιν οὐδέν ἐστι λόγος. λέγεται δὲ καὶ ταῦτα ἀντικεῖσθαι ἀλλήλοις ὡς κατάφασις καὶ ἀπόφασις· καὶ γὰρ ἐπὶ τούτων ὁ τρόπος τῆς ἀντιθέσεως ὁ αὐτός· ὡς γάρ ποτε ἡ κατάφασις πρὸς τὴν ἀπόφασιν ἀντίκειται, οἷον τὸ κάθηται—οὐ κάθηται, οὕτω καὶ τὸ ὑφ' ἑκάτερον πρᾶγμα ἀντίκειται, τὸ καθῆσθαι—μὴ καθῆσθαι.

Nor is what underlies an affirmation or negation itself an affirmation or negation: For an affirmation is an affirmative statement and a negation a negative statement, whereas none of the things underlying an affirmation or negation is a statement. These are, however, said to be opposed to one another as affirmation and negation are, for in these cases, too, the manner of opposition is the same. For in the way an affirmation is opposed to a negation, for example "he is sitting"—"he is not sitting," so are opposed also the actual things underlying each, his sitting—his not sitting. (trans., Ackrill)

Cat. 12b5–16 is situated in a discussion of privation and possession and is an argument for the claim that what underlies an affirmation and its negation, while neither affirmations nor negations themselves, are opposed to one another in the way that an affirmation and its negation are opposed (and not as privation or possession are). Thus, the opposition between the statements "He is sitting" and "He is not sitting" is the same as the opposition between an actual man combined with the actual position of sitting and an actual man separated from the actual position of sitting.

On this objectual interpretation, 1017a31–32 is to be understood as follows:

[. . .] Again "to be$_T$" and "that which is$_T$" signify that an actual thing is a true thing, "not to be$_F$" that an actual thing is not a true thing but a false thing, [. . .]

D1* and D2*, in turn, are modified as follows:

D1Obj: "To be$_T$" is equivalent to "to be a true thing," where both terms denote a kind of actual things.

D2Obj: "Not to be$_F$" is equivalent to "to be a false thing," where both terms denote a kind of actual things.

The objectual reading of the passage may seem puzzling. How can an actual thing be true or false? As we will see, proponents of the objectual reading can make ready sense of their proposal.

In summary, at *Met.* Δ 7.1017a31–32 Aristotle recognizes a use of "τὸ εἶναι" that is equivalent to a use of "ἀληθές," and a use of "τὸ μὴ εἶναι" equivalent to a use of "ψεῦδος," but it remains an open question what concepts of truth and falsehood he employs in the passage. Assertoric, explanatory, and objectual readings of the passage are possible. To make further progress, it is necessary to examine each interpretation in light of the examples at 1017a33–35.

Being True is not Being a Kind of Object

It will help to reiterate why it is important to demonstrate here that the objectual reading fails. First, the objectual interpretation has implications for how one reads the subsequent discussions about truth and falsehood in books E and Θ. In demonstrating the poverty of the objectual reading, the importance of true assertion as a kind of being is emphasized, and the way is cleared for interpreting books E and Θ in terms of true assertion. Second, a number of contemporary interpreters have defended the objectual interpretation of *Met.* Δ 7.1017a33–35. If they are correct, then Aristotle does not include true assertion among the four kinds of being in Δ 7, as is argued here. Rather, he is including another sort of objectual being explained in terms of real analogues of assertoric belonging and not belonging.

The most promising way to develop this objectual reading of 1017a31–35 is in terms of the uses of "falsehood" denoting attributes of real objects explicitly discussed by Aristotle in *Metaphysics* Δ 29, at 1024b17–26, and in *Metaphysics* Θ 10, at 1051b33–1052a1. In Δ 29, at 1024b17–26, Aristotle introduces two uses of "πρᾶγμα ψεῦδος" ("false thing"):

Τὸ ψεῦδος λέγεται ἄλλον μὲν τρόπον ὡς πρᾶγμα ψεῦδος, καὶ τούτου τὸ μὲν τῷ μὴ συγκεῖσθαι ἢ ἀδύνατον εἶναι συντεθῆναι (ὥσπερ λέγεται τὸ τὴν διάμετρον εἶναι σύμμετρον ἢ τὸ σὲ καθῆσθαι· τούτων γὰρ ψεῦδος τὸ μὲν ἀεὶ τὸ δὲ ποτέ· οὕτω γὰρ οὐκ ὄντα ταῦτα), τὰ δὲ ὅσα ἔστι μὲν ὄντα, πέφυκε μέντοι φαίνεσθαι ἢ μὴ οἷά ἐστιν ἢ ἃ μὴ ἔστιν (οἷον ἡ σκιαγραφία καὶ τὰ ἐνύπνια· ταῦτα γὰρ ἔστι μέν τι, ἀλλ' οὐχ ὧν ἐμποιεῖ τὴν φαντασίαν)—πράγματα μὲν οὖν ψευδῆ οὕτω λέγεται, ἢ τῷ μὴ εἶναι αὐτὰ ἢ τῷ τὴν ἀπ' αὐτῶν φαντασίαν μὴ ὄντος εἶναι.

We call false (1) that which is false as a thing, and that (a) because it is not combined or cannot be combined, e.g., that the diagonal of a square is commensurate with the side or that you are sitting; for one of these is false always, and the other sometimes; it is in these two senses that they are nonexistent. (b) There are things which exist, but whose nature it is to appear either not to be such as they are or to be things that do not exist, e.g., a sketch or a dream; for these are something, but are not the things the appearance of which they produce in us. We call things false in this way, then—either because they themselves do not exist, or because the appearance which results from them is that of something that does not exist. (trans., mine, following Ross)

In Δ 29.1024b17–26, Aristotle distinguishes between (1) a use of "false thing" that denotes predicative combinations that do not, in fact, exist and (2) a use of "false thing" that denotes actual things that are usually taken to be something other than what they are. It is plausible to suppose that for each use, Aristotle acknowledged a correlated use of "πρᾶγμα ἀληθές" that would denote either (1) predicative combinations of real things that, in fact, exist or (2) actual things that are usually taken to be what they are. We shall focus here only on the uses of "false thing" that denotes predicative combinations that do not, in fact, exist and the use of "true thing" that denotes predicative combinations that do, in fact, exist.

Aristotle explicitly differentiates between two sorts of real predicative combinations denoted by "false thing" in Δ 29.1024b17–26: (a) real things that are not combined, but could be (τὸ τῶι μὴ συγκεῖσθαι) and (b) real things that cannot be combined (τὸ ἀδύνατον εἶναι συντεθῆναι). At 1024b25, summarizing the general characteristic of these combinations, Aristotle emphasizes that they themselves *are not* (τῷ μὴ εἶναι αὐτά).[18] These uses of "false thing" and "true thing" are not local to Δ 29.1024b17–26. Aristotle appears to make use of them in his discussion of truth and falsehood in *Met.* Θ 10.1051b33–1052a1:

τὸ δὲ εἶναι ὡς τὸ ἀληθές, καὶ τὸ μὴ εἶναι τὸ ὡς τὸ ψεῦδος, ἓν μέν ἐστιν, εἰ σύγκειται, ἀληθές, τὸ δ' εἰ μὴ σύγκειται, ψεῦδος· τὸ δὲ ἕν, εἴπερ ὄν, οὕτως ἐστίν, εἰ δὲ μὴ οὕτως, οὐκ ἔστιν.

As regards being in the sense of what is true and not being in the manner of what is false, in one case [the case of composites] there is truth if the subject and the attribute are really combined, and falsity if they are not combined; in the other case [the case of simples], if the object is, it exists as such [in the sense that it is true], and if the object [is] not as such [in the sense that it is false], it is not; (trans., mine, following Ross)

In Θ 10.1051b33–1052a1, read objectually, Aristotle again acknowledges the uses of "false thing" and "true thing" that denote nonexistent and existent real predicative combinations.[19] If a putative real combination of a subject and its attribute are, in fact, not combined, then that putative real combination fails to exist and is a false thing. If a putative real combination of a subject and its attribute are, in fact, combined, then that putative real combination is an actual real combination and is a true thing. Of note, Aristotle also posits uses of "false thing" and "true thing" that denote nonexistent and existent real metaphysical simples.

Looking more closely at 1051b33–35, it is arguable that Aristotle is concerned with the uses of "false thing" and "true thing" in Δ 29.1024b17–26.[20] Read in relation to 1024b17–26, 1051b33–35 augments Aristotle's discussion of the uses introduced in Δ 29—which explicitly deals only with false composite things involving real predicative combination—with a use of "being$_T$" that signifies real and existing simple things and a use of "non being$_F$" that signifies real simple things but does not exist. Read this way, he is claiming that a true composite thing involves the real combination of its constituent things, a false composite thing involves the real division of its constituent things, a true simple thing exists as a simple thing, and a false simple thing doesn't exist at all. Supposing, then, that Θ 10.1051b33–1052a1 is about the uses of "true thing" and "false thing" introduced in Δ 29.1024b17–26, the things denoted by "true thing" are either composite or simple. In the former case, two real things are combined in the real world; in the latter case, a simple thing exists. The things denoted by "false thing" are either composite or simple. In the former case, two real things are divided in the real world; in the latter case, the simple thing doesn't exist at all ("false thing" in such cases signifies nothing real).

There are two interpretations current in the literature concerning the false objects in Δ 29.1024b17–24 and in Θ 10.1051b33–1052a1, a traditional interpretation that goes back at least far as Alexander and a recent interpretation proposed by Crivelli. I will argue that neither interpretation provides the basis for a plausible reading of the examples in Δ 7.1017b33–35.

In both Δ 29.1024b17–24 and in Θ 10.1051b33–1052a1, with respect to the things denoted by the uses of "false thing" and "true thing," Aristotle uses the terms "συγκεῖσθαι" and "συντεθῆναι." Both of these terms may be translated by "combined." The terms denote the real predicative relation of combination between a real subject and an attribute. Aristotle is using "συγκεῖσθαι" and "συντεθῆναι" in Δ 29.1024b17–24 and in Θ 10.1051b33–1052a1 in contrast to his use of "διηρῆσθαι" and "μὴ συγκεῖσθαι," which denote the real predicative relation of division between a real subject and an attribute. These contrasting uses of "συγκεῖσθαι" and "διηρῆσθαι" are evident in Aristotle discussion of true and false assertions about composite things in Θ 10.1051a34–b13:

> Ἐπεὶ δὲ τὸ ὂν λέγεται καὶ τὸ μὴ ὂν τὸ μὲν κατὰ σχήματα τῶν κατηγοριῶν, τὸ δὲ κατὰ δύναμιν ἢ ἐνέργειαν τούτων ἢ τἀναντία, τὸ δὲ [κυριώτατα ὄν] ἀληθὲς ἢ ψεῦδος, τοῦτο δ' ἐπὶ τῶν πραγμάτων ἐστὶ τῷ συγκεῖσθαι ἢ διῃρῆσθαι, ὥστε ἀληθεύει μὲν ὁ τὸ διῃρημένον οἰόμενος διῃρῆσθαι καὶ τὸ συγκείμενον συγκεῖσθαι, ἔψευσται δὲ ὁ ἐναντίως ἔχων ἢ τὰ πράγματα ... εἰ δὴ τὰ μὲν ἀεὶ σύγκειται καὶ ἀδύνατα διαιρεθῆναι, τὰ δ' ἀεὶ διῄρηται καὶ ἀδύνατα συντεθῆναι, τὰ δ' ἐνδέχεται τἀναντία, τὸ μὲν εἶναί ἐστι τὸ συγκεῖσθαι καὶ ἓν εἶναι, τὸ δὲ μὴ εἶναι τὸ μὴ συγκεῖσθαι ἀλλὰ πλείω εἶναι.

The terms "being" and "non-being" are employed firstly with reference to the categories, and secondly with reference to the potentiality or actuality of these or their opposites, while being and non-being in the strictest sense are truth and falsity. The condition of this in the objects is their being combined or divided, so that he who thinks the divided to be divided and the combined to be combined has the truth, while he whose thought is in a state contrary to that of the objects is in error. . . . If, then, some things are always combined and cannot be divided, and others are always divided and cannot be combined, while others are capable either of combination or of division, being is being combined and one, and not being is being not combined but more than one. . . . (trans., mine, following Ross)

Here Aristotle explains the truth conditions for assertions about real objects that are either combined or divided: If we assert of two objects that they are combined, and they are combined, then our assertion is true; if we assert of two objects that they are divided, and they are divided, then our assertion is true; if we assert of two objects that they are combined, and they are divided, then our assertion is false; if we assert of two objects that they are divided, and they are combined, then our assertion is false.[21] We saw above in *Categories* 10.12b5–16 that Aristotle acknowledges two basic real predicative relations each of which is analogous to the two basic assertions, affirmation and denial. The need for Aristotle to posit both real predicative relations cannot be overstated as they serve as the basis for his theory of contradictory opposition (a theory with logical, conceptual, and metaphysical dimensions). A clear statement of Aristotle's position is found in *De Interpretatione* 7, at 17a23–34:

Ἔστι δ' ἡ μὲν ἁπλῆ ἀπόφανσις φωνὴ σημαντικὴ περὶ τοῦ εἰ ὑπάρχει τι ἢ μὴ ὑπάρχει, ὡς οἱ χρόνοι διῄρηνται· κατάφασις δέ ἐστιν ἀπόφανσις τινὸς κατὰ τινός, ἀπόφασις δέ ἐστιν ἀπόφανσις τινὸς ἀπὸ τινός. ἐπεὶ δὲ ἔστι καὶ τὸ ὑπάρχον ἀποφαίνεσθαι ὡς μὴ ὑπάρχον καὶ τὸ μὴ ὑπάρχον ὡς ὑπάρχον καὶ τὸ ὑπάρχον ὡς ὑπάρχον καὶ τὸ μὴ ὑπάρχον ὡς μὴ ὑπάρχον, καὶ περὶ τοὺς ἐκτὸς δὲ τοῦ νῦν χρόνους ὡσαύτως, ἅπαν ἂν ἐνδέχοιτο καὶ ὃ κατέφησέ τις ἀποφῆσαι καὶ ὃ ἀπέφησε καταφῆσαι· ὥστε δῆλον ὅτι πάσῃ καταφάσει ἐστὶν ἀπόφασις ἀντικειμένη καὶ πάσῃ ἀποφάσει κατάφασις. καὶ ἔστω ἀντίφασις τοῦτο, κατάφασις καὶ ἀπόφασις αἱ ἀντικείμεναι.

The simple assertion is a significant spoken sound about whether something does or does not belong (in one of the divisions of time). An affirmation is an assertion affirming something of something, a negation is an assertion denying something of something. Now it is possible to state of what does belong that it does not belong, of what does not belong that it does belong, of what does belong that it does belong, and of what does not belong that it does not belong. Similarly for times outside the present. So it must be possible to deny whatever anyone has affirmed, and to affirm whatever anyone has denied. Thus it is clear that for every affirmation there is an opposite negation, and for every negation an opposite affirmation. Let us call an affirmation and a negation which are opposite a contradiction. (trans., mine, following Ackrill)

In this passage, real predicative combination is expressed in terms of belonging, and real predicative division is expressed in terms of not belonging. Compare these claims with the nominal definitions of "truth" and "falsehood" at *Metaphysics* Γ 7.1011b25–27:

δῆλον δὲ πρῶτον μὲν ὁρισαμένοις τί τὸ ἀληθὲς καὶ ψεῦδος. τὸ μὲν γὰρ λέγειν τὸ ὂν μὴ εἶναι ἢ τὸ μὴ ὂν εἶναι ψεῦδος, τὸ δὲ τὸ ὂν εἶναι καὶ τὸ μὴ ὂν μὴ εἶναι ἀληθές . . .

This is clear, in the first place, if we define what the true and the false are. To assert of what is that it is not, or of what is not that it is, is false, while to assert of what is that it is, and of what is not that it is not, is true. . . . (trans., mine, following Ross)

Given the nominal definitions at 1011b26–27, it is reasonable to think Aristotle is describing in *De Interpretatione* 7.17a23–34 the logical possibilities of true and false assertion in terms of predicative combination and division along the following lines: it is possible to assert of what is combined that it is divided, and of what is divided that it is combined, and to do so would be to assert what is false; and it is possible to assert of what is combined that it is combined, and of what is divided that it is divided, and to do so would be to assert what is true. These logical possibilities track Aristotle's basic assertions (affirmations and denials) in relation to his basic real predicative relations (combination and division).

Returning now to *Met.* Δ 29.1024b17–24, Aristotle offers τὸ σὲ καθῆσθαι (you sitting down) as an example of something that is not combined in the real world but could be. We may assume, for the sake of the example in Δ 29.1024b17–24, that you are a real subject, that sitting down is a real position, that you could sit down, but that you are not in fact sitting down. In the language of *De Interpretatione* 7.17a23–34, it is possible for the real sitting position to belong to you, but in fact (in the example) the sitting position does not belong to you at the time in question. The predicative combination sitting-belongs-to-you does not exist.

The example offered in Δ 29.1024b17–24 is similar to the examples Aristotle offered in *Categories* 10.12b5–16 of τὸ καθῆσθαι—μὴ καθῆσθαι (his sitting and his not sitting). In *Categories* 10.12b5–16 we have two possible real relations between the real man and the attribute of sitting: either sitting belongs to him or sitting does not belong to him. The latter case is an example of a false thing, as the use of "false thing" is explained in Δ 29.1024b17–24. The former case is an example of a true thing, according to the implicit use of "true thing" in Δ 29.1024b17–24.

It is crucial to recognize that the first use of "false thing" in Δ 29.1024b17–24 must be interpreted as denoting cases of nonexistent real predicative combinations between a real subject and a real attribute. Such real predicative combinations, were they to exist, would involve the real attribute belonging to the real subject. For an example of a real thing that *cannot* be combined, in Δ 29.1024b17–24 Aristotle offers τὸ τὴν διάμετρον εἶναι σύμμετρον (the diagonal being commensurable with its side). We may assume that, in the example, the diagonal is a real subject and that being commensurable with a side is a real predicate. In this case, using the language of *De Interpretatione* 7.17a23–34, it is impossible for the predicate being-commensurable-with-one-of-the-sides-of-a-triangle to hold of the diagonal of that triangle; the two cannot be predicatively combined in this way. The predicative combination being-commensurable-holds-of-the diagonal does not obtain. In both examples offered in Δ 29.1024b17–24, what is at issue is whether or not some real subject is predicatively combined with some real predicate.

With regard to true things, in the case that would be analogous to case (a) above, some real subjects need not be, but are, combined with certain real predicates. For example, the White House need not be in Washington, DC, but currently it is. The White House is a real subject; Washington, DC, is a real place; and although the White House could be near the Tuileries in Paris, being in Washington, DC, currently holds of the White House. Still other real subjects must be combined with certain real predicates. For example, a horse must be an animal. Being an animal holds necessarily of being a horse. Thus, Aristotle's first concept of a false thing subsumes pairs of real subjects and predicates that are not predicatively combined (whether contingently or necessarily): they are separated predicatively. The correlated concept of a true thing subsumes those pairs of real subjects and predicates that are predicatively combined (whether contingently or necessarily).[22] This is how interpreters have understood Aristotle's use of "false thing" Δ 7.1017a33–35, and they are correct.

Now, on the traditional interpretation, Aristotle uses "false thing" to denote either (1) a possible predicative combination of real things that are in fact separated predicatively or (2) an impossible predicative combination of real things. In (1) and (2), "false" is logically equivalent to "in fact not predicatively combined." The correlated use of "true thing" denotes either (1) a possible predicative combination of real things that are in fact so combined, or (2) a necessary predicative combination of real things. Here, in (1) and (2), "true" is logically equivalent to "is in fact predicatively combined."[23] This analysis yields the following provisional conceptions of true and false objects:

> TrF: For all x and y, the predicative combination of x and y is a false object if, and only if, it is not the case that x is predicatively combined with y.
>
> TrT: For all x and y, the predicative combination of x and y is a true object if, and only if, x is predicatively combined with y.[24]

If one reads the examples in Δ 7.1017a33–35 in the light of TrF and TrT, Aristotle is introducing a sense of "being$_T$" that denotes the kind of real object involving predicative combination and a sense of 'non-being$_F$' that denotes the kind of real object involving predicative division.

The traditional interpretation can make ready sense of the idea that there are false objects. Aristotle acknowledges real relations of predicative combination and division, relations he often denotes using his technical notions of predicative belonging and not-belonging. All real things are either actually combined or actually divided, from a predicative point of view. On the traditional interpretation of Δ 29.1024b17–26, a real false thing involves a real subject and a real predicate that are predicatively divided—the real predicate does not belong to the real subject—and that circumstance explains why we might say of the putative contradictory opposite circumstance that it is a false object: it is a possible object that does not in fact exist. Similarly, a real true thing involves a real subject that is predicatively combined with a real predicate—the real predicate belongs to the subject—and that circumstance explains why we might say that the object in question is true: it is a possible object that in fact exists.

Crivelli has recently proposed an alternative reading of the false objects introduced in Δ 29.1024b17–26. According to Crivelli (2004), Aristotle adopts the Fregean strategy "of explaining the truth and falsehood of certain mental states and certain sentences by appealing to the truth and falsehood of propositions (abstract entities whose nature is neither mental nor linguistic)" (2004, 7). Crivelli claims that 1024b17–26 "is the most unequivocal testimony of Aristotle's commitment to states of affairs as bearers of truth and falsehood" (2004, 46). States of affairs are defined by Crivelli as "objects of a 'propositional' nature of which it is sensible to say both that they obtain and that they do not obtain at a time" (2004, 4n4). He claims that "a state of affairs, as it is conceived by Aristotle, is best understood as being an object corresponding to a complete present-tense affirmative predicative assertion, and as being "composed of" the real beings signified by the assertion's predicate and subject." (5) According to Crivelli (2015), states of affairs are mind-dependent composite objects that are either true or false,[25] and Aristotle posits only "affirmative" states of affairs, rejecting "negative" states of affairs (2004, 5 and 2015, 200–02). All states of affairs are "composed" by means of acts of judgment out of a real subject and a real predicate. However, and importantly, the mode of composition constitutive of a state of affairs differs from the various modes of metaphysical composition familiar from Aristotle's treatises: the said-of relation, the inherence relation, the kath auto or the kata sumbebekos relations, the relations of belonging to and not belonging to, and the relations of real predicative combination and division we have been discussing above. None of these familiar Aristotelian modes of metaphysical composition is the same as Crivelli's proposed mode of composition that constitutes a state of affairs. A state of affairs is "composed" of a real subject and a real attribute and is true or false, on Crivelli's view, in virtue of whether or not the real subject and the real attribute out of which they are composed are actually metaphysically predicatively combined or divided.[26]

Following Crivelli, for the sake of the current argument, we will assume that a state of affairs has a "propositional nature" in the sense that it has a structure that "corresponds" to the structure of a complete present-tense affirmative linguistic assertion. For example, assuming that a complete present-tense affirmative linguistic assertion has the logical form "n is m" (where "n" is a linguistic subject expression, "m" is a linguistic predicate expression, and "is" signifies predicative combination) the corresponding state of affairs would have the metaphysical form x + y (where "x" is the object signified by "n," "y" is the object signified by "m," and "+" is the metaphysical relation of composition signified by "is" and essential to Crivelli's states of affairs). Every such state of affairs has the same basic structure $x + y$. This will suffice as a sketch of Crivelli's states of affairs. On Crivelli's view:

CrF: For all x and y, the state of affairs $x+ y$ is a false object if, and only if, it is not the case that x is predicatively combined with y.

CrT: For all x and y, the state of affairs of $x + y$ is a true object if, and only if, x is predicatively combined with y.

Crivelli's view can also make sense of real false objects and real true objects. The relevant objects, on Crivelli's accounts, are the affirmative states of affairs "composed" (in Crivelli's sense, see above) of real subjects and real predicates. These composite objects are real in the sense that they do not depend for their existence on minds or languages, and they are true or false in virtue of the actual real predicative combinations and separations that in fact exist.

We can assess now whether or not the examples in Δ 7.1017a33–35 make sense given the two competing objectual interpretations. According to the traditional interpretation of false objects in Δ 29, Aristotle's examples in Δ 7.1017a33–35 are to be understood as follows:

[a_{tr}] "ὅτι ἔστι Σωκράτης μουσικός, ὅτι ἀληθές" = "that the predicative combination of Socrates and being cultured *is*, that (i.e., the predicative combination of Socrates and being cultured) is a true object."

[b_{tr}] "ὅτι ἔστι Σωκράτης οὐ λευκός, ὅτι ἀληθές" = "that the predicative separation of Socrates and being pale *is*, that (i.e., the predicative separation of Socrates and being pale) is a true object."

[c_{tr}] "τό δ'οὐκ ἔστιν ἡ διάμετρος σύμμετρος, ὅτι ψεῦδος" = "that the predicative combination of the diagonal and being commensurable with one of its sides *is not*, that (i.e., the predicative combination of the diagonal and being commensurable with one of its sides) is a false object."

[d_tr] "τό δ'οὐκ ἔστιν ἡ διάμετρος οὐ ἀσύμμετρος, ὅτι ψεῦδος" = "that the predicative separation of the diagonal and being incommensurable with one of its sides *is not*, that (i.e., the predicative separation of the diagonal and being incommensurable with one of its sides) is a false object."

Adopting Crivelli's understanding of false objects in Δ 29, Aristotle's examples at 1017a33–35 would be understood as follows:

[a_c] "ὅτι ἔστι Σωκράτης μουσικός, ὅτι ἀληθὲς" = "that the state of affairs Socrates + cultured *is*, that state of affairs is a true object."

[b_c] "ὅτι ἔστι Σωκράτης οὐ λευκός, ὅτι ἀληθὲς" = "that the state of affairs Socrates + non-pale *is*, that state of affairs is a true object."

[c_c] "τό δ'οὐκ ἔστιν ἡ διάμετρος σύμμετρος, ὅτι ψεῦδος" = that the state of affairs diagonal + commensurable *is not*, that state of affairs is a false object."

[d_c] "τό δ'οὐκ ἔστιν ἡ διάμετρος οὐ ἀσύμμετρος, ὅτι ψεῦδος" = "that the state of affairs diagonal + non-incommensurable with one of its sides *is not*, that (i.e., the predicative separation of the diagonal and being incommensurable with one of its sides) is a false object."

Before addressing particular concerns about the examples, let me address two general concerns. The first has to do with the supposition of a fourth example ([d_tr] and [d_c]), which is based on a suggested interpolation by Ross (1924, 308–09) and which is intended to serve as an example of a false thing analogous to the case of a false denial. The second has to do with how we take "οὐ" in the [b_tr], [b_c], [d_tr], and [d_c], for in each case "οὐ" may operate on the copula (generating a negative assertion) or it may operate on the predicate adjective (generating what Aristotle calls "an indefinite name").

Why suppose a fourth example ([d_tr] and [d_c]) that serves as an example of a false object analogous to the case of a false denial? After all, none of the surviving manuscripts provide this case. The first argument for supplying a fourth example depends on parity of reasoning and Aristotle's claim at *Met.* Δ 7.1017a32–33 that "being$_T$" signifies that something is true and "non-being$_F$" signifies that something is false, *alike with respect to affirmation and denial*. Aristotle's point seems to be that "being$_T$" and "non-being$_F$" apply either to affirmations and denials (on an assertoric reading) or to the real analogues of affirmations and denials (on the objectual readings). He then gives two examples of the use of "being$_T$," one of which applies to the affirmation or its analogue, the other to the denial or its analogue, and he gives one example of the use of "non-being$_F$." By parity of reasoning, we expect an example of "non-being$_F$" applied to the denial or its analogue. Thus, on both objectual readings, case [a] provides an example of a true object analogous to a true affirmation. Case [b] provides an example of a true object analogous to a true denial. Case [c] in turn provides an example of a false object analogous to a false affirmation. By parity of reasoning, we should expect an example of a false object analogous to a false denial.

There is a second and more compelling argument for supposing a fourth example ([d$_{tr}$] and [d$_c$]), one of a false object analogous to the case of a false denial. If it turns out that the objectual readings cannot makes sense of false objects analogous to false denials, then this is a prima facie objection to the objectual readings. For, there is no doubting that Aristotle acknowledges false denials, and *Met.* Δ 7.1017a32–33 strongly supports the view that "non-being$_F$" applies to the case of a denial. It seems reasonable, therefore, to consider whether or not the objectual interpretations can make sense of false objects analogous to false denials. Hence, [d$_{tr}$] and [d$_c$].

Turning now to the Aristotle's use of "οὐ" in [b$_{tr}$], [b$_c$], [d$_{tr}$], and [d$_c$], we noted above that in each case "οὐ" may operate on the copula (generating a negative assertion) or it may operate on the predicate adjective (generating what Aristotle calls "an indefinite name"). Greek grammar allows for either decision. Aristotle, however, specifies at 1017a32–33 that the uses of "being$_T$" and "non-being$_F$" apply to affirmations and denials (or their objectual analogues). The examples that follow this specification at 101733–35 are therefore most naturally understood as examples of affirmations and denials (or their objectual analogues).[27] As a consequence, unless there are overriding reasons to the contrary, we should interpret Aristotle's use of "οὐ" in [b$_{tr}$], [b$_c$], [d$_{tr}$], and [d$_c$] as operating on the copula and not on the predicate adjective. Prima facie, then, [b$_{tr}$], [b$_c$], [d$_{tr}$], and [d$_c$] should be taken as examples of denials (or their objectual analogues).

We can now address the individual cases, to see how the objectual readings fare. With regard to case [a_{tr}], on the traditional reading, one may easily suppose that Socrates is predicatively combined with being-cultured, and hence that the two constitute a true object. Moreover, case [a_{tr}] is an objectual example that can be described in terms analogous to those used by Aristotle to describe the corresponding true affirmation: Being-cultured is predicated of Socrates in the case of the true thing, and analogously "being cultured" is predicated of "Socrates" in the case of the true affirmation. On Crivelli's reading, too, case [a_c] is unproblematic. One may suppose that the state of affairs composed of Socrates and being-cultured obtains, and that it is a true thing, presumably because Socrates is in fact cultured.

Case [b_{tr}] is damaging to the traditional reading. This is because, according to *Met.* Δ 29.1024b17–26, Θ 10.1051b33–1052a1, and TrF (for all x and y, the predicative combination of x and y is a false object if, and only if, it is not the case that x is predicatively combined with y), the real predicative division between the real subject Socrates and the real attribute being-pale constitutes a false object. However, on the objectual reading of Δ 7.1017a33–35, at 1017a34 Aristotle is explicitly giving an example of a true object. The traditional reading gets the example wrong. A proponent of the traditional reading might reply that the example should be understood in terms of the predicative combination constituted by being non-pale belonging to Socrates, taking "οὐ" to operate on the predicate adjective "λευκός." This predicative combination would at least appear to conform to the concept of a true object according to Δ 29.1024b17–25, Θ 10.1051b33–1052a1, and TrT (for all x and y, the predicative combination of x and y is a true object if, and only if, x is predicatively combined with y). It generates an objectual example that can be characterized in terms used by Aristotle to describe an affirmation: the real attribute being-non-pale is combined in the real world with the real subject Socrates in the case of the true thing, and "being non-pale" is syntactically combined with "Socrates" in the case of the linguistic affirmation. Note, however, that if we adopt this tactic, then on the traditional reading we cannot understand the pair [a_{tr}] and [b_{tr}] as offering examples of a true affirmation and a true denial, which is what one expects given Δ 7.1017b33–35. One expects that "is" will signify the same as "is true" in the cases analogous to an affirmation and a denial. Instead, on the proposed reading, both [a] and [b] offer examples of true things analogous to two affirmations. Moreover, adopting this tactic seems ad hoc, interpreting the use of "οὐ" in a manner that is grammatically possible but contextually forced. The traditional objectual reading flouts our reasonable expectations and undermines the natural sense of the passage.

Case [b_c] also poses a difficulty for Crivelli's view. As with the traditional objectual reading, the straightforward interpretation of the example—that the real attribute being pale is divided in the real world from the real subject Socrates—yields a false object according to Δ 29.1024b17–25, Θ 10.1051b33–1052a1, and CrF (for all x and y, the state of affairs $x + y$ is a false object if, and only if, it is not the case that x is predicatively combined with y). Again, given the sense of the passage, we expect an example of a true object. Indeed Crivelli, even more so than the proponents of the traditional objectual reading, must understand case [b_c] as involving a use of "οὐ" that operates on the indefinite predicative adjective "pale." For Crivelli only allows for affirmative states of affairs. Now, if Crivelli's affirmative states of affairs cannot be constituted out of what is signified by indefinite names, insofar as such names are themselves quasi-negative in nature, then case [b_c] would count firmly against his reading. If, however, Crivelli's affirmative states of affairs can be composed of the beings signified by such quasi-negative predicates (in the example, what would be signified by "being-non-pale"), then we may suppose that the state of affairs composed of Socrates and being-non-pale is affirmative and exists and that it is a true thing, presuming that Socrates is in fact non-pale. Case [b_c] might thus serve as an example of a true object on Crivelli's reading, but with these costs. Even so, it is clear that case [b_c] cannot be interpreted as an object analogous to a denial, for that would entail that the object be a negative state of affairs. This is itself a considerable cost, both because we expect the use of "οὐ" in the example to operate on the copula and because we expect that the example serve as a case analogous to a denial and not an affirmation involving an indefinite name.

Cases [c_c] and [c_{tr}] are examples of false objects analogous to a false affirmation. Both are straightforward on the objectual readings. On Crivelli's view, the affirmative state of affairs—the diagonal being commensurable—never obtains. The real diagonal and the real attribute of being-commensurable are always predicatively divided in the real world. The Crivellian state of affairs constituted out of the real diagonal and the real attribute of being commensurable is, therefore, always a false object. Similarly, on the traditional objectual reading the real diagonal of the square and the real attribute of being-commensurable cannot be predicatively combined, and thus their predicative combination is necessarily a false object.

Cases [d_tr] and [d_c] should provide examples of false objects analogous to false denials. The logical pattern for such an example is: τό δ'οὐκ ἔστιν S οὐ A, ὅτι ψεῦδος. We expect, therefore, examples of false objects involving a real attribute that is not predicatively combined with a real subject. The putative object in the example will be false because, in fact, the real attribute in question is predicatively combined with the real subject in question. The putative predicative division does not exist and is, therefore, false. In such an example, the false object would involve a real attribute that is predicatively combined with a real subject. According to Δ 29.1024b17–26, Θ 10.1051b33–1052a1, TrF, and CrF, however, the objects denoted by "false thing" essentially involve a real attribute that is not predicatively combined in the real world with a real subject. A false object cannot involve a real attribute that is predicatively combined in the real world with a real subject. Prima facie, both objectual readings fail to explain how there can be false objects analogous to false denials.

As with cases [b_tr] and [b_c], proponents of the objectual reading can argue that the examples [d_tr] and [d_c] are not intended as examples analogous to false denials and, rather, involve uses of "οὐ" that operate on the predicative adjectives as opposed to the copulas. This would entail that Aristotle offers no examples of uses of "being_T" or "being_F" in Δ 7.1017a33–35 that apply to a case of a denial (or its objectual analogue). All of the examples at 1017a33–35 must be interpreted as objectual analogues of affirmations. This is an untoward consequence, for reasons given above. Nevertheless, interpreting "οὐ" in the examples in this way, on Crivelli's reading [d_c] would involve the affirmative state of affairs constituted of the diagonal of a triangle and the attribute of being non-incommensurable. That state of affairs would be false, and necessarily so, because every diagonal is predicatively combined with being incommensurable with its sides. This seems to make sense on Crivelli's view if, again, his affirmative states of affairs may involve what is signified by indefinite names. Matters are much worse for the traditional objectual reading, for even if we interpret the example in [d_tr] as an objectual analogue of an affirmation, the traditional objectual reading gets the example wrong. On the traditional reading, the example would be interpreted as a false object involving a real diagonal of a triangle being predicatively combined with the real attribute of being non-incommensurable. But, given Δ 29.1024b17–26, Θ 10.1051b33–1052a1, and TrF, no false object can involve a real attribute being combined with a real subject—those sorts of composite objects are true objects.

Perhaps these objections to the objectual readings of Δ 7.1017a33–35 can be overcome, but the task is daunting. Suppose, then, that the most likely candidates for the objectual readings—the objectual notions of truth and falsehood introduced by Aristotle in Δ 29.1024b17–25 and Θ 10.1051b33–1052a1—are not what Aristotle had in mind at 1017b33–35. The objectual notions of truth and falsehood introduced in 1024b17–25 and 1051b33–1052a1 are the *only* concepts of objectual truth and falsehood explicitly introduced by Aristotle. What other objectual concepts of truth and falsehood might be proposed by the defender of the objectual reading?

Recalling the passages *Prior Analytics* I 36. 48b1–3 and I 37.49a6–10 discussed above, one might suggest that in 48b1–3 and 49a6–10 Aristotle establishes that "is true" and "is false" are used in as many ways as "is" and "is not," thereby positing as many objectual uses of "true" and "false" as there are objectual uses of "is" and "is not." Suppose one adopts this approach. It follows that in *Met.* Δ 7.1017a33–35, he is noting that "being" and "not being" are logically equivalent to "truth" and "falsehood" when these are used in the various ways that "being" and "not being" are used. The rest of Δ 7, presumably specifies these various uses of "being" and "not being." He would be explaining uses of "being$_T$" and "non-being$_F$" in terms of the other uses of "being" and "not being" introduced in Δ 7. This would surely be an unnecessarily indirect and obscure approach for him to take in explaining the uses of "being$_T$" and "non-being$_F$." But the telling objections to this suggestion are (1) that the uses of "is true" and "is false" in *Prior Analytics* I 36. 48b1–3 and *APr.* I 37.49a6–10 are correlated only with uses of "is" and "is not" denoting members of the categories and (2) that it cannot make sense of Aristotle's usage of "being$_T$" and "non-being$_F$" in *Met.* Δ 7.1017a33–35 in terms of affirmations and denials, nor can it make sense of the examples he gives there.

Matthen's Proposal

Consider now a proposal by Matthen according to which, at *Met.* Δ 7.1017a31–35, Aristotle *explains* the truth and falsehood of statements and beliefs by means of a use of the verb "to be." According to Matthen, Aristotle is proposing the following explanatory schema:

The statement or belief *p* is true (false) just in case, and because, the predicative complex signified by *p* is (is not).

On Matthen's account, the right-hand side of the schema is not only materially equivalent, but also explains why the left-hand side obtains. In support of his interpretation, Matthen introduces a monadic use of "is" and argues that it is possible to explain the truth conditions of statements involving dyadic (copular) uses of "is" in terms of this monadic use. Thus, for example, statement or belief "Socrates is sitting" is true (false) just in case "Sitting Socrates is" is true (false). The "is" in "Socrates is sitting" is copular; the "is" in "Sitting Socrates is" is monadic. Matthen also claims that Aristotle explains the truth conditions of assertions in terms of the simples and predicative complexes signified by the subject expressions in statements involving the monadic use of "is." For example, the truth value of the statement "Dog is" is a function of whether or not the simple signified by "Dog"—presumably the essence of doghood—is or is not, whereas the truth value of the statement "Sitting Fido is" depends upon whether or not the predicative complex signified by "Sitting Fido" is or is not.

There is solid textual evidence beyond Δ 7, for attributing this view—or something very much like it—to Aristotle. At *Categories* 12, 14b14–23, he makes claims that seem to entail the material equivalence of a use of the verb "to be" and the semantic predicate "is true" as applied to assertions and that also entail the explanatory relation between being and truth proposed by Matthen. Crucial here is Aristotle's explicit claim that man is [ἔστιν ἄνθρωπος] just in case the assertion "man is" is true [ἀληθὴς ὁ λόγος ᾧ λέγομεν ὅτι ἔστιν ἄνθρωπος]. In *Cat.* 12, the larger context in which the passage is found, he discusses different kinds of priority. In the passage he is considering the case of things that "reciprocate as to implication of existence" (Ackrill's phrasing) and claims that "that which is in some way the cause of the other's existence might reasonably be called prior by nature." He then seems to make the following argument: If there is a man, then the statement whereby we say that there is a man is true. If the statement whereby we say that there is a man is true, then there is a man. Hence, there is a man if and only if the statement whereby we say that there is a man is true. It is because the actual thing exists or does not that the statement is called true or false. Hence, a true statement is in no way the cause of the actual thing's [τὸ πρᾶγμα] existence, but an actual thing is in some way the cause of a statement's being true. Moreover, at *Metaphysics* Γ 5.1009a6–15, Aristotle clearly presupposes that "is" is materially equivalent with "is true" and "is not" with "is false."[28] There is, thus, strong evidence for thinking that he is committed to Matthen's explanatory schema.

However, *Met.* Δ 7.1017a31–35 is not an expression of this commitment. First, there is Matthen's claim about the relationship between the monadic and dyadic first-order uses of "is" and "is not." Again, even if one is sympathetic to Matthen's proposal, the relationship between these alternative first-order uses of "is" and "'is not" has no bearing on the proposed equivalence at 1017a31–35 between a first-order use of "being$_T$," and "not being$_F$," and a second-order use of "truth" and "falsehood." The preceding arguments against the objectual interpretation show that Aristotle is not concerned with a first-order objectual use of "truth" or "falsehood."

Moreover, Aristotle clearly *isn't* identifying a dyadic use of "truth" in the passage. Nor is he arguing that a dyadic use of "is" may be explained in terms of a monadic use of "is." And Matthen clearly recognizes that he is working with a second-order use of "is true" and "is false" that applies to assertions. That is to say, then, on Matthen's own account, at *Met.* Δ 7.1017a31–35, Aristotle identifies a first-order use of "is$_T$," that is equivalent with a second-order semantic use of "is true." It follows that he is not expressing the aspect of Matthen's account related to the different first-order uses of "is" and "is not."

The central question is whether Aristotle is proposing an explanatory schema according to which the truth-values of assertions of the form "*p* is true" are explained by the predicative complexes signified by *p*. While he may embrace this view, it is difficult to think that this is his point at 1017a31–35. When, at 1017a31–32, he claims that there is a use of "is" and "is not" that signifies that something is true or false, he seems to be saying that there is a use of "is" such that when someone predicates "is" of some subject he is saying that *that thing* is true. So, on the proposed use of "is," if someone were to assert "*p* is," one would be asserting "*p* is true," and similarly with "is not" and "false." On Matthen's reading, on the other hand, Aristotle is claiming that when someone asserts "Socrates sitting is" he signifies a predicative complex—sitting Socrates. If that predicative complex obtains, then the assertion "Socrates sitting is" is true, and the truth of *that* assertion explains the truth of *another* assertion, namely the assertion " 'Socrates is sitting' is true."

More generally, on Matthen's interpretation, at 1017a31–32 Aristotle is not claiming that there is a use of "is" that signifies that something is true. Rather, he is asserting that there is a use of "is" that signifies something (a predicative complex) which, if it obtains, explains why something else is true (the first-order assertion about the predicative complex), which in turn explains why yet another thing is true (the second-order assertion about the first-order assertion about the predicative complex). This is a tortuous line given the text. In addition, it is implausible that at 1017a31–35

Aristotle is arguing for a specific ontology of predicative complexes, and there seems to be no reason for him to presuppose a particular explanation of predicative complexes. Any account of real predicative combinations will serve his purpose in the passage.[29]

Being a True Assertion

Having rejected the objectual reading and Matthen's recent and novel interpretation of *Met.* Δ 7.1017a31–35, consider now the interpretation according to which Aristotle identifies in this passage a use of "being$_T$" that is logically equivalent to the nominal definition of "truth" presented at Γ 7.1011b26–27.[30] It is not far-fetched that, in Δ 7, Aristotle is working with the conceptions of truth and falsehood defined at 1011b26–27. It is worth repeating some salient facts about these common concepts. First, contemporary commentators generally accept that by means of them Aristotle is explicitly defining truth and falsehood. Second, the definitions have a Platonic pedigree, and Plato's use of these concepts in the *Cratylus* and the *Sophist* presupposes that they are generally accepted and applicable. Hence, apparently, the ordinary ancient Greek philosopher would recognize Aristotle's proposed nominal definitions of truth and falsehood. Third, since he explicitly defines these concepts in *Met.* book Γ, it is reasonable to think that he might have them in mind in *Met.* book Δ.[31]

If, in *Met.* Δ 7, Aristotle is concerned with the semantic concepts of truth and falsehood in *Met.* Γ 7, then he is identifying a use of "to be" and "not to be" that signifies a kind of mental and linguistic assertion. If one asserts that species evolve and, in fact, species evolve, then one has an instance of truth—one asserts of species evolving that species evolving is; one has asserted of what it is that it is. If species don't evolve, and one asserts that species evolve, then one has an instance of falsehood—one asserts of species not evolving that species evolving is. A virtue of this interpretation is that it immediately makes sense of the apposition, in the second clause at 1017a31–32, of "not truth" [οὐκ ἀληθές] and "falsehood" [ψεῦδος].

Assuming, then, that Aristotle has in mind the nominal definitions of truth and falsehood offered in Γ 7, how are we to understand the veridical use of "being" in Δ 7? How does one interpret the use of "that which is" and "that which is not" at 1017a33–35? There are various possibilities. The following paraphrase of the passage is defended here:

> Again "to be$_T$" and "that which is$_T$" signify that some simple assertion is true, and "not to be$_F$" that some simple assertion is not true but false, equally in the case of affirmation and of denial; for examples, that Socrates is cultured *is$_T$*, in the sense that this affirmation is true; or that Socrates is not pale *is$_T$*, in the sense that this denial is true; or that the diagonal is commensurable *is not$_F$*, in the sense that this affirmation is false.

First, on this reading, the clause "equally in the case of affirmation and of denial" defines the subject of the verb "to be$_T$" when it is used to signify that something is true. There is a use of "to be$_T$" that signifies of an assertion, equally in the case of affirmation and denial, that it is true. Similarly, there is a use of "not to be$_F$," equally in the case of affirmation and denial, that signifies of an assertion that it is false. That is to say, the verb signifies that some affirmation or denial is true or false.

So, second, if one assumes that Aristotle is working with the nominal definitions from *Met.* Γ 7, then to say that an affirmation or denial is true or false is to predicate "is true" or "is false" of some assertion, which generates a higher-order assertion the truth of which is a function of whether or not the embedded assertion says of what is that it is, et cetera. In the cases under consideration in Γ 7 and Δ 7, these are in every instance simple assertions.[32] The logical form of such uses will be [(A + B) is] or [(A − B) is not], et cetera, which are to be understood as logically equivalent to assertions of the form [(A + B) is true] or [(A − B) is false], et cetera. Thus, the import of the first sentence: there is a use of "to be$_T$" or "being$_T$" that signifies that something (namely some assertion) is true and a use of "not to be$_F$" or "not being$_F$" that signifies not that some assertion is true but that it is false.[33]

Now turn to the examples in Δ 7. One should complete Aristotle's examples at 1017a33–35 as follows:[34]

a. The affirmation "Socrates is cultured" is true.

b. The denial "Socrates is not pale" is true.

c. The affirmation "The diagonal is commensurable" is false.

d. The denial "The diagonal is not incommensurable" is false.

With regard to the subordinate clauses "ὅτι ἀληθές" and "ὅτι ψεῦδος," these are used in apposition in order to clarify how "ἔστι" and "οὐκ ἔστι" are used in the preceding independent clauses. In light of the first claim that there is a sense of "is$_T$" that signifies that an assertion is true, this is the most natural way to read the examples. Thus, the subordinate clauses make explicit that "is$_T$" signifies the same as "is true" and "is not$_F$" signifies the same as "is false." So, one can construe the examples as follows, producing versions that remain distant from English:

a. "That it is$_T$ Socrates cultured, that this assertion is true."

b. "That it is$_T$ Socrates not pale, that this assertion is true."

c. "That it is not$_F$ the diagonal commensurable, that this assertion is false."

d. "That it is not$_F$ the diagonal non-commensurable, that this assertion is false."

One can interpret the Greek "ἔστι" in the independent clauses in at least two ways, corresponding to two standard ways of understanding the veridical sense of the verb "to be" in semantic terms.[35] On the interpretation of the passage defended here, first, one can assume that the use of "ἔστι" and "οὐκ ἔστι" is monadic and takes for its argument the phrases that follow, "Socrates cultured" and so on. This interpretation makes the best sense of the passage. According to the account in *De Interpretatione*, these phrases may be interpreted as affirmations and denials involving implicit copulas, understanding these in terms of the ἓν κατὰ ἑν (represented by $m + n$) and the ἓν ἀπὸ ἑν (represented by $m - n$) constructions. The subordinate clauses then refer to these affirmations and denials. Read this way, the examples run as follows:

a. "That 'Socrates + cultured' is$_{T'}$ that 'Socrates + cultured' is true."

b. "That 'Socrates – pale' is$_{T'}$ that 'Socrates – pale' is true."

c. "That 'the diagonal + commensurable' is not$_{F'}$ that 'the diagonal + commensurable' is false."

d. "That 'the diagonal-non-commensurable' is not$_{F'}$ that 'the diagonal-non-commensurable' is false."

Here, it is transparent how "is$_T$" means the same as "is true" equally in the case of affirmations and denials, and how "is not$_F$" means the same as "is false" equally in the case of affirmations and denials.

Second, the Greek also allows that one interpolate an implicit copula in the phrases "Cultured Socrates" [Σωκράτης μουσικός], "Not pale Socrates" [Σωκράτης οὐ λευκός], "the commensurable diagonal" [ἡ διάμετρος σύμμετρος], and "the incommensurable diagonal" [ἡ διάμετρος οὐ ἀσύμμετρος]. Reading the passage this way, the explicit uses of "is$_T$" and "is not$_F$" are equivalent to the use of "is true" and "is false." Thus, an assertion of the form "S is$_T$ P" (where the explicit "is" is used in the veridical sense) asserts "is true" of the affirmation "S [is] P" (where this second and copular use of "is" is implicit), and it means the same as "The affirmation 'S is P' is true." A denial of the form "S is$_T$ not P" (where the explicit "is" is used in the veridical sense) asserts "is true" of the denial "S [is] not P" (where, again, this second and copular use of "is" is implicit), and it means the same as "The negation 'S is not P' is true." With regard to the veridical sense of "is not$_F$," an assertion of the form "S is not P" (where "is not" is used in the veridical sense) asserts "is false" of the affirmation "S [is] P," and means the same as "The affirmation 'S is P' is false." An assertion of the form "S is not$_F$ not P" (where "is not" is used in the veridical sense) asserts "is false" of the denial "S [is] not P," and it means the same as "The denial 'S is not P' is false." Thus, the reading defended here makes ready sense of the examples on either the monadic or implicit copular readings of "is" and "is not."

The version of the semantic reading argued for here differs from the two leading recent interpretations, those defended by Ross and Mansion. Ross proposed the following interpretation of the examples in Δ 7:

a. "Socrates is cultured" = "'Socrates is cultured' is true."

b. "Socrates is not-pale" = "'Socrates is not-pale' is true."

c. "The diagonal is not commensurate" = "'The diagonal is commensurate' is false."

d. "The diagonal is not not-commensurate." = "'The diagonal is not-commensurate' is false."

While this proposal captures the veridical uses of "is$_T$" and "is not$_F$," it entails transforming the denial "S is not P" into an affirmation of the form "S is not-P" where "not-P" is an indefinite verb. However, Aristotle clearly differentiates denials of the form "S is not P" from affirmations involving indefinite verbs of the form "S is not-P." He rejects the claim that they are logically equivalent; that is to say, they have different truth conditions. Given Aristotle's claim at 1017a31–33 that "is$_T$" signifies that an assertion is true both in the case of an affirmation and in the case of a denial, one would expect that he would give examples involving both an affirmation and a denial. On the reading defended here, this is exactly what Aristotle provides. On the contrary, on Ross's interpretation of the passage, Aristotle gives two examples of true affirmations and two examples of false denials.

In a note, Halper (2009) addresses Ross's interpretation of the examples:

> Worried about how a sentence could be a *per se* instance of being when some sentences are accidental, Ross claims that Aristotle is referring to sentences about sentences, Ross, *Aristotle's* Metaphysics, 1:308–09. It is not clear how he thinks this solves the problem, it leaves first-order being sentences unaccounted for, and Ross's application to Aristotle's examples is confused.

First, Ross is not worried about how sentences involving the veridical sense of "being" might be instances of "a *per se* instance of being." Ross is interested in discovering a kind of sentence that differs from ordinary sentences in which either accidental or *per se* uses of "being" are expressed. Second, Ross's analysis does not leave first-order sentences unaccounted for. There just are no first-order sentences involving the veridical sense of "being." For Ross, every sentence involving the veridical sense of "being" is a second-order statement attributing a semantic attribute to a first-order statement.

Mansion (1976) seems to adopt the following view: "'To be$_T$' and 'is$_T$,' signify that an assertion is true, 'is not$_F$,' that it is not true but false, equally in the case of the affirmation and the denial." This use of the verb "to be$_T$," expresses a monadic predicate of assertions. As such, "is$_T$" would signify that an assertion is true equally in the case of the affirmation and the denial, and "is not$_F$" would signify that an assertion is false, equally in the case of an affirmation and a denial. It appears, however, this is not how Mansion understands the use of the verb, since she clearly takes the use of the verb to be copular. This is the thrust of her claim "C'est donc la copule elle-même qui a le sens de 'vrai' ou 'faux' puisque dans le cas d'un jugement négatif la copule affectée d'une negation *signifie* 'faux.'" Moreover, on Mansion's reading, it would appear that only assertions having the logical form "S is$_T$ P" involve the use of "is$_T$" that signifies that an assertion is true, and only assertions having the logical form "S is not$_F$ P" involve the use of "is not$_F$" that signifies that an assertion is false. This seems to be the substance of her claim that "affirmer un prédicat d'un sujet, c'est déclarer la liaison de l'un à l'autre conforme au réel, nier un prédicat d'un subjet, c'est déclarer leur union non conforme au reel," which claim appears to be the basis for her reading of the examples.

Hence, assessing Mansion's reading of the examples, the preceding claim is the most obvious explanation for why she interprets the second of Aristotle's examples in terms of an affirmation in which an indefinite verb "non-pale" is predicatively combined with the subject Socrates. Presumably, she interprets it this way in order to preserve the claim that the copular "is$_T$" here signifies the truth of an affirmation, whereas on the view defended here, the second example is an instance of "is$_T$" signifying that a denial "Socrates is not pale" is true. Similarly, she interprets Aristotle's third example as having the logical form "S is not$_F$ P"—which is the normal form for an Aristotelian denial—but she interprets this as logically equivalent to the claim that the affirmation "S is P" is false. On the view defended here, this is straightforwardly the case, since the claim in the example is taken to have the logical form "The affirmation 'the diagonal is commensurable' is false" and at no point is the example interpreted as having the form of a denial.

A more serious problem with Mansion's approach is that the use of "is$_T$" in question does not apply equally to affirmations and denials. It applies only to affirmations. Nor does the use of "is not$_F$" in question apply equally to affirmations and negations. It, too, applies only to denials. This is odd, since both "is true" and "is false" apply to both affirmations and denials when used in the semantic sense defined at Γ 7, and this is the sense of "is true" and "is false" that Mansion must have in mind here. So, one needs an explanation as to why this restriction is now in place.

Yet another problem with Mansion's interpretation, related to the last point, is that she needs to interpret two of Aristotle's three examples in terms of indefinite verbs. This is, of course, possible, as Aristotle clearly recognizes such verbs and makes use of them in various contexts. However, simple assertions involving indefinite verbs are not Aristotle's preferred examples of affirmations and denials. Moreover, according to Aristotle, the truth conditions for an affirmation of the form "S is non-P" differ from those for a denial of the form "S is not P." Similarly, the truth conditions for a denial "S is not non-P" differ from those for a denial of the form "It is not the case that S is not P." Prima facie, when Aristotle claims that the use of "is$_T$" applies equally to affirmations and denials, one would expect Aristotle to address the case where a denial of the form "S is not P" is true, as opposed to addressing an affirmation of the form "S is non-P." Worse still, it is not clear that Aristotle can formulate claims of the form " 'S is not P' is true" using the sense of "is$_T$" in question, as understood by Mansion. Similarly, although it may not be as obvious, we would expect Aristotle to address the case where a denial of the form "It is not the case that S is not P" is false prior to considering when denials of the form "S is not non-P" are false. This latter complaint may not seem pressing to those who think that Aristotle can only make sense of negation as qualifying the copula, since the complaint presupposes that Aristotle has a sense of negation that operates on assertions (which arguably he does).

A final problem with Mansion's approach is that it presupposes that the use of "is$_T$" in question signifies both [1] that a predicate predicatively belongs to a subject and [2] that the resulting affirmation is true and, similarly, that the use of "is not$_F$" in question signifies both [3] that a predicate does not predicatively belong to a subject and [4] that the resulting denial is false. This would be fine if Mansion were explicitly endorsing the claim that in Δ 7 Aristotle is concerned with a use of "is$_T$" that is semantically complex in this fashion. However, the first sentence of the quote does not suggest that this is how she understands the use of the verb. The rest of her discussion indicates that she identifies the copular use of the verb with this veridical use. Some explanation is needed.

Truth and the Other Kinds of Being

Thus far, I have argued that in *Metaphysics* Δ 7, Aristotle identifies a use of "being$_T$" that is logically equivalent to a predicate "true" that takes assertions as subjects. I have argued that this use of "being$_T$" denotes an attribute of assertions, and have suggested that the attribute in question is the attribute of assertions denoted by the nominal definition of "truth" presented by Aristotle at *Metaphysics* Γ 7.1011b26–27—the attribute of asserting of what is that it is or of asserting of what is not that it is not. In this section I will argue that, so interpreted, Aristotle's veridical sense of "being" serves to focus metaphysical inquiry by making explicit the putative ontological commitments posited in the first-order simple assertions of which the veridical sense of "being" is predicated.

If we assume that the nominal definitions in Γ 7.1011b26–27 establish uses of "truth" and "falsehood" that denote attributes of assertions, then to say that an assertion p is true or false involves predicating "is true" or "is false" of p. If, then, we assume that p is an n-order assertion, the assertion "p is true" is a $n + 1$-order assertion, the truth of which is a function of whether or not the embedded assertion says of what is that it is, et cetera. This has interesting implications.

As noted above, Aristotle recognizes three other uses of "being" [τὸ ὄν] in Δ 7: a use that denotes coincidental beings, a use that denotes *per se* beings in the various categories of beings, and a use that denotes *per se* potential and actual beings.[36] Throughout the corpus he understands assertions involving these three uses of "being" as first-order claims about coincidental beings, beings in the various categories, and potential and actual being. Thus, the assertion ⌜ Socrates is human ⌝ is a first-order assertion about the real predicative combination of the real substantial attribute being-human and the real subject Socrates.[37] It may be properly paraphrased, employing the use of "being$_{categorial}$" in Δ 7 that denotes *per se* beings in the categories, by the first-order assertion ⌜ Socrates is$_{categorial}$ human ⌝. If this assertion is true, it is in virtue of the fact that the real subject Socrates has an essence of the sort that belongs *per se* to the substantial species being-human. ⌜ Socrates is cultured ⌝ is a first-order assertion about the real subject Socrates, the real quality of being-cultured, and their coincidental real combination. It may be properly paraphrased, employing the use of "being$_{coincidental}$" in Δ 7 that denotes coincidental beings, by the first-order assertion ⌜ Socrates is$_{coincidental}$ cultured ⌝. If the assertion is true, it is because the non-substantial attribute of being-cultured is coincidentally predicatively combined with the real subject Socrates. So, too, employing the uses of "being" in Δ 7 that denote potential and actual beings, we can paraphrase the first-order assertions ⌜ Socrates is potentially sick ⌝ and ⌜ Socrates is actually wise ⌝ as ⌜ Socrates is$_{potential}$ sick ⌝ and ⌜ Socrates is$_{actual}$ wise ⌝. If the former is true, it is virtue of the fact that the real subject Socrates has the potential to become ill. If the latter assertion is true, it is in virtue of the fact that the real subject Socrates is predicatively combined with the real attribute being wise. Each of these three uses of "being," then, is a first-order predicate denoting a real predicative relation of combination between different kinds of real beings.

In contrast to these uses of "being," assertions involving "being$_T$" are either second-order assertions about first-order assertions involving the other three uses of "being" or higher-order assertions that, ultimately, terminate in first-order assertions involving the other uses of "being" than the veridical use. There are various apparent consequences of this fact. The first consequence of the use of "being$_T$" is that it offers a metaphysically innocent starting point for the pursuit of knowledge about being insofar as it is being. With regard to any assertion, we can ask "Is the assertion true or false?" With respect to every general metaphysical assertion involving a use of "being" other than the veridical use, if one asks "Are assertions involving that use of 'being' true?" one is forced to clarify the intensional content of the assertion and then directly to investigate the world to see if what is asserted obtains. For example, when we ask "Is$_{categorial}$ Socrates human?" at the very least we need to determine what we have in mind when we use the "is$_{categorial}$." This raises the associated general questions "How is 'is$_{categorial}$' used?" and "Are assertions involving the use of 'is$_{categorial}$' true?" To answer the first of these questions, we would need to establish the philosophical usage of "is$_{categorial}$" and Aristotle is engaged in that effort in various treatises. To answer the second question, we need to figure out whether or not there are real categories of beings. Maybe the world is categorially structured, maybe not. Aristotle thinks it is. Having answered these questions, we can address the more parochial concern about whether or not Socrates is, in fact, human in the way demanded by uses of "is$_{categorial}$." This requires that we investigate the world to see if the real subject Socrates is predicatively combined with the *per se* real substantial attribute being-human. Similarly, when we consider the question "Is$_{coincidental}$ Diotima cultured?" we confront immediately the associated more general questions "How is 'is$_{coincidental}$' used" and "Are assertions involving such uses of 'is$_{coincidental}$' true?" At the very least we need to make sense of the use of "being$_{coincidental}$" and discover whether or not there are any coincidental beings. It seems there are such beings, but appearances may prove deceptive—witness Aristotle's worry over how Antisthenes handled this issue in *Metaphysics* Δ 29. And then we can investigate whether or not Diotima herself is, in fact, musical in the way demanded by uses of "is$_{coincidental}$." This requires empirical inquiry. And the same sorts of general metaphysical and particular empirical questions arise with regard to assertions involving the use of "being$_{potential}$" and "being$_{actual}$."

On the interpretation of "being$_T$" offered here, assertions involving the use of "being$_T$" are evaluated differently. Such assertions are second-order assertions about first-order assertions (or n-order assertions about $n - 1$ assertions). Thus, when we ask "The assertion ⌜ Diotima is human ⌝ is$_T$?" on my interpretation of Γ 7.1011b26–27, we know that we are asking the equivalent question "Is the assertion ⌜ Diotima is human ⌝ true?" and our first task is to investigate the truth conditions for the assertion. Given that ⌜ Diotima is human ⌝ is a first-order assertion, in part our investigation will involve determining if the first-order assertion ⌜ Diotima is human ⌝ is logically equivalent to ⌜ Diotima is$_{categorially}$ human ⌝ or ⌜ Diotima is$_{coincidentally}$ human ⌝ or ⌜ Diotima is$_{potentially}$ human ⌝ or ⌜ Diotima is$_{actually}$ human ⌝. In part our investigation will involve empirical inquiry, figuring out whether or not the real subject Diotima is predicativly combined with the attribute being-human in the way specified by the use of "is" in question. Uses of "being$_T$" are, thus, metaphysically innocent in comparison with the other uses of "is" in Δ 7. All uses of "is" in Δ 7 presuppose the significant use of language and true and false assertions. But whereas "is$_T$" presupposes only the significant use of language and the existence of true and false assertions, the other three uses of "is" in Δ 7 presuppose in addition the existence of particular and philosophically sophisticated ontological structures (categorial structures, coincidental structures, the relationship between potential and actual beings).

A second consequence of the use of "being$_T$" in Γ 7.1011b26–27 is that, on pain of a regress, assertions involving the use of "being$_T$" ultimately depend for their truth values on the truth values of assertions involving the other uses of "being" discussed in Δ 7. Adapting an idea from contemporary philosophical semantics, Aristotle can say that assertions involving the use of "being$_T$" must ultimately be *grounded* in first-order assertions that do not themselves involve the use of "being$_T$." For example, suppose ⌜ Diotima is human is$_T$ ⌝ is an affirmation involving the use of "is$_T$." Then ⌜ Diotima is human is$_T$ ⌝ is paraphrased by the second-order assertion ⌜ The assertion ⌜ Diotima is human ⌝ is true ⌝. Suppose, now, that the use of ⌜ is ⌝ predicating ⌜ human ⌝ of ⌜ Diotima ⌝ is veridical. In this case, the affirmation ⌜ The assertion ⌜ Diotima is$_T$ human ⌝ is true ⌝ would be paraphrased by the third-order affirmation ⌜ The assertion ⌜⌜ The assertion ⌜ Diotima is human ⌝ is true ⌜ is true ⌝. Suppose, again, that the use of ⌜ is ⌝ predicating ⌜ human ⌝ of ⌜ Diotima ⌝ in the third-order assertion is veridical. The regress has begun. It appears to be vicious. Unless the use of ⌜ is ⌝ predicating ⌜ human ⌝ of ⌜ Diotima ⌝ in one of the generated assertions is not veridical, there is no stopping the regress, and the assertion will not be grounded.

Conclusion

In this chapter I have argued that in *Metaphysics* Δ 7, at 1017a31–35, Aristotle identifies a use of "to be" that is logically equivalent to a predicate "to be true" that takes assertions as subjects. This use of "to be$_T$" denotes an attribute of assertions, namely the one defined by him in Γ 7, at 1011b26–27—the attribute of asserting of what is that it is or of asserting of what is not that it is not.

A number of other concerns relating to the use of "being$_T$" can only be addressed on the light of Aristotle's fuller account of this kind of truth in the *Metaphysics*. First, it is unclear in Δ 7 to which category of being in-itself one should assign this kind of truth, nor is it obvious how this kind of truth is related to coincidental being. Aristotle addresses this question in *Metaphysics* E 4. I will argue in chapter 7 that in E 4 Aristotle claims that truth and falsehood are *per se* affections of thought that depend for their existence on beings in the categories.[38] Second, from what he says about potential and actual being in Δ 7, at 1017a35ff, one can infer a distinction between potential and actual truth, but Aristotle's explanation of the basis for this distinction is put off until *Metaphysics* Θ 10. I will argue that in Θ 10 Aristotle ramifies the use of "being$_T$" in terms of potential and actual beings, both simple and composite, articulating his view in terms of the distinction he has made in Θ 1–9. Before turning Aristotle's fuller account of the kind of truth that belongs to assertions, however, it will be important to differentiate it from, and compare it with, the other kinds of truth Aristotle explicitly acknowledges in *Metaphysics* book Δ 29.

Chapter 5

Aristotle's Homonymous Truth Bearers

It was shown in part II of this book that Aristotle articulates and employs a nominal definition of "truth" in his defense of the logical axioms in *Metaphysics* book Γ, chapter 7. The sort of truth denoted by the nominal definition purports to be an attribute of assertions. In the last chapter, it was argued that true assertion is among the basic kinds of being Aristotle acknowledges in *Metaphysics* Δ 7. There, he identifies a use of "being$_T$," that logically equivalent to the nominal definition of truth presented in *Metaphysics* Γ 7.1011b26–27.

In *Metaphysics* Δ 29, Aristotle distinguishes explicitly among two kinds of truth and falsehood understood as attributes of objects, a kind of truth and falsehood understood as attributes of assertions, and two kinds of truth and falsehood that are properly predicated of persons. Are these various kinds related, and if so, how are they related?

Among leading contemporary commentators, Crivelli, De Rijk, and Whitaker have argued that there is a systematic relationship among the kinds of truth and falsehood differentiated by Aristotle, claiming that one kind of objectual truth is the most fundamental kind, the other kinds of truth being defined in terms of it.[1] Following Brentano and Modrak, in this chapter I argue that the assertoric kind of truth and falsehood is basic to Aristotle's system of homonyms. More specifically, I argue that a number of the kinds of truth and falsehood presented by Aristotle in the *Metaphysics* are homonyms.

The relationship among the various kinds of truth and falsehood Aristotle recognizes will be approached here in terms of his distinction between synonyms and homonyms. This is how he himself typically evaluates the relationship between things that are signified by the same term. Exploring the question in terms of synonymy and homonymy also yields interesting results. Insofar as there is a systematic relationship among these homonymous kinds, the assertoric kind is shown to be the "core" kind on which the others depend. In other words, among those kinds of truth that are denoted by the term "truth," but not by the same definition of "truth," all of the kinds other than the assertoric kind depend upon the assertoric kind. It turns out that the objectual kind of truth often taken to be the core kind of truth is not fundamental to the system of homonyms. Either it is disjoint altogether from the system of homonyms or it, too, depends upon the assertoric kind of truth.

The Homonymous Kinds of Truth and Falsehood

Metaphysics Δ 29 explicitly concerns falsehood [τὸ ψεῦδος]. Aristotle does not have a separate entry for "truth" in his philosophical lexicon, but he has one for "falsehood." This might seem odd, until one recalls that he has defined truth and falsehood in *Met.* Γ 7 and introduced truth as a kind of being explicitly in *Met.* Δ 7. Nor is there any reason for thinking that he divorces the concepts of falsehood and truth such that it would make sense to interpret Δ 29 as *not* having to do with truth. As a consequence, it is plausible to assume that, in Δ 29, he is concerned as much with truth as with falsehood, and that he implicitly recognizes for each concept of falsehood a correlated concept of truth.[2]

Met. Δ 29 breaks down into three parts: 1024b17-26 concerns false things, 1024b26-1025a1 concerns false accounts, and 1025a1-13 concerns false human beings.[3] Since it is obvious that the different kinds of truth and falsehood in Δ 29 share the same name, they might be synonyms or homonyms. To begin with, it is fairly straightforward to show that the various kinds are not synonyms.

True and False Assertions

At the end of Δ 29, at 1025a1-13, Aristotle distinguishes between true and false persons as follows:[4]

> τὰ μὲν οὖν οὕτω λέγεται ψευδῆ, ἄνθρωπος δὲ ψευδὴς ὁ εὐχερὴς καὶ προαιρετικὸς τῶν τοιούτων λόγων, μὴ δι' ἕτε-ρόν τι ἀλλὰ δι' αὐτό, καὶ ὁ ἄλλοις ἐμποιητικὸς τῶν τοιούτων λόγων, ὥσπερ καὶ τὰ πράγματά φαμεν ψευδῆ εἶναι ὅσα ἐμποιεῖ

φαντασίαν ψευδῆ. διὸ ὁ ἐν τῷ Ἱππίᾳ λόγος παρακρούεται ὡς ὁ αὐτὸς ψευδὴς καὶ ἀληθής. τὸν δυνάμενον γὰρ ψεύσασθαι λαμβάνει ψευδῆ (οὗτος δ' ὁ εἰδὼς καὶ ὁ φρόνιμος)· ἔτι τὸν ἑκόντα φαῦλον βελτίω. τοῦτο δὲ ψεῦδος λαμβάνει διὰ τῆς ἐπαγωγῆς—ὁ γὰρ ἑκὼν χωλαίνων τοῦ ἄκοντος κρείττων—τὸ χωλαίνειν τὸ μιμεῖσθαι λέγων, ἐπεὶ εἴ γε χωλὸς ἑκών, χείρων ἴσως, ὥσπερ ἐπὶ τοῦ ἤθους, καὶ οὗτος.

A false man is one who readily and deliberately makes such statements, for the sake of doing so and for no other reason; and one who induces such statements in others—just as we call things false which induce a false impression. Hence the proof in the *Hippias* that the same man is false and true is misleading; for it assumes (a) that the false man is he who is able to deceive, i.e., the man who knows and is intelligent; (b) that the man who is willingly bad is better. This false assumption is due to the induction; for when he says that the man who limps willingly is better than he who does so unwillingly, he means by limping pretending to limp. For if he is willingly lame, he is presumably worse in this case just as he is in the case of moral character. (trans., Tredennick)

The first kind of false person is defined as someone who readily and deliberately makes false assertions for the sake of making false assertions and for no other reason. In contrast, the true person would be someone who readily and deliberately makes true assertions for the sake of making true assertions and for no other reason. The second kind of false person is defined as someone who induces false assertions in other people. In contrast, this sort of true person would be someone who induces true assertions in other people. These concepts may properly be considered ethical concepts of truth and falsehood and may be defined as follows:

EF1: x is a false person just in case x is someone ready to use, and fond of, false assertions.

ET1: x is a true person just in case x is someone ready to use, and fond of, true assertions.

EF2: x is a false person just in case x induces false assertions in other people.

ET2: *x* is a true person just in case *x* induces true assertions in other people.

It is quite clear from the text that Aristotle explains both kinds of true and false persons in terms of true and false assertions. So, attention can be turned directly to this other sort of truth and falsehood.

At 1024b26–1025a1, Aristotle acknowledges a conception of a true and false sentence or account [λόγος ψευδής]. This kind of truth clearly applies to assertions, but it is not obviously the same as that defined in *Metaphysics* Γ 7:

> λόγος δὲ ψευδὴς ὁ τῶν μὴ ὄντων, ᾗ ψευδής, διὸ πᾶς λόγος ψευδὴς ἑτέρου ἢ οὗ ἐστὶν ἀληθής, οἷον ὁ τοῦ κύκλου ψευδὴς τριγώνου. ἑκάστου δὲ λόγος ἔστι μὲν ὡς εἷς, ὁ τοῦ τί ἦν εἶναι, ἔστι δ' ὡς πολλοί, ἐπεὶ ταὐτό πως αὐτὸ καὶ αὐτὸ πεπονθός,[5] οἷον Σωκράτης καὶ Σωκράτης μουσικός (ὁ δὲ ψευδὴς λόγος οὐθενός ἐστιν ἁπλῶς λόγος)· διὸ Ἀντισθένης ᾤετο εὐήθως μηθὲν ἀξιῶν λέγεσθαι πλὴν τῷ οἰκείῳ λόγῳ, ἓν ἐφ' ἑνός· ἐξ ὧν συνέβαινε μὴ εἶναι ἀντιλέγειν, σχεδὸν δὲ μηδὲ ψεύδεσθαι. ἔστι δ' ἕκαστον λέγειν οὐ μόνον τῷ αὑτοῦ λόγῳ ἀλλὰ καὶ τῷ ἑτέρου, ψευδῶς μὲν καὶ παντελῶς, ἔστι δ' ὡς καὶ ἀληθῶς, ὥσπερ τὰ ὀκτὼ διπλάσια τῷ τῆς δυάδος λόγῳ.

> A false formula is the formula of nonexistent objects, insofar as it is false. Hence every formula is false when applied to something other than that of which it is true, e.g., the formula of a circle is false when applied to a triangle. In a sense there is one formula of each thing, i.e., the formula of its essence, but in a sense there are many, since the thing itself and the thing itself modified in a certain way are somehow the same, e.g., Socrates and musical Socrates. The false formula is not the formula of anything, except in a qualified sense. Hence Antisthenes foolishly claimed that nothing could be described except by its own formula, one formula to one thing; from which it followed that there could be no contradiction, and almost that there could be no error. But it is possible to describe each thing not only by its own formula, but also by that of something else. This may be done altogether falsely indeed, but in some ways it may be done truly, e.g. eight may be described as a double number by the use of the formula of two. (trans., Ross)

The claims in the passage may be understood as follows, leaving "λόγος" untranslated: A false λόγος, insofar as it is false, is a λόγος of beings that are not. Every false λόγος is false of every being other than that of which it is true (as, for example, the λόγος of a circle is false of a triangle). In one sense, there is one λόγος of each being—namely, the λόγος of what it is to be it. A false λόγος of what it is to be some being is a λόγος of nothing at all. In another sense, there are many λόγοι for each being, since each being is in a way the same as itself-with-an-attribute. In this other sense, it is possible to describe each being not only by the λόγος of what it is to be that being, but also by the λόγος of what it is to be some other being. In describing a being B by a λόγος of what it is to be some other being, either the description is altogether false of B or it is true because it describes some non-essential predicate of B. Unless one allows for the latter sense of a λόγος for a being, one cannot make sense of contradiction or, practically, of falsehood.[6]

If one assumes that Aristotle uses λόγος throughout the passage to denote assertions about beings, one gets the following:[7] A false assertion, insofar as it is false, is about something other than what is. Every assertion is a false assertion about everything other than that which it is about (as, for example, the assertion "a circle is a triangle" is false of everything other than the circle that is a triangle, which is what it is about). In one sense, only one assertion is an assertion about any given being—namely, the assertion that defines the essence of that being. In this first sense, a false assertion is an assertion about nothing at all, since it cannot be an assertion that defines anything else than the essence that, by hypothesis, it doesn't define. But in another sense, many different assertions are assertions about the same thing, since each thing is in a way the same as itself combined in the real world with or separated from its predicates. Hence, the assertion about a thing combined in the real world with or separated from its predicates is about that thing. In this second sense, it is possible to make assertions about the essential predicates of something and, also, to make assertions about the coincidental predicates of that thing. In making an assertion about a being and the predicates with which it is combined or separated in the real world, either the statement is false or it is true because it describes some predicate of that thing. Unless one allow for this latter kind of assertion, one cannot make sense of contradiction or of falsity.

On this interpretation of 1024b26–1025a1, Aristotle is specifying more completely the nominal definition of assertoric truth and falsehood presented in Γ 7 and Δ 7. He is distinguishing carefully between assertions about the essences of things (i.e., the definitions of things) and assertions about one thing belonging or not belonging to another thing (i.e., simple affirmations and denials about things). Aristotle is thus explaining the truth conditions of assertions in Δ 29. This is a significant fact. Δ 29 is no oddity with respect to Aristotle's theory of truth. Quite the contrary, it fits well with the nominal definitions presented at 1011b26–27, makes sense of the relation between Δ 29 and Γ 7 (and later passages, as we shall see), integrates the preceding discussion of false things in Δ 29 at 1024b17–26, and helps one to see how Aristotle's account of the semantics of predicative statements relates to his account of the semantics of definitions.[8]

We can develop the nominal definitions presented in Γ 7, in the light of 1024b26–1025a1 along the following lines:

> For every linguistic or conceptual subject n that signifies or represents one and only one real subject x, for every linguistic or conceptual predicate d that signifies or represents one and only one real predicate y, for every linguistic or conceptual relation + that signifies or represents the real predicative relation of belonging to, and for every linguistic or conceptual relation − that signifies or represents the real predicative relation of not belonging to:
>
> [F] Falsehood is either (a) to linguistically or mentally assert that $d + n$ and y does not belong to x or (b) to linguistically or mentally assert that $d − n$ and y belongs to x.
>
> [T] Truth is either (a) to linguistically or mentally assert that $d + n$ and y belongs to x or (b) to linguistically or mentally assert that $d − n$ and y does not belong to x or (c) to linguistically or mentally asserts that n is definitionally the same as d and $x = y$.

True and False Things

In chapter 5, we discussed the two kinds of two false things introduced by Aristotle in *Met*. Δ 29.1024b17–26. Let me rehearse some of the main ideas developed there. Aristotle identifies two uses of "τὸ ψεῦδος" having the sense of "πρᾶγμα ψεῦδος" ("false thing"). "πρᾶγμα ψεῦδος" means either (1) a combination of real things that, in fact, does not obtain or (2) an actual thing that is usually taken to be something other than what it is. It is plausible to suppose that for each use, he acknowledged a correlated concept of "ἀληθές" having the sense of "πρᾶγμα ἀληθές." The correlated "πρᾶγμα ἀληθές" would mean either (1) a predicative combination of real things that, in fact, obtains or (2) an actual thing that is usually taken to be what it is.⁹

With respect to the first of these kinds of true and false things, discussed previously in relation to Δ 7, at *Met.* Δ 29.1024b18–20 Aristotle uses the terms "συγκεῖσθαι" and "συντεθῆναι." Both of these terms may be translated by "combined." He distinguishes between (a) real things that are not combined, but could be (τὸ τῶι μὴ συγκεῖσθαι) and (b) real things that cannot be combined (τὸ ἀδύνατον εἶναι συντεθῆναι). A person sitting down is given as an example of (a). The diagonal being commensurable is given as an example of (b). In both cases, what is at issue is whether or not some real subject is combined with some real predicate. Some subjects can be, but are not, combined with certain predicates. Other subjects cannot be combined with certain predicates. Still other subjects must be combined with certain predicates. For example, a horse must be an animal. Therefore, Aristotle's first concept of a false thing subsumes pairs of real subjects and predicates that are not combined (whether contingently or necessarily). The correlated concept of a true thing subsumes those pairs of real subjects and predicates that are combined (whether contingently or necessarily).¹⁰

With respect to the second kind of true and false things, Aristotle thinks that some beings in the world are properly called "true," in the sense that they appear to be what they are; others are properly called "false" because they deceptively appear to be something other than what they are.¹¹ The appearance of an illusory object does not signify what it is, but rather signifies, by its very nature, something other than what it is. Given his conception of natural signification, it makes perfect sense to call such things false because the way they appear differs from the way they actually are. Their appearance naturally asserts something other than what they are.¹²

Thus, by "false thing," Aristotle means either (1) a possible compound thing that is not actual, (2) an impossible compound thing, or (3) an actual thing that is usually imagined to be something other than what it actually is.¹³ In (1) and (2), "false" is logically equivalent to "nonexistent" or "not obtaining." Analogously, by "true thing," he means either (1) a possible compound thing that is actual, (2) a necessary compound thing, or (3) an actual thing that is usually imagined to be what it is. Here, in (1) and (2), "true" is logically equivalent to "existent" or "obtaining."[14] This analysis yields the following definitions of true and false things:

> OF1: For all actual things x, y, and z, z is a false thing if, and only if, z = (the real complex $y - x$).
>
> OT1: For all actual things x, y, and z, z is a true thing if, and only if, z = (the real complex $y + x$).
>
> OF2: For any actual thing x, x is a false thing if, and only if, the appearance generated by x either (1) is not an appearance of what x is or (2) is an appearance of what is not.
>
> OT2: For any actual thing x, x is a true thing if, and only if, the appearance generated by x is an appearance of what x is.

Aristotle's Core Kind of Truth and Falsehood

To summarize the argument in the chapter thus far, first, the various kinds of truth distinguished by Aristotle in *Met.* Δ 29 are not synonyms. The two kinds of true and false persons, the two kinds of objectual truth and falsehood, and the assertoric kind of truth and falsehood are homonymous kinds of truth and falsehood. Second, both kinds of true and false persons are defined in terms of assertoric truth and falsehood. Third, the kind of assertoric truth and falsehood presented in Δ 29 is the same as the kind denoted by the nominal definitions of assertoric truth and falsehood in Γ 7 and Δ 7. In other words, the kinds of assertoric truth and falsehood presented in *Met.* Δ 29, Γ 7, and Δ 7 are synonyms. Lastly, Aristotle posits a kind of objectual truth and falsehood, and this sort of truth and falsehood is explained in terms of the usual metaphysical suspects—real subjects and real predicates in the categories that are predicatively combined in the real world at a given time (the true objects) or are not predicatively combined in the real world at a given time (the false objects).

The main purpose of this section is to explain the relationship among the various kinds of truth and falsehood recognized by Aristotle in Δ 29. It is argued here that the different kinds of truth and falsehood are systematically related, the assertoric kind serving as the basic kind in terms of which the others are to be understood. However, to begin with, it is worth considering reasons for thinking that Aristotle does not define his core kinds of truth and falsehood in the *Metaphysics*. For one may argue that he works with *various* concepts of truth in the *Metaphysics* but does not commit himself to any particular definition of truth and falsehood.[15]

There are various ways to develop this point. One can be ruled out immediately. One may think that, *because* he works with many different concepts of truth and falsehood, he *cannot* define his core kind of truth and falsehood. There is no reason for attributing a view like this to Aristotle.[16] On the contrary, he is acutely aware that the same term can signify different things. One need only look at any chapter of *Metaphysics* Δ for examples of this fact. As introduced in the *Categories* and employed throughout the treatises, his notions of synonymy, homonymy, and paronymy seem to address the problem of equivocal terms precisely by means of distinguishing among the different definitions associated with the different things signified by the same, or grammatically derived, terms.[17] Thus, the fact that Aristotle works with many different concepts of truth and falsehood is no reason for thinking he did not or could not define them.

The most plausible argument for the claim that he does not define his core kinds of truth and falsehood takes into account the strong evidence that he does present explicit definitions of assertoric truth and falsehood at in *Met.* Γ 7.1011b26–27: The formulae at 1011b26–27 are explicit nominal definitions of the terms "truth" and "falsehood." The formulae at 1011b26–27 do not express Aristotle's real definitions of the essence of truth and falsehood. *Ipso facto*, they don't express Aristotle's core concepts of the essence of truth and falsehood. Moreover, Aristotle nowhere else explicitly defines his core concepts of truth and falsehood. Hence, Aristotle leaves his core concepts of truth and falsehood undefined. Of these, the first three claims are true and were defended earlier in this book. I reject the fourth, and I will argue Aristotle explicitly presents his real definitions of assertoric truth and falsehood in in *Met.* E 4 and Θ 10.

Thus far in this chapter, the various concepts of truth and falsehood presented by Aristotle in Δ 29 have been analyzed. In what follows, I argue that his definitions of assertoric truth and falsehood are his core kinds of truth and falsehood. The following relations among the different homonymous kinds of truth and falsehood need to be established: (1) the relation between true and false persons and the assertoric kind of truth and falsehood, (2) the relation between the different kinds of objectual truth and falsehood, (3) the relation between each of the objectual kinds and true and false persons, and (4) the relation between the assertoric kind of truth and falsehood and the two kinds of objectual truth and falsehood.

Following Shields, the following principle may be used as a criterion to establish the extent to which the homonymous kinds of truth and falsehood are associated and, in particular, to show that the assertoric kind of truth and falsehood is the core kind on which all the other kinds depend:

> (CDHT) A kind of truth d and c are *homonymously kinds of being true in a core-dependent way* iff (i) d and c have their name in common, (ii) their definitions overlap, but not completely, and (iii) necessarily, if c is a core instance of being true, then d's being true stands in one of the four causal relations to c's being true, and (iv) c's being true is asymmetrically responsible for the existence of d's being true.

As noted above, all of the different kinds of truth and falsehood currently being evaluated are homonyms. In other words, all satisfy condition (i) of CDHT. In what follows, the relations among the different kinds are evaluated in terms of clauses (ii)–(iv) of CDHT.

As noted above, Aristotle defines the two kinds of true and false persons in Δ 29 as follows:

> EF1: x is a false person$_1$ just in case x is someone ready to use, and fond of, false assertions.
>
> ET1: x is a true person$_1$ just in case x is someone ready to use, and fond of, true assertions.
>
> EF2: x is a false just in case x induces false assertions in other people.
>
> ET2: x is a true just in case x induces true assertions in other people.

We saw above that in Δ 29, Aristotle has defined the assertoric kind of truth and falsehood as follows:

> For every linguistic or conceptual subject n that signifies or represents one and only one real subject x, for every linguistic

or conceptual predicate d that signifies or represents one and only one real predicate y, for every linguistic or conceptual relation + that signifies or represents the real predicative relation of belonging to, and for every linguistic or conceptual relation − that signifies or represents the real predicative relation of not belonging to:

[F] Falsehood is either (a) to linguistically or mentally assert that $d + n$ and y does not belong to x or (b) to linguistically or mentally assert that $d − n$ and y belongs to x.

[T] Truth is either (a) to linguistically or mentally assert that $d + n$ and y belongs to x or (b) to linguistically or mentally assert that $d − n$ and y does not belong to x or (c) to linguistically or mentally asserts that n is definitionally the same as d and $x = y$.

Both kinds of true and false persons are defined in terms of true and false assertions. Thus, the definitions of these two homonymous kinds of truth and falsehood overlap, but not completely. Therefore, clause (ii) of CDHT is satisfied by these kinds.

In general, in considering clause (iii) of CDHT, one first needs to establish whether or not the homonymous kinds of truth are causally related. Second, having done so, one needs to establish that the causal relation between the two kinds necessarily obtains. There are four kinds of causal relations to consider: the material, formal, efficient, and final causal relations. For the purposes of the arguments here, the following definitions of these four causal relations will be used:[18]

(MC) "x is, or is part of, the material cause of y" $=_{df.}$ x is, or is part of, the potential that can be actualized by y.

(FC) "x is, or is part of, the formal cause of y" $=_{df.}$ x is, or is part of, the essence of y.

(EC) "x is, or is part of, the efficient cause of y" $=_{df.}$ Either (1) (a) x has the same essence as y and (b) x is what generated y or (2) there is a z such that (a) x is a part of the essence of z, (b) z has the same essence as y, and (c) z is what generated y.

(TC) "x is, or is part of, the final cause of y" $=_{df.}$ x is, or is part of, the full actualization of y.

Is the truth of the first kind of true person in any sense the cause of the truth of true assertions? Is the falsehood of the first kind of false person in any sense the cause of the falsehood of false assertions? No. First, a true person$_1$'s being true is not, and is not part of, the material cause of a true assertion's being true; a false person$_1$'s being false is not, and is not part of, the material cause of a false assertion's being false. Given (MC) above and the assumption that the material cause of assertoric truth is the genus of assertoric truth—the activity of asserting—expressed in the definition of assertoric truth, the material cause of a true assertion being true is the psychological capacity to make assertions. Neither a true person$_1$'s being true nor a false person$_1$'s being false is identical with, or is a part of, this mental capacity.

Conversely, the mental capacity to make assertions would appear to be part of the material cause of both true and false persons$_1$. Were such persons to lack the capacity to make assertions, they could not have the potential to use them or be fond of them. In other words, if a person lacks the potential to make a true or false assertion, then he or she cannot be a true or a false person$_1$. As a consequence, necessarily, the truth of an assertion is a part of the potential that can be actualized by a true person$_1$. Similarly, and necessarily, the falsehood of an assertion is a part of the potential that can be actualized by a false person$_1$.

Second, a true person$_1$'s being true is not, and is not part of, the formal cause of a true assertion's being true; a false person$_1$'s being false is not, and is not part of, the formal cause of a false assertion's being false. This is immediately evident from the definitions of the different kinds of truth and falsehood.

Conversely, it is obvious from the definitions that being a true assertion is part of the essence of being a true person$_1$ and that being a false assertion is part of the essence of being a false person$_1$. That is to say, a true assertion's being true is part of the essence of a true person$_1$'s being true, and a false assertion's being false is part of the essence of a false person$_1$'s being false.

Third, although it is perhaps less obvious than it was in the prior cases, a true person$_1$'s being true is not, and is not part of, the efficient cause of a true assertion's being true. A true person$_1$'s being true is explained in terms of being ready and deliberate in using true assertions. Given (EC) above, in order for this readiness and deliberateness to be the efficient cause of the truth of a true assertion, the readiness and deliberateness must have the same essence as the truth of a true assertion. Were that to be the case, then the two kinds of truth would be synonymous. That is clearly not so. Alternatively, for the readiness and deliberateness of a true person$_1$ to be a part of the essence of what is, in fact, the efficient cause of the truth of a true assertion, the readiness and deliberateness of a true person$_1$ would have to be a part of the essence of the truth of a true assertion. Again, this is clearly not so. The same reasoning applies in the case of a false person$_1$'s being false and a false assertion's being false.

Nor is it obvious that a true assertion's being true is, or is part of, the efficient cause of a true person$_1$'s being true. On the one hand, it is evident that the essence of assertoric truth is not the same as the essence of a true person$_1$. Hence, a true assertion's being true cannot be the efficient cause, taken as a whole, of a true person$_1$'s being true. Given (EC), one true person$_1$ would seem to be the right candidate for the efficient cause, taken as a whole, of another. On the other hand, suppose that one true person$_1$'s being true is the efficient cause, taken as a whole, of another true person$_1$'s being true. It was shown above that a true assertion's being true is part of both the material and the formal cause of a true person$_1$'s being true. It follows that a true assertion's being true is part of the essence of a true person$_1$'s being true. Hence, a true assertion's being true is part of the essence of the efficient cause of a true person$_1$'s being true, i.e., is part of the efficient cause of a true person$_1$'s being true. The same reasoning applies, mutatis mutandis, to false persons$_1$ and false assertions.

Fourth, is a true person$_1$'s being true the final cause, or part of the final cause, of a true assertion's being true? No. The full actualization of a true person$_1$ being true is the full actualization of a certain psychological disposition—the deliberateness and readiness to use true assertions. This is neither the final cause nor part of the final cause of a true assertion. The full actualization of a true assertion's being true is the full actualization of some instance of one of the following clauses from Aristotle's definition of assertoric truth. It is clear from this that the final cause of a true assertion's being true, taken as a whole or in part, is not the deliberateness and readiness to use true assertions. The same reasoning applies to the case of a false person$_1$'s being false and a false assertion's being false.

Conversely, a true assertion's being true is part of the final cause of a true person$_1$'s being true. For, the full actualization of a true person$_1$'s being true is defined in terms of a true assertion's being true. A true person$_1$

is ready to use, and deliberately uses, true assertions as opposed to false assertions. It is presumably the true assertion's being true that matters and informs the definition of a true person$_1$. The same considerations apply in the case of the false person$_1$.

Therefore, a true person$_1$'s being true and a false person$_1$'s being false are in no sense the causes of a true assertion's being true or a false assertion's' being false. However, a true assertion's being true is part of each of the four causes of a true person$_1$'s being true. As a consequence, an asymmetric relation of dependence obtains between these different kinds of truth and falsehood. True and false persons$_1$ cannot exist unless true and false assertions exist. The converse does not hold. True and false assertions can exist independently of true and false persons$_1$.

In terms of clause (iv) of CDHT, a true assertion's being true is asymmetrically responsible for the existence of true person$_1$'s being true. At least in relation to true persons$_1$, a true assertion's being true is a core instance of being true. Does it follow that, necessarily, given that assertoric truth is a core instance of being true, a true person$_1$'s being true stands in one of the four causal relations to a true assertion's being true? Yes, since the kinds of causal relation in which these two kinds of truth stand are determinate causal relations. Aristotle understands these in terms of what is necessary.[19] True persons$_1$ and assertoric truth are core-dependent homonyms, with assertoric truth serving as the core kind to which the kind of true persons$_1$ depends.

By parity of reasoning, it can be shown that a true's being true and a false's being false are in no sense the causes of a true assertion's being true or a false assertion's being false. However, as with true persons$_1$, a true assertion's being true is part of each of the four causes of a true's being true. As a consequence, an asymmetric relation of dependence obtains between the second kind of true and false person and the assertoric kind of truth and falsehood. True and false persons$_2$ cannot exist unless true and false assertions exist. As in the case of true and false persons$_1$, the converse does not hold: true and false assertions can exist independently of true and false persons$_2$. So, too, in terms of clause (iv) of CDHT, a true assertion's being true is asymmetrically responsible for the existence of true's being true. Thus, in relation to true persons$_2$, a true assertion's being true is a core instance of being true. In addition, necessarily, given that assertoric truth is a core instance of being true, a true person$_2$'s being true stands in one of the four causal relations to a true assertion's being true. For, as in the case of the first kind of true and false persons, the kinds of causal relation are determinate causal relations.

It has just been argued that the assertoric kind of truth and falsehood is the core kind on which both kinds of true and false persons depend.[20] Turning to the two different kinds of objectual truth and falsehood, it would appear that these kinds are discrete homonyms.[21] Clauses (ii)–(iv) of CDHT are false when instantiated to these kinds of truth and falsehood. Consider first instantiating CDHT to the case where the first kind of objectual truth is taken to be the core kind between them:

(ii) the definitions of the two kinds of objectual truth overlap, but not completely,

(iii) necessarily, given that the first kind of objectual truth is a core instance of being true, the second kind of objectual truth's being true stands in one of the four causal relations to the first kind's being true, and

(iv) the first kind's being true is asymmetrically responsible for the existence of the second kind's being true.

With respect to clause (ii), looking again at the definitions of the two kinds of objectual truth, the extensions of the definitions do overlap in part:

OT1: For all actual things x, y, and z, z is a true thing if, and only if, $z =$ the real complex $y + x$.

OT2: For any actual thing x, x is a true thing if, and only if, the appearance generated by x is an appearance of what x is.

OT2 is defined over all actual things. The first kind of objectual truth has actual things for members. Every instance of the first kind of objectual truth is a real complex having the form $y + x$. Since OT2 is defined over all actual things, it is defined over this kind of real complex. As a consequence, the extensions of these definitions overlap in part.

However, whether or not the extensions of the definitions overlap is not the real issue in CDHT. For Aristotle, definitional overlap has to do with overlapping intensions. It is not at all clear that the intensions of the definitions under investigation here partially overlap. To see this, first imagine a world full of real complexes in which there are no appearances of anything. In this world, there are instances of the first kind of objectual truth, but no instances of the second kind. The first kind of objectual truth can exist independently of the second kind.

Alternatively, suppose that the world is constituted entirely of real simples, none of which predicatively belong in the real world to any of the others. In this world, there are no instances of the first kind of objectual truth. Yet it seems possible that, in this world, a real simple can generate an appearance that is an appearance of what that real simple is. If so, then the intensions of these definitions do not overlap. In which case, clause (ii) does not apply to these kinds of truth. Since the same reasoning applies in the case of the two kinds of objectual falsehood, it would be reasonable to conclude that clause (ii) does not apply to these kinds of truth and falsehood and, hence, the two kinds are discrete homonyms. Therefore, the first kind of objectual truth and the second kind of objectual truth are not core-dependent homonyms.

If a relation of core-dependent homonymy obtains between either kind of objectual truth and falsehood and the kinds of true and false persons, it is because the relevant objectual kind and the assertoric kind of truth and falsehood are so related. For, in discussing true and false persons, Aristotle explicitly relates this kind of truth and falsehood to the assertoric kind and to the second kind of objectual truth and falsehood. The passage reads as follows:

> A false man is one who readily and deliberately makes such statements, for the sake of doing so and for no other reason; and one who induces such statements in others—just as we call things false which induce a false impression.

The assertoric kind of truth and falsehood is a core kind on which the kinds of true and false persons depend. Other than by way of the assertoric kind of truth and falsehood, there seems to be no connection between the objectual kinds of truth and falsehood and the kinds of true and false persons. However, if a kind of objectual truth and falsehood is a core kind on which the assertoric kind of truth and falsehood depends, the kinds of true and false persons may depend in turn on that objectual kind of truth and falsehood.[22] Therefore, before it can be established one way or another, it is necessary first to consider the relationship between the two kinds of objectual truth and falsehood and the assertoric kind.

The first kind of objectual truth and falsehood and the assertoric kind of truth and falsehood are not discrete homonyms. Recall that the first kind of objectual truth and falsehood is defined as follows:

OF1: For all actual things x, y, and z, z is a false thing if, and only if, $z =$ (the real complex $y - x$).

OT1: For all actual things x, y, and z, z is a true thing if, and only if, $z =$ (the real complex $y + x$).

The definitions of true overlap with the definitions of objectual falsehood and truth insofar as they all make reference to the real combinations $y + x$ and $y - x$. As a consequence, the definitions of the two kinds of assertoric truth and falsehood overlap in part. Therefore, clause (ii) of CDHT is satisfied.

Prior to considering clause (iii) of CDHT, it will be useful first to evaluate clause (iv) with regard to the different kinds of truth and falsehood in question. Is the being true of a true assertion asymmetrically responsible for the being true of true thing (i.e., an instance of the first kind of objectual truth)? No. Not only do we have it on Aristotle's explicit authority that he doesn't think this is so,[23] but it is also evident from the definitions. On the one hand, the truth of a true thing of the kind in question is a matter of one thing predicatively belonging in the real world to another. In almost all cases, whether or not one thing predicatively belongs in the real world to another has nothing at all to do with the truth of assertoric truths.[24] On the other hand, the truth of a true assertion is a function of the intensional content of an assertion being appropriately correlated with its real correlate. If anything is clear about Aristotle's account of assertoric truth, it is that the truth of a true assertion asymmetrically depends upon its relevant real correlate, and *not* vice versa. Therefore, the truth of a true assertion is not asymmetrically responsible for the truth of a true thing of the first sort.

Is the truth of a true thing of the first kind asymmetrically responsible for the truth of a true assertion? Again, no. First, the fact that true assertions asymmetrically depend for their truth upon their real correlates *does not imply* that the truth of a true thing of the first kind is asymmetrically responsible for the truth of a true assertion. This is implied only if the relevant real correlate of a true assertion is a true thing of the first kind. Often it is not. For, and second, with regard to every true denial, the truth of a true thing of the first kind is not asymmetrically responsible for the truth of the true denial. In fact, with regard to every denial, the falsehood of a false thing is asymmetrically responsible for the truth of a true denial. True things of the first kind have nothing to do with the truth of true denials. Therefore, in general, it cannot be the case that a true thing's being true is asymmetrically responsible for a true assertion's being true. In addition, third, in the case of every true definition, the truth of a true thing of the first kind is not asymmetrically responsible for the truth of a true definition. Not only are true things of the first kind irrelevant to the truth of definitions, but also the falsehood of false things of the first kind is irrelevant. Unlike denials, the falsehood of false things of the first kind has no relationship at all to the truth of a true definition.

It follows from the preceding that the truth of the first kind of objectual truth is not at all responsible for the truth of true denials and true definitions. *A fortiori*, the first kind of objectual truth is not asymmetrically responsible for the truth of these true assertions. Hence, the truth of the first kind of objectual truth is not asymmetrically responsible for the truth of true assertions. Much the same can be said about the relationship between the falsehood of the first kind of objectual falsehood and the falsehood of false assertions.

As a consequence, clause (iv) of CDHT fails however it is applied to the first kind of objectual truth and falsehood and the assertoric kind. Assertoric truth and falsehood and the first kind of objectual truth and falsehood are, therefore, not core-dependent homonyms according to CDHT. It is not necessary to investigate clause (iii) of CDHT in relation to these kinds.

Turning now to the relation between the second kind of objectual truth and falsehood and the assertoric kind of truth and falsehood, it is unclear whether or not they are discrete homonyms. As noted above, the second kind of objectual truth and falsehood is defined as follows:

> OF2: For any actual thing x, x is a false thing if, and only if, the appearance generated by x either (1) is not an appearance of what x is or (2) is an appearance of what is not.
>
> OT2: For any actual thing x, x is a true thing if, and only if, the appearance generated by x is an appearance of what x is.

Given Aristotle's language and examples in the passage, it is tempting to understand the relation between the appearances or impressions that are generated by the second kind of true and false thing and what those appearances are about in terms of assertoric truth and falsehood. According to him, the appearances generated by such things are not literally assertions. However, it is straightforward enough to extend the notion of assertion and interpret a dream or chiaroscuro as an assertion about some real correlate other than themselves. The idea that a dream or a painting is either true or false with regard to what it is apparently about (i.e., its seeming real correlate) would have been obvious to Aristotle's contemporaries and is familiar to us.

Extending the notion of assertion to the appearances generated by true and false things of the second kind is explicitly supported by Aristotle's claims about the second kind of true and false person discussed above. There, in responding to the problem raised in Plato's *Hippias Minor* at 365–75, he compares the appearances generated by the second kind of true and false thing with the false assertions induced in other people by the second kind of true and false person. Clearly this is intended to suggest that the appearances generated by the second kind of true and false thing are analogous to true and false assertions.

If one assumes that Aristotle understands the appearances, generated by the second kind of true and false thing, in terms of assertoric truth and falsehood, then these kinds of truth and falsehood are not discrete homonyms. Their definitions overlap in part. In order to understand the appearances involved in the definition of the second kind of objectual truth and falsehood, one needs to understand the nature of assertoric truth and falsehood. Therefore, clause (ii) of CDHT applies to them.

In addition, given that the second kind of objectual truth and falsehood is defined in terms of assertoric truth and falsehood, the truth and falsehood of the latter is asymmetrically responsible for the truth and falsehood of the former. Hence, clause (iv) of CDHT applies with respect to the relation between these kinds of truth and falsehood.

Lastly, it is possible to show that clause (iii) is also satisfied. The assertoric kind serves as the core kind on which the second kind of objectual truth and falsehood depends. The argument is similar to that given for the first kind of true and false person given above. It will suffice here to state the conclusions of the argument. A true assertion's being true is part of each of the four causes of a true thing$_2$'s being true. Given that assertoric truth is a core instance of being true, it is necessary that a true thing$_2$'s being true stands in these four causal relations to a true assertion's being true because the kinds of causal relation in which these two kinds of truth stand are *determinate* causal relations.

Conclusion

A number of the kinds of truth and falsehood presented by Aristotle in the *Metaphysics* are homonyms. In this chapter, I have shown that there is a systematic relationship among these homonymous kinds and that the assertoric kind is the "core" kind on which the others depend. The objectual kind of truth identified by Aristotle in Δ 29, and often taken to be the core kind of truth, is not fundamental to his system of homonyms.

In the next chapter, I consider Aristotle's claims about being true and being false in book E, chapter 4, and I interpret them in terms of the kind of truth that belongs to assertions. I argue that Aristotle explicitly identifies the genus of this kind of truth in E 4, specifying the genus in terms of his account of simple assertions and identifying the place of this kind of truth in his general metaphysical scheme.

Chapter 6

The Genus of Truth

In this chapter, I interpret Aristotle's claims in *Metaphysics* E 4 about truth and falsehood in terms of the uses of "being$_T$" and "non-being$_F$" explained at *Metaphysics* Δ 7, at 1017a31–35 and the nominal definitions of "truth" and "falsehood" in *Metaphysics* Γ 7, at 1011b26–27. My reading resolves a number of longstanding interpretive difficulties, improves upon recent alternatives, and opens up the possibility of a novel approach to interpreting *Metaphysics* Θ 10.

I argue that in *Metaphysics* E 4 Aristotle explicitly identifies the genus of his core kind of truth, the kind that belongs to assertions, and I explain the precise sense in which we ought to take Aristotle's claim in *Metaphysics* E 4, at 1028a1–3, that "being true is concerned with the remaining kind of being [substance] and does not indicate the existence of any extra nature of being."[1] He thus articulates the generic aspect of his real definition of the kind of truth that belongs to assertions and locates this kind of truth in his general metaphysical scheme.[2] In so doing Aristotle completes an important part of Stage 3 of his inquiry into the essence of his core kind of truth.

Identifying the Genus

At *Metaphysics* E 4.1027b18–19, Aristotle makes two related claims: "being" in the sense of being true and "not-being" in the sense of being false are about combination and separation,[3] and taken together, being true and being false are about the apportionment of a contradiction.[4] He then explains these assertions at 1027b19–25. The passage from 1027b18–25 reads as follows:

τὸ δὲ ὡς ἀληθὲς ὄν, καὶ μὴ ὂν ὡς ψεῦδος, ἐπειδὴ παρὰ σύνθεσίν ἐστι καὶ διαίρεσιν, τὸ δὲ σύνολον περὶ μερισμὸν ἀντιφάσεως (τὸ μὲν γὰρ ἀληθὲς τὴν κατάφασιν ἐπὶ τῷ συγκειμένῳ ἔχει τὴν δ' ἀπόφασιν ἐπὶ τῷ διῃρημένῳ, τὸ δὲ ψεῦδος τούτου τοῦ μερισμοῦ τὴν ἀντίφασιν· πῶς δὲ τὸ ἅμα ἢ τὸ χωρὶς νοεῖν συμβαίνει, ἄλλος λόγος, λέγω δὲ τὸ ἅμα καὶ τὸ χωρὶς ὥστε μὴ τὸ ἐφεξῆς ἀλλ' ἕν τι γίγνεσθαι).

But since that which is in the sense of being true, or is not in the sense of being false, depends on combination and separation, and truth and falsehood together are concerned with the apportionment of a contradiction (for truth has the affirmation in the case of what is compounded and the negation in the case of what is divided, while falsity has the contradictory of this apportionment—it is another question, how it happens that we think things together or apart; by "together" and "apart" I mean thinking them so that there is no succession in the thoughts but they become a unity). (trans., mine, following Ross)

Aristotle's reasoning in these lines may be understood as follows: With respect to a real combination $y + x$, being true is properly applied to the affirmation that asserts that $y + x$. With respect to a real division $y - x$, being true is properly applied to the denial that asserts that $y - x$. With respect to a real combination $y + x$, being false is properly applied to the denial that asserts that $y - x$. With respect to a real division $y - x$, being false is properly applied to the affirmation that asserts that $y + x$. Here, the first and second statements capture Aristotle's assertion at 1027b20–22 that "truth has the affirmation in the case of what is compounded and the denial in the case of what is divided." The second and third statements spell out his idea at 1027b22–23 that falsehood has the contradictory of this apportionment.

Interpreting the passage in terms of the definitions at *Metaphysics* Γ 7.1011b26–27, we can see how being-as-truth *has* ["ἔχει"] the affirmation in the case of what is compounded and *has* the denial in the case of what is divided, and the same with not-being-as-falsehood. In E 4, Aristotle is primarily concerned with mental assertions as opposed to linguistic assertions, but the discussion applies to the latter as well. As a consequence, Aristotle's reasoning in the passage corresponds with the following truth conditions:

> "Socrates is white" is true iff being-white belongs to Socrates.
>
> "Socrates is white" is false iff being-white does not belong to Socrates.
>
> "Socrates is not white" is true iff being-white does not belong to Socrates.
>
> "Socrates is not white" is false iff being-white belongs to Socrates.

At 1027b25–28, Aristotle shifts to a discussion of combination and separation in thought:

> οὐ γάρ ἐστι τὸ ψεῦδος καὶ τὸ ἀληθὲς ἐν τοῖς πράγμασιν, οἷον τὸ μὲν ἀγαθὸν ἀληθὲς τὸ δὲ κακὸν εὐθὺς ψεῦδος, ἀλλ' ἐν διανοίᾳ, περὶ δὲ τὰ ἁπλᾶ καὶ τὰ τί ἐστιν οὐδ' ἐν διανοίᾳ.
>
> For falsehood and truth are not in the things, as if the good were true and the bad straightaway false, but in thought, and with regard to simple things and the what-it-ises, not even in thought. (trans., Reeve)

In this passage, Aristotle makes the following substantive claims: Truth and falsehood are not in the actual things. Rather, truth and falsehood are in thought. It is important to note that the former claim explicitly rules out—and the latter implicitly rules out—the possibility that Aristotle is concerned with the true and false things discussed in Δ 29.[5]

Aristotle continues his discussion of combinations and separations in thought at 1027b29–33:

> ὅσα μὲν οὖν δεῖ θεωρῆσαι περὶ τὸ οὕτως ὂν καὶ μὴ ὄν, ὕστερον ἐπισκεπτέον· ἐπεὶ δὲ ἡ συμπλοκή ἐστιν καὶ ἡ διαίρεσις ἐν διανοίᾳ ἀλλ' οὐκ ἐν τοῖς πράγμασι, τὸ δ' οὕτως ὂν ἕτερον ὂν τῶν κυρίως (ἢ γὰρ τὸ τί ἐστιν ἢ ὅτι ποιὸν ἢ ὅτι ποσὸν ἤ τι ἄλλο συνάπτει ἢ ἀφαιρεῖ ἡ διάνοια), τὸ μὲν ὡς συμβεβηκὸς καὶ τὸ ὡς ἀληθὲς ὂν ἀφετέον.

> Since all this is so, what should be done to get a theoretical grasp on this way of being and not being must be investigated later. But since the connection and division are in thought and not in the objects, being in this way is a different thing from being in the full way (since thought joins or subtracts either the what-it-is or a quality or a quantity or whatever else it may be), being coincidentally and being as being true may be left aside. (trans., Reeve)

Here Aristotle reiterates his assertion that the sort of combination and separation involved in affirmations and denials are in the mind, and not in the actual things. Given his ontology, he does not and indeed *cannot* mean by this that there are no combinations and divisions among actual things. Rather, his point is that the combinations and divisions constituting mental assertions are not in actual things but in the mind. In other words, truth and falsehood, insofar as they are attributes of assertions, are *not* attributes of mind and language independent objects. They are attributes of assertions that involve conceptual combination and division. This is why he goes on to say at 1027b34–1028a1 that the cause of assertoric truth and falsehood is a certain affection of thought: Truth and falsehood are about such conceptual combinations and divisions insofar as they are related to their correlative real combinations and divisions. Thought connects or divides things in the various categories of being, which combinations and divisions constitute mental affirmations and denials and are either true or false in virtue of the way things in the various categories of being in fact are combined or divided. Hence, this sort of being (namely, true and false assertion) is different from the fundamental sort of being (namely, the being of the categories, which ultimately is explained in terms of substance). It is worth stressing here that Aristotle's claim at 1027b29–31 ought to be interpreted in light of his earlier claims in the passage about conceptual combinations and divisions.[6]

It is important at this point to digress briefly and discuss Aristotle's account of the intensional contents involves in mental assertions. Aristotle claims at *De Interpretatione* 1.16a6–8 that the affections of the psyche signified by spoken sounds are likenesses of real things in virtue of being like real things.[7] These affections of the soul are likenesses of the real things in the world in virtue of having the same qualities had by the real things in the world—there is some quality had by both the affection of the soul and some real thing with respect to which they are alike. Some crucial remarks in *De Anima* III about the role of mental images in our cognitive life make this clear. Having provisionally described imagination at *DA* 428a1–2 as "that in virtue of which we say that an image occurs to us," (trans., Hamlyn)[8] he proceeds to distinguish it from sense perception, belief, knowledge, or intellect, summarizing his findings at *DA* 428b30–429a4 as follows:

> εἰ οὖν μηθὲν ἄλλο ἔχει τὰ εἰρημένα ἢ φαντασία (τοῦτο δ' ἐστὶ τὸ λεχθέν), ἡ φαντασία ἂν εἴη κίνησις ὑπὸ τῆς αἰσθήσεως τῆς κατ' ἐνέργειαν γιγνομένη. ἐπεὶ δ' ἡ ὄψις μάλιστα αἴσθησίς ἐστι, καὶ τὸ ὄνομα ἀπὸ τοῦ φάους εἴληφεν, ὅτι ἄνευ φωτὸς οὐκ ἔστιν ἰδεῖν.

> If, then, nothing other than imagination has the features mentioned (and this is what was claimed), then imagination would be a motion effected by actual perception. Since sight is the principal sense, the name imagination (*phantasia*) was derived from light (*phaos*), because without light it is not possible to see. (trans., Shields)

Relating this passage to *DA* 428a1–2, we get the conception that imagination is a movement in the soul arising as a result of sense perceptions in virtue of which we say that an image occurs to us. These images play a central role in our cognitive life. Aristotle claims that the soul cannot think or contemplate without a mental image, and mental images are to the thinking soul what sense perceptions are to the perceiving soul (see *DA* 431a14–16, 431b6–8 and 432a7–14). As one cannot see without light, for Aristotle one cannot think without images.

This suggests that mental images are the intensional contents of acts of assertion.[9] Moreover, Aristotle believes that the mental images employed by the thinking soul are images of essences, necessary for but somehow distinct from acts of thought (see *DA* 431b2 and 432a7–14). Mental images are supposed to be like real things because both the images and the things have qualities in common. These qualities are the perceptible and intelligible qualities had by real things and represented by mental images. Further support and clarification of this view comes from *DA* III 8.431b26–432a6 where the perceiving soul and the thinking soul are said to *become* the various forms of real things, ranging from the forms which are dispositions and affections of perceptible objects to those spoken of in abstraction (such as the mathematical objects) to the forms of perceptible objects themselves.

The intensional contents of acts of assertion are, thus, likenesses of their real correlates in virtue of instantiating a perceptible or intelligible quality that is like a perceptible or intelligible quality instantiated by the real correlate. According to this view, Aristotle embraces a strong representational theory whereby intensional contents actually have the qualities possessed by the things in the world of which they are likenesses.[10]

Returning now to the main discussion, one might be tempted to read *Met.* E 4.1027b29–31 as supporting the bald claim that assertoric truth and falsehood *just are* conceptual combination and division. Aristotle explicitly rejects this reading by emphasizing the relationship between what is combined and divided in the psyche (images of beings in the world) and what is combined and divided in the world (beings in the various categories of substance).[11] The psyche combines or divides images of things in the various categories of being, which combinations and divisions of images constitute the cognitive content of assertions and are either true or false in virtue of the way things in the world are combined or divided.

Importantly, Aristotle tells us at 1027b28–29 that he will investigate later the nature of truth and falsehood as they relate to the simples and what-things-are. In short, he will discuss elsewhere assertoric truth and falsehood in the case of definitions. He appears to deny in *Met.* E 4 that that the concepts of assertoric truth and falsehood apply in the case of the simples and what-things-are, but this appearance is deceptive. In *Met.* Θ 10, Aristotle ramifies his account of assertoric truth and falsehood. It becomes clear that the concept of assertoric truth does apply in the case of definitions of simples, although not insofar as assertoric truth involves combination and separation of one thing and another. Aristotle also explains why the concept of assertoric falsehood fails to apply in such cases and, thus, why assertoric truth and falsehood do not *both* apply in such cases. However, in E 4 it remains an open question how Aristotle understands truth and falsehood in the case of simples.

The Category of the Genus of Truth

On the reading proposed here, Aristotle has warrant to talk about the use of "is" in *Met.* E 4, in terms of truth and falsehood. Someone might doubt this. Pearson (2005) has, for example. On the one hand, one might ask why Aristotle would tie an assertion that things are compounded to truth and an assertion that things are divided to falsity? First, he doesn't. He ties truth [a] to affirmations (which assert that some *y* belongs to some *x*) in the case that what they assert obtains (i.e., the relevant *y* belongs to the relevant *x*) and [b] to denials (which assert that some *y* does not belong to some *x*) in the case that what they assert obtains (i.e., the relevant *y* does not belong to the relevant *x*). He similarly ties falsehood to the contradictory of these. Second, Aristotle would not tie assertions that things are compounded to falsehood and assertions that things are divided to truth. Why? To do so would contradict the nominal definitions of assertoric of truth and falsehood at 1011b26–27 and—although this gets ahead of the argument—his real definitions based on them.

On the other hand, why does Aristotle speak of truth or falsity in the context of *Met*. E 4, at all? He does so because the passage is about assertoric truth and falsehood as commonly understood in *Met*. Γ 7 and developed in E 4. On the view defended here, the relations between assertions and real compounds just are truth and falsehood, as defined in *Met*. Γ 7.1011b26–27. The examples expressed by the biconditionals above are instances of the conceptions of truth and falsehood at 1011b26–27. The instances illustrate how truth and falsehood *are* by providing examples of the correlatives that constitute these instances of the relations of truth and falsehood. The relationships illustrate how the conceptions of truth and falsehood are exemplified in the case of simple assertions. Aristotle is thus indicating, by means of the relations, the *being* of truth and the *not-being* of falsehood defined at 1011b26–27. For him, the *being* of truth essentially involves an act of assertion and the realization of the real correlate of that act. Assertoric truth just *is* the actuality that obtains between an assertion and what makes it true.[12]

It is precisely because the relations introduced in the second sentence constitute truth and falsehood in the context of simple assertions *that* the relations can justify or explain the fact that truth and falsity depend on combination and separation and taken together concern the apportionment of contradiction. Aristotle is focusing on the conceptions of truth and falsehood defined at 1011b26–27, with a specific focus on simple assertions and their correlative real complexes. He is addressing truth and falsehood in the context of these relations. The relations he introduces in the second sentence explain why simple assertions depend on combination and separation. Taken together, truth, falsehood, combination, and separation concern the apportionment of contradiction.

It is possible that "is" and "is not" have two functions in the passage. On the one hand, one may think that they indicate that the statements in which they appear make truth claims. On the other hand, one may think that they make claims about whether an attribute belongs to a subject or not.[13] More specifically, following Pearson 2005, one may think that " 'is' asserts that y belongs to x and 'is not' asserts that y does not belong to x." Here, "x" stands for some real subject and the variable "y" stands for some real attribute. Thus, according to this thesis, the simple assertions "x is y" and "x is not y" would have the senses:

[Pi] "x is y" = df. It is the case that y belongs to x.

[Pii] "x is not y" = df. It is the case that y does not belong to x.

It will now be argued that the first proposed function of "is" and "is not" is not one of the functions Aristotle attributes to these terms.

First, it cannot be the function of "being" in the sense of truth introduced in *Met.* Δ 7. At 1017a31–32, he states that "is" indicates that a statement is true, whether in relation to an affirmation or a denial, and that "is not" indicates that a statement is false, whether in relation to an affirmation or a denial. Second, the proposed function does not seem to fit well with the relevant part of E 4. The analysis suffers from being divorced from Aristotle's claims in Δ 7. "Is$_T$" and "is not$_F$" are understood here in the senses of being-as-truth and not-being-as-falsehood in Δ 7. The proper analysis of simple assertions involving these senses of "is$_T$" and "is not$_F$" runs as follows:

i. "x is y is$_T$" = df. It is true that y and x are combined.

ii. "x is not y is$_T$" = df. It is true that y and x are divided.

iii. "x is y is not$_F$" = df. It is false that y and x are combined.

iv. "x is not y is not$_F$" = df. It is false that y and x are divided.

The fact that the very same assertions are susceptible to analyses in terms of being-as-truth and not-being-as-falsehood may seem untoward. However, it is entailed by Aristotle's explicit claim at 1017a31–33: " 'to be$_T$' and 'is$_T$' signify that a thing is true, and 'not to be$_F$' [and 'is not$_F$'] that it is not true but a falsehood, equally in the case of affirmation and of denial." The sense of 1027b18–25 conforms exactly to that of 1017a31ff. It is difficult to interpret the claim in terms of the proposed function.

In both *Met.* Δ 7 and E 4, on the view proposed here, "is" (used in the sense of being-as-truth) signifies that the assertion with which it is combined is true, and "is not" (used in the sense of not-being-as-falsehood) signifies that the assertion with which it is combined is false.

Turn now to the second function "is" and "is not" are supposed to have in assertions of the form "x is y" and "x is not y." According to this proposal, "is" asserts that y belongs to x and "is not" asserts that y does not belong to x. For Aristotle, the copular use of "is" does not assert that x belongs to y, nor does it make claims about states of affairs. Strictly speaking, "is" doesn't *assert* or *claim* anything—it signifies. Nor does the copular use of "is not" assert or claim that x does not belong to y. Rather, in the context of an assertion "x is y," "is" serves to signify that what is signified by "y" belongs to what is signified by "x," and in the context of an assertion "x is not y," "is not" signifies that what is signified by "y" belongs to what is signified by "x."

Aristotle certainly acknowledges a copulative function of "is." It indicates that what is signified by the predicate expression of an assertion belongs to what is signified by the subject expression of that assertion. Similarly, there is a copulative sense of "is not."[14] The question here is whether or not he identifies the copulative use with being-as-truth and not-being-as-falsehood in *Met.* E 4. The answer is "No." In E 4, he explicitly relates being-as-truth and not-being-as-falsehood to real combination and division. He does so by noting that [i] true affirmations are related to real combinations, [ii] true denials are related to real divisions, [iii] false affirmations are related to real divisions, and [iv] false denials are related to real combinations. In other words, he explains truth and falsehood in terms of assertions and what makes them true. (This, of course, makes it plain how he can justifiably speak of an "is" of truth and an "is not" of falsehood in E 4.)[15]

It is worthwhile to consider briefly the relationship between being true and coincidental being and being in-itself.[16] To begin with, it is important to emphasize the fact that Aristotle repeatedly differentiates coincidental being from being true. He nowhere suggests they might be the same. Why this is so is evident from what he says in *Met.* E 2–3? There he argues that there can be no science of coincidental being because it is defined as that which neither always, nor for the most part, is. Some assertoric truths and falsehoods are surely coincidental beings. Indeed, with one exception, it seems that no assertoric truth always or for the most part obtains, since almost every act of assertion comes into being and passes away within a short compass of time. According to Aristotle, however, there is at least one assertoric truth that always obtains: the truth realized by thought eternally thinking itself. Therefore, assertoric truth is not in general the same as coincidental being.

With respect to the being in-itself of the categories, Aristotle notes in E 4 that being true in the case of affirmations and denials is always a function of the rational part of the psyche, by means of acts of thought, combining or separating images of beings in the various categories themselves. Thus, the rational part of the psyche asserts, by means of images of beings in the world, that some being in some category belongs to another being in some category, or denies that some being in some category belongs to another being in some category. Being true itself, then, would seem to be a kind of relative. It obtains whenever the rational part of the psyche makes assertions about the beings in the world by means of affirmation and denials. In E 4, Aristotle defines being true in terms of, and distinguishes it from, being in-itself.

On the basis of the reading of E 4 defended here, and recognizing that Aristotle needs to complete his account of assertoric truth and falsehood at least with respect to definitions simples and what-things-are, we can revise the common conceptions of assertoric truth and falsehood as follows:

> For every linguistic or conceptual subject n that signifies or represents one and only one real subject x, for every linguistic or conceptual predicate d that signifies or represents one and only one real predicate y, for every linguistic or conceptual relation + that signifies or represents the real predicative relation of belonging to, and for every linguistic or conceptual relation − that signifies or represents the real predicative relation of not belonging to:
>
> [F] Falsehood is *for a psyche* either (a) to linguistically or mentally assert that $d + n$ and y does not belong to x or (b) to linguistically or mentally assert that $d - n$ and y belongs to x.
>
> [T] Truth is *for a psyche* either (a) to linguistically or mentally assert that $d + n$ and y belongs to x or (b) to linguistically or mentally assert that $d - n$ and y does not belong to x or

(c) to linguistically or mentally asserts that n is definitionally the same as d and $x = y$.

Here, emphasis is placed on Aristotle's explanation of the genus of assertoric truth and falsehood: acts of assertion by means of the rational part of the psyche about beings in the categories of being in-itself. Some of these mental acts constitute one species of assertoric truth and falsehood, namely, the species involving the combination and separation of concepts by means of affirmation and denial.

An Outstanding Problem: True Definitions of Essences

We can now see how the concepts of assertoric truth and falsehood inform Aristotle's account of sensible substance in the *Metaphysics* and help us to see how he solves an outstanding problem from his theory of definition in the *Analytics*. As was made clear in chapter 1 of this book, first principles are crucial to his conception of philosophical wisdom as well as to his account of comprehension and demonstrative knowledge. In chapters 2 and 3, his arguments in support of the common first principles—the logical principles shared by all the special sciences—were evaluated. In the *Posterior Analytics*, he explains that the first principles of the various special sciences are expressed through definitions. More precisely, the first principle of a science is a definition that provides an indemonstrable account of the essence of the subject matter of the science. Since one possesses a first principle only if one possesses a definition, any problem that threatens to undermine his theory of definition is a threat to the project of Aristotelian science.

That his analysis of sensible substance in *Met.* book Z gives rise to difficulties in connection with his theory of definition is well known. His attempt to reconcile his analysis of sensible substance with his theory of definition as presented in his other works, particularly the *Posterior Analytics*, leads him in the *Metaphysics* to reconsider his account of definitions that express indemonstrable essences. See, for example, 1030b4–23, 1031b18–22, 1037a17–20, 1037b8–27, 1038a28–30, 1038b6–15, and 1040b16–27.

It will be helpful to review the central claims in book Z about definitions that generate the problem. At 1029b29ff, he tells us that definitions are true assertions about essences; definitions are not assertions of one thing predicatively belonging to another; definitions are of metaphysically primary things. From 1030b3ff, it becomes clear that a definition is an assertion about one thing, where any of the proper senses of "one" is appropriate other than "oneness by continuity" and "oneness by coincidence." The real units denoted by true definitions are essences. He says as much at 1031a12ff, for example: It is obvious, then, that the definition is the formula of the essence, and that the essence belongs either only to substances, or especially and primarily and simply. At 1034a31ff, the importance of definitions for demonstrative knowledge in the special sciences is made apparent. Without definitions of essences, there can be no demonstrative knowledge of anything.

At 1034b20ff, the question of how the parts of a definition are related to the whole definition such that the various parts of the *definiens* form a unity is an outstanding question for Aristotle's theory of definition as presented in the *Posterior Analytics*, 93b35ff. His claims in the *Metaphysics* about the unity of the essences of sensible substances make this problem even more pressing. For example, see 1034b20ff.

To get at the fundamental problem as Aristotle understands it in Z, it will help to consider a reductio ad absurdum Aristotle constructs at end of Z.13. The relevant passage at 1039a15–23 reads as follows:

> εἰ γὰρ μήτε ἐκ τῶν καθόλου οἷόν τ' εἶναι μηδεμίαν οὐσίαν διὰ τὸ τοιόνδε ἀλλὰ μὴ τόδε τι σημαίνειν, μήτ' ἐξ οὐσιῶν ἐνδέχεται ἐντελεχείᾳ εἶναι μηδεμίαν οὐσίαν σύνθετον, ἀσύνθετον ἂν εἴη οὐσία πᾶσα, ὥστ' οὐδὲ λόγος ἂν εἴη οὐδεμιᾶς οὐσίας. ἀλλὰ μὴν δοκεῖ γε πᾶσι καὶ ἐλέχθη πάλαι ἢ μόνον οὐσίας εἶναι ὅρον ἢ μάλιστα· νῦν δ' οὐδὲ ταύτης. οὐδενὸς ἄρ' ἔσται ὁρισμός· ἢ τρόπον μέν τινα ἔσται τρόπον δέ τινα οὔ. δῆλον δ' ἔσται τὸ λεγόμενον ἐκ τῶν ὕστερον μᾶλλον.

> For if no substance whatsoever can be composed of universals because they signify such-and-such sort but not this something, and if also no substance can be actually composed of substances, then every substance would be incomposite, so that there could not even be an account of any substance whatsoever. But then it *seems* to everyone, and was stated long ago, that definition is either of substance only or of it most of all, whereas now it seems not even to be of it. So there will not be a definition of anything at all. Or else in one way there will be one, but in another way there will not. What is being said will be more clear on the basis of what comes later. (trans., Reeve)

The first feature of this passage worth noting is Aristotle's recognition that some of his assumptions concerning substance in the *Metaphysics* seem to entail that there can be no definition of substance. The second feature is that he claims that, at least in one sense of what he means by "definition," there can be a definition of substance, which he promises to make clear what he means by this in the sequel.

A preliminary reconstruction of the argument in the above passage reveals that the following premises apparently entail the claim that there can be no definition of substance: all substances are incomposite; all definitions are composite; all the parts of true definitions correspond to the parts of that of which they are definitions. Before explaining this reconstruction in some detail, it is necessary to state two general assumptions that will be made in evaluating the problem.

First, it is assumed in what follows that Aristotle's claims concerning definitions in the passage from Z 13 are to be understood in the sense of an indemonstrable account of the essence. He has already dismissed definitions of the matter (understood as indeterminate stuff), definitions of accidental compounds, and definitions of concrete particulars prior to Z 13. From the point of view of his theory of science, indemonstrable accounts of the essence are of particular importance. It is assumed, therefore, that the two competing conceptions of definition with which he concerns himself in resolving his problem are kinds of indemonstrable accounts of the essence.

Second, when he puzzles over the connection between definitions and substance in Z 13, it is assumed that he is concerned with the essences of sensible substances. He already has concluded that there can be no definitions of the matter (construed as indeterminate stuff) or of the concrete particular. He has argued that, prior to Z 13, the essence is substance in the primary sense of the term. Moreover, his claims in *Met.* books H, Θ, and I concerning both substance and definition concern the essences of sensible substances and the definitions of these, not those of indeterminate matter or of concrete particulars.

In virtue of these general assumptions, one may reformulate the three premises mentioned before as follows: all essences of sensible substances are incomposite; all definitions are composite; all the parts of true definitions correspond to the parts of the essences of which they are true definitions.

The first premise is presented in the passage from Z 13 as the conclusion of an argument which goes as follows: either an essence of a sensible substance can be composed of universals, or an essence of a sensible substance can be composed actually of substances, or every essence of a sensible substance is incomposite. Since no essence of a sensible substance can be composed of universals and no essence of a sensible substance can be composed actually of essences of sensible substances, every essence of a sensible substance is incomposite.

The second premise concerns definitions and asserts that all definitions have parts. This is a corollary of Aristotle's claim, made in various places, that all formulae have parts (see, e.g., *Metaphysics* 1034b20 and 1042a20). It is sufficient in this context to state that the parts of formulae and, hence, of definitions are nouns. All definitions are formulae of essences, and he states that the formula of the essence is the formula composed of the ultimate differentia and its primary genus (see, e.g., *Met.* 1038a5, 1038a19, and 1038a25). The ultimate differentia (e.g., "rational") and the primary genus (e.g., "animal") constitute the parts of the definition (in this case, the definition of man), and in what follows the terms "primary genus" and "ultimate differentiae" will be used to refer to these linguistic entities. Thus, definitions satisfy Aristotle's requirement that all formulae have parts, and one can restate the second premise to read "All definitions are composed of the ultimate differentia and its primary genus."

The third premise is directly supported by the following passage, at *Met.* E 1034b20ff, concerning definitions and formulae: "Since a definition is a formula, and every formula has parts; and since the formula is related to the thing in the same way as the part of the formula to the part of the thing, the question now arises; Must the formula of the parts be contained in the formula of the whole, or not?" (trans., Tredennick). This passage explains in full neither how formulae are related to the things of which they are formulae nor how the parts of formulae are related to the parts of things to which they refer. Aristotle does present here a compositional account of the latter relation whereby, insofar as formulae are related to things, so too the parts of formulae are related to the parts of things. Since the whole of the definition is related to the whole of the essence, the parts of the definition likewise refer to parts of the essence.

The most important point to emphasize here is that the problem hardly seems well motivated unless one accepts something like Aristotle's real definition of assertoric truth with respect to definitions. Recall his definition of assertoric truth:

> For every linguistic or conceptual subject n that signifies or represents one and only one real subject x, for every linguistic or conceptual predicate d that signifies or represents one and

only one real predicate y, for every linguistic or conceptual relation + that signifies or represents the real predicative relation of belonging to, and for every linguistic or conceptual relation − that signifies or represents the real predicative relation of not belonging to:

[F] Falsehood is for a psyche either (a) to linguistically or mentally assert that $d + n$ and y does not belong to x or (b) to linguistically or mentally assert that $d - n$ and y belongs to x.

[T] Truth is for a psyche either (a) to linguistically or mentally assert that $d + n$ and y belongs to x or (b) to linguistically or mentally assert that $d - n$ and y does not belong to x or (c) to linguistically or mentally asserts that n is definitionally the same as d and $x = y$.

Given the preceding, clause (c) of part [T] can now be reformulated to reflect the complexity involved in a *definiens* (i.e., every such *definiens* includes a term denoting the genus and a term denoting at least one differential characteristic of the species) and the putative simplicity of the essence denoted by the *definiens*:

(c) to linguistically or mentally asserts that n is definitionally the same as d and $x = y = s \otimes g$ (where s and g are, respectively, the species differential characteristic and the proximate generic characteristic that constitute the essence being defined, and where "$\otimes$" represents the fact that the unity of the species is different from the other kinds of predicative unity we have discussed thus far).

Were it not for the fact that clause (c) requires both that the real correlate of the definition be a real simple and that the intensional content expressed by the definition be a mental representation of that real simple, there would be no problem of the parts of the definition corresponding with the parts of the essence.

In *Met.* book H 6, Aristotle identifies the primary genus with matter and the ultimate differentia with form. The crucial passage comes at 1045a15. Aristotle claims in the passage that the essence of man is composed of a part that is matter and a part which is form. In book H, he develops his position that the essences of sensible substances involve a part which is matter [i.e., potentiality] and part which is form [i.e., actuality]; the case of man in the above quote is intended as an instance of this general claim. Without attempting here to explain the precise nature of the unity of the parts of a definition and the unity of the parts of an essence, book H strongly suggests that the nature of this unity is tied to Aristotle's account of unity and number (see, for example, 1043b27ff). As he did in *De Interpretatione*, he grounds the oneness of the definition in the oneness of the thing it signifies. The relationship between his account of assertoric truth, unity, and number will be addressed below.

Conclusion

In this chapter I argued that in *Met.* E 4 Aristotle identifies and specifies the genus of the kind of truth that belongs to assertion. His claims in E 4 about truth and falsehood were interpreted in terms of the veridical uses of "being$_T$" and "non-being$_F$," explained at *Met.* Δ 7.1017a31–35 and in terms of the nominal definitions of "truth" and "falsehood" in *Met.* Γ 7.1011b26–27. Interpreting E 4 in this way, we see that it serves to specify the genus of truth and falsehood—generically speaking, truth and falsehood are powers of the psyche to assert affirmations and denials about beings in the categories of being in-itself. My reading of *Metaphysics* E 4 opens up the possibility of a novel approach to interpreting *Metaphysics* Θ 10, an important and difficult text concerning truth and falsehood.

I also argued that Aristotle's account of his core kind of truth explains why definitions of the essences of sensible substances are problematic. Given his real definition of the kind of truth that belongs to asserted definitions and his hylomorphic account of sensible substance, he needs to explain how there can be a true semantically complex definition of a metaphysically simple essence. It was suggested that, in books Z and H of the *Metaphysics*, Aristotle uses his concepts of potential and actual being to explain how the essence of a sensible substance is at once simple and yet properly signified by a definition composed of a part signifies potential being and a part that signifies actual being. It was also noted that in books Z and H Aristotle apparently understands the oneness of a definition and the oneness of an essence in terms of the kind of oneness possessed by a number. Hence, on the one hand, in Z and H, Aristotle appears to solve various problems for his account of the definitions of essences, problems that are best understood in terms of the requirements imposed by Aristotle's definitions of true and false assertions. On the other hand, the interpretation defended in this section points to books Θ, I, M, and N insofar as these books provide insight into potential and actual being and the kind of oneness proper to numbers.

Chapter 7

The Activity of Truth

The nominal definition of "truth" presented in *Metaphysics* Γ 7.1011b26–27, the kind of truth that belongs to assertions that is addressed in *Metaphysics* Δ 7 and 29, and Aristotle's discussion in *Metaphysics* E 4 of the genus of this kind of truth all indicate the likely differential characteristics involved in Aristotle's real definition of his core kind of truth. In this chapter I argue that in *Metaphysics* book Θ Aristotle articulates the differential characteristics of the essence of truth, extending his real definition of truth to assertions about simples and essences. I thus resolve a longstanding worry concerning the relationship between Aristotle's account of assertoric truth and falsehood in *Metaphysics* Γ 7, and his account of the truth of simple thoughts in *Metaphysics* Θ 10 and *De Anima* III. I also show how the discussion in Θ 10 fits neatly into the overall discussion of power and activity in *Metaphysics* Θ 1–9 and argue that Θ 10 is best interpreted in terms of assertoric truth and falsehood and not in terms of an objectual conception of truth.

True Assertions about Simples

In E 4, at 1027b29, Aristotle had stated that he will consider the nature of being-as-truth elsewhere. He never explicitly indicated to us where he would undertake this investigation. Did he do so in *Metaphysics* Θ 10?[1] The proof that he does lies in how well Θ 10 illuminates the nature of being-as-truth.

Recall that at *De Interpretatione* 4 (17a1–7) Aristotle defines assertion as follows:

ἔστι δὲ λόγος ἅπας μὲν σημαντικός, οὐχ ὡς ὄργανον δέ, ἀλλ᾽ ὥσπερ εἴρηται κατὰ συνθήκην· ἀποφαντικὸς δὲ οὐ πᾶς, ἀλλ᾽ ἐν ᾧ τὸ ἀληθεύειν ἢ ψεύδεσθαι ὑπάρχει· οὐκ ἐν ἅπασι δὲ ὑπάρχει, οἷον ἡ εὐχὴ λόγος μέν, ἀλλ᾽ οὔτ᾽ ἀληθὴς οὔτε ψευδής. οἱ μὲν οὖν ἄλλοι ἀφείσθωσαν,—ῥητορικῆς γὰρ ἢ ποιητικῆς οἰκειοτέρα ἡ σκέψις,—ὁ δὲ ἀποφαντικὸς τῆς νῦν θεωρίας.

Every sentence is significant (not as a tool but, as we said, by convention), but not every sentence is an assertion, but only those in which there is truth or falsity. There is not truth or falsity in all sentences: a prayer is a sentence but is neither true nor false. The present investigation deals with assertion; the others we can dismiss, since consideration of them belongs rather to the study of rhetoric or poetry. (trans., mine, following Ackrill)

Here Aristotle appears to be concerned primarily with linguistic assertion. In *De Anima* III.430b26–30, Aristotle focuses on mental assertion:

ἔστι δ᾽ ἡ μὲν φάσις τι κατά τινος, ὥσπερ καὶ ἡ ἀπόφασις, καὶ ἀληθὴς ἢ ψευδὴς πᾶσα· ὁ δὲ νοῦς οὐ πᾶς, ἀλλ᾽ ὁ τοῦ τί ἐστι κατὰ τὸ τί ἦν εἶναι ἀληθής, καὶ οὐ τὶ κατὰ τινος· ἀλλ᾽ ὥσπερ τὸ ὁρᾶν †τοῦ ἰδίου ἀληθές, εἰ δ᾽ ἄνθρωπος τὸ λευκὸν† ἢ μή, οὐκ ἀληθὲς ἀεί, οὕτως ἔχει ὅσα ἄνευ ὕλης.

An affirmation involves one thing in relation to another, as is the case with denial, and is in every case either true or false. This is not always the case with thought: the thinking of the definition in the sense of what it is for something to be is never in error nor is it an assertion of one thing in relation to another; but, just as while the seeing of the special object of sight can never be in error, seeing whether the white object is a man or not may be mistaken, so too in the case of objects which are without matter. (trans., mine, following Smith)

Aristotle's definition of truth applies to both linguistic and mental assertions. Both sorts of assertions are true or false in virtue of asserting either (i) of what is that it is, (ii) of what is not that it is not, (iii) of what is that it is not, or (iv) of what is not that it is. Aristotle has yet to explain how he understands these essential differential characteristics of truth and falsehood in terms of the ontology he has developed in the preceding books of the treatise.

Having established generically how assertoric truth and falsehood relate to both categorical being and being *per accidens* in E 2–4, and having developed his account of categorial being in books Z and H, it remains for him to explain how it is possible to assert of what is that it is, of what is not that it is not, of what is that it is not, and of what is not that it is. Part of this explanation requires Aristotle's distinction between potential being and actual being. All of these issues lead us to consider *Metaphysics* Θ 10.

Truth involves both an objectual dimension (what the assertion is about) and a subjective dimension (the psychological activity of asserting intensional contents). Aristotle addresses both dimensions in *Met.* Θ 10. He discusses combinations and divisions of beings in the categories and the mental assertions associated with these combinations and division, and he discusses simple beings and the mental assertions associated with these. The whole of Θ 10 should be seen as an explication of the differential characteristics of the kind of truth and falsehood that belong to assertions.

If *Met.* Θ 10 develops ideas about truth introduced but set aside in *Met.* E 4, one encounters two immediate interpretive difficulties. First, recall that in E 4, at 1027b25–29, Aristotle distinguishes between the sense of "being" that applies to combinations and divisions in thought from the sense that applies to things in the categories:

> οὐ γάρ ἐστι τὸ ψεῦδος καὶ τὸ ἀληθὲς ἐν τοῖς πράγμασιν, οἷον τὸ μὲν ἀγαθὸν ἀληθὲς τὸ δὲ κακὸν εὐθὺς ψεῦδος, ἀλλ' ἐν διανοίᾳ, περὶ δὲ τὰ ἁπλᾶ καὶ τὰ τί ἐστιν οὐδ' ἐν διανοίᾳ.

> For falsehood and truth are not in objects, as if the good were true and the bad were immediately false, but in thought, and with regard to simple items and the "what it is's" [sic] they are not even in thought—then what needs to be considered about what "is" and "is not" in this sense must be investigated later, [. . .] (trans. Crivelli)

But in Θ 10, at 1051b17–1052a4, he claims:

> Then in connection with the incomposites, what is it to be or not to be and what is truth and falsity? [. . .] There is truth

or falsity in the following way, to make contact and to state is the truth (for affirmation and stating are not the same) while to be ignorant is not to make contact. (trans., Makin)

If in using "the incomposites" [τὰ ἀσύνθετα] at 1051b17and "the simple items and the what it is" [τὰ ἁπλᾶ καὶ τὰ τί ἐστιν] at 1027b27–28, Aristotle has in mind the same things, then it would appear that he is contradicting himself, asserting and denying that thoughts about simple things are neither true nor false.[2]

Crivelli (2004, 64) has offered a way out of this first difficulty. First, as *Met.* Θ 10, and *De Anima* III 6, make clear, thoughts concerning simple items are only true and cannot be false. Second, one can interpret *Met.* E 4, at 1027b27–28 as the claim that truth and falsehood are not *both* present in thoughts concerning simple items, although truth is present. Hence, the clash between E 4, at 1027b27–28 and Θ 10, and *De Anima* book III 6 is only apparent. The first premise is correct, but we ought to reject the second. 1027b27–28 is best understood as the claim that, in the case of simple items, neither truth nor falsehood *understood in terms of combination and division* exist even in thought. Aristotle is stressing the fact that, with respect to simple items, there is absolutely no combination or division, not even in thought. This leaves it open for him to claim in Θ 10 that thoughts about simples can be true, even though they do not involve any sort of combination or division which amounts to asserting that, in Θ 10, simple items are thought by means of intuitive thought [νόησις] and not by means of discursive thought [διάνοια]. Hence, in the case of simple items, it seems best to interpret 1027b27–28 as making the claim that *discursive* thought [διάνοια] has no application.

Turning now to the second interpretive difficulty, recall that in *Met.* E 4, at 1027b29–33, Aristotle distinguishes between the sense of "being" that applies to combinations and divisions in thought from the sense that applies to things in the categories. But in *Met.* Θ 10, at 1051a34–b2, he apparently distinguishes among three senses of "being" and "non-being." Now if, in the phrases "the strictest sense of being true or false" [τὸ δὲ κυριώτατα ὂν ἀληθὲς ἢ ψεῦδος] at 1051b1–2 and "the sense of being differs from the strict sense of being" [τὸ δ' οὕτως ὂν ἕτερον ὂν τῶν κυρίως] at 1027b31, he has in mind the same sense of "being," again he would appear to contradict himself, both asserting and denying that the strict sense of "being" signifies the attribute of being true.

The standard argument—see, for example, Crivelli (2004, 234ff.)—is straightforward for thinking that "the strictest sense of being true or false" at *Met.* Θ 10.1051b1–2 is problematic. At *Met.* E 4.1027b31, Aristotle claims that "being" in the sense of "being true" is different from "being" in the strict [κυρίως] sense. At 1051b1, he claims that the strictest sense of "being" is the sense of "being true." At *Met.* E 4.1027b31, he refers to 1051b1, and at *De Anima* 412b8–9, he claims that the strict sense of "unity and being" is the sense of "being actual." Therefore, with respect to the strict sense of "being," 1051b1 is inconsistent with 1027b31 and with what his claims at *De Anima* 412b8–9. Hence, either he contradicts himself, or the text at 1051b1–2 must be emended.

Crivelli (2004, 234ff.) has proposed to resolve this second difficulty in two steps. First, he argues that the phrase, "the strictest sense of being true or false" at 1051b1–2, should be translated by "being true or false in the strictest sense." Whereas he thinks the phrase, "the sense of being differs from the strict sense of being" at 1027b31, has the sense of " 'being true' differs from the strict sense of 'being.' " In addition, he argues that being in the strictest sense true or false at 1051b1–2 is an attribute of objects, whereas the sense of "being true or false" at 1027b31 is an attribute of thoughts. Second, Crivelli rejects the usual reading of 1027b31, arguing that "κυριώτατα ὂν ἀληθὲς ἢ ψεῦδος" should be interpreted as a single clause "by being in the strictest sense true or false." Crivelli notes that, even though Aristotle is distinguishing among various senses of "being" in the passage, the adjective "κυριώτατα" modifies "being" and may well be taken as modifying "being true or false."

A review of Aristotle's reasoning is appropriate here. In the first place, he goes on in the chapter to dilate on the different modes of being true or false. In the second place, the taking "ὄν" in "ὂν ἀληθὲς ἢ ψεῦδος" to modify "ἀληθὲς ἢ ψεῦδος" parallels the structure of the preceding clauses in which the other senses of "ὄν" are characterized with using the term. In using the single clause "being in the strictest sense true or false," he is making a claim about the strictest sense of "being true or false." He does not claim that "being" in the sense of "being true" is the strictest sense of "being." Hence, the standard argument for thinking that "the strictest sense of being true or false" at 1051b1–2 is problematic is incorrect. Whereas the phrase "τὸ δὲ κυριώτατα ὂν ἀληθὲς ἢ ψεῦδος" at 1051b1–2 is a claim about the strictest sense of "being true or false," " 'ὁ δ' " οὕτως ὂν ἕτερον ὂν τῶν κυρίως" at 1027b31 is a claim about the strict sense of "being," and the apparent conflict between *Met.* E 4 and Θ 10 is resolved.

If Aristotle picks up in Θ 10 the discussion left off in E 4, it is reasonable to assume that "τὸ οὕτως ὂν καὶ μὴ ὄν" means "what 'is' in the sense of being true and 'what is not' in the sense of being false."[3] Thus, at 1027b28–29 he notes that he will discuss in the sequel what "is" in the sense of being true and what "is not" in the sense of being false.[4] At 1051b2–17, he claims that:

> τοῦτο δ' ἐπὶ τῶν πραγμάτων ἐστὶ τῷ συγκεῖσθαι ἢ διῃρῆσθαι, ὥστε ἀληθεύει μὲν ὁ τὸ διῃρημένον οἰόμενος διῃρῆσθαι καὶ τὸ συγκείμενον συγκεῖσθαι, ἔψευσται δὲ ὁ ἐναντίως ἔχων ἢ τὰ πράγματα, πότ' ἔστιν ἢ οὐκ ἔστι τὸ ἀληθὲς λεγόμενον ἢ ψεῦδος; τοῦτο γὰρ σκεπτέον τί λέγομεν. οὐ γὰρ διὰ τὸ ἡμᾶς οἴεσθαι ἀληθῶς σε λευκὸν εἶναι εἶ σὺ λευκός, ἀλλὰ διὰ τὸ σὲ εἶναι λευκὸν ἡμεῖς οἱ φάντες τοῦτο ἀληθεύομεν. εἰ δὴ τὰ μὲν ἀεὶ σύγκειται καὶ ἀδύνατα διαιρεθῆναι, τὰ δ' ἀεὶ διῄρηται καὶ ἀδύνατα συντεθῆναι, τὰ δ' ἐνδέχεται τἀναντία, τὸ μὲν εἶναί ἐστι τὸ συγκεῖσθαι καὶ ἓν εἶναι, τὸ δὲ μὴ εἶναι τὸ μὴ συγκεῖσθαι ἀλλὰ πλείω εἶναι· περὶ μὲν οὖν τὰ ἐνδεχόμενα ἡ αὐτὴ γίγνεται ψευδὴς καὶ ἀληθὴς δόξα καὶ ὁ λόγος ὁ αὐτός, καὶ ἐνδέχεται ὁτὲ μὲν ἀληθεύειν ὁτὲ δὲ ψεύδεσθαι· περὶ δὲ τὰ ἀδύνατα ἄλλως ἔχειν οὐ γίγνεται ὁτὲ μὲν ἀληθὲς ὁτὲ δὲ ψεῦδος, ἀλλ' ἀεὶ ταὐτὰ ἀληθῆ καὶ ψευδῆ.

> If some things are always combined and it is impossible for them to be divided, and others are always divided and it is impossible for them to be combined, and yet others can be either of the opposites, then on the one hand to be is to be combined and to be one, while on the other not to be is not to be combined but to be more; and therefore in connection with those which can be either of the opposites the same belief and the same statement come to be both false and true, and someone can at one time speak the truth and at another time speak falsely. (trans., Makin)

Aristotle is asserting, with respect to things in the various categories that can be combined or divided, that for such things to be is to be combined and not to be is not to be combined.[5] For example, with respect to the pair of things, Socrates and being white, to be is to be combined and one thing (that is, being-white belongs to Socrates) and not to be is not to be combined, but many things (that is, being-white does not belong to Socrates). The passage may be understood as follows: Truth and falsehood with respect to things is being combined or separated (1051b2–3). To think the separated to be separated and the combined to be combined is to have the truth. To think the separated to be combined and the combined to be separated is to have the false (1051b3–5).[6] It is not because we think truly that F*a* that F*a* is the case (1051b6–8).[7] It is because F*a* is the case that we who say F*a* say what is true (1051b8–9). Being is being combined and one. (1051b11–12) Not being is being not combined but more than one (1051b12–13). Regarding what is capable of both combination and separation, the same opinion or the same statement comes to be false and true (1051b13–14). Regarding what is capable of both combination and separation, it is possible at one time to have the truth and at another time to have falsehood (1051b14–15). Regarding what cannot be otherwise, the same opinion or the same statement does not come to be true at one time and false at another time (1051b15–16). Regarding what cannot be otherwise, the same opinion or the same statement is always true or always false (1051b15–16). It is clear on this reading that Aristotle is concerned with the kind of truth that belongs to assertions, and not the objectual conception in *Metaphysics* Δ 29.[8]

The passage provides important information about one set of differential characteristics concerning assertoric truth, those having to do with affirmations and denials. It is already clear from *Metaphysics* E 4, that some "atomic" assertions involve asserting that one thing belongs to another (i.e., affirmations) or that one thing does not belong to another (i.e., denials). The chief innovation here is the emphasis on temporality. Sometimes what one asserts is true, sometimes what one asserts is false, and some assertions are always true or always false, while others are sometimes true and sometimes false. Aristotle clarifies how he understands the real correlates of such assertions, both in terms of their modal status and in terms of unity and plurality. In some cases, two things y and x are always combined in the real world and, hence, always form a real unity. This can be because y always belongs to x, or because x always belongs to y, or because both always belong to each other. In other cases, two things are always separated in the real world and, hence, always constitute a real plurality. In such cases, neither ever belongs to other and vice versa. In yet other cases, two things are sometimes combined and sometimes separated; they are sometimes unified and sometimes a plurality.

It is now possible to articulate the truth conditions for both sorts of simple assertions (affirmations and denials). Suppose for the following that n signifies or represents one and only one being x, that d represents one and only one being y, that + signifies or represents the real relation of belonging to, and that − signifies or represents the real relation not belonging to:

- To assert $d + n$ when $y + x$, is true.
- To assert $d − n$ when $y − x$, is true.
- To assert $d + n$ when $y − x$, is false.
- To assert $d − n$ when $y + x$, is false.
- If it is always the case that $y + x$, then it is always true to assert $d + n$ and it is always false to assert $d − n$.
- If it is always the case that $y − x$, then it is always true to assert $d − n$ and it is always false to assert $d + n$.

Before developing this further, it will be useful first to return to the main line of argument. At *Met.* Θ 10.1051b17–25, Aristotle claims that:

περὶ δὲ δὴ τὰ ἀσύνθετα τί τὸ εἶναι ἢ μὴ εἶναι καὶ τὸ ἀληθὲς καὶ τὸ ψεῦδος; οὐ γάρ ἐστι σύνθετον, ὥστε εἶναι μὲν ὅταν συγκέηται, μὴ εἶναι δὲ ἐὰν διῃρημένον ᾖ, ὥσπερ τὸ λευκὸν <τὸ> ξύλον ἢ τὸ ἀσύμμετρον τὴν διάμετρον· οὐδὲ τὸ ἀληθὲς καὶ τὸ ψεῦδος ὁμοίως ἔτι ὑπάρ- ξει καὶ ἐπ' ἐκείνων. ἢ ὥσπερ οὐδὲ τὸ ἀληθὲς ἐπὶ τούτων τὸ αὐτό, οὕτως οὐδὲ τὸ εἶναι, ἀλλ' ἔστι τὸ μὲν ἀληθὲς ἢ ψεῦδος, τὸ μὲν θιγεῖν καὶ φάναι ἀληθές (οὐ γὰρ ταὐτὸ κατάφασις καὶ φάσις), τὸ δ' ἀγνοεῖν μὴ θιγγάνειν.

Then in connection with the incomposites, what is it to be or not to be and what is truth and falsity? For it is not composite in this case, to that they would be when put together and not be when separated, as it is in the case of the wood being white or the diagonal being incommensurable; nor will truth and falsity still obtain in the same way as in those cases. Rather, just as truth is not the same as regards these, so too neither is to be [the same as regards incomposites]; instead there is truth or falsity in the following way, to make contact and to state is truth (for affirmation and stating are not the same), while to be ignorant is not to make contact. (trans., Makin)

As with 1051b9–15, it is best to interpret "to be" and "not to be" here in terms of the things in the figures of the categories, and to take "true" and "false" in the sense that applies to assertions.⁹ Thus, Aristotle's example of wood being white involves a substance combined with a quality, and his example of the diagonal being incommensurable involves two quantities.

How, though, should we understand his claim at Θ 10.1051b17–25 that truth and falsehood are present with regard to incomposites? On the one hand, he claims that assertions about incomposites are true *and* false in a way different from assertions about real combinations and separations. Whereas the latter are true and false because the assertoric combinations and separations in thought track those in the world, the former are true by virtue of "contact and assertion" [τὸ θιγεῖν καὶ φάναι] and false because of "ignorance and lack of contact" [τὸ ἀγνοεῖν μὴ θιγγάνειν]. He is contrasting the mode of assertoric truth with regard to incomposites, described in terms of assertoric contact, with the mode of assertoric falsehood in such cases, which he explains in terms of a lack of assertoric contact or ignorance. Therefore, it is plausible that he extends the strictest sense of "truth" and "falsehood" to include true and false assertions about incomposites, since they are like true and false assertions about composites insofar as both are kinds of assertoric truth conforming to the common philosophical conception of assertoric truth.

On the other hand, Aristotle may wish to differentiate the two sorts, introducing a sense of "truth" that denotes truth about incomposites by virtue of assertoric contact, and explaining it on the basis of the strictest sense. One might adopt this approach because one thinks that he rejects assertoric falsehood in the case of assertions about incomposites. Textual evidence for this may be found at 1051b33–35:

> τὸ δὲ εἶναι ὡς τὸ ἀληθές, καὶ τὸ μὴ εἶναι τὸ ὡς τὸ ψεῦδος, ἓν μέν ἐστιν, εἰ σύγκειται, ἀληθές, τὸ δ' εἰ μὴ σύγκειται, ψεῦδος· τὸ δὲ ἕν, εἴπερ ὄν, οὕτως ἐστίν, εἰ δὲ μὴ οὕτως, οὐκ ἔστιν· τὸ δὲ ἀληθὲς τὸ νοεῖν ταῦτα· τὸ δὲ ψεῦδος οὐκ ἔστιν, οὐδὲ ἀπάτη, ἀλλὰ ἄγνοια.

> Being as what is true, and non-being as what is false, on the one hand one is, if combined, true, on the other hand, if not combined, false; yet again, the one, if it is, thus it is; and again

if not thus, it isn't. And truth is to think these. And there is no falsehood, nor any mistake, but ignorance. (trans., mine)

If Aristotle's claim that "there is no falsehood" is meant to include all sorts of falsehood, and this certainly seems to be the thrust of similar claims made in *De Anima* III 6, then it seems clear that there is no falsehood in cases of assertions about incomposites.

All things considered, however, the inclusive reading seems preferable. First, his question at *Met.* Θ 10.1051b5–6—"This being so, when is what is called truth and falsity present, and when is it not? We must consider what we mean by these terms?"—signals the fact that, although he has introduced the strictest sense of "truth" and "falsehood" in terms of affirmations and denials, the full extent of the strictest sense is not yet clear. Θ 10, as I understand it, is devoted to completing his real definition of assertoric truth and falsehood. Part of what Aristotle does is incorporate into this definition his account of assertions about incomposites, as promised in E 4. As a consequence, one need not think that *Met.* Θ 10.1051b1–5 rules out including assertions about incomposites in the scope of the strictest sense. Nor need one infer from the fact that he denies one can be in error [ἀπατηθῆναι] with regard to incomposites that he denies assertions about incomposites can be false. Denying that one can be in error is best understood as a claim about the impossibility of approximating the truth in the case of assertions about incomposites, which approximation he thinks is indeed impossible. (Fleshing out this claim requires developing Aristotle's account of measurement and error, discussed in the next chapter.) Moreover, he clearly thinks that there is some sense in which claims about incomposites are false, since as we saw above, at 1051b21–25, Aristotle is explicit that *both* truth and falsity will be present in the case of assertions about incomposites, just not in the same way as in the case of assertions about composites and separations. Moreover, he identifies the mode of assertoric falsehood by means of which assertions about incomposites are to be understood: assertions about incomposites are false when the assertion fails to make contact, rendering us ignorant.[10]

Looking more closely at 1051b33–35, we see that the passage is a complicated discussion of the homonymous kinds of truth and falsehood recognized by Aristotle. First, it is plausible, following Ross and Crivelli, that Aristotle is referring to true and false things, and in the sense he discussed in Δ 29, at 1024b17–26. At 1051b33–35 he augments his discussion in Δ 29, which explicitly deals only with false composite things involving composition, with the claim that a true simple thing exists as simple thing and a false simple thing does not exist. Read this way, he is claiming that a true composite thing involves the combination of its constituent things, a false composite thing involves the division of its constituent things, a true simple thing exists as a simple thing, and a false simple thing doesn't exist at all. The point is to make clear, first, that a thought about a true simple object is true by virtue of its object existing. Second, a thought about a false simple object is a thought about nothing at all. Hence, it is not false in the sense having to do with combinations and separations, not mistaken because merely approximately true, but false in the sense of sheer ignorance. In other words, it is false because there is a total lack of assertoric contact.

Suppose, then, that 1051b23–33 is about true and false things as well as true and false assertions. True things are either composite or simple. In the former case, two things are combined. In the latter case, a simple thing exists. False things are either composite or simple. In the former case, two things are divided. In the latter case, the simple thing doesn't exist. Understanding things this way, affirmations are true in virtue of objectually true composite things, and false in virtue of objectually false composite things. Negations are true in virtue of objectually false composite things and false in virtue of objectually true composite things. A thought about a simple thing is true in virtue of assertoric contact with that existing simple thing. A thought about a putative but nonexistent simple thing is false because such a thought has no assertoric contact with anything.

The Core Kind of Truth *Redux*

I explained in the last chapter why we ought to interpret Aristotle's claims in *Metaphysics* E 4 in terms of the nominal definitions of truth and falsehood in *Metaphysics* Γ 7, at 1011b26–27. Thus far in this chapter I have interpreted *Metaphysics* Θ 10 in terms of assertoric truth and falsehood. I have argued that Aristotle completes his exposition of the real definitions of assertoric truth and falsehood in Θ 10, articulating their differentiae, and I have shown how he extends his conception of assertoric truth to assertions about simples and that he is not concerned primarily with an objectual conception of truth in Θ 10.

The apparently different kinds of assertoric truth discussed by Aristotle in *Met.* Δ 29, E 4, and Θ 10 are in fact synonymous kinds. That is to say, each of these kinds of assertoric truth is both denoted by the term "truth" and by the same definition of the term "truth." The kinds denoted by his real definitions of assertoric truth and falsehood and the nominal definitions of assertoric truth and falsehood are best understood as synonyms, even though there is a sense in which they can plausibly be called homonyms.

Aristotle's real definitions of assertoric truth and falsehood, developed in books E–Θ, are related ancestrally to the nominal definitions of assertoric truth and falsehood explicitly stated in Γ 7 and are tied to Aristotle's theory of being in Δ 7. It is necessary to consider more carefully how the various kinds of assertoric truth and falsehood in Γ 7, Δ 7, E 4, and Θ 10 are related. I will now establish that Aristotle explicitly takes the kind of assertoric truth and falsehood denoted by his real definitions to be the most fundamental.

Following Crivelli, it was argued above that whereas the phrase "τὸ δὲ κυριώτατα ὂν ἀληθὲς ἢ ψεῦδος" at 1051b1–2 is a claim about the strictest sense of "being true or false," "τὸ δ' οὕτως ὂν ἕτερον ὂν τῶν κυρίως" at 1027b31 is a claim about the strict sense of "being."[11] The apparent conflict between E 4 and Θ 10 is thereby resolved. However, granting this approach to interpreting the phrases "τὸ δὲ κυριώτατα ὂν ἀληθὲς ἢ ψεῦδος" at 1051b1–2 and "τὸ δ' οὕτως ὂν ἕτερον ὂν τῶν κυρίως" at 1027b31, another interpretive difficulty is generated.

According to Crivelli, on the one hand, the strict sense of "being true" in *Metaphysics* Θ 10 signifies an attribute of objects.[12] On the other hand, according to Crivelli, the sense of "being true" at E 4.1027b31 signifies an attribute of thoughts. Hence, the kind of truth signified by "being true," in its strict sense, is not the kind of truth signified by "being true" at 1027b31. Indeed, as Crivelli notes, the kind of truth at 1051b1–2 does not even entail the kind of truth signified by "being true" at 1027b31. Crivelli thinks that Aristotle appeals to the strict sense of "being true" in defining the sense of "being true" at 1027b31 and, therefore, that "being true" in its strict sense is the most fundamental sense of "being true" in Aristotle's theory of truth. Crivelli provides the definitions he has in mind:

> In an affirmative predicative belief a state of affairs is thought "to be" in the sense of being true. The belief is true (false) when and only when this state of affairs in fact "is" in the sense of being true ("is not" in the sense of being false).

In a negative predicative belief a state of affairs is thought "not to be" in the sense of being false. The belief is true (false) when and only when this state of affairs in fact "is not" in the sense of being false ("is" in the sense of being true).

According to Crivelli, the strict sense of "being true" is a "theoretical construct" introduced to set up a better theory of truth. Citing Modrak, Crivelli argues that this may be why, in Δ 29, Aristotle mentions neither false beliefs nor false assertions but false objects, which latter are appealed to in the definition of the two former.

As was shown in the previous chapter, Aristotle does *not* work with a sense of "being true" at 1051b1–2 that signifies an attribute of objects.[13] Rather, at 1051b1–2, Aristotle employs the same sense of "being true" that he uses at 1027b31—namely, the semantic sense defined at 1011b26–27. Call the sense of "being true" at 1051b1–2 "the strictest sense" and the sense of "being true" at 1027b31 "the common philosophical sense." Understood this way, one can interpret the passage at 1050a34–1051b6 as follows:

Ἐπεὶ δὲ τὸ ὂν λέγεται καὶ τὸ μὴ ὂν τὸ μὲν κατὰ τὰ σχήματα τῶν κατηγοριῶν, τὸ δὲ κατὰ δύναμιν ἢ ἐνέργειαν τούτων ἢ τἀναντία, τὸ δὲ [κυριώτατα ὂν] ἀληθὲς ἢ ψεῦδος, τοῦτο δ' ἐπὶ τῶν πραγμάτων ἐστὶ τῷ συγκεῖσθαι ἢ διῃρῆσθαι, ὥστε ἀληθεύει μὲν ὁ τὸ διῃρημένον οἰόμενος διῃρῆσθαι καὶ τὸ συγκείμενον συγκεῖσθαι, ἔψευσται δὲ ὁ ἐναντίως ἔχων ἢ τὰ πράγματα.

The terms "being" and "non-being" are employed first with reference to the categories, and second with reference to the potentiality and actuality of these and their opposites, while being true and being false, in the strictest sense, occur when beings are combined or separated so that he who thinks the separated to be separated and the combined to be combined has the truth, while he whose thought is in a state contrary to that of the beings is in error. (trans., Makin)

Read in this way, the rest of Θ 10 is best interpreted as an explanation of how Aristotle understands assertoric truth and falsehood in terms of categorial being and the being of potentiality and actuality, an explanation that yields his real definition of the strictest sense of "truth" and "falsehood."[14]

On the reading of Θ 10 urged here, the strictest sense of truth is the assertoric sense. One might think that the precise claim at 1051b1–5 is that the strictest sense of "truth" and "falsehood" is the sense in which affirmations and negations are true and false. On this reading, Aristotle limits the strictest sense to assertions involving assertoric combination and separation. Thus interpreted, he would leave aside those assertions that do not involve assertoric combination or separation, namely those assertions that are definitions of simples. As was argued in the previous chapter, however, the appearance of a limitation is misleading. Aristotle includes assertions about incomposites as instances of his real definition of assertoric truth and, hence, his real definitions have unrestricted scope over all simple assertions.[15]

As a consequence of these arguments, it is reasonable to infer that Aristotle's real definitions of assertoric truth and falsehood—his definitions of "the strictest sense of truth and falsehood"—denote the core kind of truth and falsehood on which other kinds of truth and falsehood depend. This claim is corroborated by the system of homonymous kinds of truth and falsehood introduced by Aristotle in Δ 29 and discussed previously in chapter 6.

A brief summary of the arguments made in chapter 6 may be helpful. First, the various kinds of truth distinguished by Aristotle in Δ 29—the two kinds of true and false persons, the two kinds of objectual truth and falsehood, and the assertoric kind of truth and falsehood are homonymous kinds of truth and falsehood—are not synonyms. Second, both kinds of true and false persons are defined in terms of assertoric truth and falsehood. Third, the kind of assertoric truth and falsehood presented by Aristotle in Δ 29 is the same as the kind denoted by the nominal definitions of assertoric truth and falsehood in Γ 7 and Δ 7; in other words, the kinds of assertoric truth and falsehood presented in Δ 29, Γ 7 and Δ 7 are synonyms. Fourth, I argued that the kind of assertoric truth and falsehood denoted is the core kind on which the other kinds in Δ 29 depend. We have just seen that in Θ 10 Aristotle explicitly claims that the use of "truth" and "falsehood" denoting the assertoric kind of truth and falsehood defined in E 4 and Θ 10 is the strictest use of the terms "truth" and "falsehood."

I will now consider the relationship between the kind of assertoric truth and falsehood denoted by Aristotle's real definitions in *Met.* E 4 and Θ 10 and the kind denoted by the nominal definitions of assertoric truth and falsehood in *Met.* Δ 29, Γ 7 and Δ 7. I have argued that Aristotle presents the following nominal definitions of "truth" and "falsehood":

> (Nominal Definitions of Falsehood and Truth "NFT'") For every linguistic or conceptual subject n that signifies or represents one and only one real subject x, for every linguistic or conceptual predicate d that signifies or represents one and only one real predicate y, for every linguistic or conceptual relation + that signifies or represents the real predicative relation of belonging to, and for every linguistic or conceptual relation − that signifies or represents the real predicative relation of not belonging to:
>
> [F] Falsehood, in the case of a simple assertion, is either (a) to linguistically or mentally assert that $d + n$ and y does not belong to x or (b) to linguistically or mentally assert that $d - n$ and y belongs to x.
>
> [T] Truth, in the case of a simple assertion, is either (a) to linguistically or mentally assert that $d + n$ and y belongs to x or (b) to linguistically or mentally assert that $d - n$ and y does not belong to x.

I have argued that Aristotle develops his real definitions on the basis of these nominal definitions and in the light of his account of assertions, intensional contents, and correlates in the real world. These developments are reflected in (RFT):

> (Real Definitions of Falsehood and Truth "RFT") For every linguistic or conceptual subject n that signifies or represents one and only one real subject x, for every linguistic or conceptual predicate d that signifies or represents one and only one real predicate y, for every linguistic or conceptual relation + that signifies or represents the real predicative relation of belonging to, and for every linguistic or conceptual relation − that signifies or represents the real predicative relation of not belonging to:
>
> [F] Falsehood is for a psyche either (a) to linguistically or mentally assert at time t that $d + n$ and y does not belong to x

at time t or (b) to linguistically or mentally assert at time t that d-n and y belongs to x at time t or (c) to linguistically or mentally assert at time t that n is definitionally the same as d and the simple thing $x = y$ does not exist at time t.

[T] Truth is for a psyche either (a) to linguistically or mentally assert at time t that $d + n$ and y belongs to x at time t or (b) to linguistically or mentally assert at time t that $d - n$ and y does not belong to x at time t or (c) to linguistically or mentally assert at time t that n is definitionally the same as d and $x = y = s \otimes g$ at time t (where s and g are, respectively, the species differential characteristic, i.e., the form or actuality, and the proximate generic characteristic, i.e., the matter or potentiality, that constitute the essence being defined, and where "$\otimes$" represents the fact that the unity of the form and matter is different from the other kinds of predicative unity).

If these arguments are sound, then the nominal definitions overlap at least in part with the real definitions. This is because the concepts involved in the *definientia* of Aristotle's real definitions are specifications of the concepts involved in the *definientia* of the definitions of the nominal philosophical concepts.

Whether one thinks that the kinds denoted by Aristotle's real definitions and those denoted by the nominal definitions are synonyms depends, in part, on how one understands the relationship between nominal and real definitions. The relationship between nominal and real definitions is complicated. This is not the place to argue about the alternative approaches to Aristotle's account of nominal and real definitions. However, something more can be said.

The nominal and the real definitions denote either synonymous kinds of assertoric truth and falsehood or homonymous kinds. In the first case, the assertoric kind of truth and falsehood denoted by both is the core kind of truth and falsehood among the associated homonyms Aristotle recognizes. In the second case, the question is left open as to which of the two kinds of assertoric truth and falsehood is the core kind, the kind denoted by Aristotle's real definitions or the kind denoted by the definitions of the common concepts. In either case, one or the other kind of assertoric truth and falsehood is the core kind of truth and falsehood in Aristotle's system.

There is an argument available to Aristotle by means of which he can show that the kinds denoted by his real definitions are the core kinds on which the kinds denoted by the nominal definitions depend. This argument is independent of his theory of definition.

First, there is a clear sense in which RFT subsume NFT as a special case. Aristotle's contemporaries may have explained assertions, intensional contents, and real correlates in ways essentially different from the ways in which Aristotle explains these phenomena. These alternative ways in which the nominal definitions may be specified by Aristotle's contemporaries would constitute alternative definitions of assertoric truth and falsehood. These alternative definitions and Aristotle's own definitions would all be specifications consistent with, and subsumed by, the nominal definitions. Another way of putting this point is that the logical extension of NFT is included in the logical extension of RFT.

Second, that said, suppose Aristotle is correct in thinking that RFT denotes the essences of assertoric truth and falsehood. Then, insofar as NFT denotes true and false assertions, they denote all and only those denoted by RFT. NFT must denote all those denoted by RFT for the reasons given in the prior paragraph. NFT must denote only those true and false assertions denoted by RFT because, other than these—on the assumption that Aristotle's real definitions in fact denote all and only true and false assertions—there simply are no other true and false assertions.

Third, if one supposes that Aristotle is correct in thinking that RFT denotes the essences of assertoric truth and falsehood, then there is a sense in which the being true of true assertions and the being false of false assertions as defined by RFT, are asymmetrically responsible for the being true and the being false of true and false assertions as defined by NFT. By our supposition, it is because the true and false assertions denoted by RFT are true and false that the true and false assertions denoted by NFT are true and false.

The converse claims do not hold. It is axiomatic for Aristotle that fully determinate actualized natural kinds are metaphysically fundamental.[16] RFT articulates fully what must be actualized in order to have fully determinate instances of true and false assertions. NFT falls short of this mark, articulating only generic and more fully determinable characteristics of true and false assertions. According to Aristotle, for the same reason that the existence of primary substances is asymmetrically responsible for the existence of their generic and differential characteristic, the truth of true assertions denoted by RFT is asymmetrically responsible for the truth of those denoted by NFT. Unless all of the differential characteristics of a true assertion are realized, there is no actual true assertion, only a potentially true assertion. The same reasoning applies to in the case of false assertions. NFT signifies generic characteristics of true and false assertions. It does not express the specific and fully determinate differential characteristics that must be realized in order for a true or false assertion to be actualized. As a consequence, it is reasonable to conclude that the truth and falsehood of the fully determinate kinds denoted by the RFT are asymmetrically responsible for the truth and falsehood of the determinable kinds denoted by the generic NFT. Clause (iv) of CDHT is, thus, satisfied with regard to these homonymous kinds. Recall CDHT:

> (CDHT) A kind of truth d and c are *homonymously kinds of being true in a core-dependent way* iff (i) d and c have their name in common, (ii) their definitions overlap, but not completely, and (iii) necessarily, if c is a core instance of being true, then d's being true stands in one of the four causal relations to c's being true, and (iv) c's being true is asymmetrically responsible for the existence of d's being true.

Again, assuming that RFT denotes the core kinds of truth and falsehood, and assuming that they denote the essences of assertoric truth and falsehood, we can also show that the truth and falsehood of the kinds denoted by NFT necessarily stand in at least one of the four causal relations. As a consequence, clause (iii) of CDHT is satisfied.

Given this argument and the arguments in the preceding sections, it is reasonable to conclude that the kinds denoted by Aristotle's real definition RFT are the core kinds of truth and falsehood on which the kinds denoted by the nominal definitions depend.

The Power and Activity of Truth

I have argued that the kinds of assertoric truth and falsehood denoted by Aristotle's real definitions are the core kinds on which all the other homonymous kinds depend. We saw in this and the last chapter that the concepts of power and activity inform an accurate interpretation of the real definitions of assertoric truth and falsehood presented in *Met.* Θ 10. If, as Aristotle argues in *Met.* books Z, H, and Θ, the essence of a substance is identical with its matter and form, the matter is understood in terms of power, and the form in terms of activity, then truth and falsehood are species of the power and activity of mental assertion.[17]

In *Metaphysics* Θ 1–9 Aristotle analyzes his concepts of power and activity and uses them to explain the nature of the cognitive activities that essentially involve assertoric truth and falsehood.[18] If we read Θ 1–9 and Θ 10 in each other's light—an approach to Θ often neglected but suggested by Jaeger 1934, 262n3—we deepen our understanding of Aristotle's account of the essence of truth and falsehood.

It is common for recent commentators to think that Θ 10 is exogenous to the rest of book Θ.[19] Focusing as it does on truth and falsehood, Θ 10 appears to be an outlier in an otherwise well focused discussion of potentiality and actuality in book Θ.[20] Following Burnyeat and others, we might conclude that it is implausible "to try and link Θ 10 as a whole to the theme of potentiality and actuality . . . ,"[21] and we might think it best to sever the two parts.

Met. Θ 1–9 and Θ 10 are, I think, more closely related than is usually thought. In defense of my reading, I will consider first reasons for thinking that Θ 1–9 and Θ 10 are not thematically linked. Then I defend the relatively weak claim that throughout much of Θ 1–9 Aristotle's discussion of potential and actual being crucially depends upon his account of truth and falsehood. Finally, I argue that there is a strong case for thinking that each chapter of Θ 1–9 involves claims that bear directly on Aristotle's account of truth and falsehood in Θ 10. As a consequence, Θ 10 as a whole can and should be linked to the discussion of potential and actual being in Θ 1–9.

Seeing the connection between *Met.* Θ 1–9 and Θ 10 is important because, on the one hand, for Aristotle, truth and falsehood are kinds of complete activities—namely, they are the exclusive and exhaustive kinds of the complete psychological activity of assertion. In Θ 10, Aristotle describes the nature of these kinds of complete activities, differentiating between true and false assertions about composites and true and false assertions about incomposites. Thus, the discussion in Θ 1–9 concerning potentialities, incomplete activities, and complete activities—the most extensive such discussion in the corpus—directly informs Aristotle's account of truth and falsehood in Θ 10. On the other hand, Aristotle thinks that the various kinds of true and false assertion discussed in Θ 10 serve as the clearest and, perhaps, the most important examples of complete activity, using the different kinds of psychological capacities for true and false assertion throughout Θ 1–9 to exemplify and explain the differences among powers, incomplete activities, and complete activities. Thus, the discussion of truth and falsehood in Θ 10—again, arguably, the most extensive discussion of these topics in the corpus—directly informs the account of potential and actual being in Θ 1–9.

Why might one ignore Θ 10 in thinking about book Θ 1–9? I take it that the following sort of argument for ignoring Θ 10 is seriously problematic: There is evidence Θ 10 was appended to the rest of Θ. Hence, Θ 10 is not a part of the original Θ. Therefore, the project pursued in Θ 10 is not related to the project pursued in the rest of Θ. So far as I can tell, there isn't much solid evidence that someone other than Aristotle appended Θ 10 to the rest of Θ, and if Aristotle himself appended Θ 10 to the rest of Θ, then the argument is weakened considerably: there is a perfectly good sense in which Θ 10 is really a part of book Θ, if Aristotle himself added it. Indeed, Aristotle appending Θ 10 to the rest of Θ would serve as strong prima facie evidence in favor of the claim that the project he is pursuing in Θ 10 is related to what he had to say in the rest of Θ.

Supposing, though, that someone other than Aristotle added Θ 10 to the rest of Θ, would this, by itself, entail that the project pursued in Θ 10 is not related to the project pursued in the rest of Θ? No. For it may be that the rest of Θ was put together by an editor other than Aristotle, and if so, then even if Θ 1–9 was put together by editors before Θ 10 was added to it, Θ 1–9 may have no greater claim to thematic unity than Θ 1–10. But suppose that Θ 1–9 constitute a suitably original and thematically unified Θ and Θ 10 was appended to it. (I'm not at all sure about this. Insofar as I have doubts about the relationship between Θ 10 and Θ 1–9, I also have doubts about the relationship among the parts of Θ 1–9. Claims about an original Θ seem to me to be underdetermined by the available evidence.) The inference from there being an original and unified Θ which did not include Θ 10 to the conclusion that Θ 1–9 and Θ 10 are thematically heterogenous is nevertheless fallacious—the projects pursued in 1–9 and 10 may be related.[22]

In the end, only a close reading comparing *Met*. Θ 1–9 and Θ 10 provides adequate reasons for thinking that the subject matter in Θ 10 is related or unrelated to the rest of Θ. There are however (and this is true even on a not so close reading of Θ) quite apparent textual grounds for thinking that Θ 1–9 and Θ 10 are thematically unrelated. In the first place, Θ 1–9 quite clearly focuses on the nature of potentiality and actuality, whereas Θ 10 focuses on truth and falsehood, and these distinct foci are quite emphatically articulated—Aristotle announces the topic of potential and actual being at the beginning of Θ 1, which topic quite obviously dominates Θ 1–9, and then again he announces the topic of truth and falsehood at the beginning of Θ 10. And then there is his seeming lack of interest in truth and falsehood in Θ 1–9 and his at best muted claims in Θ.10 about potentiality and actuality. Add to this the fact that, in Θ 1.1046a4–9, Aristotle reminds us of his discussion of the different senses of potentiality in *Met.* Δ 12, apparently with the express purpose of dismissing the sense of potentiality defined there from 1019b21–32 in terms of truth and falsehood. In so doing, he seems to explicitly set aside an interest in truth and falsehood in discussing potentiality and actuality.

I accept that Θ 1–9 focuses on the nature of power and activity and that Θ 10 focuses on truth and falsehood. I grant that these distinct foci are quite emphatically articulated. In what follows, however, I aim to diminish our sense that Aristotle is not interested in truth and falsehood in Θ 1–9. More importantly, I demonstrate that Aristotle's discussion of truth and falsehood in Θ 10 is informed by Aristotle's claims about potentiality and actuality in Θ 1–9, so much so that it is difficult to imagine how we might make sense of Θ 10 independently of Θ 1–9.

No one doubts that Θ 10 is about truth and falsehood. Aristotle reminds us at 1051a34–b2 that one of the ways in which "being" and "non-being" are used is to denote truth and falsehood. From 1051b2–17 Aristotle explains the nature of truth and falsehood when we make assertions about composite objects. Then, from 1051b17–33, Aristotle explains the nature of truth and falsehood when we make assertions about incomposite objects. At 1051b33–1052a4, Aristotle relates his discussion thus far in Θ 10 to his discussion of truth and falsehood in *Met.* Δ 29 and E 4. Last, at 1052a4–14, Aristotle concludes Θ 10 with a discussion of assertions about unchanging objects.[23] Aristotle is, thus, focused exclusively on the nature of truth and falsehood throughout Θ 10.

There are prima facie reasons for thinking that, in Θ 10, Aristotle is concerned to develop his account of truth and falsehood in light of his discussion of power and activity in Θ 1–9. To begin with, in addressing truth and falsehood in the case of assertions about composite objects, and having rehearsed his familiar account of truth and falsehood for simple assertions, Aristotle asks *when* simple assertions are true or false. He develops his answer in terms of possible and impossible combinations and divisions. Whereas Aristotle's earlier discussions of truth and falsehood in *Met.* Γ 7, Δ 7, Δ 29, and E 4 were focused solely on synchronic cases of simple assertions, he here extends the earlier discussion to the diachronic cases using distinctions he has made in Θ 3–4.

Second, in considering truth and falsehood in the case of assertions about incomposite objects, Aristotle explains incomposite objects in terms of power and activity. The distinction Aristotle makes here between existing as a power and existing in activity refers us to his discussion of power, incomplete activity, and complete activity in Θ 5–7.

Third, having explained incomposite objects in terms of power and activity, Aristotle now focuses on the nature of truth and falsehood in cases where we are thinking about such objects. Here Aristotle distinguishes between an ignorance that is like blindness and an ignorance that differs from blindness. This distinction depends upon, or is at least illuminated by, Aristotle's discussion of potentiality and privation in Θ 1–2: In Θ 1, Aristotle explains the different sorts of privation in terms of potentiality. In Θ 2, Aristotle explains how the same account can be applied by a rational power to both the thing itself and its primary privation (i.e., its contrary).

Fourth, the last part of Θ 10 focuses on unchanging objects, whether composite or incomposite. Aristotle ends his discussion of truth and falsehood by asking when thoughts about unchanging objects are true or false. The notion of an unchanging object is best understood in terms of the distinctions made in Θ 1–9 among powers, incomplete activities, and complete activities. In addition, Aristotle's examples of truths about unchanging mathematical objects refers us back to his discussion of the relationship between the activity of thought and the activity of mathematical relations in Θ 9.

All of this suggests that there is a stronger connection between Θ 10 and Θ 1–9 than the received view admits. I will now argue that, without exception, each chapter of Θ 1–9 develops or, at least, exemplifies the distinctions among potentialities, incomplete activities, and complete activities in terms of nonrational and rational powers. It may not be obvious how demonstrating that fact effectively ties the distinctions between potentiality and actuality to Aristotle's account of truth and falsehood. Recall, however, that the distinction between nonrational and rational powers just is the distinction between powers essentially involving the power to assert what is true or false and powers that do not involve the power to assert what is true or false.

Our discussion in chapter 1 of *Metaphysics* A.1 revealed that Aristotle referred us to his discussion of rational powers in *Nicomachean Ethics* VI.3, where he lists at 1139b15 the five ways "the soul possesses truth by way of affirmation and denial." These five ways of possessing the truth by way of affirmation and denial are, again: art, demonstrative knowledge, practical wisdom, philosophical wisdom, and comprehension. Each of these kinds of cognition and, hence, both the productive and theoretical rational activities essentially involve the soul possessing truth by means of acts of assertion. Given the importance of the arts in Θ 1–9, it is worth stressing that, according to Aristotle in the *Nicomachean Ethics* VI.1140a20–23, art in general is defined in terms of true and false accounts:

ἡ μὲν οὖν τέχνη, ὥσπερ εἴρηται, ἕξις τις μετὰ λόγου ἀληθοῦς ποιητική ἐστιν, ἡ δ' ἀτεχνία τοὐναντίον μετὰ λόγου ψευδοῦς ποιητικὴ ἕξις, περὶ τὸ ἐνδεχόμενον ἄλλως ἔχειν.

Art, then, as has been said, is a state concerned with making, involving a true account, and lack of art on the contrary is a state concerned with making, involving a false account; both are concerned with what can be otherwise. (trans., mine)

Theoretical activity is also discussed in *Met.* Θ 1–9. It follows from all of this that, insofar as each chapter of Θ 1–9 develops or exemplifies the distinctions among potentialites, incomplete activities, and complete activities in terms of rational potentialities and activities, Aristotle is thereby indicating the importance of these distinctions for his account of truth and falsehood.

Nor does this seem to be an accidental feature of Aristotle's discussion: it seems that Θ 1–9 is driven by a need to understand rational activities, in particular, and hence activities essentially involving truth and falsehood. This is borne out in each of the chapters.

There are two passages in Θ 1 that bear directly on whether or not there is a tie between the topic of potential and actual being and truth and falsehood.[24] The first is Aristotle's aforementioned reference at 1046a4–9 to the discussion of potentiality in *Met.* Δ 12. There, at 1019b21–35, he dismisses the sense of "potentiality" and "possibility," relates directly to truth and falsehood, and again in Θ 1, at 1045b27, Aristotle states explicitly that he will ignore this senses in Θ. This would appear to be damaging evidence, but in fact I don't think it is too damaging. I will return to this point. The second passage that bears on truth and falsehood comes at 1046b26–28 where Aristotle uses the examples of heat (a nonrational power) and the art of building (a rational power) to explain the sort of power found in an agent to act on something else. While merely examples and at best obliquely related to truth and falsehood, viewed with an eye to the larger context, the examples point to a distinction that is fundamentally important in Θ.

Of note here, also, is the claim in Θ 1 that the strictest sense of potentiality is not the most useful for Aristotle's present purposes.[25] What are those purposes? Arguably Aristotle is principally concerned to discuss the sorts of potentiality and actuality manifested by the sorts of form/matter compounds discussed at length in books Z and H and the sorts of rational powers and activities that Aristotle has yet to explain adequately elsewhere in terms of potentiality and actuality. Aristotle's discussion of powers and activities in the *Physics*, while perhaps sufficient for an account of powers and incomplete activities (i.e., movements), is not adequate to explain the nature either of form/matter compounds or the complete activities of rational potentialities. Similarly, Aristotle's analyses of the different senses of "power" in *Met.* Δ 12 leave form/matter compounds and the specifically rational powers and activities unexplained.

Now turning to Θ 2, Aristotle takes pains to distinguish nonrational from rational capacities, explaining in particular and at length that rational capacities can produce opposites while nonrational capacities cannot (at least not in the same way, see Aristotle's caveat in Θ 8). Throughout, Aristotle's claims turn on his claim that a rational capacity is a capacity for change that is accompanied by a λόγος. In the context of Θ 2, Aristotle is using of λόγος is the sense of a true or false account, what he elsewhere calls a λόγος ἀποφαντικος. This use makes the best sense of each of the four ways Aristotle uses the term λόγος in Θ 2.

Aristotle explains in Θ 3 how it is possible to retain rational capacities involving assertion when not employing them. There are many fascinating questions raised by Aristotle's attack on the Megarian position. Here I wish only to highlight the fact that Aristotle develops his first argument against the Megaric position in terms of the potentiality and actuality of the arts (using the art of building as an example of these) and of the perceptual organs.

Θ 4 divides into two main arguments. One has to do with the pair of claims "this is capable of being but will not be" and "there is nothing incapable of being." The other argument relates to the modal claim "If (if A is, then it is necessary that B is), then (if A is possible, then it is necessary that B is possible)." At the end of the first argument, Aristotle explicitly addresses the relation between falsehood and impossibility, claiming that falsehood is not the same as impossibility. Aristotle here clearly connects his discussion of possibility and impossibility to a concern with truth and falsehood.

Aristotle returns in Θ 5 to the question raised in Θ 2 about how a rational capacity can cause opposite results. Here he argues that, in addition to the fact that all such capacities involve a λόγος that serves as the basis for producing opposite results, there must be something else that decides which of these opposites will actually be produced. Again, the most plausible way to understand λόγος in the context of Θ 5 is that Aristotle is using it to denote a linguistic or mental assertion.

Aristotle explains the difference between incomplete actualities and complete actualities in Θ 6. Many of the examples Aristotle gives of complete actualities are cognitive activities that essentially involve true assertions. Θ 7 focuses on when a thing has potential and when it does not. Aristotle provides a general explanation of how thought has the potential to produce a result, using the art of medicine as his example of such a potentiality of thought.

Aristotle explains in Θ 8 how what is actual is prior to what is potential. It bears on the topic of truth and falsehood in a variety of ways. First, the discussion of priority in knowledge and in λόγος requires an understanding of Aristotle's account of truth and falsehood. Second, depending on how we understand the nature of the unmoved mover, it may be that the claims here about the priority in time and becoming of the unmoved mover has bearing on Aristotle's account of truth and falsehood. Third, Aristotle's claims about becoming an artist or a scientist have presuppose an account of how we acquire of true and false assertions. Fourth, the account of the substantial priority of actuality in relation to potentiality relates to the actuality of thought and, hence, to truth in the case of human and divine life. So does the claim about imperishable things that exist actually and without potentiality as such.

In Θ 9, Aristotle explains why actuality is better than a good potentiality, and how it is that thinking makes certain sorts of potential mathematical constructions actual. Aristotle's argument for why actuality is better than a good potentiality reverts to his claims in Θ 2 and 5 about capacities to produce opposites and, thus, implicitly makes reference to the distinction between rational and nonrational capacities. His claims about mathematical actualities make it evident that it is by means of the activity of thought that the potentially existing mathematical entities become actual.

I have so far made the case that we if read Θ 1–9 through truth-tinted glasses, we can see that Aristotle is concerned throughout to tie his claims about potentiality and actuality to his distinction between rational and nonrational capacities and, hence, to the distinction between capacities for different kinds of true and false assertions. I will now defend the more demanding thesis that the concepts and arguments developed in Θ 1–9 are propaedeutic to Aristotle's account of the activity of assertoric truth in Θ 10. I will do this by way of reverse-engineering—analyzing Θ 1–10 as if it were a unified whole with Θ 10 as its *terminus ad quem*, to see how, were that true, Θ 10 would be related plausibly to Θ 1–9.

To begin, then, the introduction to Θ 10 serves as a transition from the discussion of powers and activities to the topic of truth and falsehood. From 1051b2–5, Aristotle recapitulates the truth conditions for simple assertions familiar from his earlier discussions of truth and falsehood. He then poses a question at 1051b5–6 about the diachronic truth conditions for simple assertions about composite objects: When do truth or falsehood exist or not exist? After reminding us of his familiar truth-maker condition at 1051b6–9, Aristotle explains at 1051b9–17 that the same opinion or account (i.e., how the same mental or linguistic assertion) about a contingent composite object can be true at one time and false at another time but that an opinion about a composite object that cannot be otherwise is always either true or false.

Aristotle's earlier discussions of truth and falsehood in *Met.* Γ 7, Δ 7, Δ 29, and E 4 were focused solely on synchronic cases of combination and division. It is already clear from these earlier passages that some "atomic" assertions involve asserting that one thing belongs to another (i.e., affirmations) or that one thing does not belong to another (i.e., denials). The chief innovation in Θ 10 is the emphasis on temporality. Sometimes what one asserts is true, sometimes what one asserts is false, and some assertions are always true or always false, while others are sometimes true and sometimes false. Aristotle clarifies how he understands the real correlates of such assertions, both in terms of their modal status and in terms of unity and plurality. His claims here rely upon the distinctions he has made in Θ 3–4.

Aristotle's claims in Θ 3 bear on his discussion of the diachronic truth conditions of simple assertions in three major ways. First, Aristotle takes on the Megaric claim that something has a given power to be F only when it is F in activity. Aristotle develops his refutation of the Megaric position in terms of the rational powers and activities of the arts (using the art of building as an example of these) and of the perceptual organs. Second, Aristotle demonstrates that the Megaric view undermines the possibility of movement and becoming. In so doing, he elaborates on how something can be actually combined or separated and also have the power not to be so combined or separated and also how it is possible for something not actually combined or not actually separated to have the power to be combined or separated. Third, Aristotle clarifies to some extent how composite objects that do not exist except in the mind can be said to have the power to exist. Similarly, in Θ 4, Aristotle explores some of the consequences of the view developed in Θ 3, explicitly addressing the relationship between assertoric falsehood and impossibility. I think the claims in Θ 4 are best understood in terms of combinatorial possibilities and impossibilities, on the one hand, and the entailment relations among assertions about such combinations.

Although I cannot make the full case here, I propose that the obscurity of the arguments in Θ 4 is lessened if we read them in light of the account of truth and falsehood in Θ 10. I would also venture here to say that in Θ 3 and 4 Aristotle provides us with evidence that the sense of possibility and impossibility directly related to claims about truth and falsehood in *Met.* Δ 12 are relevant to his discussion of potentiality and actuality in Θ, even if they are homonymously related to the core notion of potentiality. And this is in spite of Aristotle's apparent dismissal of this sense as homonymous—the senses of the possible and impossible having to do with determinate truth and falsehood are, I submit, the senses in play in Θ 3 and 4.

At *Met.* Θ 10.1051b17–33 Aristotle turns to the case of incomposite objects. Aristotle explains incomposite objects in terms of potentiality and actuality. The distinction Aristotle makes here between existing potentially and existing actually refers us to his discussion of potentiality, incomplete actuality, and complete actuality in Θ 5–7. Although all of Θ 5–7 is germane, the discussion of actuality in Θ 6 is most obviously crucial. Aristotle there differentiates between incomplete and complete activities from 1048b18–36:

Ἐπεὶ δὲ τῶν πράξεων ὧν ἔστι πέρας οὐδεμία τέλος ἀλλὰ τῶν περὶ τὸ τέλος, οἷον τὸ ἰσχναίνειν ἢ ἰσχνασία [αὐτό], αὐτὰ δὲ ὅταν ἰσχναίνῃ οὕτως ἐστὶν ἐν κινήσει, μὴ ὑπάρχοντα ὧν ἕνεκα ἡ κίνησις, οὐκ ἔστι ταῦτα πρᾶξις ἢ οὐ τελεία γε (οὐ γὰρ τέλος)· ἀλλ' ἐκείνη <ᾗ> ἐνυπάρχει τὸ τέλος καὶ [ἡ] πρᾶξις.

οἷον ὁρᾷ ἅμα <καὶ ἑώρακε,> καὶ φρονεῖ <καὶ πεφρόνηκε,> καὶ νοεῖ καὶ νενόηκεν, ἀλλ' οὐ μανθάνει καὶ μεμάθηκεν οὐδ' ὑγιάζεται καὶ ὑγίασται· εὖ ζῇ καὶ εὖ ἔζηκεν ἅμα, καὶ εὐδαιμονεῖ καὶ εὐδαιμόνηκεν. εἰ δὲ μή, ἔδει ἄν ποτε παύεσθαι ὥσπερ ὅταν ἰσχναίνῃ, νῦν δ' οὔ, ἀλλὰ ζῇ καὶ ἔζηκεν. τούτων δὴ <δεῖ> τὰς μὲν κινήσεις λέγειν, τὰς δ' ἐνεργείας. πᾶσα γὰρ κίνησις ἀτελής, ἰσχνασία μάθησις βάδισις οἰκοδόμησις· αὗται δὴ κινήσεις, καὶ ἀτελεῖς γε. οὐ γὰρ ἅμα βαδίζει καὶ βεβάδικεν, οὐδ' οἰκοδομεῖ καὶ ᾠκοδόμηκεν, οὐδὲ γίγνεται καὶ γέγονεν ἢ κινεῖται καὶ κεκίνηται, ἀλλ' ἕτερον, καὶ κινεῖ καὶ κεκίνηκεν· ἑώρακε δὲ καὶ ὁρᾷ ἅμα τὸ αὐτό, καὶ νοεῖ καὶ νενόηκεν. τὴν μὲν οὖν τοιαύτην ἐνέργειαν λέγω, ἐκείνην δὲ κίνησιν. τὸ μὲν οὖν ἐνεργείᾳ τί τέ ἐστι καὶ ποῖον, ἐκ τούτων καὶ τῶν τοιούτων δῆλον ἡμῖν ἔστω.

Since of the actions which have a limit none is an end but all are relative to the end, e.g., the process of making thin is of this sort, and the things themselves when one is making them thin are in movement in this way (i.e., without being already that at which the movement aims), this is not an action or at least not a complete one (for it is not an end); but that in which the end is present is an action. E.g., at the same time we are seeing and have seen, are understanding and have understood, are thinking and have thought. At the same time we are living well and have lived well, and are happy and have been happy. For every movement is incomplete—making thin, learning, walking, building; these are movements, and incomplete movements. For it is not true that at the same time we are walking and have walked, or are building and have built, or are coming to be and have come to be—it is a different thing that is being moved and that has been moved, and that is moving and that has moved; but it is the same thing that at the same time has seen and is seeing, or is thinking and has thought. The latter sort of process, then, I call an actuality, and the former a movement. (trans., Ross)

Also, in Θ 9, in explaining why actuality is better than a good potentiality, and how it is that thinking makes certain sorts of potential mathematical constructions actual, Aristotle in effect explains to us why it is that assertoric truth is good: The acquisition of such truth is the fulfillment of our rational capacities and the fulfillment is better than the potential for that fulfillment and better than the contrary opposite of that fulfillment.

Aristotle claims that assertions about incomposites are true *and* false in a way different from assertions about real combinations and separations. Whereas the latter are true and false because the assertoric combinations and separations in thought track those in the world, the former are true by virtue of "assertion and contact" [τὸ θιγεῖν καὶ φάναι] and false because of "ignorance and lack of contact" [τὸ ἀγνοεῖν μὴ θιγγάνειν].

Having explained incomposite objects in terms of potentiality and actuality, Aristotle then focuses on the nature of truth and falsehood in cases where we are thinking about such objects, at 1051b33–1052a4. Here Aristotle distinguishes between an ignorance that is like blindness and an ignorance that differs from blindness. As noted above, this distinction depends upon Aristotle's discussion of potentiality and privation in Θ 1 and 2. And here we have a natural way into the topic of how a given assertion can serve as a principle for producing opposite consequences, a topic noted earlier and addressed at length in Θ 2 and 5. In Θ 2, at 1046b1ff, Aristotle explains how rational capacities essentially involving true and false assertions are capacities for opposites. In Θ 5, at 1048a1ff, he explains acting in accordance with reason, given that rational capacities are capacities for opposites.

The last part of Θ 10 focuses on unchanging objects, whether composite or incomposite. Aristotle ends his discussion of truth and falsehood by asking when thoughts about unchanging objects are true or false, from 1052a4–14. The notion of an unchanging object is best understood in terms of the distinctions made in Θ 1–9 among potentialities, incomplete actualities, and complete actualities. In addition, Aristotle uses for his examples of truths about unchanging objects geometrical and arithmetical objects, which examples cannot help but refer us back to the discussion of the relationship between the actuality of thought and the actuality of geometrical relations in Θ 9. That discussion offers us a prima facie reasonable way of reading the end of last part of Θ 10: If we suppose that a given mathematical object does not change, then we shall not suppose that at one time the mathematical relations it instantiates are thus-and-so while at another time they are not-thus-and-so (for that would imply change). It is possible, however, to suppose that one instance of a kind of mathematical object has a certain attribute and another instance does not have it, e.g., we may suppose by means of one act of thinking that no even number is prime, and we may suppose by means of another act of thinking that some even numbers are and some are not prime. But regarding a single instance of a mathematical object not even this form of error is possible; for we cannot in this case suppose that one instance has an attribute and another has not; but whether our judgment be true or false, it is implied that the fact is eternal.

I have argued that Θ 1–9 and Θ 10 are more closely related than is usually thought. I began by defending the modest claim that throughout much of Θ 1–9 Aristotle's discussion of potential and actual being depends upon his account of truth and falsehood. I then argued for the stronger thesis that Θ 1–9 prepare us for the novel claims Aristotle wishes to make about truth and falsehood in Θ 10. Thus, I hope to have persuaded you that we can and should read Θ 1–10 as a unified whole having to do with potential and actual being, especially as this kind of being bears on the nature of truth and falsehood.

I also hope that the preceding arguments make it plausible that Aristotle's discussion of truth and falsehood in Θ 10 is very strongly informed by Aristotle's claims about potentiality and actuality in Θ 1–9. The two parts of Θ are complementary, and it is difficult to imagine how one might parse correctly the claims in Θ 10 independently of those in Θ 1–9.

Aristotle's definitions of the essences of assertoric truth and falsehood may be revised on the basis of my reading of Θ 1–10 as follows:

> (Real Definitions of Falsehood and Truth "RFT") For every linguistic or conceptual subject n that signifies or represents one and only one real subject x, for every linguistic or conceptual predicate d that signifies or represents one and only one real predicate y, for every linguistic or conceptual relation + that signifies or represents the real predicative relation of belonging to, and for every linguistic or conceptual relation − that signifies or represents the real predicative relation of not belonging to:

> [F] Falsehood is *a privation of a complete activity of a psyche in which that psyche* either (a) linguistically or mentally asserts at time t that $d + n$ and y does not belong to x at time t or (b) linguistically or mentally asserts at time t that $d − n$ and y belongs to x at time t (c) linguistically or mentally asserts at time t that n is definitionally the same as d and the simple thing $x = y$ does not exist at time t.

[T] Truth is *a complete activity of a psyche in which that psyche either (a) linguistically or mentally asserts at time t that $d + n$ and y belongs to x at time t or (b) linguistically or mentally asserts at time t that $d - n$ and y does not belong to x at time t or (c) linguistically or mentally asserts at time t that n is definitionally the same as d and $x = y = s \otimes g$ at time t (where s and g are, respectively, the species differential characteristic, i.e., the form or actuality, and the proximate generic characteristic, i.e., the matter or potentiality, that constitute the essence being defined, and where "$\otimes$" represents the fact that the unity of the form and matter is different from the other kinds of predicative unity).*

Conclusion

Looking now at the larger context of the *Metaphysics*, Aristotle's theory of being in the *Metaphysics* generates two problems for his theory of truth. First, how does Aristotle explain the apparent fact that God's essence involves the activity of assertoric truth? Second, how does Aristotle explain the truth of assertions about essences? Aristotle solves both problems on the basis of his discussion of potential and actual being in book Θ.

Aristotle needs to explain how the kind of truth that belongs to assertions helps us to make sense of the essence of Aristotle's God as specified in book Λ—the perfect activity of thought thinking thought. In the concluding chapter, I will develop the ideas that Aristotle's God is the first cause and principal of all that there is, that God is essentially the activity of thought thinking thought and, as such, that God would seem to essentially involve the kind of truth that belongs to assertions. If I am right about this, then there is a case to be made that the concepts and arguments in Θ 1–9 and those in Θ 10 are part of the same project, and not part of different projects. In the *Metaphysics*, taken as a unified whole, Aristotle is concerned with the nature of philosophical wisdom itself and with its proper objects, the most important first principles and causes. If we assume that Aristotle's claims and arguments in Θ 1–9 and Θ 10 relate to his conclusions in book Λ, then we can see more clearly how Aristotle's focus on rational powers and activities is intended ultimately to help us understand the nature of Aristotle's God: If we assume that God is thought thinking thought, and hence the perfect exemplar of the kind of truth that belongs to assertions, and if we assume (1) that God is the ultimate cause of all activity other than itself, (2) that God is prior in being to all other things, and (3) that God is perfectly good, then the concepts developed in Θ 1–9 and Θ 10 help us to understand the fulfillment that constitutes the essence of Aristotle's God.

Aristotle also needed to explain how true definitions of the essences of sensible substances are semantic unities that correspond with metaphysical unities well described in terms of potential and actual being. This was an outstanding and pressing concern left over from the discussion in books Z and H. I agree with Owen and others that books E–Θ form a continuous whole addressing the various kinds of being differentiated by Aristotle in Δ 7. If so, then it would make sense that Aristotle would use the distinctions made in book Θ to resolve difficulties remaining from books Z and H.[26] In this chapter, I have argued that Aristotle specifies the differential characteristics of the kind of truth that belongs to assertions. Taken in combination with his account of the genus of this kind of truth in *Met.* E 4, this yields a complete specification of the essence of his core kind of truth and, thus, complete Stage 3 of Aristotle's inquiry into the essence of the kind signified by the nominal definition of "truth" in *Met.* Γ 7. In this way, *Met.* Θ 10 can be seen as the capstone of Aristotle's account of the essence of the kind of truth that belongs to assertions. Yet there remains a difficulty: How does Aristotle understand the oneness presupposed by real definition of his core kind of truth, and how does his account of oneness help us to understand the nature of the relationship between the intensional contents of assertions and their correlates in the real world? I turn to this issue in the final two chapters.

Part III

Truth and Measurement

Chapter 8

Truth, Oneness, and Measurement

We have seen that in *Metaphysics* books Γ–Θ Aristotle explicates his account of the essence of truth as part of his inquiry into the nature of philosophical wisdom. He presents his developing analyses of truth and falsehood in Γ 7, Δ 7, Δ 29, E 4, and Θ 10. These analyses are informed by their respective contexts. Aristotle presents nominal definitions of "truth" and "falsehood" in Γ 7 in the context of arguing elenctically for the axioms of argument. In Δ 7 he relates the being of truth to the other kinds of being he takes seriously in the *Metaphysics*: the beings-in-themselves that belong to the categories, the coincidental beings that depend on the beings-in-themselves, and potential and active being. In Δ 29 Aristotle identifies various kinds of truth and falsehood, differentiating them and enabling us to establish that the kind of truth that belongs to assertions is the core kind on which the other kinds of truth depend. Lastly, in E 4 and Θ 10 he specifies the genus and the differentiae of the essence of his core kind of truth.

Aristotle's real definitions of truth and falsehood involve more consequential metaphysical commitments than did the nominal definitions presented in Γ 7. The real definitions presuppose the existence of the real predicative relations of belonging, not-belonging, and definitional sameness. Each of the real relata of these real predicative relations is assumed to be one and only one being falling under one of the categories. The real definitions also presuppose the existence of intensional contents of acts of assertion and their correlates in the real world. It is *in virtue of* the correlates in the real world obtaining and *not* in virtue of the intensional contents obtaining—Aristotle is emphatic about this—that truth and falsehood obtains. The real definitions also presuppose the existence of a more robust form of correspondence than the nominal definitions did. According to the real definitions, true and false linguistic affirmations, denials, and definitions are at least structurally isomorphic with the mental assertions they immediately signify. The intensional contents of true and false mental affirmations, denials, and definitions are at least structurally isomorphic with their real correlates. The real definitions entail, therefore, the existence of some sort of correspondence-as-congruence relation. In all of these ways the real definitions are intrinsically metaphysical in a robust sense.

These metaphysical posits generate three outstanding questions concerning Aristotle's account of truth in the *Metaphysics*. First, when Aristotle tells us that each of the correlates of a true assertion is one and only one being subsumed by one of the categories, how does he understand the oneness of these correlates in the real world? Second, why does he think that truth or falsehood obtain in virtue of the correlates in the real world obtaining and not in virtue of associated intensional contents obtaining? And third, how does he explain the correspondence-as-congruence relation essentially involved in truth? I argue that Aristotle answers each of these questions in terms of his account of oneness and measurement in the *Metaphysics*.

In this chapter I defend the view that Aristotle explains oneness—what it is to be one, the essence of oneness—in terms of measurement and not in terms of indivisibility, as is sometimes thought. To be more precise I claim that to be one, for Aristotle, is essentially to be the first measure of a kind. To be one and only one being is to be an instance of the first measure of a kind. This account of oneness directly informs Aristotle's real definitions of truth and falsehood: the core kinds of truth and falsehood essentially involve assertions about individual first measures of kinds (in the case of a true definition) or assertions about combinations of such first measures of kinds (in the cases of affirmations and denials). In other words, ultimately and strictly speaking, individual first measures of kinds—or combinations of these—are always the beings in virtue of which assertions are true or false.

The Extension of the Term "One"

In *Metaphysics* Λ 7.1072a32–34, Aristotle makes an interesting claim that sets the theme for my interpretation of his account of oneness and measurement:

ἔστι δὲ τὸ ἓν καὶ τὸ ἁπλοῦν οὐ τὸ αὐτό· τὸ μὲν γὰρ ἓν μέτρον σημαίνει, τὸ δὲ ἁπλοῦν πῶς ἔχον αὐτό.

Oneness and simplicity are not the same, since unity signifies a measure, whereas simplicity signifies that the thing itself is a certain way. (trans., Reeve)

The immediate claims at 1072a32–34 are: (1) the one [τὸ ἕν] and the simple [τὸ ἁπλοῦν] are not the same; (2) the one signifies a measure [τὸ μὲν γὰρ ἓν μέτρον σημαίνει]; and (3) the simple signifies how it is for something to be itself [τὸ δὲ ἁπλοῦν πῶς ἔχον αὐτό]. All of these claims, given the context, are reasonably taken to reflect Aristotle's own positions: they are neither merely entertained for the sake of argument nor presented by him as a part of an aporematic problem that needs to be solved. Taken in the context of the surrounding argument, (1) is intended to clarify the difference between substance and being one being, on the one hand, and what is simple and exists actually, on the other.[1] With regard to (2) and (3), his remarks are asides about oneness and measurement isolated from the main discussion of the unmoved mover in *Metaphysics* Λ 7.[2] They are consonant, however, with his introductory discussion of oneness in *Metaphysics* Δ 6 and his considered account of oneness in book I. In both of these latter texts he asserts that oneness is to be understood in terms of measurement. His point in Λ 7 is that a thing being a measure is different from its being itself in a certain condition. Being a measure is not like being white or like being seated or like—in the example offered in the passage—being simple.[3] As we will see, being a measure is being a certain kind of relative.

What exactly does Aristotle have in mind when he claims in *Metaphysics* Λ 7 that the one signifies a measure [τὸ μὲν γὰρ ἓν μέτρον σημαίνει]? In what way does the one "signify" a measure? How are being one and being a measure related?

To answer these questions, I turn to *Metaphysics* book I, where Aristotle presents his most well developed account of oneness. The account in book I is not the only account of oneness offered by Aristotle in the *Metaphsyics* or elsewhere. He begins I 1 with a reminder at 1052a15–16 that he has discussed elsewhere the many kinds of oneness. There are a number of discussions to which he might be referring. The most likely is *Metaphysics* Δ.6, although *Metaphysics* Λ 7, N 1, and *Physics* A 2 are candidates. With Elders, Jaeger, and Ross, I assume that at 1052a15–16 Aristotle is referring to his discussion of oneness in *Metaphysics* Δ 6.[4] I will compare the account of oneness in *Metaphysics* book I with that in Δ 6 and with Aristotle's other discussions, but we can and should evaluate first the distinctions he makes in *Metaphysics* book I.

Early on in I 1, from 1052b1–1053b8, Aristotle presents and defends his account of the essence of oneness in terms of measurement.[5] In doing so he first distinguishes at 1052b1–3 between two different questions we might ask about the use of the term "one" [τὸ ἕν]. On the one hand, we can ask what sorts of things are said to be one [λέγεσθαι ποῖά τε ἓν λέγεται]. This is a question about the extension of the term "one." On the other hand, we can ask about the account of the essence signified by the term [τί ἐστι τὸ ἑνὶ εἶναι καὶ τίς αὐτοῦ λόγος]. This is a question about the intension of the term.[6]

Aristotle then clarifies this semantic distinction. When we ask about the intension of the term "one," we are concerned more nearly with what is expressed or signified by the term itself than when we ask about the extension of the term. Whereas, when we ask about the extension of the term "one"—the kinds of things of which the term "one" is properly said—what we seek "approximates to its [the term's] force" [τῇ δυνάμει δ' ἐκεῖνα]. Aristotle implies that the extension of the term is farther from what is expressed or signified by the term itself than is the intension.[7]

To drive home the semantic distinction he has in mind, at 1052b7–15 Aristotle briefly discusses the semantics of the term "element" (one of the terms discussed in *Metaphysics* book Δ, in chapter 3), and he extends this case to the terms "cause" and "one," (both of which are also discussed in book Δ, in chapters 2 and 6, respectively) and "other such terms." He distinguishes quite explicitly between the things of which a term is said (i.e., predicated) and the definition of the term itself [εἰ δέοι λέγειν ἐπί τε τοῖς πράγμασι διορίζοντα καὶ τοῦ ὀνόματος ὅρον ἀποδιδόντα]. Developing his example of the semantics of the term "element," he notes that in one sense it is true to assert that fire or the indefinite or something else of the sort is by its own nature the element, but that in another sense it is false to assert this. For, on the one hand, fire and the indefinite and the rest are particular things that may well have the coincidental attribute of being elements. In this sense, it is true to say that the attribute of being an element belongs to these things. But, on the other hand, what it is to be fire or what it is to be the indefinite or what it is to be something of this sort—even considering the very nature of each—is *not* what it is to be an element. For fire and the indefinite and the like are particular things with natures distinct from the nature of being an element itself. Whereas what it is to be an element—the signification of the term "element" expressed by its definition and which is the attribute of being and element itself coinciding with fire and the indefinite and the other things of which it is predicated—is to be a primary constituent out of which something is made.

As Aristotle himself notes at 1052b3–5, he has asked and has answered the question about the extension of the term "one" at 1052a15–b1, the very beginning of book I 1. There, in describing the extension of the term, Aristotle distinguishes four kinds of things of which "one" is said primarily, in virtue of their own nature, and not coincidentally—these four are the naturally continuous, the whole, the individual, and the universal.

From 1052a19–29, Aristotle explains the oneness of what is continuous by nature and the oneness of what is whole. He ultimately explains both kinds of oneness in terms of indivisibility. He begins with his explanation of what is continuous by nature at 1052a19–21. He differentiates between that which is continuous ἁπλῶς (which has the sense here of "taken simply" or "taken generically") and that which is continuous by nature and not by contact or by bonds.[8] As I read 1052a20–21, Aristotle has identified one of the kinds of things "one" is said of primarily and in virtue of its own nature and not coincidentally: the kind of things that are continuous by nature and not because of contact or bonds. He explains the oneness of things of this sort—things that are continuous by nature—in terms of movement. More precisely, he claims that things that are continuous by nature can be more or less one, and the extent of their oneness is a function of the degree to which their movement is indivisible and simple.

At 1052a22–29 Aristotle identifies the next kind of thing of which "one" is said—the things that are continuous because they are wholes and have a definite shape and form. As with the first kind of thing said to be "one," things in this second kind are called one because they are continuous. But *continuous wholes*—things that have a definite form and shape—are one, according to Aristotle, "to a greater extent" than what is merely continuous by virtue of simple and indivisible movement. The relevant difference between things that are continuous by nature and things that are continuous wholes cannot be the fact that they are both continuous by nature. Aristotle takes this for granted. It is the way in which the different kinds of thing are continuous by nature that matters, and he explains the difference in their continuity in terms of a difference in their simple and indivisible movement.[9] Continuous wholes, he tells us, whose movement is more indivisible and simpler are more unified than others, but continuous wholes by nature are themselves the causes of their own indivisible movement and, hence, their own continuity. As a consequence, they are unified to a greater extent than things that are merely continuous by nature but that are not the causes of their own movement.

Aristotle then discusses the oneness of the individual and the oneness of the universal from 1052a29–34. He explains these sorts of oneness in terms of the indivisible formulae by means of which each is thought and not in terms of indivisible movement.[10] The oneness of the individual and the universal is a function of the oneness of the formula or thought we have of them. This may suggest that the oneness of an individual or of a universal depends on our having formulae or thoughts about them. But Aristotle explains the oneness of the formula or thought about an individual in terms of being indivisible in number, and he explains the oneness of the formula or thought about a universal in terms of being indivisible in intelligibility and in knowledge. As we will see, for Aristotle, both being indivisible in number and being indivisible in intelligibility and in knowledge are a function of being a mind and language independent first measure. Hence, he explains the oneness of formulae and thoughts about individuals and universals in terms of mind and language independent measures.

Aristotle concludes his discussion of the kinds of things of which "one" is said, his discussion of the *extension* of the term, at 1052a36–b1. There are two basic kinds of things of which "one" is predicated—those things the movement of which is indivisible and those things the thought of which is indivisible. He makes his general explanatory principle explicit at 1052a36–b1: ". . . And all these are one because in some cases the movement, in others the thought or the account, is indivisible [. . . πάντα δὲ ταῦτα ἓν τῷ ἀδιαίρετον εἶναι τῶν μὲν τὴν κίνησιν τῶν δὲ τὴν νόησιν ἢ τὸν λόγον.][11] This might lead one to think that Aristotle ultimately defines oneness in terms of indivisibility. This expectation is immediately dashed.

Given Aristotle's real definitions of truth and falsehood, and given that he never rescinds this general account of the extension of the term "one," it is plausible to assume that any beings falling within the extension of the term "one" may be among the correlates in the real world in virtue of which assertions are true or false. Although plausible, this assumption is also imprecise—it fails to explain *why* the beings in question fall within the extension of the term "one." Aristotle thinks there is a more precise explanation of the nature of the beings that are the proper correlates in the real world of true and false assertions.

The Intension of the Term "One"

Having explained the extension of the term "one," Aristotle examines the intension of the term from 1052b1–1053a14, asking and answering the questions: What is it *to be* one and what is *the account of oneness*? Aristotle explains at 1052b15–19 that although it is true to say of oneness that it is indivisible—since to be one is to be a this and capable of existing apart either in place or in kind or in thought (the marks of indivisibility, already introduced)—most of all what it is to be one is to be the first measure of each genus and, most strictly, to be the first measure of the genus quantity. That is to say, although the term "one" is properly predicated of things that are indivisible, what it is to be one differs from what it is to be indivisible. Aristotle does not define oneness in terms of indivisibility. Rather, he defines it by the formula "the first measure of a genus." Thus, for Aristotle, the terms "one" and "indivisible" are coextensive, but they have different intensions. They signify different essences or quiddities.

Having made these points, at 1052b20–24 Aristotle goes on to develop his claim at 1052b18–19 that to be one is most strictly to be the first measure in the genus of quantity and, by extension, the first measure in the other genera. It is important to see that Aristotle, in developing this idea, does not define oneness in terms of quantity. He assumes the definition of oneness in terms of being the first measure of a genus, and then explains at 1052b20–24 why this definition applies most strictly in the genus of quantity yet also applies just as well in the other genera. Aristotle begins by stating that measure is that by which quantity is known. As it turns out, this is not unique to quantity—measure is that by which anything is known—but unlike things that are not in the genera of quantity, quantities insofar as they are quantities (and not quantities *of* something or other) are primarily known by means of the one itself and not something else. In contrast to this, as Aristotle argues in book I 2, things other than quantities are primarily known not by measure itself—not by the one itself—but by things that serve as the measures and the ones in the genera for those things. Aristotle's argument at 1052b20–24 is swift and needs to be augmented by what he has to say in books M and N of the *Metaphysics*, yet his argument is clear: every quantity insofar as it is a quantity is known either by oneness or number; but every number insofar as it is number is known by oneness; so every quantity insofar as it is quantity is known by oneness; hence, that by which quantities are primarily known is oneness itself; therefore oneness is the starting point of number insofar as it is number. I will address the most pertinent passage in book N below, but for my purposes here what needs to be emphasized is that quantities insofar as they are quantities are primarily known by oneness itself and—since oneness itself just is, by definition, measure itself—quantities insofar as they are quantities are primarily known by measure itself. As Aristotle puts it, the first measure of number is the *starting-point* for all knowledge of quantity. Aristotle will address measures in genera other than the genus of quantity in I 2. Prior to that discussion, in I 1, at 1052b24–31, he gives weight and speed as examples of measures in the genus of quantity, which examples are meant to highlight measures of kinds of quantity other than the measure of the kind number insofar as it is number. I will not develop these examples. The point I wish to highlight now is that each of these kinds of quantity has a first measure by which it is known—some measure of gravity in the case of weight and some measure of movement in the case of speed—and that these first measures define the unit for that kind.

Thus far in book I 1, Aristotle has explained the relationship among indivisibility, oneness, quantity, and measure. Indivisibility and oneness are coextensive, but what it is to be indivisible differs from what it is to be one. "One" is said of everything that is primarily and by its nature indivisible (and of other indivisible things too), but the formula that defines the essence signified by "one" differs from the formula of the essence signified by "indivisible." What it is to be one—the formula that defines the essence signified by "one"—is to be a first measure of a genus. What it is to be a one and a measure also differs from what it is to be a quantity. To be one is to be the first measure of a genus, and this holds of every genus in every category of being. Hence, the extension of oneness far exceeds the extension of the genus of quantity. But oneness itself is indeed the first measure of number itself, and so oneness itself, according to Aristotle, is the starting point for knowledge of all kinds of quantity—it is the first principle for all knowledge of quantity. And this is not true about beings in the other genera. Oneness *itself* is not the first principle of knowledge for genera in the categories of substance, quality, place, and the rest. For each of these genera, however, there is some first measure or other that *is* the first principle of knowledge of that genus.

As we might predict, given the discussion in I 1, Aristotle argues in I 2 that oneness itself is not a substance. Let us turn to that argument in order to help us better understand what Aristotle says in I 1 about oneness and measures. In I 2, Aristotle offers two main arguments against the claim that oneness is a substance, each of which also serves to explain how it is that in each category other than quantity oneness is explained in terms of something the nature of which is not itself oneness but some particular thing in that category. But if the substance and nature of oneness just is to be the first measure of a genus, and if the substance and nature of oneness is *not* to be a substance or a genus, then the substance and nature of being a first measure of a genus is *not* to be a substance or a genus. What, then, is the substance and nature of the first measure of a genus?

Aristotle begins to answer this question at I 2.1053b25–28. He notes that in the categories of quality and quantity the one is always some thing, some particular nature. Since "one" is said in as many ways as "being" is said, and "being" is said in as many ways as there are categories of being, Aristotle seeks to determine what the one is with respect to each of the categories and not just with respect to quality and quantity. Presumably he is looking for a general way of describing the substance and nature of the one in terms of being a particular nature, and he rejects out of hand as inadequate a description along the lines of "the substance and nature of oneness is to be one."

Aristotle enumerates and analyzes at I 2.1053b28–1054a5 various particular ones in different categories and genera. He begins with the one in the genus of color and then applies the same analysis to the genera of tunes, articulate sounds, and rectilinear figures. Aristotle's pattern of argument here is interesting. First, he specifies a genus of beings for the sake of the argument. The genera he actually identifies in the passage are colors, tunes, articulate sounds, and rectilinear figures, but he makes it evident that he thinks the pattern applies to all genera. Second, he identifies for each genus a particular infima species within that genus: white for color, quarter-tone for tunes, letter for articulate sounds, and triangle for rectilinear figures. We know from I 1.1053a24–25 that the first measure of every genus is itself an infima species of that genus, and we also know from I 1.1053a14–20 that there need not be just one infima species serving as the only measure of a given genus. Aristotle is taking these claims from I 1 for granted in I 2. Third, he asks us to assume, for the sake of the arguments, that the genus under investigation is the only genus of being—first that every being is a color, and next that every being is a tune, et cetera—and he claims that, were this the case, there would have been a number of that genus of being (i.e., first a number of colors, and then a number of tunes, et cetera). Fourth, he encourages us to recognize that in each of these hypothesized cases, the substance of the one and number of that genus would not be the one itself and number itself but would be the one thing that serves as the first measure of the genus in question: the substance of the one and number of color would not be the one itself and number itself but would be the one thing in the genus of color that serves as the first measure of color, the substance of the one and the number of tunes would not be the one itself and number itself but would be the one thing in the genus of tunes that serves as the first measure of tunes, et cetera. Fifth, he reminds us that what it is to be one in a given genus is not to be oneness itself—he has already secured this point in I.1—but to be the first measure of the genus: the substance of the one in the genus of color would not be itself oneness but would be the white, for example; the one in the genus of articulate sound would not be oneness itself but would be the vowel; and the substance of the one in the genus of rectilinear figures would not be oneness itself but would be the triangle; and in general the substance of the one in a genus is not oneness itself but the particular first measure (or first measures) of that genus. As we might expect, given that Aristotle has defined what it is to be one in terms of being the first measure of a genus, he here identifies the substance and the nature of oneness in general in terms of being a particular first measure of a given genus.

Next at I 2.1054a5–9, Arisotle tells us that in every category of being—affections, qualities, quantities, movements, and substance—the numbers of things in the category will be numbers of particular things. These particular things are the units of measure (the ones) by means of which things in the various categories are numbered, and in every category including that of substance, the substance of these units is not oneness itself but to be a particular nature that serves as the first measure of its genus. I take it that he has raised the discussion to the level of the categories of beings, having made the case in the preceding lines that the number of things in any given genus in any given category is a function of a unit of measure which is a particular nature of that genus.

Aristotle thinks he has made it obvious by I 2.1054a9–19 that in every genus the one is a particular nature and, emphatically, that the nature of these ones is never just to be oneness itself. He makes it more evident in his concluding remarks at 1054a9–19 what he means when he says that each one in every genus (i.e., each unit of measure in every genus) is a *particular nature*: in colors the one itself is one color, and in substance the one itself is a single substance. I take it this means that each *species* in every genus serves as a unit of measure for that genus.

Aristotle ends the discussion of the nature and substance of oneness in I.2 at 1054a13–19, arguing that his view of oneness explains how it is that "one" and "being" signify the same things. On his view, what it is *to be one* is to be a particular nature in a given genus, and what it is *to be* is to be a particular nature in a given genus. Hence, with respect to every genus of being in every category, both "one" and "being" signify the same thing—a particular nature in that genus. Both predicates apply in the same way in all of the categories; neither is limited to any given category or to a limited number of categories. Nor is either oneness or being something apart from—in the sense of being a oneness itself or being itself that transcends—the particular natures in the various genera of being.

Returning to I.1 and Aristotle's explanation of the essence of oneness in terms of measure at 1052b31–34, Aristotle reiterates the points he thinks he has established earlier in the chapter. In all of the genera of quantities he has considered, the measure of each genus is a starting point for knowledge of that genus, is one, and is indivisible. At 1052b34–36 he extends his analysis of measure in terms of simplicity and exactness:

τοῦτο δὲ τὸ ἁπλοῦν ἢ τῷ ποιῷ ἢ τῷ ποσῷ. ὅπου μὲν οὖν δοκεῖ μὴ εἶναι ἀφελεῖν ἢ προσθεῖναι, τοῦτο ἀκριβὲς τὸ μέτρον.

And this is the simple in either quality or quantity. Now, where it seems impossible to take away or to add, this measure is exact. (trans., Reeve)

The measure we seek is, by definition, something one. By virtue of the co-extension of the terms "one" and "indivisible" the measure is something indivisible. Aristotle tells us that such a measure is simple in quality or quantity and that what is simple in quality or quantity is what is exact.

He now spells out exactness in terms of addition or subtraction: that is exact from which nothing can be subtracted and to which nothing can be added. From I 1.1052b36–1053a14, he provides examples intended to illustrate this understanding of measurement and exactness. The measure of number insofar as it is number is the most exact measure because it is absolutely indivisible—nothing can possibly be subtracted from it, and nothing can be added to it insofar as it is what it is. This most exact measure is the paradigm for all other measures, which are imitations of it insofar as they are exact. The examples of a furlong and a talent are offered as instances of measures from which nothing can be subtracted and to which nothing can be added, at least from the point of view of our perception of these sorts of magnitude. The example of the movement of the heavens is similarly offered as a measure from which nothing can be subtracted and to which nothing can be added, at least from the point of view time. So too the cases of the quarter-tone in music and the letter in speech (both of which are measures of quantity, according to Aristotle in the *Categories*). These are measures because they are the least of their genera to which nothing can be added insofar as they are what they are. All of his proffered examples are measures of genera of quantity and hence are units in their genera, even though—and Aristotle himself stresses this point—none is the same measure as any of the others.

Aristotle then digresses at I 1.1053a14–20 to address whether or not there is always only one measure for each genus. For a given genus, he tells us there may be many measures. How many will depend on how many elements constitute the infima species of that genus. To find this out we have to divide the genus into its constituent quantities or its constituent genera. In general, spatial magnitudes are divisible into more than one measure—the triangle serves as an example of this. Articulate sound is divisible into a large number of constituent phonemes. Musical sound is divisible into many different tones.

Aristotle explains, at I 1.1053a20–24, why oneness is properly said of what is indivisible both primarily and in virtue of its own nature. He states that the one is indivisible because the first of each genus is. His reasoning may be reconstructed in a straightforward way from his earlier claims in I.1: the first of each genus of things is indivisible; the measure of each genus of things is the first of each genus; what is one for each genus of things is the measure of each genus; therefore, what is one for each genus of things is indivisible.

At I 1.1053a24–25 Aristotle claims that a measure is always "συγγενὲς." Ross translates this with "homogeneous," rendering the whole phrase "ἀεὶ δὲ συγγενὲς τὸ μέτρον" by "the measure is always homogenous with the thing measured." Ross's choice makes sense given the Aristotle's subsequent claims. First Aristotle claims that the measure of each genus of things is itself a member of that genus of things, and he provides a series of examples of genera of quantities intended to illustrate how the measure of each of these genera of quantity is itself a member of that genus of quantity. Then he goes on to claim that it would be a mistake to say that the measure of number is itself a number. He explains why this would be a mistake: a number is a plurality of units; hence, were one to claim that the measure of number is itself a number, one would be saying that the measure of a plurality of units is itself a plurality of units; but this is impossible on Aristotle's account: the measure of a plurality of units is *a* unit. A plurality of units *presupposes* the unit of which it is a plurality.

By the ends of I 1 and I 2, Aristotle appears to offer us criteria by means of which to identify the correlates in the real world for true and false assertions made in the context of philosophical inquiry. True and false assertions, strictly speaking, are about exact first measures in the genera of the categories of being. To corroborate this reading of I 1 and I 2, it will be necessary to first to compare what Aristotle says about oneness and measures in other passages.

Metaphysics Δ 6 on Oneness and Measure

In I 1 and I 2 Aristotle explains the essence oneness in terms of being an exact first measure of a genus. Let me now compare what Aristotle says about oneness and measure in *Metaphysics* Δ 6 with my analysis of I 1 and 2.[12] As we will see, in Δ 6 he effects the same semantic distinction between the extension and the intension of the term "one" as he did in I.1, and he identifies the essence of oneness Δ 6 in terms of measurement, just as he did I.1.[13] At Δ 6.1015b16–1015b34, he tells us that we call "one" that which is one by coincidence and that which is one by its own nature and that two things are coincidentally one either because they both are coincidents of one substance, because one is an coincident of the other, because one of the parts in the formula of one is a coincident of the other, because both have parts which are coincidents of one and the same subject. At Δ 6.1015b35–1016a17 Aristotle claims that things are called one in virtue of their own nature because they are continuous, and a thing is called continuous which has by its own nature one movement and cannot have any other. A movement, he continues, is one when it is indivisible, and indivisible in time. Those things are continuous by their own nature which are one not merely by contact. Of things that are continuous, the continuous by nature are more one than the continuous by art.

As I read Δ 6.1015b16–1017a2, Aristotle offers us an analysis of the signification of the term "one" as he did in I 1. At Δ 6.1015b16–1016b17 he describes the extension of the term "one." He distinguishes among various kinds of things that are properly called "one." Some things are called "one" because they are coincidentally one; others are called "one" because they are one by their very nature. There are various kinds of coincidental unities and various genera of natural unities. Things in all these different genera fall within the extension of the term "one." From 1016b17–1017a2, Aristotle shifts his attention from the extension to the intension of the term "one." He defines what it is to be one, giving an account of the essence of oneness. As I understand lines 1017b17–21, Aristotle tells us that what it is to be one is to be the first measure of a genus. This is his definition of the term "one" in Δ 6. This is the account of the essence signified by the term "one" in Δ 6.

At Δ 6.1016a17–1017a17, for my purposes, the major claim here is that some things are called one because the substratum of each does not differ in genus, i.e., where the genus of the substratum of each is indivisible to the sense, where the relevant substratum is either the genus nearest to or furthest from the final state of the things in question. At 1016a24–32, Aristotle states that the genus which underlies the differentiae is one in a way similar to that in which the matter is one.

Turning now to Δ 6.1016a32–1016b3, in his note on line1016a32, Ross claims that this is a discussion of specific oneness. Insofar as specific oneness is identical with oneness of essence—and this is plausible given the argument in the middle books of the *Metaphyiscs*—I agree. Aristotle is explicitly concerned with oneness of essence in the *Metaphysics* and in Δ 6. At Δ 6.1016a33–35, Aristotle claims that a formula in itself is divisible (lines 1016a34–35) even though in cases of essential oneness the formula of one thing is indivisible (line 1016a33) in relation to the formula of another thing. I take it that Aristotle is here relying upon the distinction he draws in the *De Anima* III 6.430b6ff in the context of discussing thoughts about what is indivisible. There he distinguishes between being indivisible in the sense of not capable of being divided and indivisible in the sense of what is not actually divided. In Δ 6 his point is that, although in itself the formula of the essence is divisible because it can be divided, insofar as the formula of the essence is the basis for essential oneness it is indivisible because it is not actually divided. Ross, in his note on line 1016a35, explains the parenthetical remark at 1016a34–35 as follows: "Every definition must be analyzed into genus and differentia." That is to say, and as we saw in chapter 6 above, for Aristotle every definition can be divided into genus and differentiae, but not every definition is actually so divided.[14]

Ross (1924) understands lines Δ 6.1016b2–3 in terms of the identity of individuals. He notes that (i) an individual at one time is more one with itself than it is at different times, (ii) an individual of a given genus is more one than are two spatially distinct individuals of that genus, and (iii) different aspects of the same individual may be distinguished from each other by means of their formulae, even though they will be spatially and temporally coincidental. If Ross is correct, then at 1016b2–3 Aristotle is explicitly claiming that there are thoughts of the essences of things, which thoughts include the formula of the essence of the thing as well as information about its location and time. This would entail that Aristotle posited individual essences that are constituted out of the species essence of the thing as well as its spatial and temporal attributes. I do not think, however, Aristotle posited these sorts of individual essences, although I think he can make sense of these sorts of coincidental compounds. Nor do I think 1016b2–3 is about these sorts of things. I think Ross misreads the force of Aristotle's claim at the end of the passage. Throughout the passage, Aristotle is concerned with the oneness of two things. His main point is that two things are most one when the thought of the formula of the essence of one cannot be distinguished from the thought of the formula of the essence of the other. Such thoughts, because they are thoughts about the formulae of the essences of things, do not include spatial or temporal content sufficient to distinguish individuals possessing the essences in question. These thoughts cannot separate the two things spatially, temporally, in terms of other coincidental attributes, *or* in terms of their essences. Such thoughts will include, however, insofar as they are thoughts about essentially spatiotemporal things, content to that effect—the formulae of the essences of these genera will entail that individuals of those genera are spatiotemporal individuals.[15]

At Δ 6.1016b3–6 Aristotle explains why it is that 'one' is said of all of the different genera of things he has discussed thus far in the chapter. In general, he says, 'one' is said of things that are not divisible insofar as they are not divisible.[16] At 1016b6–11, having made the general point about oneness and indivisibility, Aristotle returns to his initial distinction at 1015b16 between what is one by coincidence and what is one by nature. He tells us that the majority of things of which "one" is said are so-called because they are one by coincidence. Nevertheless, he thinks this is not the primary use of "one." In its primary use, "one" is said of things one by nature—those whose substance is one—in the three ways he has delineated in Δ 6: in continuity, in form, or in formula.[17] Some things are called one because the formula of the essence of one thing is indivisible from the formula of the essence of the other thing (though *in itself* every formula is divisible). In general, those things the thought of whose essence is indivisible, which thought cannot separate the things either in time or in place or in formula, are most of all one. And of such things the thought of whose essence is indivisible, those which are substances are especially one. In other words, those things that do not admit of division are one insofar as they do not admit of it, and the things that are primarily called one are those whose substance is one either in continuity or in form or in formula.

At 1016b12–1016b17, Aristotle offers a number of assertions important for our purposes here. He tells us that, in one sense, we call something one if it is a quantity and continuous and, in another sense, we call something one only if it is a whole (i.e., only if it has one form). These assertions are familiar from our discussion of book I. Δ 6.1016b17–21, however, is a crucial passage:

τὸ δὲ ἑνὶ εἶναι ἀρχῇ τινί ἐστιν ἀριθμοῦ εἶναι· τὸ γὰρ πρῶτον μέτρον ἀρχή, ᾧ γὰρ πρώτῳ γνωρίζομεν, τοῦτο πρῶτον μέτρον ἑκάστου γένους· ἀρχὴ οὖν τοῦ γνωστοῦ περὶ ἕκαστον τὸ ἕν.

To be one, however, is to be a sort of starting-point of number. For the first measure is a starting-point, since that by which we first know it is the first measure of each kind. The starting-point, then, of what is knowable about each kind is what is one. (trans., Reeve)

Aristotle affirms that what it is to be one [τὸ δὲ ἑνὶ εἶναι] is to be a beginning of number [ἀρχῇ τινί ἐστιν ἀριθμοῦ εἶναι], that the first measure is the beginning [τὸ πρῶτον μέτρον ἀρχή], and that by which we first know each genus [γένους] is the first measure of the genus. The one is the beginning of the knowable regarding each genus.[18] These claims reinforce what Aristotle has argued in book I, chapters 1 and 2. And at Δ

6.1016b21–23, for my purposes the important point here is that the one not the same in different genera.[19] This is because the one in any genus is the first measure of *that* genus and not another. The first measure of a genus is a part of *that* genus. If the genus is music, the first measure will be a unit of music and not a unit of speech, not a unit of weight, and not a unit of movement. All of this is an important point because Aristotle conceives of first measures as real beings. The first measure is a real part of the genus it measures.

At Δ 6.1016b23–31 Aristotle asserts that everywhere the one is indivisible either in quantity or in kind [τῷ εἴδει]. That which is indivisible in quantity and *qua* quantity is called either (i) a unit [μονάς] if it is not divisible in any dimension and is without position, or (ii) a point if it is not divisible in any dimension and has position, or (iii) a line if it is divisible in one dimension, or (iv) a plane if in two, or (v) a body if divisible in quantity in all—i.e., in three—dimensions. Aristotle is not concerned here with the earlier distinctions among kinds of oneness.[20] He is neither concerned with the difference between oneness by coincidence and oneness by nature nor with the varieties of oneness by nature—oneness by continuity, by substratum, by genus, and by formula. Lines 1016b23–31 are primarily about indivisibility in the category of quantity, and secondarily about indivisibility in the other genera (this is the focus of 1016b31–1017a6). More specifically, at 1016b23–31 Aristotle specifies the different units of measure of quantity-insofar-as-it-is-quantity in terms of divisibility and dimensionality. The examples of the unit and the point make it obvious that not all of these units of measure involve oneness by continuity.[21]

At 1016b31–1017a6 Aristotle explicitly commits himself to the following: Some things are one in number, others in species, others in genus, others by analogy. Things are one in number whose matter is one; things are one in species whose formula is one; things are one in genus to which the same figure of predication applies; things are one by analogy which are related as a third thing to a fourth thing. Moreover, he tells us, if there is generic oneness, then there is analogical oneness; if specific oneness, then generic oneness; and if numerical oneness, then specific oneness. *Pace* Ross, I very much doubt Aristotle wishes to claim here that only the categories are proper genera. The proper sense is "things in the same scheme of a category," where appropriate weight needs to be given to the sense of "scheme" (σχῆμα). In the context of understanding oneness in terms of measurement, we need to know the measure in virtue of which two things are counted as one in a given genus. The measure cannot be the proximate genus, since this is identical with the measure of the matter of the things. The measure cannot be all of the genera and specific differentiae within a given category, since two things may be generically the same without being in the same species. Aristotle's claim here is that the proper measure of a genus is the scheme of predicates that are predicated of and define it within its category. For example, if a dog and a plant are one insofar as they are both living things, the measure of the genus of living things will be the *scheme* of predicates in the category of substance that is predicated of and defines the genus living things. Again, such a scheme will not define the two things that are generically one. It is not the formula of a living thing that would serve to define the essence of a dog or the essence of a plant. The measure of the genus of living things would not serve as the measure of the essential oneness of a dog or a plant. The scheme of predicates defines the genus in question, and nothing else.

Aristotle is saying quite a lot about measures in these passages. First, the measure of the matter is the basis of numerical oneness. Second, the measure of the formula is the basis of specific oneness. Third, the measure of the scheme of a category is the basis of generic oneness. Lastly, the measure of the relations between two pairs of relatives is the basis for analogical oneness. If this interpretation of Δ 6.1015b16–1017a2 is correct, we can expect the account of the intension of "one" to *explain* the account of the extension of the term. Is this expectation met? Not in *Metaphysics* Δ 6, and given Aristotle's purposes in book Δ and how he proceeds, this is unsurprising. Instead, at Δ 6.1016a21–1017a3, Aristotle introduces a *new* topic, and he never returns to the issue of the extension or the intension of the term "one" in *Metaphysics* Δ 6. However, as we have seen, he does return to both topics in I.1. If the analyses I have offered of *Metaphysics* I 1 and 2 are correct, and if the analysis I will offer below of *Metaphysics* I 6 is correct, then our expectation is met—the intension of the term "one" explains why the term is properly predicated of each of the things in its extension.

Conclusion

Let me now summarize the analysis of being one and being a measure offered thus far on the basis of *Metaphysics* I 1 and 2 and *Metaphysics* Δ 6. Oneness is predicated properly of what is indivisible primarily and in virtue of its own nature. Things that are indivisible primarily and in virtue of their own nature constitute the extension of the term "one." But what it is to be one is to be a measure. What it is to be a measure is to be a quality or quantity from which nothing can be subtracted and to which nothing can be added. Such a quality or quantity is exact, one, indivisible, and a starting point for the knowledge of a genus. Thus, the intension of the term "one" is to be an exact first measure of a genus. These considerations inform Aristotle's real definitions of assertoric truth and falsehood.

Recall that, according to Aristotle, the essence of truth involves making assertions either about predicative combinations of two things—each of which is one and only one thing—or about one and only one simple thing. In *De Interpretione* and *De Anima* and in the *Metaphysics*, as we saw in chapters 2 and 3, Aristotle repeatedly emphasizes this fact about the essence of truth (and the concomitant facts about falsehood). We are now in a position to understand what Aristotle has in mind when he says that each true assertion is about either one and only one being or two such beings that are predicatively combined. Properly speaking, in the context of assertion:

1. Every linguistic or conceptual subject n signifies or represents a real subject *which is an exact first measure of a genus in one of the categories*, and every linguistic or conceptual predicate signifies or represents a real predicate *which is an exact first measure of a genus in one of the categories.*

2. Truth is a complete activity of a psyche in which that psyche either

   a. linguistically or mentally asserts that *one exact first measure of a genus in one of the categories* belongs to *another exact first measure of a genus in one of the categories* at time t and the predicative combination of the one exact first measure belonging to the other obtains at t or

   b. linguistically or mentally asserts *one exact first measure of a genus in one of the categories* does not belong to *another exact first measure of a genus in one of the categories* at time t and the predicative combination of the one exact first measure not belonging to the other obtains or

c. linguistically or mentally asserts that *one exact first measure of a genus in one of the categories is definitionally the same as another exact first measure of a genus in one of the categories* at time *t* and the one exact first measure is numerically the same as the other, both of which are numerically the same as some species defined by a differential characteristic (or more than one) and a proximate generic characteristic.

Thus, for example, in the context of dialectical inquiry, we might assert at time *t* that Socrates is cultured. If we suppose that Socrates is an exact first measure of a genus in the category of substance, if we suppose that being cultured is an exact first measure of a genus in the category of quality, and if we further suppose that the attribute of being cultured belongs to Socrates at *t*, then our assertion at *t* that Socrates is cultured is true. For another example, in the context of philosophical inquiry, we might assert that human beings are essentially rational social animals. Perhaps we propose this as a definition of what it is to be human. Suppose, for the sake of the example, that being human is an exact first measure of a genus in the category of substance. Suppose further that being a rational social animal is an exact first measure of a genus in the category of substance. Now, if it turns out that being human *is the same exact first measure of a genus in the category of substance as* being a rational social animal. Then the assertion that human beings are essentially rational social animals is true.

In the next chapter, on the basis of the analysis of oneness and measure offered here, I consider how Aristotle understands the nature of the relation that obtains between the intensional contents of assertions and the real correlates in virtue of which they are true. We now know that, for Aristotle, the proper real correlates of assertions are exact first measures of genera in the categories of being, and we also know that Aristotle understands the intensional contents of assertions in terms of likenesses. How, on Aristotle's view, are the contents and the correlates related such that the former are true in virtue of the latter?

Chapter 9

The Ground of Truth

Aristotle is committed to the view that assertions are true or false in virtue of the way the world is and *not* in virtue of the fact of assertion. If someone asserts that Socrates is sitting and, as a matter of fact, Socrates is sitting, then as Aristotle sees it the assertion is true in virtue of the fact that Socrates is sitting and not because someone asserts that Socrates is sitting. How does he explain this?

In this chapter, I argue that Aristotle understands the relation between the intensional contents of assertions and their correlates in the real world in terms of accurate measurement.[1] Someone may think that if Aristotle conceives of truth in terms of measurement, he commits himself to an essentially relativistic epistemology and semantics along the lines of Protagoras's measure doctrine. I will explain why this thought, though tempting, is incorrect. Knowledge, for Aristotle, essentially involves and aims at truth. Truth, he thinks, essentially involves measurement. But he rejects the idea that our cognitions and assertions are the measures of beings. He propounds instead the doctrine that our cognitions and assertions are measured by mind and language independent exact first measures of genera in the categories of being.

The Measure and the Measured

Aristotle makes an important point at I 1.1053a5–8. He tells us that "the first thing from which, *as far as our perception goes*, nothing can be subtracted, all men make the measure, whether of liquids or of solids, whether of weight or of size; and they think they know the quantity when they know it by means of *this* measure" (trans., Ross, my emphasis). Prior to this in I 1 Aristotle has been talking about oneness, measure, and exactness without specifying whether or not he defines these *relative to our perception* or not. At 1053a5–8, he flatly asserts that human beings take as their measure the first thing from which nothing can be subtracted *as far as our perception goes* and that we take this measure (the one based on what we perceive as the most exact measure) as the starting point for our knowledge of the kind in question. This suggests that what it is to be a measure—and, hence, what it is to be exact and one—*just is* to be a quality or quantity from which *relative to human perception* nothing can be subtracted and to which nothing can be added. Aristotle rejects this suggestion outright.

Two claims at 1053a14–20 bear on the suggestion that measurement is relativized to human perception. First, at 1053a16, Aristotle tells us that the measure of the musical tones is not made according to the human perception of the tones through the ears but rather according to the accounts of the tones [αἱ μὴ κατὰ τὴν ἀκοὴν ἀλλ' ἐν τοῖς λόγοις]. This may mean that the measure is not relative to human perception but is instead grounded in an objective account. This will depend on whether or not the accounts themselves are relativized to human perception. Second, at 1053a19–20, Aristotle claims that we come to know the beings out of which a substance is constituted by dividing with respect to quantity or kind [γνωρίζομεν ἐξ ὧν ἐστὶν ἡ οὐσία διαιροῦντες ἢ κατὰ τὸ ποσὸν ἢ κατὰ τὸ εἶδος]. On the one hand, if we place the stress here on the fact that *we* are coming to know because *we* divide according to quantity or kind, the passage may support the idea that the first measures of things are relative to our perception of the beings into which things are divided. On the other hand, if we place the stress on the fact the we come to *know* because we divide according to *quantity or kind*, then the passage may allow for reading according to which measure is defined by the beings themselves out of which the substance is constituted and not by our perception of them.

Aristotle directly responds to these worries at the end of I 1. At 1053a31–b8 he considers the following question: Are perception and knowledge the measures of the things they are about, or are our perceivings and knowings measured by the things we claim to perceive and know? Aristotle tells us at 1053a35–b3 that Protagoras defended the first alternative—that human perception and knowledge measure all things:[2]

Πρωταγόρας δ' ἄνθρωπόν φησι πάντων εἶναι μέτρον, ὥσπερ ἂν εἰ τὸν ἐπιστήμονα εἰπὼν ἢ τὸν αἰσθανόμενον· τούτους δ' ὅτι ἔχουσιν ὁ μὲν αἴσθησιν ὁ δὲ ἐπιστήμην, ἅ φαμεν εἶναι μέτρα τῶν ὑποκειμένων. οὐθὲν δὴ λέγοντες περιττὸν φαίνονταί τι λέγειν.

But Protagoras says that "man is the measure of all things," as if he had said "the man who has scientific knowledge" or "the man who perceives," and that these are the measure because they have in the one case perception and in the other case scientific knowledge, which we say are measures of the underlying object. People who say what Protagoras says, then, are saying nothing, though they appear to be saying an extraordinary thing. (trans., Reeve)

Aristotle attributes to Protagoras the following: (1) that human beings who perceive or know—and not just any human beings—are the measures of all things, (2) that these people are the measures of all things *because* they have perception or knowledge (and not for any other reason), and (3) that their having perception or knowledge explains their being measures *because* perception or knowledge themselves are said to be measures of objects. The most fundamental and salient point is that, according to Aristotle, Protagoras believed that perception and knowledge are themselves the measures of objects. Of which objects? According to the passage, all objects. As Aristotle presents Protagoras's view, perception and knowledge are the measures of all objects.

This much can be said about the view Aristotle attributes to Protagoras at 1051a35–b3. What is Aristotle's take? Already at 1053a35–b3, as a preface to his recapitulation of Protagoras's doctrine, Aristotle had stated his own understanding of the relationship between perception, knowledge, and measure, implicitly dismantling Protagoras's approach in advance of presenting it:

καὶ τὴν ἐπιστήμην δὲ μέτρον τῶν πραγμάτων λέγομεν καὶ τὴν αἴσθησιν διὰ τὸ αὐτό, ὅτι γνωρίζομέν τι αὐταῖς, ἐπεὶ μετροῦνται μᾶλλον ἢ μετροῦσιν. ἀλλὰ συμβαίνει ἡμῖν ὥςπερ ἂν εἰ ἄλλου ἡμᾶς μετροῦντος ἐγνωρίσαμεν πηλίκοι ἐσμὲν τῷ τὸν πῆχυν ἐπὶ τοσοῦτον ἡμῶν ἐπιβάλλειν.

Also, we say that scientific knowledge is a measure of things, as is perception, because of the same thing, namely, that we come to know something by them, since really they are measured more than they measure. It is as if someone else measured us and we came to know how big we are by seeing that he applied the cubit-measure to such-and-such a fraction of us. (trans., Reeve)

Aristotle here grants that perception and knowledge are said to be measures of things [μέτρον τῶν πραγμάτων], and that the reason they are said to be measures is because we come to know something [γνωρίζομέν τι αὐταῖς] by means of them. Thus far it would seem that he and Protagoras could agree. But Protagoras—according to Aristotle—thought that perception and knowledge are the measures and the things we come to know are the measured. Whereas Aristotle claims on the contrary that the things we come to know are the measures and perception and knowledge are the measured.

Aristotle's Measure Doctrine

Aristotle's claim that the things we come to know are the measures of human perception and knowledge has profound implications for his account of the essence of assertoric truth and falsehood. As I will argue below, Aristotle here establishes that the correspondence-as-congruence relation between the intensional contents of mental acts of assertion and the correlates in the real world of these is best understood in terms of his account of measurement.

In I 1, Aristotle explains his understanding of how measurement, perception, and knowledge are related by means of an analogy. He says it is as if we were able to watch some third party measuring our height (the thing to be measured) with a ruler (the unit of measure), learning thereby what our height is. The third party measuring our height is analogous to the philosopher evaluating our claims to perception and knowledge of objects in the world. The intensional contents of our perceptions and knowings—the cognitive content of our perceptions and knowledge—are analogous to our height. The things we claim to perceive or know are analogous to the cubit; these are the real correlates of the intensional contents of our perceptions and knowings that we yearn to come to know. We learn whether or not we actually perceive or know by comparing the real correlates we claim to perceive or know with the intensional contents of our perceptions and knowledge just as, according to the analogy, we learn how tall we are by comparing the length of the cubit measure to our height.

Aristotle's rendering of the analogy may be contrasted with how Protagoras would draw it. For Protagoras, it is as if we were able to watch some third party measuring the length of a ruler (the thing to be measured) with our height (the measure), learning thereby what the length of the ruler is. By way of the analogy, then, Protagoras would be saying that we should evaluate the real correlates (the things to be measured) of our perceptions and knowledge claims with the intensional contents of our perceptions and knowledge claims (the measures), learning thereby what the real correlates are. The intensional contents of our perceptions and knowledge claims become the standards by means of which things in the world are measured. Insofar as something fails to conform to the measures expressed in our mental assertions, to that extent it fails to be one thing and, indeed, fails to be.

To use a contemporary way of distinguishing the approaches: Protagoras's measure doctrine insists on world-to-mind fitness—things in the world must conform to our perceptions and knowledge claims; Aristotle's measure doctrine insists on mind-to-world fitness—our perceptions and knowledge claims must conform to the things in the world.

Given Aristotle's measure doctrine, what aspect of perception and knowledge is measured by the things in the world that we claim to perceive and know? With Ross, I take it Aristotle asserts in the prior passage that perception and knowledge are the things to be measured for accuracy, and that the things we are supposed to perceive and know are the measures of the accuracy our perception and knowledge. Given Aristotle's account of perception and knowledge, nothing other than the intensional contents of perception and knowledge could plausibly serve as what gets measured against real correlates for accuracy. The psyche asserts whatever it asserts by means of intensional contents that are putative likenesses of things in the world.

On the basis of these comparisons between Protagoras's view and Aristotle's view, we can see how Aristotle's real definitions of assertoric truth and falsehood invoke his measure doctrine. The intensional contents of linguistic and mental assertions are exact likenesses of exact first measures of genera in the categories of being. The exactness of the intensional contents, or the lack of exactness, is determined by comparing the intensional contents with their real correlates, each of which is itself an exact first measure of a genus in one of the categories of being. These exact first measures in the world are the measures of our assertions about them. Thus, for example, if someone asserts, in the context of philosophical inquiry, that to flourish is to engage in philosophical thought, we would need to determine first whether or not the intensional contents of our assertions about flourishing and philosophical inquiry *are likenesses of first measures* of the genus of living beings in the category of substance. If our assertions are not about exact first measures, then strictly speaking they are not well-formed assertions in the context of philosophical inquiry. Then, second, we would need to determine if the intensional contents of our assertions about flourishing and philosophical inquiry are *exact* likeness of the first measures they signify or represent. This would be a matter of comparing the intensional contents of our assertions with the exact first measures themselves, using the latter as the bases for determining whether or not the former are exact likenesses.

The important development here is that the relation between the intensional contents and their real correlates is spelled out in terms of exact likeness—the intensional content of an affirmation, a denial, or a definition is an exact likeness of the first measure of a genus with which it is correlated. And the meaning of "exact likeness" has a quite definite meaning for Aristotle: a mental act of assertoric truth obtains just in case nothing can be added or subtracted from the intensional content of the act without thereby undermining the sameness of essence that obtains between the intensional content and the real correlate. Assertoric falsehood is now explicable in terms of the failure of exact likeness—the intensional content of a false assertion adds or subtracts something from the first measure or the combined first measures that are its real correlates.

Recall that in chapter 1 we saw that Aristotle explains the essence and ultimate purpose of all cognitive states—perceptions, memories, experience, and the various kinds of knowledge he recognizes—in terms of assertoric truth and falsehood. We are now in a position to see that the essence and ultimate purpose of all cognitive states is to assert intensional contents that are exact likenesses of first measures of kinds in the categories. Truth obtains whenever we achieve this complete activity of the psyche.

Aristotle's Metrical Account of the Correspondence Relation

If truth and falsehood are functions of the relation between intensional contents of assertions and their correlates in the real world, how did

Aristotle understand this relation? The analogy of the cubit measure at I 1.1053a31–b3 clarifies Aristotle's main claim: the objects of perception and knowledge are the measures of the assertoric content of perception and knowledge. The analogy and the more general discussion of oneness and measure in I.1 indicate that Aristotle conceives of measurement in terms of the correlative pair: the measure and the measured. To better understand his account of measurement and truth, therefore, it will help to consider how he understands relatives of this sort in the *Metaphysics*.

In this section I offer additional reasons for thinking that Aristotle rejects the idea that, in general, relatives of the sort that subsumes the correlative pair {measure, the measured} are intrinsically quantitative. As a consequence, he would deny that perception, knowledge, and truth are intrinsically quantitative. I also explain why he would reject the idea that the kind of relation that obtains between an intensional content of an assertion *insofar as that content is what is measured* and the being that is correlated with that intensional content *insofar as that being is a measure* is a species of the kind of relation that obtains between a patient and an agent. He does not think that the intensional contents of assertions are "made true" by their real correlates in the sense that the real correlates actively make the intensional contents true and those contents are passively made true. Instead he explains the relation between the intensional contents of assertions and their real correlates in terms of the measurement relation, a sort of relation essentially different from the relation that obtains between an agent and a patient.[3]

Aristotle discusses the nature of relatives at length in *Metaphysics* Δ 15 and *Categories* 7. I will focus my attention on Δ 15, but it will be useful first to summarize here the most germane parts of *Cat.* 7.[4] First, in *Cat.* 7, Aristotle offers two general definitions of what it is to be a relative—one at 6a36–37 and one at 8a31–32. At 6a36–37 he tells us that "we call relatives all such things as are said to be just what they are, of or than other things, or in some other way in relation to something else." [Πρός τι δὲ τὰ τοιαῦτα λέγεται, ὅσα αὐτὰ ἅπερ ἐστὶν ἑτέρων εἶναι λέγεται ἢ ὁπωσοῦν ἄλλως πρὸς ἕτερον.][5] At *Cat.* 8a28–37 he rejects this way of defining relatives because it fails to explain why no substance is a relative, and instead he defines relatives as those things "for which being is the same as being somehow related to something" [ἔστι τὰ πρός τι οἷς τὸ εἶναι ταὐτόν ἐστι τῷ πρός τί πως ἔχειν]. This definition explains the plausibility of the definition at *Cat.* 6a36–37—if the being of a relative just is being somehow related to something else, then it is likely we will say just what it is in terms of how it is related to that correlative—but it also entails that no substance is a relative, since the being of a substance is not the same as being somehow related to something else. The being of a relative, then, according to Aristotle in *Cat.* 7, is essentially the being related somehow to something else.

From 6b28–7b14 in *Cat.* 7, Aristotle makes the case that every relative, without exception, is said in relation to a correlative: "All relatives are spoken of in relation to correlatives that reciprocate." [πάντα δὲ τὰ πρός τι πρὸς ἀντιστρέφοντα λέγεται, . . .][6] He makes the point in this passage in terms of the first definition of a relative, but it can be made in terms of his considered definition at *Cat.* 8a31–32: all relatives are what they are in relation to some relative. The change in register from how we talk about the relative to how the relative is in-itself—from, as Carnap would put it, the formal to the material mode of discourse—is straightforward.

On the basis of his definition at *Cat.* 8a31–32, Aristotle argues at 8a37–b4 that knowing a relative entails knowing its correlative.[7] This is of particular interest because Aristotle claims at *Cat.* 7, 6b2–6, that perception and knowledge are relatives. Aristotle has quite a bit to say about the pairs of relatives {knowledge, what is knowable} and {perception, what is perceptible} in *Cat.* 7. For my purposes here the most important information pertains to how the relatives in each pair depend on each other for their being. At 7b22–8a12 Aristotle argues that the being of every perception depends on the being of its correlative perceptible, but the converse does not hold: most of what is perceptible can exist independently of its being perceived. The same holds for knowledge and what is knowable. What is perceptible is metaphysically prior to and independent of the perception of it; what is knowable is metaphysically prior to and independent of the knowledge of it.

Returning now to the discussion in the *Metaphysics*, Aristotle introduces three senses of relatives at the beginning of Δ 15 at 1020b26–32. Which sort of relative is a measure? He discusses the first sort of relative at Δ 15.1020b32–1021a14. He says that every relative of this kind is related, either definitely or indefinitely, to some number or to the one [λέγεται δὲ τὰ μὲν πρῶτα κατ' ἀριθμὸν ἢ ἁπλῶς ἢ ὡρισμένως, πρὸς αὑτοὺς ἢ πρὸς ἕν] and that they are all of them said of some number and are determinations of some number [ταῦτά τε οὖν τὰ πρός τι πάντα κατ' ἀριθμὸν λέγεται καὶ ἀριθμοῦ πάθη]. At Δ 15.1021a12–14 he reaffirms what we have learned from I.1 that "the one is the beginning and measure of number, so that all these relations imply number, though not in the same way." [τὸ δ' ἕν τοῦ ἀριθμοῦ ἀρχὴ καὶ μέτρον, ὥστε ταῦτα πάντα πρός τι λέγεται κατ᾽ ἀριθμὸν μέν, οὐ τὸν αὐτὸν δὲ τρόπον.]

I take it therefore that what it is to be a relative of this first kind is to be a definite or indefinite determination of some number or of the one itself in the genus of quantity. And the correlatives of relatives of this sort will be definite or indefinite determinations of numbers or of the one itself. All such relatives and all their correlatives therefore will be subsumed by the genus of quantity, and the relations in which they stand will all be quantitative relations. But we know from I 1 (and Δ 6, see below) that Aristotle's account of measurement is intended to apply to first measures in all the categories of being as well as all the things that are measured by these first measures. So the first sort of relative introduced by Aristotle would not include all it would need to include were it to be the sort of relative that subsumes either first measures or what they measure.

Aristotle discusses the second sort of relative at Δ 15.1021a14–1021a26. Aristotle here fills out what he had in mind at 1020b30 when he explained the second kind of relative by means of the phrase "and generally the active relative to the passive" [ὅλως τὸ ποιητικὸν πρὸς τὸ παθητικόν]. The phrase may also be rendered by "the agent relative to the patient" or "the maker relative to the made." At 1021a14–16 Aristotle analyzes what is active and what is passive in terms of powers:

τὰ δὲ ποιητικὰ καὶ παθητικὰ κατὰ δύναμιν ποιητικὴν καὶ παθητικὴν καὶ ἐνεργείας τὰς τῶν δυνάμεων,

Things that can act or be acted on are said to be relative with reference to a capacity to act or be acted on and to the activations of the capacities. (trans., Reeve)

In specifying here the kind of relative he has in mind, he carefully differentiates between, on the one hand, correlative pairs of what is active and what is passive considered insofar as these are powers and, on the other hand, the same correlative pairs considered insofar as they are activities of these powers ["τὰ δὲ ποιητικὰ καὶ παθητικὰ κατὰ δύναμιν ποιητικὴν καὶ παθητικὴν καὶ ἐνεργείας τὰς τῶν δυνάμεων"]. Aristotle's examples at 1021a16–19 make it fairly evident that each correlative pair of agents and patients needs to be understood in terms of his basic metaphysical distinction between correlative powers and activities. His first example is of the correlative pair {that which heats, that which is heated}. First he considers this pair insofar as it includes powers: {that which is capable of heating, that which is capable of being heated}; then he considers the same pair insofar as it includes the activity of these powers: {that which is heating, that which is being heated}. His second example is truncated—explicitly involving only the correlative pair {that which cuts, that which is cut} insofar as these are activities actually undertaken—but it can be understood along the lines of the first example: the pair can be understood in terms of potential activity {that which is capable of cutting, that which is capable of being cut} and in terms of actual activity (that which is cutting, that which is being cut}.

Thus, Aristotle understands relatives of the second sort in terms of what is active or what is passive, conceived either potentially or actually. Aristotle uses this basic characterization to clarify the way in which relatives of this sort differ from relatives of the first sort, the way they may entail reference to time, and the way they may involve privation. In each case, his remarks bear on his account of measurement and truth.

First, at Δ 15.1021a19–21 Aristotle differentiates relatives of the second sort from relatives of the first sort. Unlike relatives of the second kind, relatives of the first kind "are not activities except in the sense which has been elsewhere stated; activities in the sense of movement they have not." Determinations of numbers do not—because they cannot—move. Insofar as it makes sense to say that they are activities, it will not be because they move. In what sense are they activities? Aristotle tells us he has discussed the relevant sense elsewhere. With Ross I take it that Aristotle is referring to his discussion of the mathematical activities at the end of *Metaphysics* Θ 9 and the end of *Metaphysics* Θ 10. Recall that Aristotle had explained there the activity of mathematical objects in terms of the complete activity of thought. Relatives of the first kind, then, are a kind of complete activity.

Aristotle's main point seems to be that mathematical objects (relatives of the first sort) are not activities in the sense relevant to being a relative of the second kind—relatives of the first kind may be activities in some sense, but they are not activities in the sense of movement, which is the sense that applies to relatives of the second kind. If this is correct, then Aristotle understands relatives of the second kind in terms of kinetic activity. What is active or what is passive (conceived either potentially or actually) is so in the kinetic sense: it is a mover or it is moved.

We saw above that according to Aristotle's measure doctrine, the intensional contents of assertions are measured by their objective correlates. We also know that it is in virtue of the objective correlates obtaining, and not in virtue of the intensional contents obtaining, that assertoric truth obtains. As a consequence, if Aristotle explains what measures and what is measured in terms of what is active or what is passive, whether conceived potentially or actually, then the objective correlates must be what is active in a kinetic sense and the intensional contents must be what is passive in a kinetic sense. This would entail that he conceives of assertoric truth and falsehood as kinds of incomplete activity perception and, as a consequence, that he conceives of perception and knowledge as kinds of incomplete activities. But it is patent that he thinks perceptions and knowledge are complete activities, and as we saw in the last chapter, he thinks truth and falsehood are kinds of complete activity. These are grounds for thinking that assertoric truth and falsehood are not relatives of the second sort.

At Δ 15.1021a26–b3, Aristotle discusses the last of the three sorts of relatives introduced at 1020b26–32. The first sort included determinations of number; the second sort included powers to act and be acted upon. Aristotle tells us that all relatives in these sorts are relatives because what they are essentially is to be related to something else. They are not what they are essentially because something else is related to them. As he puts it at 1021a26–29:

> τὰ μὲν οὖν κατ' ἀριθμὸν καὶ δύναμιν λεγόμενα πρός τι πάντα ἐστὶ πρός τι τῷ ὅπερ ἐστὶν ἄλλου λέγεσθαι αὐτὸ ὅ ἐστιν, ἀλλὰ μὴ τῷ ἄλλο πρὸς ἐκεῖνο.

> Things that are said to be relative with reference to a number or a capacity, then, are all relative because of being said to be just what they are of another thing, not because of the other thing's being relative to them. (trans., Reeve)

In contrast to this, Aristotle tells us at 1021a29–30 that the relatives subsumed by the third sort are relatives because what they are essentially is for something else to be related to them:

> τὸ δὲ μετρητὸν καὶ τὸ ἐπιστητὸν καὶ τὸ διανοητὸν τῷ ἄλλο πρὸς αὐτὸ λέγεσθαι πρός τι λέγονται.

> But what is measurable or scientifically knowable or thinkable is said to be relative because of another thing's being said to be [what it is] relative to them. (trans., Reeve)

As examples of relatives in this third sort, Aristotle offers that which is measured, that which is known, and that which is thought [τὸ δὲ μετρητὸν καὶ τὸ ἐπιστητὸν καὶ τὸ διανοητὸν]. Each of these is a relative *not* because what each is just is to be said of something else but, rather, because what each is just is to have something else said of it.

Thus, to spell out the consequences of the passage, a being that is measured is measured because something else—viz., the measure—is essentially related to it and *not* because it is essentially related to its measure; in other words, being measured is essentially being measured by some measure. Similarly, a being that is known is known because something else—viz., some assertion—is essentially related to it and *not* because it is essentially related to that by which it is known; in other words, being known is essentially being known by means of some assertion. Again, a being that is perceived is perceived because something else—viz., some perception—is essentially related to it and *not* because it is essentially related to some perception.

Aristotle explains what he has in mind at 1 Δ 15.021a29–30 by way of two examples at 1021a30–b3: thought and the object of thought, and sight and the object of sight. Let me begin with his second example at 1021a34–b3—the example of sight and the object of sight—since it is better developed:

> ὁμοίως δὲ καὶ τινός ἐστιν ἡ ὄψις, οὐχ οὗ ἐστιν ὄψις (καίτοι γ' ἀληθὲς τοῦτο εἰπεῖν) ἀλλὰ πρὸς χρῶμα ἢ πρὸς ἄλλο τι τοιοῦτον. ἐκείνως δὲ δὶς τὸ αὐτὸ λεχθήσεται, ὅτι ἐστὶν οὗ ἐστιν ἡ ὄψις.

> Similarly sight is the sight of something, not of what it is the sight of (though of course it is true to say this). Instead, it is relative to color or something of that sort. But the other way the same thing will be said twice: sight is of what sight is of. (trans., Reeve)

Aristotle understands objects of the senses in much the same way as he understands objects of knowledge and thought. He takes it for granted that sight is essentially the sight of an object. Indeed, as he reminds us, on his account sight is essentially related to a specific sort of object (the "proper sensible of sight") which is color or something of that sort. But the sight of an object is not essentially what it is *because* the object of sight is said of it. If someone wishes to know what the sight of an object is, we would not do well to tell her that the sight of an object is the sight *of an object of which there is sight*. This may seem so obviously unhelpful that one might wonder why anyone would suggest saying it.

To see why someone would suggest it, we need to consider how we would explain the nature of an object of sight. According to Aristotle, an object of sight is essentially an object *of which there is sight*. Were someone to ask us what an object of sight is, we *would* do well to tell her that an object of sight is essentially an object of which there is sight. An object of sight is what it is because something other than it—sight—is related to it. Sight itself is not like this. Sight is not what it is because something other than it—an object of sight—is related to it. Here Aristotle makes use of distinctions familiar to us from Plato's *Euthyphro*, particularly the claims about seeing and being seen at 10b–c, and we can apply those insights to Aristotle's second example involving objects of thought and thought.

At 1021a30–31 Aristotle contrasts what it is to be the object of thought with what it is to be the thought of an object in a way similar to how he contrasted what it is to be the object of sight with what it is to be the sight of an object:

> τό τε γὰρ διανοητὸν σημαίνει ὅτι ἔστιν αὐτοῦ διάνοια, οὐκ ἔστι δ' ἡ διάνοια πρὸς τοῦτο οὗ ἐστὶ διάνοια (δὶς γὰρ ταὐτὸν εἰρημένον ἂν εἴη.)

> For what is thinkable signifies that there can be a thought of it, but the thought is not relative to what it is a thought of, since we would then have said the same thing twice. (trans., Reeve)

σημαίνει at 1021a30 has the sense of "indicates that." If someone were to ask what we mean by the phrase "the object of thought" (or what we mean by the term "τό διανοητὸν"), an appropriate explanation would be that by "the object of thought" we intend to indicate the object of which there is a thought. This is all well and good. An object of thought, according to Aristotle, *is what it is* because something other than it—thought—is related to it. After all, that is the point of using it as an example of the third kind of relative.

But Aristotle denies that a similar explanation will help someone understand what we have in mind when we use the phrase "the thought" [ἡ διάνοια]. The phrase "the thought" may well be extensionally equivalent to the phrase "the thought of an object"—this is analogous to the fact that the phrase "sight" is extensionally equivalent to "sight of an object," which is part of the lesson of the example at 1021a31–b3—but were someone to ask what we mean by the phrase "the thought" we ought not say that we intend to indicate the thought of an object of thought. This would not be an acceptable explanation of the semantic intension of the phrase. Yet this *would* be the explanation we should need to give supposing that the thought of an object *is what it is* because something other than it—an object of thought—is related to it. But the thought of an object is *not* what it is because an object of thought is related to it. According to Aristotle, an indication of this fact is that we are apparently saying the same thing twice in offering the definition of the phrase—we are explaining the intension of the term "thought" with a phrase that includes the term "thought." (See the *Topics* here on Aristotle's proscription of circular definitions.) But this is merely an indication that there is a problem with the proposed explanation. The real problem with the proposed explanation is that it flouts the teaching of the *Euthyphro*.

Why is the explanation of "the object of thought" informative, while that proposed for "the thought of an object" trivial? Because in fact, according to Aristotle, an object of thought is a relative of the third kind, whereas the intensional content of a thought itself is not. While it is true, according to 1021a29–30, that an object of thought is essentially an object of thought because something else—the intensional content of the thought about that object—is related to it and not because it is related to the intensional content of the thought about it. On the contrary, the intensional object of a thought of an object is essentially what it is, according to Aristotle, because in part *it* is related to something else (namely, the object of which it is a thought). According to *De Anima* III.3–8 thought is essentially what it is because it—thought—is essentially a kind of mental discrimination involving imagination and assertion in relation to an object.

Aristotle's Asymmetrical Measurement Relation

Aristotle understands true and false assertion in terms of what is measured (the intensional content of a thought) and what measures it (the first measure of some kind in one of the categories). According to *Metaphysics* Δ 15 a true or false assertion is what is measured and is a relative of the third kind: a true or false assertion is essentially what it is because something else—viz., the first measure(s) in virtue of which it is true or false—is related to it. A true or false assertion is not essentially what it is because it is related to something else. And what measures in the case of a true or false assertion is not similarly a relative of the third kind; the first measures in virtue of which assertions are true or false are not essentially what they are because something else—the intensional contents of an assertions—is related to them. As we have seen in chapter 8, according to Aristotle the first measures of genera in the categories are first measures whether or not assertions are made about them. And as we saw in the preceding sections of this chapter, these mind and language independent first measures are metaphysically prior to and independent of our assertions about them.

Aristotle confirms my proposed reading of *Metaphysics* Δ 15 in I 6. He again addresses the relationship between what measures and what is measured. I 6 is principally about the nature of the opposition between the one and the many. Aristotle had raised this question initially in I 5 in conjunction with the question of how the equal was related to the greater and the lesser. He returns to the question about the one and the many at the beginning of I 6, and from 1056b3–16 he argues that impossible consequences follow from the assumption that the one and the many are absolutely opposed.[8]

Wishing to avoid these consequences, at I 6.1056b16–32 Aristotle distinguishes different senses in which things are said to be many. First he notes at 1056b16–17 that things that are divisible are said to be many. I take it that he means by that, that only things that are divisible are said to be many. Then, second, at 1056b17–20 he distinguishes the two senses in which divisible things are said to be many. In one sense, "many" means the same as "a plurality which is excessive either absolutely or relatively," where for Aristotle every plurality is a plurality of ones into which it is divisible. In this sense, "many" is similar in meaning to "few" when used with the sense "a plurality which is deficient [either absolutely or relatively]." In another sense "many" means the same as "number," and when it is used with this sense "many" is opposed to "one." Aristotle explores this latter sense from I 6.1056b20–1057a17. In doing so he makes additional and important claims about the relationship between things that are measured and their measures.

To begin with Aristotle reminds us of his view of the relationship between number and oneness—a view we saw he defended in I.1—according to which every number is a plurality of ones and, for every kind, the first measure of that kind is the one for that kind. Thus, every number insofar as it is a quantity is a plurality of units and, for the kind number, the first measure of number is the unit; every number of white things is a plurality of individual whites, and for the kind white, the first measure is some one white thing; and, importantly, every number of measured things is a plurality of ones, and for a kind of measured things, the first measure is the one for that kind. As Aristotle puts it at 1056b20–22:

> οὕτως γὰρ λέγομεν ἓν ἢ πολλά, ὥσπερ εἴ τις εἴποι ἓν καὶ ἕνα ἢ λευκὸν καὶ λευκά, καὶ τὰ μεμετρημένα πρὸς τὸ μέτρον [καὶ τὸ μετρητόν]·

> For it is in this way that we say that something is one or many, just as if we had said one and ones, or white thing and white things, or things measured relative to the measure. (trans., Reeve)

Aristotle's claim here compresses three different and related points on which he expatiated in I 1. The first and second of these points are fairly straightforward. The third—which has to do with the measure and the measured—is a bit more complicated. Let me quickly address the first and second points and then I will consider the third point more carefully. First, he tactily reminds of the relationship between oneness and number insofar as it is a kind of quantity, claiming that were we to say "one or many"—where "many" has the sense of "number," and "number" is understood to denote the kind of quantity named "number"—we would say the same as "one and ones." Second, he reminds us of the relationship between oneness and number in kinds not in the category of quantity, telling us that were we to say "one or many"—where we are referring to many white things, and "many" has the sense of "number"—we would say the same as "white thing and white things." As I mentioned above, these claims follow from what we have learned in I 1.

Turning now to the third point, there is a textual difficulty and then a question of interpretation. On the one hand, if we don't accept καὶ τὸ μετρητόν at I 6.1056b22, then the phrase "οὕτως γὰρ λέγομεν ἓν ἢ πολλά, ὥσπερ εἴ τις εἴποι . . . τὰ μεμετρημένα πρὸς τὸ μέτρον" has a sense similar to that of the first second examples: "For we say 'one or many' just as if one were to say 'that which has been measured relative to the measure.'"

In which case Aristotle is reminding us of the relationship between oneness and number (and hence "many" when it has the sense of "number") insofar as what it is to be one is to be a first measure of a kind. He claims that were we to say "one or many"—where we are referring to many measured things, and "many" has the sense of "number"—we would say the same as "the things that have been measured and the measure," where here "τὰ μεμετρημένα" corresponds with "many" and "τὸ μέτρον" with "one" and the intended point is that "one or many" has the sense of "the measure and the things measured." On the other hand, if we accept καὶ τὸ μετρητόν at 1056b22, then the phrase "οὕτως γὰρ λέγομεν ἓν ἢ πολλά, ὥσπερ εἴ τις εἴποι . . . τὰ μεμετρημένα πρὸς τὸ μέτρον [καὶ τὸ μετρητόν]" has the sense of "For we say 'one or many' " just as if as if one were to say that which has been measured relative to the measure and the measured.

Either way we decide on the text, Aristotle's point is that the relevant sense of "one" at 1056b20 is the same as that of "the measure" at 156b22 and the relevant sense of "many" at 1056b20 is the same as "that which has been measured" at 1056b21. The idea here is that when we use "many" in the sense of "number," it is properly opposed to the use of "one" in the sense of the first measure of number, and in these senses the one is opposed to the many in the same way that the measure is opposed to the things measured.

Aristotle has reminded us in cryptic fashion at 1056b20–22 of the various ways in which oneness and number are related in the different categories and are related insofar as what it is to be one is to be a first measure and what it is to be a number is to be a plurality of measured things. He has explained at 1056b22–32 how the use of "many" in the sense of "number" explains the senses of "multiple," "two," and "few" (and using his insights to criticize Anaxagoras). At 1056b32–33 Aristotle comes right out and says that the one is opposed to that which is many in number as measure is opposed to things measured:

– ἀντίκειται δὴ τὸ ἓν καὶ τὰ πολλὰ τὰ ἐν ἀριθμοῖς ὡς μέτρον μετρητῷ· ταῦτα δὲ ὡς τὰ πρός τι, ὅσα μὴ καθ᾽ αὑτὰ τῶν πρός τι.

The one is opposed to the many in the case of numbers, then, as measure to the measurable. But these are opposed as those relatives are that are not intrinsically relatives. (trans., Reeve)

From the grammatical point of view ταῦτα here may have a narrow or wide anaphoric scope. It could refer back only to the opposed pair including the measure and the things measured, or to both pairs of opposites (the one and the many, the measure and the things measured). In the first case, Aristotle would be claiming that only the measure and the things measured are opposed as relatives that are not from their very nature relative. In the second case, in addition to the measure and the things measured, the one and the many in number would also be opposed as relatives that are not by their very nature relative.

The larger context however suggests that these are only apparent alternatives. Aristotle is in the process of explaining the way in which the one and the many are opposed. He has told us at 1056b16–20 that the only way in which the many is opposed to the one is when "many" is used in the sense of many in number and is opposed to the one. At 1056b32–33 Aristotle is telling us *how* the one is opposed to the many in number—they are opposed as measure to things measured. Therefore, the one is opposed to the many in number in exactly the way that measure is opposed things measured *because* the one just is a first measure and the many in number just are the things measured by such a measure. As a consequence of this equivalence, in telling us at 1056b32–33 that the measure and the measured are opposed as relatives that are not by their very nature relative, Aristotle is telling us that the one and the many are opposed as relatives that are not by their very nature relatives. Thus either way we read ταῦτα at 1056b33 the force of the subordinate clause is the same. Nor are the claims at I 6.1056b32–33 surprising, given how Aristotle understands oneness, measure, and number in I.1 and I.2, and it is to these earlier chapters of I to which we should look if we wish to better understand why Aristotle thinks the one is opposed to the many in number as measure is to things measured.

The fact that a measure and the things measured by it are opposed as relatives that are *not* by their nature relatives—the important point made at 1056b32–33 for my purposes here—leaves it open which of the two relatives is a relative because the other is related to it and not vice versa. Aristotle goes on to say at 1056b33–1057a1 that he has discussed elsewhere that there are two ways in which things are said to be relative. He briefly recapitulates these two ways by means of examples and a terse gloss:

> ἡμῖν ἐν ἄλλοις ὅτι διχῶς λέγεται τὰ πρός τι, τὰ μὲν ὡς ἐναντία, τὰ δ' ὡς ἐπιστήμη πρὸς ἐπιστητόν, τῷ λέγεσθαί τι ἄλλο πρὸς αὐτό.

We have determined elsewhere that things are said to be relatives in two ways, some as contraries, others in the way that scientific knowledge is related to the scientifically knowable, where something is said to be a relative because something else is relative to it. (trans., Reeve)

I take it that Aristotle is adverting here to *Metaphysics* Δ 15. According to his brief summary of the discussion, on the one hand he had identified some things as relatives because they are contraries, and on the other hand he had identified others as relatives because something else is said in relation to it. As an example of this latter case, Aristotle offers the familiar example of knowledge relative to the thing known. He says that, in the case of knowledge relative to what is known, one thing is said relative to another [τῷ λέγεσθαί τι ἄλλο πρὸς αὐτό]. Aristotle brings up these distinctions at I 6.1056b33–1057a1 in order to clarify his immediately prior claim at 1056b32–33 about the opposition between a measure and what it measures. We should infer therefore, first, that the relatives that are not from their nature relatives at 1056b33 are the relatives at 1056b36–1057a1 that are relatives because one thing is said of another, and second that a measure and the things it measures are relatives of the same sort as knowledge and what is known. It is also safe to assume, third, that the first sort of relatives at 1056b35–36—those that are contraries—would subsume relatives that *are* by their very nature relatives.[9]

In *Metaphysics* Δ 15, 1021a26–30 Aristotle had used both things measured and things known as examples of things that are relative because something else is related to them and *not* because their very essence includes being related to something else. If so and if we assume for the moment that what Aristotle says from I 6.1056b32–1057a1 parallels exactly what he says in *Metaphysics* Δ 15, then the example at I 6.1056b32–33 of knowledge and the thing known and the example at I 6.1056b33–1057a1 of the measure and the things measured should be interpreted as follows: the thing known and the thing measured are relatives because something else—knowledge and a measure, respectively—is related to each and *not* because the very essence of each includes being related to something else.

Regardless of which discussion of relatives Aristotle has in mind at I 6.1056b32, and regardless of how we should understand the relationship between numerical and functional relatives and relatives that are opposed as contraries, of immediate interest is how Aristotle intends us to interpret the opposed pairs of relatives {knowledge and thing known} and {measure and thing measured} at 1056b32–1057a1. Aristotle settles the matter at 1057a4–17.

At I 6.1057a4–6 Aristotle draws out the main implication of the points made at 1056b32–a1—namely, that the one and the many in number are opposed not as contraries but as relatives that are not from their very nature relative but, instead, because one of the relatives is said of the other:

> ἔστι γὰρ ἀριθμὸς πλῆθος ἑνὶ μετρητόν, καὶ ἀντίκειταί πως τὸ ἓν καὶ ἀριθμός, οὐχ ὡς ἐναντίον ἀλλ' ὥσπερ εἴρηται τῶν πρός τι ἔνια· ᾗ γὰρ μέτρον τὸ δὲ μετρητόν, ταύτῃ ἀντίκειται, διὸ οὐ πᾶν ὃ ἂν ᾖ ἓν ἀριθμός ἐστιν, οἷον εἴ τι ἀδιαίρετόν ἐστιν.

> For number is plurality that is measurable by one, and so the one and number are in a way opposed—not as contrary, but in the way we said certain relatives are. (For insofar as one is a measure and the other measurable, in that way they are opposed, which is why not everything that is one is a number—for example, if something is indivisible it is not a number.) (trans., Reeve)

To illustrate his point, Aristotle reminds us that the one is the measure and number is what is measured. Given what he has said about measures and things measured in I 1 and I 2, we are prepared for the claim at I 6.1056a6–7 that not everything that is one is a measure of number. Different kinds of things have different measures, but each measure of a kind is the one for that kind.

Given what we have learned from Δ 15, we might immediately infer from I 6.1056a4–7 that what is measured is a relative because the measure is said of it and, hence, that number is a relative because the one is said of it. What Aristotle goes on to say at 1057a6–12 about the relationship between knowledge and the thing known and a measure and the thing measured vindicates this inference:

> ὁμοίως δὲ λεγομένη ἡ ἐπιστήμη πρὸς τὸ ἐπιστητὸν οὐχ ὁμοίως ἀποδίδωσιν. δόξειε μὲν γὰρ ἂν μέτρον ἡ ἐπιστήμη εἶναι τὸ δὲ ἐπιστητὸν τὸ μετρούμενον, συμβαίνει δὲ ἐπιστήμην μὲν πᾶσαν ἐπιστητὸν εἶναι τὸ δὲ ἐπιστητὸν μὴ πᾶν ἐπιστήμην, ὅτι τρόπον τινὰ ἡ ἐπιστήμη μετρεῖται τῷ ἐπιστητῷ.

And though scientific knowledge is said to be in the same way relative to the scientifically knowable, the way does not turn out to be the same. For whereas scientific knowledge may seem to be the measure and the scientifically knowable what is measured, the fact is that all scientific knowledge is scientifically knowable but not all that is scientifically knowable is scientific knowledge, because in a way it is scientific knowledge that is measured by the scientifically knowable. (trans., Reeve)

As he did in I 1.1053a1–b3, so here Aristotle acknowledges that the relatives involved in the opposed pair {knowledge, what is knowable} can be understood in terms of the relatives in the opposed pair {what measures, what is measurable}. He also reminds us, as he did in I 1 as part of his discussion of Protagoras's view, that people tend to think that the pair of opposed relatives {knowledge, what is knowable} is just another way of talking about the more general pair of opposed relatives {what measures, what is measurable}, where the tendency to talk this way is based on the following assumptions: (i) knowledge = what measures, and (ii) what is knowable = what is measurable. Aristotle denies (i) and (ii); he made his case against both in I 1. Rather, according to Aristotle, "in a sense knowledge is measured by what is knowable." The pairs of opposed relatives are related by means of the following rules: (iii) what is knowable is a species of what measures and (iv) knowledge is a species of what is measured. The pairs of opposed relatives are similar, but not by means of the identities expressed in (i) and (ii). There are related by virtue of transposition by means of the inclusion rules expressed by (iii) and (iv).

What does Aristotle mean when he states that "*in a sense* knowledge is measured by what is known" [ὅτι τρόπον τινὰ ἡ ἐπιστήμη μετρεῖται τῷ ἐπιστητῷ]? Aristotle uses this fact to explain his preceding claims that all knowledge is knowable but not all that is knowable is knowledge. How are we to understand his explanation? What is being explained? The fact that not all of what is knowable is knowledge, the fact that all knowledge is knowable, or both? And how do we explain the apparent suggestion that there is a sense in which knowledge is *not* measured by what is knowable.

If we assume that in general and paradigmatically for Aristotle *human* knowledge is *knowledge of* something other than knowledge, then it cannot be true that all that is knowable is the same as knowledge.[10] There must be some things that are knowable, that aren't the same as knowledge itself, and that we are aiming to know. In such cases—which are the majority of cases for human beings—Aristotle thinks that the knowable serves as the measure of knowledge and not vice versa. To use David Charles's way of putting it in Charles (2004), we have knowledge because the formal causal content actualized in that epistemic state is the same as the formal causal content of what is knowable in the world, and if the formal causal content actualized in the mind differs from the formal causal content of what is knowable in the world, we need to eliminate the difference so that the formal causal content in our minds conforms to that of the knowable in the world.

But at the same time, if all knowledge is knowable, there may be cases where someone's knowledge *insofar as it is taken as an instance of what is knowable* serves itself as a measure of knowledge. For Aristotle, knowledge *insofar as it is knowledge* is essentially an activity of the mind in which the formal causal content in actualized in that mental activity is identical with the formal causal content of what is knowable in the world. Hence, if I know something, then I can use my knowledge *qua* the actualization of what is knowable in my mind as a measure of what you claim to know.

Thus, at I 6.1057a7–12 Aristotle is reaffirming his claims in *Metaphysics* Δ 15 that (1) the knowable is a relative because knowledge is said of it and (2) what is measurable is a relative because some measure is said of it. Aristotle here clarifies how we should interpret both claims in epistemic contexts: (1') the knowable *insofar as it is what is knowable and not insofar as it is a measure* is a relative because knowledge *insofar as it is a mental state that is about what is knowable* is said of it and (2') knowledge *insofar as it is what is measurable by what it is about* is a relative because what is knowable *insofar as it is a measure and not insofar as it is what is knowable* is said of it. (2') captures Aristotle's point that "*in a sense* knowledge is measured by what is known" [ὅτι τρόπον τινὰ ἡ ἐπιστήμη μετρεῖται τῷ ἐπιστητῷ].

Aristotle reinforces this at I 6.1057a12–17 when he says that there is a sense in which plurality (when used in the sense of "many in number") is relative to oneness just as knowledge (insofar as it, like plurality, is what is measured) is to what is knowable (insofar as it, like the one, is what measures):

τὸ δὲ πλῆθος οὔτε τῷ ὀλίγῳ ἐναντίον—ἀλλὰ τούτῳ μὲν τὸ πολὺ ὡς ὑπερέχον πλῆθος ὑπερεχομένῳ πλήθει—οὔτε τῷ ἑνὶ πάντως· ἀλλὰ τὸ μὲν ὥσπερ εἴρηται, ὅτι διαιρετὸν τὸ δ' ἀδιαίρετον, τὸ δ' ὡς πρός τι ὥσπερ ἡ ἐπιστήμη ἐπιστητῷ, ἐὰν ᾖ ἀριθμὸς τὸ δ' ἓν μέτρον.

Plurality, though, is contrary neither to the few (instead, the much is contrary to it, as plurality that exceeds is to plurality that is exceeded) nor in all ways to the one. One way, however, in which they are contrary, as has been said, is because a plurality is divisible, whereas the one is indivisible, but in another way they are relative, just as scientific knowledge is to the scientifically knowable, if plurality is number and the one a measure. (trans., Reeve)

Aristotle has argued that what it is to be one is to be the first measure of a kind. In the case of the kind number, the unit is the one that is the first measure. The unit is the one that serves as the measure of number. Hence, if we assume that plurality is used in the sense of "number," then the unit is the one that is the measure of plurality. And he emphasizes here that knowledge is to the knowable as what is measured is what measures.

In *Metaphysics* Δ 15, I 1, and I 6, Aristotle is unwavering in his belief that the measureable is a relative that is relative because some measure is related to it and not because it is related to some measure. In Δ 15, he tells us that what is knowable is a relative because knowledge is related to it and not because it is related to knowledge. This claim might appear to conflict with what Aristotle says in I 1 and I 6 where he rejects the Protagorean view that knowledge is the measure of the knowable and argues on the contrary that knowledge is measurable by the knowable. Thus, according to I 1 and I 6, knowledge *insofar as it is measurable* is a relative because the knowable is said of it and not because it is said of the knowable. The conflict is merely apparent however. Knowledge and the knowable may be, and in fact are, related in two different ways. On the one hand, knowledge and the knowable are related as intentional state and object of intentional state; on the other hand, they are related as measureable and measure.

On my reading of *Metaphysics* Δ 15, I 1, and I 6, Aristotle is committed to the following claims: (1) knowledge is a relative because it is said in relation to the object of knowledge and not because the object of knowledge is said in relation to it; (2) the measure is a relative because it is said in relation to the thing measured and not because the thing measured is said in relation to it; (3) the object of knowledge is a relative because knowledge is said in relation to it and not because it is said in relation to knowledge; (4) the thing measured is a relative because the measure is said in relation to it and not because it is said in relation to the measure; and (5) knowledge is the thing measured and the object of knowledge is the measure of knowledge.

Someone might think that these claims entail either that Aristotle gives up (1) and (3) or that he gives up (2) and (4). For, if knowledge is the thing measured and the object of knowledge is the measure, then in the first place, it seems that knowledge is a relative because the object of knowledge is said in relation to it and not because it is said in relation to the object of knowledge (which flatly contradict (1)), and in the second place it seems that the object of knowledge is a relative because it is said in relation to the object of knowledge and not because the knowledge is said in relation to it (which flatly contradicts (3)). Understood this way, since Aristotle remains committed to (1) and (3), he must reject (2) and (4).

As I read *Metaphysics* Δ 15 and I 1, 2 and 6, Aristotle can consistently maintain (1)–(5). The correlative pair {knowledge, object of knowledge} is different than the correlative pair {measure, thing measured}. Two things—Aristotle and the equine essence, say—can instantiate both correlative pairs at the same time. Indeed, given how Aristotle understands knowledge and measurement, if x is knowledge of y, then (i) y is the measure of x and (ii) it is not the case that x is the measure of y.

Let me be more precise about these relations. As Aristotle understands it, the correlative pair {knowledge, object of knowledge} is instantiated by x and y such that x is knowledge of y only when the correlative pair {measure, thing measured} is instantiated by x and y such that y measures x. Let's assume that Aristotle has knowledge of the equine essence. It follows from this that the equine essence instantiates the relative {object of knowledge} and Aristotle instantiates the relative {knowledge}. The relative {object-of-knowledge} belongs to the equine essence because the relative {knowledge} that belongs to Aristotle is said in relation to the relative {object of knowledge} that belongs to the equine essence and not because the relative {object of knowledge} that belongs to the equine essence is said in relation to the relative {knowledge} that belongs to Aristotle. At the same time, the fact that the equine essence is the object of Aristotle's knowledge entails that it—the equine essence—instantiates the relative {measure} and Aristotle instantiates the relative {thing measured}. The relative {thing measured} belongs to Aristotle because the relative {measure} that belongs to the equine essence is said in relation to the relative {thing measured} that belongs to Aristotle and not because the relative {thing measured} that belongs to the Aristotle is said in relation to the relative {measure} that belongs to the equine essence.

On my view, knowledge entails measurement. The fact that x is knowledge of y—the fact that x instantiates the relative {knowledge} and y instantiates the relative {thing known}—entails the fact that y measures x—entails that y instantiates the relative {measure} and x instantiates the relative {thing measured}. There is nothing unusual about the claim that one relation entails another, and I cannot imagine Aristotle denying it. For example, suppose x is the sibling of y, then there is some z such that z is the parent of x and z is the parent of y. The sibling relation is not the same as the parent-child relation, although the fact of the former entails the fact of the latter: if there are siblings, then there are parents. (Here I am supposing a timeless use of "is.") Nor is there anything strange in thinking that a relation r entails that its relata are related to each other by means of other relations at the same time. Suppose that x is a male, y is a female, and x is the brother of y. These facts entail the facts, among others, that (i) y is the sister of x, (ii) it is not the case that y is the brother of x, and (iii) it is not the case that x is the sister of y. Being a brother is not the same as being a sister.

Aristotle's account of relations allows him to talk both about the things that are related and about the relatives that inhere in the things that are related by means of them. If Aristotle knows the equine essence, then two beings—Aristotle and the equine essence—are related by means of the correlative pair {knowledge, thing known} that constitutes the knowledge relation, the first of which inheres in Aristotle, the second in the equine essence.

Nothing Aristotle says about relations rules out the possibility that a relation is a complex in the sense that it is actualized just in case and because other relations out of which it is constituted are actualized. The most interesting and important relations in Aristotle's system are complex in just this sense. Consider a rough approximation of Aristotle's conception of friendship based on virtue:

> x and y are friends in the primary sense of "friend" only if (i) x has affection for y, (ii) y has affection for x, (iii) x has goodwill for y for y's sake because y is virtuous, (iv) y has goodwill for x for x's sake because x is virtuous, (v) x knows

that y has goodwill for x because x is virtuous, (vi) y knows that x has goodwill for y because y is virtuous, (vii) x knows that y knows that x has goodwill for y because y is virtuous, and (viii) y knows that x knows that y has goodwill for x because x is virtuous.

The friendship based on virtue between x and y is a relation between x and y. The goodwill that x has for y is a relation between x and y, and it is not the same as—although it is in part constitutive of—the relation of friendship that obtains between them. Similarly, the goodwill that y has for x is a relation between x and y that differs from—but is in part constitutive of—the relation of friendship between x and y. In addition, the goodwill that y has for x differs from the goodwill that x has for y: the particular relation of goodwill that obtains when x has goodwill for y is not the same as the particular relation of goodwill that obtains when y has goodwill for x. The type of relation is the same but the token relations are different. So, too, x knowing that y has goodwill for x for x's sake because x is virtuous is a relation between x and y yet again different from—but in part constitutive of—the relation of friendship that obtains between them. I could continue, but my point has already been made: the actualization of the relation of friendship entails the actualization of a number of other relations that are in part constitutive of friendship.

As Aristotle conceives it, knowledge is like this. The actualization of knowledge—a relative, according to Aristotle—itself entails the actualization of a number of other relations out of which it is partially constituted. Thus, consider Aristotle's concept of demonstrative knowledge as presented in *Posterior Analytics* A 1–2:

> s has demonstrative knowledge of the assertion that all x are y only if (1) s asserts that all x are y and it is necessary that all x are y, (2) s has the ability to demonstrate that the assertion that all x are y follows from the noetic grasp s has of the essence of y and the essence of y.

Suppose Aristotle has demonstrative knowledge that, for example, all horses are quadrupeds. Aristotle's demonstrative knowledge that all horses are quadrupeds is ultimately grounded in his noetic grasp of the equine essence and is about the equine essence, specifically the part of the equine essence having to do with how many legs a horse has by nature. Thus, the relative {the knowledge that all horses are quadrupeds} inheres in Aristotle, and the correlative {the known fact that all horses are quadrupeds} inheres in the equine essence.

Let me now apply the distinctions about relatives made in *Metaphysics* Δ 15 and *Categories* 7 to Aristotle's claims at 1053a31–b3. Insofar as perception and knowledge are things that are measured, they are relatives of the third kind because (1) what they are essentially is for something else—the objects of perception or of knowledge—to be said of them, and (2) they are not what they are essentially because they are said of something else. Aristotle seems to think his brief discussion settles the question about whether human perception or knowledge measures, or is measured by, things in the world.

On the contrary, according to Protagoras, perception and knowledge measure objects and objects are measured by perception and knowledge. Applying the account in *Metaphysics* Δ 15 of that which is measured to Protagoras's view, since objects of perception and knowledge are among the things that are measured, they are relatives of the third kind and, hence, (1) what they are essentially is for something else—perception or knowledge—to be said of them, and (2) they are not what they are essentially because they are related to something else.

Aristotle thinks this reflects a fundamental confusion about the nature of perception and cognition. By their very nature, perception and cognition aim at truth. Truth, as we now see, essentially involves the psyche asserting of some first measures of being an intensional content that is an exact likeness of those first measures. The ultimate purpose of this sort of complete activity, as Aristotle understands it, is to grasp the essences of the first measures themselves. The point is not to make the world conform to the intensional contents of our thoughts. The point is to ensure that our intensional contents are exact likenesses of the first measures of being.

In *Metaphysics* Δ 15 Aristotle had offered as examples three species of the third kind—that which is measured, that which is known, and that which is thought. Things in each of these three sorts are relatives of the third kind. Therefore, since that which is known is an object of knowledge, objects of knowledge are relatives of the third kind: something is an object of knowledge because knowledge is said of it and not because it is said of knowledge.

However, given what Aristotle says in *Metaphysics* I 1 the things in the world that are the objects of knowledge measure knowledge. From which claim two consequences appear to follow: First, in I 1 objects of knowledge are measures, whereas in *Metaphysics* Δ 15 it would appear that they are what is measured. Second, in I 1 knowledge is measured by objects of knowledge; hence knowledge is among the things that are measured; therefore, knowledge is among the things that are relatives of the third kind discussed in Δ 15. But in Δ 15 it would appear that knowledge is not among the things that are relatives of the third kind.

These apparent consequences are merely apparent. On the one hand, insofar as something is an object of knowledge, it is an object of knowledge because knowledge is said of it and not because it is said of knowledge. On the other hand, insofar as something is a measure of knowledge, it is a measure of knowledge because it is said of the intensional content essentially involved in knowledge and not because the intensional content of knowledge is said of it. Can one and the same thing be both an object of knowledge and a measure of knowledge? Yes. It can be an object of knowledge because knowledge is said of it, and it can be a measure of knowledge because it is said of knowledge; insofar as it is an object of knowledge, it is not said of knowledge, and insofar as it is a measure of knowledge, knowledge is not said of it.

This becomes clearer when we see that the reasons why knowledge is said of an object of knowledge are different from the reasons why a measure of knowledge is said to be a measure of knowledge. The middle term differs in each case. Aristotle thinks that something is an object of knowledge because some mind makes an assertion about it on the basis of either noetic comprehension or epistemic demonstration. Being the target of that sort of mental activity explains what it is to be an object of knowledge. But that is not what explains what it is to be a measure of knowledge. Something is a measure of knowledge, for Aristotle, because it is a first principle or a cause of some kind of being.

Hence, when the psyche actively asserts some intensional content of some first measure of being, the essence of this psychological activity involves—indeed generates—a relation defined by the first measure being said of (related to, in an asymmetrical way) the intensional contents of the assertion. There is a clear sense, then, in which truth obtains in virtue of the first measures of being obtaining and *not* in virtue of the intensional contents obtaining—when we make assertions, we thereby take the first measures of being to be the measures of the intensional contents of our assertions. This is to say, in contemporary jargon, in making assertions we thereby take the first measures of being the truth-makers of our assertions. But the first measures of being are not essentially truth-makers. They become truth-makers when noetic agents engage in the activity of making assertions.

Conclusion

To conclude my analysis of Aristotle's account of oneness and measurement, let me turn to a passage in *Metaphysics* N 1, at, 1087b33ff, that bolsters my way of construing Aristotle's account of the way in which first measures of being—and not intensional contents—are responsible for the realization of truth and falsehood without being themselves intrinsically related to the intensional contents of acts of assertion.

At the beginning of this passage Aristotle repeats almost word for word the claim he made at 1072a32–34 ("τὸ δ' ἓν ὅτι μέτρον σημαίνει"), and in the midst of the passage he again makes the same point, importantly amplifying it ("σημαίνει γὰρ τὸ ἓν ὅτι μέτρον πλήθους τινός"). In addition to reaffirming the claim that "one" signifies a measure, Aristotle makes three claims that are fundamental to his account of unity and measurement—(1) measures and things measured are subjects with natures of their own, (2) what is one and a measure is a first principle [ἀρχὴ καὶ τὸ μέτρον καὶ τὸ ἕν], and (3) a measure is necessarily and always the same thing as that to which it belongs as a measure [δεῖ δὲ ἀεὶ τὸ αὐτό τι ὑπάρχειν πᾶσι τὸ μέτρον].

The passage at N 1.1087b33–1088a14 reads as follows:

τὸ δ' ἓν ὅτι μέτρον σημαίνει, φανερόν. καὶ ἐν παντὶ ἔστι τι ἕτερον ὑποκείμενον, οἷον ἐν ἁρμονίᾳ δίεσις, ἐν δὲ μεγέθει δάκτυλος ἢ ποὺς ἤ τι τοιοῦτον, ἐν δὲ ῥυθμοῖς βάσις ἢ συλλαβή· ὁμοίως δὲ καὶ ἐν βάρει σταθμός τις ὡρισμένος ἐστίν· καὶ κατὰ πάντων δὲ τὸν αὐτὸν τρόπον, ἐν μὲν τοῖς ποιοῖς ποιόν τι, ἐν δὲ τοῖς ποσοῖς ποσόν τι, καὶ ἀδιαίρετον τὸ μέτρον, τὸ μὲν κατὰ τὸ εἶδος τὸ δὲ πρὸς τὴν αἴσθησιν, ὡς οὐκ ὄντος τινὸς τοῦ ἑνὸς καθ' αὑτὸ οὐσίας. καὶ τοῦτο κατὰ λόγον· σημαίνει γὰρ τὸ ἓν ὅτι μέτρον πλήθους τινός, καὶ ὁ ἀριθμὸς ὅτι πλῆθος μεμετρημένον καὶ πλῆθος μέτρων (διὸ καὶ εὐλόγως οὐκ ἔστι τὸ ἓν ἀριθμός· οὐδὲ γὰρ τὸ μέτρον μέτρα, ἀλλ' ἀρχὴ καὶ τὸ μέτρον καὶ τὸ ἕν). δεῖ δὲ ἀεὶ τὸ αὐτό τι ὑπάρχειν πᾶσι τὸ μέτρον, οἷον εἰ ἵπποι, τὸ μέτρον ἵππος, καὶ εἰ ἄνθρωποι, ἄνθρωπος. εἰ δ' ἄνθρωπος καὶ ἵππος καὶ θεός, ζῷον ἴσως, καὶ ὁ ἀριθμὸς αὐτῶν ἔσται ζῷα. εἰ δ' ἄνθρωπος καὶ λευκὸν καὶ βαδίζον, ἥκιστα μὲν ἀριθμὸς τούτων διὰ τὸ ταὐτῷ πάντα ὑπάρχειν καὶ ἑνὶ κατὰ ἀριθμόν, ὅμως δὲ γενῶν ἔσται ὁ ἀριθμὸς ὁ τούτων, ἢ τινος ἄλλης τοιαύτης προσηγορίας.

It is evident, however, that the one signifies a measure. And in every case there is another thing, an underlying subject— for example, in a musical scale, it is a quarter-tone, in spatial magnitude, a finger or a foot or something else of the sort, in rhythms, a beat or a syllable, and similarly in weight, some standard weight. And in all cases it is the same way, in qualities it is a quality, in quantities a quantity. And the measure is indivisible, in kind for qualities and perceptually for quantities, as the one is not intrinsically substance of anything. And this stands to reason. For the one signifies the measure of some plurality, and number signifies a measured plurality and a plurality of measures. That is why it is quite reasonable for the one not to be a number, since the measure is not measures, on the contrary, what both the measure and the one are is a starting-point. The measure, thought, must always be some self-same thing belonging to all [the relevant cases]—for example, if horse is the measure, to horses, and if human, to humans, and if human or horse or god, perhaps to living being, and the number of them will be a number of living beings. But if the things are human, pale, and walking, there will scarcely be a number of them, because they all belong to the same thing, which is one and the same in number—nonetheless, there will be a number of kinds of them, or of some other such term.[11] (trans., Reeve)

At 1088b37–a4, Aristotle extends the preceding point about the nature of the one in each genus to every case, explicitly mentioning the categories of quality and quantity: For my purposes, the most important claim comes at 1088a2–3: ἀδιαίρετον τὸ μέτρον, τὸ μὲν κατὰ τὸ εἶδος τὸ δὲ πρὸς τὴν αἴσθησιν. Aristotle has just claimed that "one" signifies the measure; he now states that the measure is indivisible, noting at 1088a3–4 that the measure is indivisible in kind in the category of quality and indivisible in perception in the category of quantity. This reinforces and explains

Aristotle's claims elsewhere that "one" signifies the first measure of a genus—what it is to be one is to be the first measure of a genus—but denotes things that are indivisible—all the things that are by their very nature called "one" are indivisible.[12]

At N 1.1088a10–11 there are two related issues having to do with the manuscripts. Both bear on my reading of the passage. First, based on his understanding of the sense of 1088a10–11, Ross follows Bonitz's conjecture that the εἰ clause in 1088a9 "should relate not to the measure but to the things measured," contrary to the sense of Codd. Γ which reads as follows: εἰ ἵππος τὸ μέτρον ἵπποθς, καὶ εἰ ἄνθρωπος, ἀνθρώπους. As a consequence, second, Ross rejects Bywater's decision to excise τὸ μέτρον at 1088a8, claiming that it "does not meet the whole difficulty."

Bonitz sees a difficulty at lines N 1.1088a8–11 because he assumes that things measured ground their measures and that this grounding relation is asymmetrical. Given these assumptions, it makes sense to think that the things measured must be prior to and determine their measure, and that they serve as the basis for the selection of the measure. In the examples at lines 1088a10–11 Aristotle begins with given sets of things to be measured and then uses these sets as the grounds on the bases of which to identify the proper measures that are the same as all those things. This conforms with what we would expect of Bontiz's interpretation. However, in the examples in line 1088a9, if we accept the text in Codd. Γ, Aristotle begins with given measures and then uses *the measures* as the grounds on the basis of which to identify the things with which they are the same to which they are properly applied. This violates the asymmetry of the presumed grounding relation.

Bywater attempts to solve the problem by eliminating reference at 1088a8 to the measure—and hence eliminating the need to read what follows in terms of the presumed grounding relation entailed by it. He has this to say about the sense of the passage:

> If we ignore it [τὸ μέτρον] as an emblema, the sense of the second sentence (δεῖ δὲ ἀεὶ κτέ.) will be practically this: There must always be an element of identity (τὸ αὐτό τι) in the group of objects counted together horses, for instance, if the unit of measurement with which one starts be a horse, and men, if it be a man. But if one starts with a man, a horse, and a god, as the units in the group, these dissimilars have to be brought under a common term, say ζῷον, and the sum of them, when counted together, will be so many ζῷα.

As I understand the sense of the passage, we can follow Ross in rejecting Bywater's proposed excision and also accept the text in Codd. Γ. Bonitz is incorrect in thinking that Aristotle is committed to the asymmetrical grounding relation. The sameness between measure and things measured is symmetrical—as we should expect given that it is a sameness relation. At 1088a8, Aristotle states a rule for which he has argued in Iota: a measure applies to each thing measured in virtue of being something common to them all. The examples offered in 1088a9 are, on the one hand, applications of this rule where we know the measure in question—a horse; a man—and infer what is measured from the measure and the rule—horses and men, respectively, are measured by the supposed measures. The examples at 1088a10-11, on the other hand, begin with things that are to be measured—man, horse, god; man, white, walking—and involve using the rule to determine which measure properly applies to all of the things to be measured—a living being and a class, respectively, are proper measures of these sets of things to be measured. Given this interpretation, we can make sense of the received text without excision or emendation.

Note that none of this conflicts with Aristotle's claim that things measured ground, asymmetrically, the correctness of measures. At lines 1088a8–a11, Aristotle is not concerned with whether or not a given measure is an accurate measure of the things it measures. Rather, he is asserting a condition for such accuracy—a given measure must be the same as the things it measures.[13]

On the basis of these considerations, we can again reformulate Aristotle real definition of assertoric truth and falsehood, specifying more fully the relevant conception of exact likeness in terms of exact measurement:

> (Real Definitions of Falsehood and Truth "RFT") For every linguistic or conceptual subject *n* that signifies or *is an exact measurement of x*, which is a particular nature that is an exact first measure of a genus in one of the categories, for every linguistic or conceptual predicate *d* that signifies or *is an exact measurement of y*, which is a particular nature that is an exact first measure of a genus in one of the categories, for every linguistic or conceptual relation + that signifies or *is an exact measurement of* the real predicative relation of belonging to, and for every linguistic or conceptual relation – that signifies or *is an exact measurement of* the real predicative relation of not belonging to:

[F] Falsehood is a privation of a complete activity of a psyche in which that psyche either (a) linguistically or mentally asserts at time t that $d + n$ and y does not belong to x at time t or (b) linguistically or mentally asserts at time t that $d - n$ and y belongs to x at time t (c) linguistically or mentally asserts at time t that n is definitionally the same as d and the simple thing $x = y$ does not exist at time t.

[T] Truth is a complete activity of a psyche in which that psyche either (a) linguistically or mentally asserts at time t that $d + n$ and y belongs to x at time t or (b) linguistically or mentally asserts at time t that $d - n$ and y does not belong to x at time t or (c) linguistically or mentally asserts at time t that n is definitionally the same as d and $x = y = s \otimes g$ at time t (where s and g are, respectively, the species differential characteristic, i.e., the form or actuality, and the proximate generic characteristic, i.e., the matter or potentiality, that constitute the essence being defined, and where "$\otimes$" represents the fact that the unity of the form and matter is different from the other kinds of predicative unity).

Conclusion

The Subsequent Free Play of Thought

If you have stayed with me this far, I am thankful. I realize that we have worked through some thorny textual exegesis, some quasi-technical reconstructions of Aristotle's analyses and arguments, and a fair bit of scholarly debate. In concluding the book, I would like to step back from the details of the argument and offer some general remarks.

I have attempted to demonstrate that in the *Metaphysics* Aristotle systematically investigates and methodically defines the essence of his core kind of truth, the kind of truth that belongs to acts of assertion. Aristotle's exposition apparently conforms to the stages of inquiry he recommends in the *Posterior Analytics* for defining the essence of an object of inquiry. In *Metaphysics* book Γ, chapter 7, he offers nominal definitions of what the terms "truth" and "falsehood" signify, and in books A–Γ he offers arguments and examples that reveal that truth and falsehood so defined exist. In *Metaphysics* Δ 7 and 29 Aristotle differentiates the kind of truth that belongs to assertions from other kinds of being and other kinds of truth. He then carefully explains the nature of the kind of truth that belongs to assertions as part of his theory of being in books E–N, unfolding for us the fabric of his account of the essence of truth. Even if we resist the idea that the *Metaphysics* is a unified philosophical work, I hope to have shown that his investigation of truth directly informs the main arguments of the treatise, and that the resulting definition of truth is a major philosophical achievement.

Having offered an analysis of Aristotle's real definition of truth, it may be helpful to return to some of the outstanding questions raised earlier in the book and to consider how the definition of truth is relevant to answering them. I cannot hope here to answer fully any of these questions, but I can say something about how Aristotle's real definition of truth indicates the shape—as Wilfrid Sellars might have put it—of the correct answers.

Beginning with questions having to do with the semantics of assertion, the conception of truth that emerges in the *Metaphysics* would seems to differ from contemporary coherentist, pragmatist, minimalist, correspondence, and supervaluation theories of truth. As Aristotle understands it, truth is the full realization of the psyche's ability to accurately measure, by means of assertions, the fundamental units of being. Falsehood is a privation of this ability, explicable in terms of the gap in likeness between the exact first measures of genera in the categories of being and the intensional contents of our assertions that are about them and that are measured by them. The analyses I have defended entail that both linguistic and mental assertions *bear* truth—the kind of truth that belongs to assertions belongs to both linguistic and mental assertions. I have explained how Aristotle understands the sort of relations that obtain among linguistic assertions, mental assertions, the intensional contents of assertions, and the real correlates that make assertions true or false, but I have not endeavored here to formalize these semantic relations. Nor have I addressed how Aristotle's understanding of the asymmetrical relation that obtains between the intensional contents of assertions and the real things in virtue of which they are true (or false) might illuminate contemporary accounts of the relation in terms of a correspondence relation or a truth-making relation. That is work for the future.

Aristotle's definitions of truth and falsehood place very tight restrictions on the assertions that, strictly speaking, can be true or false. The semantic constraints may seem *so* extreme that the definitions are useless. After all, how many linguistic or mental assertions involve subject and predicate expressions that are intended to signify, in fact do signify, or are exact measurements of exact first measures in the genera of the categories? Aristotle would reply to this concern, I think, by noting that he is offering his definition of truth in the context of explaining the norms for philosophical inquiry and, in particular, the ideal conditions for the assertions that will constitute the content of philosophical wisdom. He is not concerned (or, at least, he is not *primarily* concerned) to define a conception of truth that will serve in ordinary language contexts or ordinary doxastic contexts. Rather, his definition is intended to establish the norm for assertions in the rigorous theoretical disciplines of philosophy, theology, mathematics, and the natural sciences. And arguably, it is this definition that has since set the agenda for these disciplines and, perhaps, continues to do so.

This suggests that we are well advised to compare Aristotle's account of truth with accounts—such as those devised by Frege, Russell, Carnap, Tarski, Montague, Kripke, Kaplan, and Soames—devised with an eye toward understanding truth in the context of philosophical semantics, the formal languages of logic and mathematics, and natural scientific and social scientific theories. For example, Aristotle's account of truth and falsehood enables him to make sense of approximate truth and falsehood in terms of measurement, accuracy, and error. The theory of approximate truth is notoriously difficult topic in contemporary philosophy of science. (See Weston 1987, 1988, and 1992 for insight into the contemporary discussion.) The fact that Aristotle's account of truth is both rigorous and naturally extended to assertions that require measures of approximation and error suggests that his account should be assessed in the "extraordinary" contexts of philosophical, mathematical, and scientific theorizing.[1] Were Aristotle presenting his ideas about truth to contemporary philosophers of science, he might talk about it in terms of the relationship between a model and the world, where the model is intended to be a more or less accurate representation of the way the world is. The accuracy of the model might be described mathematically in terms of error, and the real correlates of the assertions made within the model might serve as the basis for measuring the accuracy of the model.

Although Aristotle's definition of truth establishes a norm for assertions made in the context of seeking philosophical wisdom—which context sets the highest high epistemological bar—Aristotle may also wish to argue that all assertions, regardless of context, ought to be held to this high standard to the extent possible. (See Elgin 2017 for a discussion of the epistemic acceptability of assertions that are "close to the truth" and related issues as they arise in the context of contemporary philosophy.) Given the vagaries and ambiguities of ordinary language use and everyday beliefs, most ordinary assertions will fall far short of what the definition of truth, taken strictly, requires. Most assertions in most contexts will not signify exact first measures in genera of the categories of being, nor will they be intended to do so. But Aristotle may nevertheless insist that all assertions in all contexts aim at truth as he understands it to the extent possible and that, for example, we should at least ensure that the terms in our assertions each signify one and only one being, carving reality at its various joints as it were, even if we may not succeed in making assertions about the exact first measures of reality. After all, it is plausible that Aristotle would insist that *philosophers* consider carefully the extent to which any assertion accurately measures the things in the world it purports to be about, whether or not these things turn out to be fundamental measures of being. For Aristotle, in every case the pursuit of truth will require disambiguating and diminishing the vagueness of our terms and concepts, using the techniques painstakingly elaborated in the *Organon*, particularly in the *Topics* and the *Sophistical Refutations*. In both the theoretical and practical treatises Aristotle seems unreservedly committed to the application of these techniques in the pursuit of truth—using them in any context will bring us closer to understanding whether or not the assertions we are testing for truth give us accurate information about real things in the world.

In developing his conceptions of truth and falsehood and in thereby defending an account of language and thought aimed at accurately measuring the way the world is, Aristotle need not deny that language and thought can serve purposes other than securing theoretical truth, and he does not. He considers alternative ends served by language and thought in the ethical treatises, the *Rhetoric*, and the *Poetics*. Chief among these is the role Aristotle attributes to thought and language in his account of practical wisdom. Olfert 2017, for example, argues that Aristotle's account of truth is crucial to his understanding of practical reasoning and action, identifying practical truth as an essential part of acting well and urging us to reconsider the importance of truth in Aristotle's normative theory. I agree with Olfert that truth is fundamental to Aristotle's accounts of practical wisdom, deliberation, decision, and virtuous activity, and would argue that Aristotle's metrical definition of truth not only conforms to what he has to say about practical truth but enables him to cash out the apparently metrical requirements of his ethical doctrine of the mean. Castelli (2008) is suggestive of how this latter idea might be developed (see, especially, 211–14).

It is, therefore, an interesting question whether or not and how Aristotle's definition of truth will apply in the various contexts within which we make linguistic and mental assertions about the world. Another and related question has to do with the nature of the activity of assertion. In this book, I have not attempted to distinguish between Aristotle's understanding of linguistic assertion, on the one hand, and his understanding of mental assertion, on the other. The distinction, however, is important and needs to be emphasized. For Aristotle, the semantics of these two kinds of assertion—the linguistic and the mental—differ in fundamental ways, and Aristotle would urge us not to conflate them. The details of these differences and a thorough discussion of how Aristotle understood the nature of assertion must be pursued elsewhere, but Charles (2000), Crivelli (2004), Hestir (2013 and 2016), Modrak (1987 and 2001), and Wheeler (1999) offer ways into that discussion.

In addition to informing answers to questions about the semantics of assertions, Aristotle's real definition of truth also gives us insight into fundamental questions in Aristotle's metaphysics. Among these, for example, there is the principal theological question: What is the essence of God? We broached this question in chapter 1, and I can only hope to sketch here how the results of my analysis may help us to better understand Aristotle's answer. Menn (1992) and his online manuscript (not dated), Charles and Frede (2001), Gabriel (2009), De Koninck (2012), and Olson (2012) provide a sense of the difficulties, which are serious. Let us assume here, though, that any interpretation of Aristotle's theology must accept as data the following claims: The heavens and the sublunary world of nature depend upon an unmoved first mover. (See Λ.7, 1072b13–14.) This unmoved first mover is the first cause of the motion of everything else, which motion it causes by being loved [ὡς ἐρώμενον] as a good. (See Λ.7, 1072b2–4 and 1072b10–11.) This beloved first cause is properly considered God [ὁ θεός], who is an exact first measure in the genus of living beings in the category of substance. (See Λ.7, 1072b24–30.) God's essential activity [ἐνέργεια ἡ καθ' αὑτήν] is either identical with or involves thought [ἡ νοῦς ἐνέργεια ζωή]. (See Λ.7, 1072b26–27.) And God's thinking is a thinking on thinking [ἡ νόησις νοήσεως νόησις]. (See Λ.9, 1074b34–35.) I have argued that Aristotle defines thinking in terms of noetic acts of assertion, and that he defines truth as the noetic activity of accurately making assertions about the exact first measures of genera in the categories of being. If all of these premises hold, and we add the plausible claim that all of God's assertions are true, then it seems reasonable to conclude that God's essence involves truth. Indeed, God's essence would appear to involve, at the very least, God asserting of itself that it is the exact first measure that it in fact *is* in the genus of living beings in the category of substance. The suggestion that God engages in assertion may strike some as puzzling or absurd, but I think it is entailed by what Aristotle says: Aristotle conceives of thought in terms of assertion, and the purpose and ultimate good of assertion is truth. If my analysis of truth is correct, then God both measures itself and is measured by itself. Perhaps God thinks about other things as well—perhaps God is the genuine measure of all things, for Aristotle—but that is contested. All of this is speculative, of course, but suggests that Aristotle's definition of truth may help us to identify the key issues to address in order better understand the nature of Aristotle's God, the proper object of philosophical wisdom.

Aristotle's real definitions of truth and falsehood may also offer us deeper insight into how he understands and justifies his confidence in the logical axioms. Although his elenctic arguments in book Γ succeed in vindicating the axioms against his philosophical opponents, they do not of themselves provide us with his considered defense of the axioms in terms of his own philosophical system. We are now in a position to see better how Aristotle himself would argue for the axioms by recasting his elenctic arguments using his real definitions of truth and falsehood instead of the nominal definitions he uses in Γ. For although I cannot present my reconstructions of the arguments here, even if we only modify the arguments this much, the arguments are more sophisticated and more properly Aristotelian elenctic demonstrations of the axioms.

I noted in chapter 1 that, for Aristotle, truth is the proper function and ultimate good of the intellect. All intellectual activity aims at the truth. We can expect, therefore, that a proper understanding of Aristotle's definition of truth will give us insight into his epistemology. Recall that Aristotle explains the various modes of cognition in *Nicomachean Ethics* VI.1139b15–17, defining each as a kind of activity of the psyche by means of which it possesses truth by way of affirmation and denial. Given how Aristotle defines truth, we can now see clearly and distinctly that he understands every kind of knowledge in terms of true assertion and, hence, accurate measurement. Thus, it is hard to overstate the importance of Aristotle's theory of measurement for any adequate understanding of his epistemology. Since his theory of measurement is bound up with his account of oneness and number, it also suggests that Aristotle's philosophy of mathematics is more relevant to his epistemology and metaphysics than is usually thought. And if, as Olfert 2017 seems to argue, Aristotle's account of practical reasoning and practical truth is developed with his real definition of truth in mind—and this seems quite plausible, given that practical wisdom is a kind of *wisdom*—it appears that Aristotle's account of measurement, oneness, and number may help us to better understand his normative ethical theory.

When therefore in the *Metaphysics* and elsewhere Aristotle warmly recommends philosophical wisdom as the most wonderful sort of knowledge, our highest calling, the sort of thing that perhaps only God can possess, we should not be surprised. Aristotle's evaluation of the importance of philosophical wisdom depends upon his estimation of the value of truth, and his estimation of the value of truth could not be higher. In the *Nicomachean Ethics*, at 1096a14–17, Aristotle tells us that:

> ... it would perhaps be thought to be better, indeed to be our duty, for the sake of maintaining the truth [τῆς ἀληθείας] even to destroy what touches us closely [τὰ οἰκεῖα ἀναιρεῖν], especially as we are philosophers; for, while both are dear, piety requires us to honour truth [τὴν ἀλήθειαν] above our friends.

Aristotle does not offer his "it would perhaps be thought" here as a disclaimer—he is earnest about the preeminence of truth over friendship. And this is vaulting praise indeed. Aristotle extols friendship in relation to all the other so-called "external" goods in human life—wealth, physical beauty, good birth, political office, power over others, etc. (See, for example, *NE* 1169b7–10 and following, where Aristotle explicitly makes this claim.) And when Aristotle compares friendship with *all* the other human excellences, he claims it is the most necessary for human flourishing. He is quite emphatic about this—see, for example, *NE*, 1055a3–6—and yet the passage just quoted makes it clear that the virtue of piety demands that we value truth more than friendship. Perhaps though, given Aristotle's distinction between external and internal goods, there is an internal good (pleasure or some other activity of the psyche) more important than truth? Not so. Aristotle explains the proper function and ultimate good of the intellect in terms of truth, and he insists that there is no psychological activity more important than intellectual activity. Indeed, not only is truth more important for *human happiness* than anything else, according to Aristotle, it seems he thinks truth is among the most important things *all things considered*. For, again, if God's essential activity is or essentially involves the intellectual activity that constitutes philosophical wisdom—as Aristotle insists in *NE* X.8 for example—and if the proper purpose and ultimate good of all intellectual activity (including God's) *just is* truth, then since God is the most important of all beings, truth is the proper purpose and ultimate good of the most important of all beings.

All of which leaves us with an interesting question: Given how Aristotle defines truth, why would he—and why might we—value it more highly than friendship and, indeed, more highly than anything else?

Notes

Introduction

1. Charles (2000, 24). There is scholarly debate about how many stages of inquiry Aristotle acknowledges. See Bronstein (2016), (Ferejohn, unpublished), and Charles (2000) for details. I adopt Charles's view here.

2. As is customary, throughout this book I translate "ἀλήθεια" and "ψεῦδος" and their cognates by "truth" and "falsehood" and their cognates.

3. See also the first paragraph of Crivelli's chapter on Aristotle's account of signification and truth in Anagnostopolous (2008).

4. When I began this research in the 1990s only one book devoted to Aristotle's theory of truth had been published—*'Wahres Sein' in der Philosophie des Aristoteles* by Johannes G. Deninger in (1961). Maybe some of Heidegger's early and posthumously published lectures on Aristotle's philosophy are understood best as interpretations of Aristotle's theory of truth. I am unsure. (It is well known how difficult it is to interpret Heidegger's published works, never mind his posthumously published lectures. In some circles this is a notorious fact; in others merely a fact.) After Deninger's effort, if we consider books expressly written as expositions of Aristotle's account of truth, Crivelli (2004) was the second such book published, and Long (2010) was the third. In the last century, only four doctoral dissertations on the topic—Carson (1996), Carretero (1983), Harvey (1975), and Miller (1971). Various important articles and chapters were published on the topic in the last 100 years, although the majority have been published since the turn of this century.

5. See, for example, Pritzl (1998).

6. I would call these mental acts of assertion *apophantic acts*—which is the terminology Aristotle coined to discuss them—were it not for the fact that both Husserl and Heidegger used the term "apophantic" in developing their own phenomenological conceptions of true assertion. I do not want readers to conflate my interpretation of Aristotle's account of true assertion with the rich and difficult

ideas crafted by Husserl and Heidegger. Of course, the use of "assertion" involves its own risks. But I believe these risks are easier to manage.

7. Important recent work—especially that done by Primavesi and his colleagues—has improved dramatically our understanding of the manuscript transmission. I have benefitted enormously from Kotwick (2016) and the papers collected in Steel (2012).

8. Some think the title was coined by Andronicus in the first century BCE. Jaeger thought it was struck by a Peripatetic other than Aristotle and earlier than Andronicus.

9. Of these, some claim that the treatise involves a single conception of the science of metaphysics but contradictory conceptions of the object of this science; some claim (Natorp, Jaeger, Zürcher) that it involves contradictory conceptions of the science of metaphysics; some (A. Mansion, Dhondt, Aubenque) claim that it involves two different conceptions of the science of metaphysics, each studying a different object.

10. Of these, some (Natorp, Mansion, Aubenque) have argued that—in order both to avoid the philosophical disunity and to explain its origin—the treatises should be separated into two groups, one which would consist of the treatises authored by Aristotle, the other containing those added to the first set by later thinkers. Book K in particular is singled out for excision as inauthentic by many (A. Mansion, Aubenque) because the account of metaphysics therein is taken to conflict with that in E. Owens (1978, 18–22) doubts this reading. The Greek commentators, with the possible exception of Alexander of Aphrodisias, the medieval commentators, most commentators writing before the nineteenth century, and some commentators throughout the nineteenth and twentieth centuries accepted the authenticity and the philosophical unity of the *Metaphysics*. (Here I am extrapolating from Owens 1978, 16–17, based on my sense of the tradition.) Most scholars accept most of the books to be authentic.

11. Jaeger (1934, 192) argued that the *Metaphysics* as we have it is a synthesis of earlier and later parts and that these parts contain different notions of the science of metaphysics. The early view focuses on first principles; the later view focuses on substance. As he puts it:

> It may be stated here, although the inevitability of the assertion will not be clear until we have analyzed the later passages, that the view of metaphysics as a study of first principles, an aetiology of the real—a view which is connected with Plato's latest phase—is a sign of the earliest version of the *Metaphysics*, whereas the later formulation always devotes more attention to the problem of substance as such. Even in the doctrine of supersensible reality (M 1–9) we can clearly detect the aspect of principles yielding place in the later version to that of substance itself.

For an introductory overview of the current debate on these issues, see chapters 2 and 8 in Anagnostopoulos (2009).

12. Menn's online manuscript (*The Aim and the Argument of Aristotle's Metaphysics*) contains not only the best discussion of these issues but the most compelling case for the unity of the argument in the treatise.

13. I offer no new arguments here about how the *Metaphysics* was put together. I do not assume that Aristotle himself put the pieces together in the way they are now arranged, although I do assume that the various parts of the treatise are genuine.

14. All of the commentators agree on this point of interpretation. I provide textual arguments for these claims in the next chapter, but see *Posterior Analytics* I.1–4 and II.10–12 and 19; *Metaphysics* A.1; and *Nicomachean Ethics* VI, 1139b15f.

15. Of the passages about truth and falsehood outside the *Metaphysics*, none involve definitions of truth or falsehood. See below for my arguments in defense of this claim.

16. It is worth noting that, for the reasons just given, even if truth were not among the candidate kinds of being, Aristotle would still need to define truth in the *Metaphysics*. In contrast, he would not need to define each of the other sorts of being—the being of the categories, coincidental being, and potential and actual being—were any shown to be irrelevant to philosophical wisdom. Arguably, in fact, Aristotle dismisses coincidental being on these very grounds in E 2–3 and never returns to it in order to define it.

Chapter 1

1. He would raise relevant concerns about substituting extensionally equivalent expressions in intensional contexts. He was well aware of these difficulties. See Peterson (1969).

2. For passages related to sensory perception, see *DA* 418a5, 421a20, 424a20, 426b20, 427a20, 427b7, 428a5; for memory, see 449b20. For a recent and extended discussion of Aristotle's account of sense perception see Marmodoro (2014).

3. The Greek ἕξις, especially in the context of Aristotle's ethical works, has the sense of "a stable capacity to act, which capacity is the product of training."

4. Jaeger connects the discussion of knowledge in *Metaphysics* A 1 to Aristotle's *Protrepticus*, going so far as to say that A 1 is merely a précis of the latter, grafted—albeit poorly—to the *Metaphysics*:

> Knowledge has never been understood and recommended more purely, more earnestly, or more sublimely [than in the *Protrepticus*]; and it is still a dead letter today for those who cannot pursue it in this spirit. Now to teach us to understand it in this profound sense was what

Aristotle aimed at in the *Protrepticus*, and the famous introduction [A 1] to the *Metaphysics* is in essence nothing but an abbreviated version of his classical exposition of the matter there . . . We find that the introductory chapter of the *Metaphysics* is simply a collection of material extracted from this source for the purpose of a lecture, and that it is not even quite firmly cemented into place. (Jaeger, 1948, 69)

Following Jaeger's lead, we can see that in the *Protrepticus* Aristotle conceives of philosophical wisdom in terms of truth and values it for the sake of truth. In the *Protrepticus* Aristotle uses φρώνησις to denote philosophical wisdom; in the *Metaphysics* and the ethical works he opts instead for σωφία, reserving φρώνησις as a technical term for practical wisdom. Jaeger's and related discussions of Aristotle's use of φρώνησις in the *Protrepticus* and σωφία in the *Metaphysics* are of interest here. But regardless of his terminology, in all of these works he insists that philosophical wisdom is the most excellent activity of the human intellect. If Jaeger's conjecture about the relationship between the *Protrepticus* and A 1 is accurate, Aristotle's account of philosophical wisdom in the *Protrepticus* confirms that truth is the final cause of intellectual activity, and it also serves as a precedent for the importance of truth in Aristotle's investigation of philosophical wisdom the *Metaphysics*. See Nightingale (2009), the chapter on the *Protrepticus*, for a contemporary discussion of the fragmentary work as it relates to the topic of truth. Hutchinson and Johnson have developed a very useful web resource for the *Protrepticus*, <http://www.protrepticus.info/index.html>, at which you can find drafts of their reconstruction, translation, and commentary on the dialogue.

5. For excellent and recent discussions of the various parts of *Metaphysics* Book A, see the papers collected in Steele (2012).

6. 982a6–19. I follow Reale (1980) in thinking that σοφία, φιλοσοφία and πρώτη φιλοσοφία have the same sense in the *Metaphysics*.

7. Jaeger (1948, 166n1) thinks the passages warrant the claim that knowledge of God is identical with God's knowledge. In *NE* VI.7, Aristotle rejects the idea that human beings are the best among living things in the world, noting at 1141b1 that the heavenly bodies are more divine than human beings. Taken with the claims in *Metaphysics* A.1 and Λ.7, it is prima facie plausible that Aristotle's God is the proper object of philosophical wisdom. See the papers collected in Charles and Frede (2001, especially chapters 7–10).

8. Following Reale (1980, 21–22), I take it that according to A 2 the study of God is the study of the ultimate good of nature, and that God is personal and knows all things (and not just itself).

9. Aristotle's God is by nature the most important being of all. God is, thus, the proper object of philosophical wisdom, if not the sole object.

10. It is worth noting the connection here with the methodology Aristotle uses earlier in the *Metaphysics*, in the *Physics*, and in other works, where he

looks at the "pieces" of truth acquired by his predecessors in order to get at the "whole" truth.

11. For further details, see the *Posterior Analytics* and McKirahan (1992).

12. For a thorough overview of the difficulties surrounding the interpretation of *Metaphysics* book B, see the papers collected in Crubellier and Laks (2009).

Chapter 2

1. Aristotle specifically discusses the nature of priority in *Categories* 12 and *Metaphysics* Δ 11. For an excellent recent discussion of the difficulties, see Peramatzis (2011).

2. Of passages outside the *Metaphysics*, the following are crucial for an understanding of Aristotle's concepts of truth: *Categories*: 2a4–10, 4a23–b10, 13a37–b35, 14b11–23; *De Interpretatione*: 16a9–19, 16a32–b5, 16b26–17a7, 17a38–18a7, 18a12–27, 18a28–19b4, 21b18–19, 23a27–24b9; *Analytics*: 47a8–9, 52a24–38, 53b4–57b17, 64b9–10, 81b18–29; *Topics*: 111a14–20, 139a37–b3, 149b4–9, 157b26–31, 160a24–28; *Sophistical Refutations*: 178b24–9; *De Anima*: 427b8–20, 428a11–18, 428b2–17, 428b10–429a2, 430a26–b6, 430b26–30, 431b10–18, 432a10–14; *Nicomachean Ethics*: 1111b31–4, 1124b6, 1127b2, 1139b15–18, 1141a3–8, 1142b10–11; *Rhetoric*: 1355a14–19.2. None of these passages involve definitions of truth. Moreover, the claims made about truth in each passage conform to and are best explained in terms of the definitions Aristotle presents in the *Metaphysics*, although the proof for this must wait until I have completed the arguments in this book. *Categories* 14b11–23 may be an exception to the claim that no passage outside the *Metaphysics* presents a definition of truth. In that passage, Aristotle claims that true assertions and what they are about "reciprocate as to implication of existence," and that what an assertion is about, "causes" that assertion to be true. One might think this is an instance of the following schema: an assertion that *p* obtains is true just in case, and because, *p* obtains. In fact, Aristotle's claim at 14b11–23 conforms to and is best explained by the definition of the essence of truth in the *Metaphysics*.

3. Jaeger was keenly aware that Aristotle is arguing for the possibility philosophical wisdom in the *Metaphysics*; see for example, Jaeger (1948, 379).

4. The nominal definitions of "truth" and "falsehood" deployed in *Metaphysics* book Γ 3–8 express the main ideas on the basis of which, in *Metaphysics* books Δ-N, Aristotle develops his full account of the essence of truth and falsehood, i.e., his real definitions. I explain the distinction between nominal and real definitions below.

5. In his comprehensive and detailed assessment of Aristotle's theory of truth, Crivelli (2004, 132) analyzes the definitions presented at 1011b26–27, and claims that "in *Metaphysics* Γ.7 Aristotle defines truth and falsehood." De Rijk

(2002, vol. 2, 89) notes that the formulae express "operational" or "conventional" definitions of truth and falsehood. Whitaker (1996, 27) assumes that the formulae are definitions. Brown (1994, 212) accepts that Aristotle "propounded" definitions at 1011b26–27. Kahn (1973, 336n7) claims that the formulae at 1011b26–27 capture the "classical formula for truth in ancient Greek philosophy"; and see also Fiorentino 2001, 282. The definitions at 1011b26–27 are commonly viewed as *the* Aristotelian definitions of truth and falsehood.

6. This is the text printed in the *Thesaurus Linguae Graecae* (TLG). Bekker's text has a period at b28 instead of a colon, but is otherwise the same.

7. ἀντιφάσεως E A^b Al^1 Asc^1: ἀποφάσεως J.

8. e3n E J G Al Asc: om A^b.

9. τί E J Al^p Asc^c: om. A^b Asc^1.

10. τὸ μὴ ὄν A^b Asc^c Syr^p: τοῦτο E S T J G.

11. τὸ δὲ τὸ ὄν A^b Al^p Asc^c: τὸ post δὲ omitted E J.

12. καὶ τὸ A^b Al^p Asc^p: τὸ δὲ E J T.

13. καὶ ὁ λέγων E J Γ Asc^c: ἐκεῖνο λέγων A^b: καὶ ὁ λέγων τοῦτο Al^c.

14. μὴ] μὴ εἶναι S.

15. λέγεται A^b: λέγει E J Al^p Asc^c.

16. Keeping in mind the point made above about the force of "ὁρισαμένοις" at 1011b25. Perhaps it means the same as "were we to define," but it may mean something more like "were we to provide a distinguishing mark of" or "were we to provide distinguishing criteria for."

17. Thus Parmenides and Plato. Also Protagoras. See Denyer, Pelletier, and Hestir on Plato's conceptions. Plato's *Euthydemus* and *Sophist* are the best dialogues with which to begin. These unquestioned assumptions ground Cassin's and Narcy's claim (1989, 259) that the proposed conception of falsehood is absurd. Ordinarily the charge of absurdity is grounded either in manifest contradiction or total lack of meaning. In the context of arguing for the logical axioms, we cannot presume that a claim is absurd in virtue of violating LNC. But were Aristotle to define falsehood in terms of what is paradigmatically true, flouting what everyone assumes is axiomatic about truth and falsehood, we might think he has veered into the utterly senseless.

18. Cassin and Narcy note (1989, 259) that the proposed understanding of the accounts "complique inutilement l'argument, beaucoup plus rigoreux dans sa simplicité."

19. Here agreeing with Crivelli (2004, 132). I assume that "ἐξ ὁρισμοῦ" at 1012a3 refers to the definition at 1011b26–27.

20. In the cited passage Aristotle is focusing on the definientia, which are parts of full definitions but are appropriately called definitions when considered separately, both by us and by Aristotle, and definientia are not assertions but possible parts of assertions. This explains why at 1011b25 Aristotle claims that

definitions stated by themselves are not propositions or problems, but that propositions and problems can be constituted out of them.

21. In the *Metaphysics*, Aristotle identifies definitions with accounts of essences, but seems to limit his discussion to immediate definitions. The central passages in the *Metaphysics* are: 1012a22–25; 1030a2–1031a13; 1034b20–1038a36; 1042a16–23; 1043a12–1044a14; 1045a7–20. We will consider briefly Aristotle's discussion of definitions in the *Metaphysics* when we address books Z and H. The distinctions he has made in the *Topics* and the *Analytics* will suffice for our assessment of book Γ.

22. There is disagreement concerning how many kinds of definitions Aristotle presents in *Apo.* B 10 and which are "genuine" definitions. It would require another work to fairly treat all the issues involved. Following Barnes (1994, 222–25), I assume the traditional explanation of B 10—that Aristotle distinguishes among four kinds of definitions—is correct.

23. For recent discussions of the problems related to nominal and real definitions in Aristotle's philosophy, see Deslauriers (2007) and Modrak (2010).

24. According to Deslauriers (2007), ". . . the nominal definitions of 2.10 do not *assume* or *state* that the object of definition exists, but . . . nominal definitions do nonetheless give us some knowledge of the existence of that object."

25. From what Aristotle claims at *Apo.* 93a27–29, it would appear that we can know *that* something exists without having a grasp on *what* something but knowing *that* something exists implies that we are somehow related to what it is.

26. The phrase "first principle" translates Aristotle's ἀρχή. This phrase is, at the very least, ambiguous between an objectual and an assertoric sense. As De Rijk has argued in various places, the ambiguity does not reflect confusion on Aristotle's part. See, for example, De Rijk (2002). As long as one is sensitive to the context, it is usually clear which sense Aristotle intends. There is controversy about the relationship between metaphysical first principles and assertoric first principles. For discussion of Aristotle's first principles, see Terence Irwin (1988) and McKirahan (1992).

27. Aristotle may be willing to admit views like this one put forward in Dancy (1975): "articulate thinking and talking are not games we play. It is possible to disobey these rules [the laws of logic] without ceasing to think or talk articulately." (42) Perhaps there are non-philosophical contexts within which Aristotle would acknowledge that LNC and other laws fail. In the context of the *Metaphysics*, where he is pursuing philosophical wisdom itself, he seems unwilling to bend.

Menn, discussing Γ 3–8, dismisses the value of the arguments in 3–8 insofar as they are supposed to be arguments for the axioms: "The arguments are meant to support, not so much their ostensible conclusions, as the meta-conclusion that the scientific understanding of the axioms is necessarily connected with the science of substance, and specifically with the knowledge that there are eternally unmoved substances" (n.d., 38). Specifically with respect to the arguments for LEM, Menn claims that "Aristotle continues to develop this connection in G7–8, trying to connect denial of the principle of excluded middle with the physical doctrine that 'all things are together,' so that neither P nor not-P could be affirmed of the mixture (again, presumably the absurdity arises from supposing that whiteness itself is neither white nor not-white) . . ." (n.d., 40). Summing up his reading of 3–8, he concludes that "G is not claiming to give a 'scientific' understanding of the axioms, but rather (besides supporting them by showing that their denials are self-refuting) to show that the science of the axioms is the science of being, specifically the science of substance, and more specifically the science of eternally unmoving substance, and that the path to a scientific understanding of the axioms requires the detailed investigation of being, substance, and unmoved substance to which Aristotle will now turn. (n.d., 41).

28. For recent discussions of the development of dialectic from Plato to Aristotle, see the papers collected in J. L. Fink (ed.) (2012). The account of dialectic accepted here follows that in Smith 1993.

29. *Metaphysics* book Γ at 1006a11 and 1006a15–16.

30. For discussions of Aristotle's account of linguistic signification and cognitive content, see Charles (2000), Modrak (2001), and Wheeler (1995 and 1999).

31. Of course, he might so commit himself, and a number of the elenctic demonstrations proceed on the basis of hypotheses of this sort. See *Apr.* I 23, 44, and 46 and *Apo.* II 11–15, 17, and 20.

32. My thanks to Rusty Jones, who suggested that the passage allows for both readings.

33. 1006a26–8. Not all of the manuscripts have this sentence. Bonitz (1960) deletes it.

34. *Metaphysics* 1006a31–b18. See Reeve 2002, specifically his discussion of principle S. 1003b22–1004a2 establish that being and oneness are coextensive. So, to say of what is that it is, is to say of one thing that it is one thing. Thus, the passage informs the arguments about LNC and LEM, all of which have to do with signifying one thing.

35. This is not to suggest that Aristotle's assumptions about univocal signification and truth are unproblematic. They face serious objections. For the difficulties, Lukasiewicz (1971), Dancy (1975), Priest (1998). Here it need only be shown how Aristotle's assumptions about truth and signification are supposed to function inferentially in the elenctic demonstrations.

36. 1006a13–15 and 1006a22–24. He makes a related point in the *Protrepticus*, "man deprived of perception and mind is reduced to the condition of a plant; deprived of mind alone he is turned into a brute; deprived of irrationality but retaining mind, he becomes like god" (Iamblichus, *Protrepticus* 34.5–35.18 Pistelli).

37. This is to say, in responding to the dialectical question with the answer "Yes" or "No" the opponent commits himself to the truth or falsehood of the

claim in question. This commitment could be solely for the sake of the dialectical argument, or it could reflect the opponent's considered opinion about what is true or false. The dialectical decision to accept or reject a claim is the decision to assume that the claim is true or false. See Whitaker 1996, 106–08 *et passim*, for the claim that dialectic practice involves accepting a claim as either true or false.

38. Lear considers whether or not Aristotle's opponents could reasonably reject these semantic constraints; see Lear (1980, 104ff.). Lear seems to agree with the view advanced here that dialectic presupposes univocal signification and the distinction between true and false assertions (see, for examples, Lear 1980, 106–07 and 112).

39. Ward describes this constraint on dialectic in terms of its being "oriented toward the truth insofar as it sketches a procedure through which false beliefs are revealed as such and rejected, even if it cannot prove which propsitions are true"; see Ward (2008, 55–56).

40. See Irwin (1988) for a discussion of different kinds of dialectic.

41. Contrary to De Rijk (2002), not only is Aristotle presenting semantic concepts of truth and falsehood at 1011b26–27, but also all of the arguments in book Γ are best understood as based on these semantic conceptions of truth and falsehood. De Rijk chides Kahn (1971) for thinking that the definitions at 1011b26–27 are semantic, claiming that such a reading diminishes the importance of being-as-truth and fails to cohere with Aristotle's claims in books Δ and E and, presumably, Θ. However, Kahn is correct. Chapter 4 of this book demonstrates that the definitions at 1011b26–27 present semantic concepts. Part III of this book argues that this fact in no way diminishes the importance of being-as-truth in books Δ, E, and Θ.

42. There are real difficulties concerning the relationship between Plato's and Aristotle's theories of assertion. It is unclear to what extent the two accounts agree. For an insightful and entertaining general overview, see Denyer (1991). The recent books by Crivelli (2011) and by Hestir (2016) provide the best entries into the current debate.

43. Priest (1992) thinks Aristotle main historical targets are the Heracliteans and the Protagoreans. Menn declares that "many of the arguments seem designed to refute only the most extreme form of the opponent's view, e.g., not that some pair of contradictories are true together but that all contradictories are true together and thus that all propositions are true, so that even if the arguments succeed they will not establish any seriously controversial doctrines or refute any historically plausible opponents, but only illustrate general strategies that might work against such an opponent" (n.d., 32–33). With regard to the form of Protagoreanism Aristotle attacks, Menn thinks that "what Protagoras actually said was that man is the measure of all things, but Aristotle takes him to mean that everything which appears or seems is true" (n.d., 34).

44. On nominal and full possession of concepts, see Bealer (1998).

45. That is to say, to use Shields's terminology, all parties might agree that the proposed definitions express the shallow signification of the terms without thereby agreeing on their deep signification.

46. For discussion of Plato's concept of falsehood, see Denyer (1991).

47. In discussing Plato's views about falsehood, Denyer (1991, 9) translates λέγειν by "speak" or "speech," and similar worries to those I discuss apply to his choice.

48. See Kahn (1971, 345–46) and Mourelatos (1970). Contemporary philosophers of language distinguish two senses of the phrase "What is said," a pragmatic sense and a semantic sense.

49. In general, Aristotle appears interested in the conventional meanings of written statements and speech acts, i.e., what is said in the semantic sense of the phrase. However, Aristotle may have the resources to develop an account of what is said from the pragmatic point of view, and he is obviously sensitive to the pragmatics of rhetoric.

50. For orthodox explanations of the use of the infinitive in indirect discourse with verbs of saying or thinking, see Smyth sections 2016–2024, also sections 1866–1867 and Goodwin sections 664, 746, 751, 877, and 904.

51. Here I follow Shields (1999, 217–19), in distinguishing these two problems. Kahn's work defines the contemporary debate about the philosophical uses of the ancient Greek verb from Parmenides to Aristotle. Denyer (1991), considers various uses of the verb in Plato's dialogues.

52. I follow Kahn in taking the "is" of identity (where "is" means the same as "is identical with") to be a case of the copulative "is."

53. See Brentano (1975), Owen's "Aristotle on the Snares of Ontology" in Owen and Nussbaum (eds.) (1986), Owens (1978); and Mansion (1976). At *Met.* 1003a33ff, Aristotle distinguishes among different senses of "being" in terms of the categories and negation.

54. Kirwan had claimed that v3 "alone makes the definitions cover all truths and falsehoods, as Aristotle's argument requires"; see Kirwan (1993, 117). Graeser agrees (1986, 85–97). Neither Graeser nor Kirwan explain why taking "is" in the other senses cannot cover all truths and falsehoods. Presumably v2 leaves out existential claims, and v1 leaves out predicative claims. Neither Kirwan nor Graeser consider the inclusive sense. Pearson argues that Aristotle has a very specific concept of being-as-truth in the *Metaphysics*, which diverges from the way Kahn and others understand veridical sense of "being"; see Pearson (2005). I think it is clear that we can't interpret the definitions at 1011b26–27 using Pearson's proposed sense of "being."

55. Here I am assuming that linguistic statements are a kind of sentence, which is Aristotle's view. Someone inclined to a deflationary concept of truth might wish to interpret the definitions using this variant, arguing that so doing minimizes unwanted metaphysical commitments. Someone motivated by coherentism might

also wish to interpret the definitions this way, making truth solely a function of relations among statements. Modrak (2001, 59–62) has argued effectively against interpreting Aristotle as a coherentist.

56. Wolenski (2004, 357) argues that Aristotle's definitions go beyond the equivalence asserted by the T-Criterion because they incorporate what Wolenski calls a "causal nexus" that isn't incorporated in the T-Criterion. I do not see how the definitions incorporate a causal nexus, but I agree that the definitions go beyond Tarski's T-Criterion for a different reason: Aristotle isn't interested (at least not primarily) in formulating definitions that are adequate (materially and formally) for formal languages of the sort Tarski has in mind.

57. Perhaps Aristotle's linguistic veridical sense of "to be" is a primitive concept of the object language in terms of which, for the sake of metaphysical investigation, he is defining a meta-linguistic predicate "is true" at 1011b26–27.

58. Some might think this a virtue, viewing truth as an indefinable and basic concept. But Aristotle nowhere suggests that truth is indefinable. To the contrary, he claims to define it at 1011b26–27.

59. This construction captures what I am calling the "worldly" veridical sense. See Kahn 1971, 335–36.

60. See, in particular, Rijk (2001, vol. 1); Kahn (1971, xii–xiv); and (Matthen 1983). Bäck (2000) has argued the same is true for Aristotle.

61. Owen (1986, "Snares") takes Aristotle to maintain that "to be is to be something or other." For Bäck (2000) "S is P" means "S is (existent) as a P."

62. As argued above, Aristotle is defining the Greek terms "τὸ ἀληθές" and "τὸ ψεῦδος." According to the formulae at 1011b26–27, the terms "truth" and "falsehood" are nouns that denote contrary triadic relational states essentially involving acts of assertion, the semantic content of such acts, and what the semantic content of such acts is about.

63. Tarski, in discussing what he calls "the so-called *classical* conception of truth ('true—corresponding with reality')," clearly takes Aristotle's definitions to express a correspondence conception of truth and falsehood; see Tarski, "The Concept of Truth in Formalized Languages," in Tarski and Corcoran (1983, 153 and 155n). Modrak (2001) attributes a correspondence conception to Aristotle. In his book, Crivelli (2004, 132–36) claims that the definitions "expound" a correspondence theory of truth.

64. Davidson (2005) bluntly asserts that "Aristotle was no correspondence theorist." David (1994, 17–18) asks us to "notice that Aristotle's famous definition in *Metaphysics* 1011b25 has a rather deflationary flavor . . . This formulation does not invoke any correspondence-like relations, nor does it make any explicit reference to anything like facts."

65. Alston (1996, 6) claims that Aristotle's definitions express a conception he calls "alethic realism" according to which "a statement (proposition, belief . . .) is true if and only if what the statement says to be the case actually is the case,"

where "actually" is intended to capture the fact that what is the case is *mind independent*.

66. It seems plain that Aristotle's definitions do not express prosentential, pragmatist, supervaluational, or coherence conceptions of truth or falsehood. Perhaps there is some way to stretch his definitions to fit one or another of these, but I don't see how. Less obvious is whether or not the definitions are deflationary conceptions, Realist conceptions, or correspondence conceptions. Many contemporary semantic theorists are concerned to formulate "scientific" definitions of truth and falsehood. Perhaps the most interesting questions to answer in this context would be: Why might a contemporary theorist deny that Aristotle's definitions are scientific? The possibilities are: (1) Science cannot explain assertions; (2) Science cannot explain the intentional contents of assertions; (3) Science cannot explain the real correlates of the intentional contents of assertions; and (4) Science cannot explain the relation between the intentional content of assertions and their real correlates. I won't consider the arguments for and against these possibilities. It suffices to note that, if any of these obtain, Aristotle's definitions are unscientific.

67. Following Kirkham (1995, 78), but modifying his account so that I may assess Realist and Nonrealist conceptions of truth. Kirkham discusses Realism and Nonrealism in terms of theories of truth and not conceptions of truth.

68. My formulation of correspondence-as-correlation does not require that the relation of correlation is governed by rules or principles, and thus it differs from Pitcher's formulation (Pitcher 1964, 9), and follows Kirkham's (1995, 119). If we impose Pitcher's constraint, then Aristotle's definitions do not entail a relation of correspondence-as-correlation—they don't of themselves entail that intentional contents and their real correlates are related by means of rules or principles.

69. Davidson (1996, 267) is incorrect to say that a ". . . reason for preferring Aristotle's characterization is that it makes clear, what the other formulations do not, that the truth of a sentence depends on the inner structure of the sentence, that is, on the semantic features of the parts." Aristotle's definitions entail neither syntactical nor semantical complexity with respect to the inner structure of an assertion. It would be a mistake to think that the comprehensive sense of "to be," which I have translated by "to exist as an *F*," presupposes either syntactic or semantical complexity.

Chapter 3

1. Insight into Aristotle's reasons for accepting LEM also bears directly on a proper evaluation of his understanding of the relationship between LNC, LEM, and the Principle of Bivalence (PB), his arguments in *De Interpretatione* 9 concerning LNC, LEM, and PB, and his general account of the truth values of

tensed statements. For a recent and excellent discussion of truth and the logical axioms in *De Interpretatione* 6–9, see Jones 2010, 26–67.

2. Aristotle explicitly argues for LNC and LEM in book Γ. LI is asserted at 1055b8–10:

διὸ ἀντιφάσεως μὲν οὐκ ἔστι μεταξύ, στερήσεως δέ τινος ἔστιν· ἴσον μὲν γὰρ ἢ οὐκ ἴσον πᾶν, ἴσον δ' ἢ ἄνισον οὐ πᾶν, ἀλλ' εἴπερ, μόνον ἐν τῷ δεκτικῷ τοῦ ἴσου.

This is the reason why, while contradiction does not admit of an intermediate, privation sometimes does; for everything is equal or not equal, but not everything is equal or unequal. (trans., Ross)

Aristotle notes that LI is among the common axioms at 76a41f. I understand LI as follows:

LI: For every pair of beings x and y, either $x = y$ or $x \neq y$.

Aristotle also notes that LI is to be distinguished from a similar claim: For every pair of beings x and y, either $x = y$ or $x < y$ or $x > y$. This latter principle is false in the case where the beings are incommensurable.

3. At 1009a16–1011a13 Aristotle offers an explanation of the difficulties that lead people to reject LNC.

4. The articles collected in *Apeiron* Vol. XXXII, No. 3, Sept. 1999 provide an excellent introduction to the various problems. See also Charles (2000, esp. Appendix I), Dancy (1975); Lukasiewicz (1971), Priest (1998), and Wedin (1999, 2000, 2003, 2004).

5. The Greek passage at 1011b23–29, with discussion of textual difficulties, may be found at the beginning of chapter 2.

6. Agreeing with Cavini (1998). Thus, for some examples, see 71a14, 77a22–23, 77a30, 88b1. These typical formulations "πᾶν φάναι ἢ ἀποφάναι" or "πᾶν ἀναγκαιον ἢ φάναι ἢ ἀποφάναι" differ from [LEM$_2$] in that "πᾶν" replaces "ἓν καθ' ἑνός." The relevant senses of the Greek verbs "φημί" and "ἀπόφημι" are "to affirm" and "to deny," respectively. None of these formulations of LEM explicitly exclude an intermediate between contradictories.

7. See Whitaker (1996) for a discussion of the rules of dialectical argument.

8. We will consider with care what it means, according to Aristotle, for something to be one thing when we discuss Aristotle's account of measurement and number in chapters 8 and 9.

9. The notions of mediate signification and immediate signification are borrowed from Charles (2000).

10. See Charles and Crivelli (2011) for a recent and careful discussion of Aristotle's use of πρότασις in the *Prior Analytics*.

11. *Pace* Cavini (1998) who claims that at 24a17 Aristotle presents a variant of LEM.

12. Kirwan (1971) argues that Aristotle's "formulation of PEM [at b23–24] is incautious." If, as Kirwan contends, the formulation at 1011b23–24 is incautious, Aristotle is generally incautious in formulating LEM. As will be shown, he is generally quite cautious in formulating LEM.

13. The following passages relate to Aristotle's account of assertions purported to be intermediate between contradictory assertions: 1011b29ff, 1012a5ff, 1012a9ff, 1012b21ff.

14. Here, "et cetera" is intended to include all other parameters that might generate ambiguous denotation. The phrase "object-theoretical" is borrowed from Lukasiewicz (1971), who notes that the passage expresses a metaphysical formulation of LNC.

15. Lukasiewicz (1971) argues that, for Aristotle, the metaphysical and the logical formulations of LNC are logically equivalent. He claims that "the equivalence of the logical and the ontological principle of contradiction come necessarily from the one-one correlation between assertions [propositions] and objective facts." He suggests, but does not develop, the argument for the claim that the one-one correlation between assertions and objective facts follows from the definitions of truth and falsehood at 1011b26–27. It is unclear how he would develop this line of thought.

16. This question shall be left aside here. Lukasiewicz (1971) is right in thinking that each version of LNC differs in meaning from the other.

17. Kirwan (1993), thinks the opponent of LEM may either (i) accept that, if there is a third operation between asserting and denying, the products of the operation cannot be either true or false, or (ii) claim that her statement—denying both that that which is, is and that, that which is, is not—is a denial and does say that that which is not is not.

18. As Kirwan (1993), notes, LEM excludes the following "middle" options: (1) affirming and denying a given predicate of some subject (i.e., [y belongs to x] ∧ [y does not belong to x]) and (2) neither affirming nor denying a given predicate of some subject (i.e., [(y belongs to x) ∨ (y does not belong to x)]).

19. Thus, Mignucci (1975) and Cavini (1998) are correct in thinking that the conclusion of the argument at 1011b23ff is that LEM "is not only false but impossible, i.e., necessarily false."

20. There is no need here to become embroiled in the difficulties surrounding Aristotle's account of modality. I am persuaded by Waterlow's (1982) account, but nothing here hinges on which interpretation of Aristotle's account of modality one adopts. Crivelli's (2004) account of modality is developed in direct relation to his interpretation of Aristotle's theory of truth and, as a consequence, provides an interesting perspective on the issues discussed here.

21. Twentieth-century logicians tended to formulate LEM propositionally. For examples, see Church (1956) and Tarski (1952).

22. Complications that might limit the scope of the logical axioms will be ignored here. For example, in *De Interpretatione* 9, Aristotle appears to deny the LEM holds in the case of assertions about future contingent circumstances. It is assumed in what follows that the logical axioms hold in all cases relevant to philosophical wisdom.

23. The first, defended by Alexander of Aphrodisias and Bonitz depends, primarily, on accepting "ἐκεῖνο λέγων" (or "καὶ ὁ λέγων τοῦτο") at 1011b28 instead of accepting "καὶ ὁ λέγων"; see Alexander of Aphrodisias, *In Aristotelis Metaphysica Commentaria*, M. Hayduck (ed.), (Berlin, 1891), 328.23, and H. Bonitz, *Aristotelis Metaphysica: Commentarius*, (Hildesheim, G. Olms, 1960), 212. Ross disagrees with this reading, arguing that at b28 "καὶ ὁ λέγων τοῦτο" makes less sense than "καὶ ὁ λέγων," if we take "τοῦτο" to mean the same as "τὸ μεταξὺ ἀντιφάσεως." The second version of the argument has been defended by Ross (Ross, *Metaphysics*, 284) and Kirwan (Kirwan, *Metaphysics*, 117), accepting "καὶ ὁ λέγων" at 1011b28 instead of "ἐκεῖνο λέγων" (or "καὶ ὁ λέγων τοῦτο"), where no reference to the middle between contradictories is assumed, but only reference to some subject or other.

24. Aristotle's arguments for LNC remain among the most important. Since Lucasiewicz's (1971) analyses, Priest has done the most to reinvigorate arguments for and against LNC. Kirwan (1993) has noted that Aristotle devotes far less attention to LEM than LNC. He claims this is because [1] Aristotle thinks that, among his predecessors, only Anaxagoras expressed doubt about LEM and [2] Aristotle thinks the arguments in support of LNC apply equally to LEM. Insofar as [2] is true, [1] seems unlikely, since all those who deny LNC will ipso facto, given [2], deny LEM. However, [2] is correct.

25. Dancy's (1975) discussion remains helpful for the reader interested in whether or not Aristotle's argument succeeds. My focus here is only on the inferential roles of truth and falsehood in the argument.

Chapter 4

1. The arguments I present here bolster the claims made by Charles and Peramatzis (2016, 103) that the claims made in *Met*. Δ 7 are important and support the idea that assertions (my way of talking about their "propositional items") are the fundamental truth bearers for Aristotle.

2. Again, in *Metaphysics* book E 2, Aristotle distinguishes among the same four kinds of being: the coincidental, the veridical, the καθ' αὑτὸ uses corresponding to the categories, and the senses corresponding to potentiality and actuality. Ross in his commentary notes the relation between Δ 7, 1017a31–35 and E 2, E 4, Θ 10, Λ 1069b27, and N 1089a26–28.

3. Crivelli (2004) takes the veridical use of 'being' at 1017a31–35 to denote mind and language independent states of affairs. Crivelli does not analyze the passage in Δ 7 in either Crivelli (2004) or Crivelli (2015), but claims in a note (2015, 219n142) that the uses of being-as-truth and being-as-false introduced at 1017a31–35 apply to states of affairs as defined by Aristotle in Δ 29 at 1024b17–25. In his more recent article, Crivelli (2015), Crivelli argues that the states of affairs denoted by the veridical use of "being" at 1017a31–35 are mind dependent. I discuss Crivelli's views below. Halper (2009, 78–80) claims the veridical use of "being" in Δ 7 denote real objects. Whitaker (1996, 27–28, see esp. n. 34) takes Δ 7 objectually and thinks it conforms to the objectual notions of truth and falsehood in Δ 29. Aristotle, at Δ 29, 1024b17–26, explicitly defines a kind of false object and, by implication, a kind of true object. Crivelli (2004) has done the most to draw our attention to these kinds of objects and their importance in Aristotle's philosophical system. Aristotle would appear to use these kinds of objects in a variety of explanatory contexts in and beyond the *Metaphysics*. For example, looking at *Categories* 10 and at the examples Aristotle provides at 11b23, one notes that the pair of things offered at 12b15–16 is a good example of a pair of things involving combination or division, both of which are sometimes false, as false things are defined at *Met.* 1024b17–26. I consider the relevant passages below.

4. Following Künne's usage of the term "objectual" in Künne (2005).

5. Aristotle defines and discusses the linguistic and mental ranges of "ἀπόφασις," "κατάφασις," "ἀπόφανσις," and "λόγος" in *De Interpretatione* (see especially 16a8–13 and 16b33–17a26) and in *De Anima* III (see especially III 3; III 6.430a27–b5 and 430b27–33; and III 8.432a10–14). My usage of "assertion" here is similar to the use of "propositional items" adopted by Charles and Peramatzis (2016, 103).

6. In this chapter, by "truth-bearer" I mean any entity to which either only truth belongs, only falsehood belongs, or both truth or falsehood may belong. This usage differs from that in Charles and Peramatzis (2016) who limit the use of "truth-bearer" to propositional entities to which "truth and falsity together (*as a whole*) belong" (their emphasis).

7. I shy away from using the term "proposition" because of the theoretical baggage it has acquired in contemporary philosophical semantics and the metaphysics of meaning, baggage I don't think Aristotle would wish to carry. Of course, the use of "assertion" involves its own risks. But I believe these risks are easier to manage than those that arise with "proposition."

8. See Menn's (n.d.) for a defense of the importance of *Met.* book Δ quite generally, and see Charles and Peramatzis (2016) on the importance of Δ 7. Charles and Peramatzis (2016, see 103 et passim) offer the most extensive recent discussion of Δ 7 as it relates to Aristotle's theory of truth, yet this amounts to little more than two short paragraphs. Crivelli (2004) does not analyze the passage in

Δ 7, and in Crivelli (2015, see especially, 219n142), he but notes that the uses of being-as-truth and being-as-false introduced at 1017a31–35 apply to mind and language independent objects (which are states of affairs, in his sense) as defined by Aristotle in Δ 29 at 1024b17–26. Modrak (2001) does not address Δ 7.

9. See Menn's arguments in his (n.d.) and (2008) for attributing this sort of conception to Al-Farabi and for a discussion of Al-Farabi's interpretation of Δ 7.

10. Pearson (2005) claims that he is following Ross's interpretation of the examples of being-as-truth in Δ 7. However, where Ross in his commentary would extend his understanding of being-as-truth to E 2 and E 4, Pearson does not.

11. There are various problems with *Metaphysics* book Δ. It is assumed here that it is authentic and properly considered a part of the *Metaphysics*. It makes sense that Δ is placed after *Metaphysics* Γ and prior to *Metaphysics* E, although the issue of placement is not essential to the arguments here. See Baltzy (1999, 201)—contra Ross and Bonitz, and with Alexander—on the proper placement of Δ in the treatise.

12. Mansion (1976) compares Δ 7 with E 2 and claims that the lists in each are of the uses of the word "being."

13. Halper, following Aquinas and others, has argued recently that in *Metaphysics* Δ 7, Aristotle [1] distinguishes between the accidental and the essential senses of "being" and [2] differentiates among three essential senses of "being"—the categorial, the veridical, and that related to potentiality and actuality; see Halper (2009). He claims that each of the ways in which being is *per se* "is itself a schema of multiple *per se* beings" and claims that "the problematic schema is true/false." The use at 1017a31–35 may be problematic for Halper's schema. However, this is a mark against Halper's proposal, but not a problem for Aristotle's usage.

14. The subscripts in 1 and 2 and elsewhere ensure that focus is restricted to the veridical use of "being," as opposed to the other uses of being discussed by Aristotle in Δ 7.

15. Kirwan (1993) notes that "it was a common Greek idiom to use 'is' and 'is not' in the sense 'is the case' and 'is not the case.'" Kahn's work on the veridical use of "to be" is obviously relevant here.

16. In her commentary, Striker (2009) notes that Aristotle here recognizes a use of "is" that "can be paraphrased with the expression 'it is true to say (of B) that . . .'" Smith (1989) is right in thinking that "there is little if any connection between this sentence and the famous doctrine of the homonymy of 'is' as found in *Metaphysics* Γ.2, 1003a33–b15, Z.1, 1028a10–31, I.3, 1060b31–1061a10" It nonetheless seems that there is a connection between this sentence and Aristotle's discussion of "is" and "is true" in Δ 7.

17. The Greek: Ἐπεὶ δὲ δῆλον ὅτι ἕτερον σημαίνει τὸ ἔστιν οὐ λευκόν καὶ οὐκ ἔστι λευκόν, καὶ τὸ μὲν κατάφασις τὸ δ' ἀπόφασις, φανερὸν ὡς οὐχ ὁ αὐτὸς τρόπος τοῦ δεικνύναι ἑκάτερον, οἷον ὅτι ὃ ἂν ᾖ ζῷον οὐκ ἔστι λευκὸν ἢ ἐνδέχεται μὴ εἶναι λευκόν, καὶ ὅτι ἀληθὲς εἰπεῖν μὴ λευκόν· τοῦτο γάρ ἐστιν εἶναι μὴ

λευκόν. ἀλλὰ τὸ μὲν ἀληθὲς εἰπεῖν ἔστι λευκὸν εἴτε μὴ λευκὸν ὁ αὐτὸς τρόπος· κατασκευαστικῶς γὰρ ἄμφω διὰ τοῦ πρώτου δείκνυται σχήματος· τὸ γὰρ ἀληθὲς τῷ ἔστιν ὁμοίως τάττεται· τοῦ γὰρ ἀληθὲς εἰπεῖν λευκὸν οὐ τὸ ἀληθὲς εἰπεῖν μὴ λευκὸν ἀπόφασις, ἀλλὰ τὸ μὴ ἀληθὲς εἰπεῖν λευκόν. εἰ δὴ ἔσται ἀληθὲς εἰπεῖν ὃ ἂν ᾖ ἄνθρωπος μουσικὸν εἶναι ἢ μὴ μουσικὸν εἶναι, ὃ ἂν ᾖ ζῷον ληπτέον ἢ εἶναι μουσικὸν ἢ εἶναι μὴ μουσικόν, καὶ δέδεικται.

18. Here agreeing with Charles and Peramatzis (2016, 107).

19. See Charles and Peramatizis (2016) for a reading of the passage in terms of true assertions. I develop my analysis of the passage in terms of true assertion below.

20. Ross (1924) and Crivelli (2004) adopt this approach, as against that defended in Charles and Peramatzis (2016).

21. Here agreeing with Charles and Peramatzis (2016, 114) against Crivelli (2004).

22. Pearson (2005) notes that in *De Interpretatione* Aristotle posits real compounds and divisions correlated with the logical combinations and separations involved in assertions. Kirwan (1971, 178) notes that the main distinction is not between (1) things that are not as they seem and (2) false statements and beliefs. He sees the main distinction as between (a) false actual things, which include false states of affairs and things that are not as they seem, and (b) false descriptions.

23. As Rangos (2009, 9) stresses, Aristotle is not talking about combinations of terms or concepts. He is concerned with actual things. Rangos argues that Aristotle introduces these false things in order to explain the falsehood of a false proposition. According Whitaker (1996), Δ 29 introduces a use of "truth" and "falsehood" that denotes real features of the world. He notes that E 4 dismisses this sense from the study of being *qua* being because it doesn't introduce a new kind of basic entity. I disagree, but see Crivelli (2015) for a sustained development of Whitaker's line.

24. TrF and TrT are presented in terms of predicative combinations, and not in terms of states of affairs. This is because the term of art, "state of affairs," is potentially misleading. There *is* a generic notion of a state of affairs according to which a state of affairs is a way things might be. Aristotle apparently allows that one thing can be combined with another without actually being so combined, that one thing can be separated from another without actually being so separated, and that one thing can exist as an essential unity without actually so existing. According to him, these are ways things can be. As a consequence, it seems that he allows for states of affairs generically defined. A fact is a state of affairs of this generic sort that obtains. He clearly allows for one thing actually to be combined with another, for one thing actually to be separated from another, and that one thing actually is an essential unity. According to Aristotle, these are ways things might be that actually obtain. In this attenuated sense, Aristotle posits facts. If one conceives of states of affairs as accidental and essential predicative combina-

tions and divisions of actual things in the various categories, then one is clearly dealing with Aristotelian entities and relations. As such, there is, in principle, no objection to this way of talking about his composite actual things. Crivelli (2004, 2009, and 2015) introduces a quasi-Fregean/quasi-Russellian conception of states of affairs in his interpretation of Δ. 29. According to Crivelli, states of affairs as he conceives of them are the fundamental bearers of truth in Aristotle's system. I will address this reading below.

25. In Crivelli (2004, 6, see especially his schema), Crivelli claim that states of affairs are mind- and language-independent objects. In the more recent Crivelli (2015, 21–19) he argues that states of affairs depend for their existence on minds insofar as states of affairs are composed by means of acts of judging. On both of his views, Crivelli maintains that his states of affairs are objects, enitites that are distinct from assertions that "target" them, and that they are different from the real predicative combinations and divisions in virtue of which that are true or false. If Crivelli (2015) entails that states of affairs are a sort of assertion (as I am using that term here), then Crivelli's view devolves into a version of the assertoric reading.

26. Thus, suppose someone asserts "Socrates is a poet." On Crivelli's view, this assertion is true just in case the state of affairs composed of Socrates and being-a-poet is true. The state of affairs composed of Socrates and being-a-poet is true just in case universal being-a-poet belongs to the individual substance Socrates. The state of affairs composed of Socrates and being-a-poet is false just in case the attribute of being-a-poet does not belong to the individual Socrates. The composition of Socrates and being-a-poet *is not identical with* the predicative complex constituted out of the universal being-a-poet belonging to the individual Socrates. For one thing, the state of affairs composed of Socrates and being-a-poet obtains even if the predicative complex constituted out of the universal being-a-poet belonging to the individual Socrates does not obtain.

27. At *De Interpretatione* 17a25–26 Aristotle defines a denial as follows: κατάφασις δέ ἐστιν ἀπόφανσις τινὸς κατὰ τινός, ἀπόφασις δέ ἐστιν ἀπόφανσις τινὸς ἀπό τινός ("An affirmation is an assertion of one thing belonging to another, and a denial is an assertion of one thing not belonging to another" (trans., mine)). Aristotle then gives the same examples of opposed affirmations and denials involving Socrates as the subject at 17b27–28 and 18a2–3: ἔστι Σωκράτης λευκός—οὐκ ἔστι Σωκράτης λευκός.

28. Kirwan (1993) cites this passage as an example of Aristotle using "is" and "is not" in the sense of "is the case" and "is not the case." As long as these latter phrases are not taken to be *logically equivalent* to the semantic predicates "is true" and "is false" as used in the passage, there is no reason to disagree. Aristotle does not use "is true" or "is false" in an objectual sense in the passage from book Γ. One can easily extend this reading to Matthen's preferred ontology of predicative complexes.

29. In defense of his proposal, Matthen (1983) argues against Kahn's (2003) reading of Δ 7, who cites 1017a31–35 as a passage in which Aristotle explicitly recognizes the veridical use of "is."

30. De Rijk (2002, volume 2, 138) rightly argues that the semantic use of "is" should be taken as an assertoric operator.

31. Modrak (2001) has doubted that Aristotle accepts the definitions at Γ 7.1011b26–27. It is hoped that the arguments presented in this book diminish the grounds for such worries.

32. There may be no need to limit the target assertions to these, but for the time being it will suffice to deal with the cases Aristotle clearly has in mind.

33. De Rijk (2002) argues that "is" and "is not" are not used veridically in the passage, but as higher-order existential concepts that operate on his "assertibles." The details of his account assertibles cannot be addressed here.

34. The analysis of *Metaphysics* book E 4 (defended below) confirms this approach.

35. One may assume that "ἔστι" may be used both in a copular and a veridical sense. This is how Ross, Mansion, Kahn, and Bäck understand the passage. Kirwan (1993) has proposed an argument that, if sound, undermines the semantic approach. He has argued that the examples in Δ 7 "can have no tendency to show that 'is' can mean the same as 'is true,' or 'is not' as 'is false,'" because the examples fail to exhibit the grammatical structures "it is (the case) that . . ." and "it is not (the case) that [. . .]." In fact, however, as will become clear from my analysis of Aristotle's examples in the passage, Aristotle's proposed usage exhibits fairly well the grammatical structure Kirwan denies them.

36. Halper (2009), following Aquinas and others, has argued recently that in Δ 7 Aristotle first distinguishes between the uses of "being" that signify coincidental and *per se* beings and then he differentiates among three uses of "being"—the categorial, the veridical, and that related to potentiality and actuality—that denote *per se* beings of different kinds. Halper claims that each of these uses denoting *per se* beings "is itself a schema of multiple *per se* beings," and claims that "the problematic schema is true/false." On my reading, Aristotle distinguishes between three uses of "being" that denote different kinds of mind and language independent beings—categorial, coincidental, and potential and actual beings—and one use of "being" that denotes mind and language dependent beings—assertions. Although I cannot make the case here, I think my reading reduces the problematic nature of what Halper calls the true/false schema of *per se* beings. I take it that Aristotle's uses of "being$_{T}$" and "non-being$_{F}$" denote attributes of assertions (here agreeing with Charles and Peramatzis (2016, 105)), and these attributes are subsumed by the true/false schema of *per se* beings.

37. I use Quine corners here to indicate that what is bracketed by the corners is an assertion or a part of an assertion.

38. Agreeing with Charles and Peramatzis (2016).

Chapter 5

1. As in chapter 4 of this book, "objectual" is used here, following Künne (2005), to denote attributes of real things (i.e., substances and other kinds of being).

2. Here I differ with the view defended in Charles and Peramatzis (2016), who reserve the disjunction "true or false" for what they term "propositional items" (in my terms, linguistic and mental assertions and their intensional contents). I agree with Charles and Peramatzis that assertions (propositional items) are the primary truth bearers for Aristotle. I also am open to the idea that Aristotle restricts the disjunction "true or false" to such items. I am unsure. If they are correct, then this is a devastating objection to Crivelli's way of understanding Aristotle's fundamental truth-bearers in terms of his conception of states of affairs (see below and chapter 4). As we will see shortly, Charles and Peramatizis are certainly correct that impossible real combinations are always false objects and never true. The disjunction "true or false" does not apply to them, except trivially through the standard inference rule of addition. I have my doubts, however with regard to contingent real combinations (Aristotle seems to want to say that the real combination Socrates + sitting may be true at one time and false at another, and so may be either true or false) and also with regard to the true and false persons discussed below in this chapter (Aristotle seems committed to the claim that the same person could be a true person during one part of her life and a false person during another phase). Crucial here is the following: even if we were to grant that the disjunction "true or false" applies to no individual items other than individual assertions, on my view Aristotle posits two sorts of true and false objects, true and false assertions of both simple and combined sorts, and true and false persons, and the predicates "true" and "false" apply to individuals in *both sorts* of objects, to individuals in *both sorts* of assertions, and to individual persons.

3. De Rijk (2002, volume 2) interprets Δ 29 as throughout concerned with falsehood understood as "a mental state of affairs that is not actually the case in the outside world." De Rijk rebukes Kirwan and Wolff—and many others, by implication—for thinking that Aristotle is concerned with false things as opposed to false thoughts. Kirwan (1993) is correct in expecting Aristotle to discuss true and false assertions. It would be surprising were Aristotle to ignores these and to discuss instead false actual things, false accounts, and false persons, after having discussed true and false assertions in Γ 7 and Δ 7. On the view defended here, Aristotle is concerned with true and false assertions. That is the import of his discussion of true and false accounts. Kirwan and others are correct, of course, that Aristotle addresses these only after considering false things. Although one need not accept Kirwan's assessment of Aristotle's account of states of affairs in Δ 29, Kirwan is correct, against Rijk, that Aristotle is concerned with actual things at 1024b17–20 and that "πρᾶγμα" is to be taken to denote actual things in the

passage. De Rijk himself interprets the phrase "as meaning falsehood-as-a-state," by which he seems to mean "false state of affairs."

4. There is an obvious connection between this passage and Plato's *Hippias minor* and the discussion of the virtue of truthfulness in the ethical treatises (*Nicomachean Ethics* 1108a19–23, 1127a13–32). These points are set aside here; see Rangos (2009).

5. Here accepting αὐτὸ πεπονθός, which Ross translates by "itself-with-an-attribute."

6. A great deal can be said about the proper interpretation of both "πρᾶγμα" and "λόγος." The details are unimportant here. See De Rijk (2002, volume 2, 129, and sections 2.22ff, 8.43 for the former and 130ff and section 3.41 for the latter).

7. Rangos (2009) claims that "obviously, λόγος denotes a propositional statement or ἀποφαντικὸς λόγος." He claims that definitions are the paradigmatic kind of statement.

8. Crivelli (2004, 57n42) claims that Aristotle omitted reference to predicative beliefs and assertions in his discussion of falsehood in Δ 29 because the "truth" and "falsehood" of these can be explained in terms of the truth and falsehood of states of affairs which, he thinks, are discussed in Δ 29. Crivelli claims that the true and false λόγοι at 1024b26–1025a1 "are probably not assertions, but *definientia* of definitions or descriptions." With respect to Aristotle not mentioning predicative beliefs and assertions, Crivelli thinks "the omission might be due to the fact that 'true' and 'false' as applied to beliefs and assertions are definable in terms of their application to states of affairs." He refers the reader to Modrak's interpretation of the passage, suggesting that his account is similar to hers. It is instructive to see why Crivelli's account is not similar to Modrak's. Modrak 2001, 58ff. interprets "λόγος" in Δ 29 as denoting "an expression that states what a thing is, either strictly speaking or coincidentally" and, more generally, as "the content of the thought accompanying the spoken sound." Modrak notes that "the odd thing about the chapter is that there is no discussion of garden-variety false statements." Modrak refers the reader to Kirwan's discussion of the matter (see below). It will be helpful to reproduce Modrak's (2001, 58–59) full explanation of the lacuna:

> With respect to meaning, the two crucial elements are the external *pragma* and the *logos*, the content of the thought accompanying the spoken sound. It is not surprising then to find Aristotle analyzing the notion of falsity in terms of these two items. This is why he talks about states of affairs and definitions when we might expect him to speak of statements that fail to correspond to actual states of affairs . . . The tension arises precisely because of Aristotle's commitment to truth as correspondence.

Modrak, then, is not claiming that the omission of a discussion of predicative beliefs and assertions is, as Crivelli's note suggests, "due to the fact that 'true' and 'false' as applied to beliefs and assertions are definable in terms of their application to states of affairs." Rather, Modrak thinks there is a tension between Aristotle's "desire to make words and phrases the ultimate bearers of meaning and to makes statements (certain concatenations of words and phrases) the ultimate bearers of truth, while making both meaning and truth dependent on the relation between linguistic expressions and the world." As she puts it:

> The eccentricity of *Metaphysics* D 29's account of falsity signals Aristotle's recognition of this tension within his semantics and his desire to lessen it by diagnosing the failure of a sentence to be true in terms of the relation between its constituent terms or the relation between the objects signified by the terms.

In the first place, Modrak understands the passage in terms of πρᾶγμα (i.e., states of affairs as she conceives them, which is *not* how Crivelli conceives them) and λόγος (i.e., as she puts it, "the content of the thought accompanying the spoken sound"), where the λόγος is the cognitive content associated with a term and expressible as a definition. On Modrak's reading, the passage *does* mention beliefs, contrary to what Crivelli suggests. Specifically, on her reading, the passage is about those thoughts associated with terms (1) that constitute the beliefs that correspond to predicative statements involving those terms and (2) that, when false, explain the falsehood of those statements.

Note that on this analysis, at 1024b26ff Aristotle explains the truth and falsehood of statements and beliefs in terms of the truth and falsehood of λόγοι, and not πράγματα. Of course, this explanation fits nicely with the preceding discussion of false πρᾶγμα, at least on Modrak's reading, and on the interpretation defended here. However, the explanation does not involve defining the truth conditions of predicative assertions in terms of true and false things as Crivelli conceives of them, i.e., as a sort of abstract object.

In the second place, Modrak explains the odd fact that Aristotle discusses falsehood with respect to πρᾶγμα and λόγος—and not with respect to assertions—by pointing out that the "two crucial elements of meaning" (and, hence, the two crucial elements of truth and falsehood) are the πρᾶγμα and λόγος. Her point is that Aristotle may assume that a discussion of falsehood with respect to πρᾶγμα and λόγος will suffice for clarifying falsehood with respect to statements. Suppose this is so. It follows that, on Modrak's interpretation, Aristotle explains the truth conditions of statements in terms of the thoughts and things associated with the terms that constitute statements. As argued above, the odd fact is explained differently here: it is no fact at all.

9. The interpretation offered here should be compared with that in Crivelli (2004).

10. Pearson (2005) notes that in *De Interpretatione* Aristotle posits real compounds and divisions correlated with the logical combinations and separations involved in assertions. Kirwan (1993, 178) notes that the main distinction is not between (1) things that are not as they seem and (2) false statements and beliefs. He sees the main distinction as between (a) false actual things, which include false states of affairs and things that are not as they seem, and (b) false descriptions.

11. Here I follow Rangos (2009) in calling these "illusory objects." According to Rangos, illusory objects are false neither because of how we take them to be nor because of how they affect us but, rather, because by their very nature they appear to be different than they are.

12. Rangos (2009) thinks that Aristotle talks first about false things in order to indicate that "falsity does not begin with human discourse but with the (necessary or contingent) *actuality* of the world, and the *presence* in it of relations (that *exclude* other relations) and of illusion (that casts a veil, breaking the continuity of essence and manifestation)."

13. Rangos (2009, 16) notes that "ordinary Greek usage cannot fully account for the fact that Aristotle included the sense of false 'as a thing' [. . .] Nor can linguistic usage easily explain why this sense precedes the sense of false *qua* 'false statement' [. . .]."

14. As Rangos (2009, 9) stresses, Aristotle is not talking about combinations of terms or concepts. He is concerned with actual things. Rangos argues that Aristotle introduces these false things in order to explain the falsehood of a false proposition. According Whitaker (1996) Δ 29 introduces a use of "truth" and "falsehood" that denotes real features of the world. He notes that *Met*. E 4 dismisses this sense from the study of being *qua* being because it doesn't introduce a new kind of basic entity. He takes *Met*. Δ 29, E 2-4, and Θ 10 to support the claim that only compound things can be true or false. Simple things cannot be true or false. I argue that this is incorrect.

15. This may well be Modrak's point. Modrak acknowledges that the account presented at 1011b26-27 expresses a "conception of truth," but would appear to deny that it expresses *Aristotle's* conception of truth (2001, 54). She argues that Aristotle has a "broad notion of truth" according to which "being true is synonymous with correctly representing what is," a core concept of truth underlying Aristotle's various remarks on the topic of truth (65). Although Modrak does not elaborate on the point, in making reference to a "core conception of truth" it is reasonable to assume she has something like Owen's notion of focal meaning (1986, "Logic"), Irwin's (1981) conception of "focal connection," or the conception of "core dependent homonymy" recently developed by Shields (1999) and Ward (2008). Presumably, Modrak's point is that Aristotle's core concept of truth is implicit in his treatises, but that Aristotle nowhere defines this core concept of truth, and in particular that he doesn't define it at 1011b26-27.

16. Certainly, Modrak (2001, 152 and 187) does not attribute such a principle to Aristotle, since she clearly thinks that some multivocal terms (for example, "being") can be defined. Modrak uses Aristotle's notion of πρὸς ἕν predication to explain Aristotle's account of multivocal terms related by means of a core notion.

17. For recent and excellent studies of Aristotle's understanding of synonymy and homonymy, see Shields (1999) and Ward (2008).

18. These analyses differ from, but are meant to track the reasoning behind, the account of the four causes offered in Shields (2007). It is not possible here to argue for these analyses. It is assumed that they capture Aristotle's accounts of the four determinate causes in the *Physics* and the *Metaphysics*.

19. To be precise, according to Aristotle, the four determinate causal relations hold necessarily *or for the most part*. The rider "for the most part" is set aside here for the sake of simplicity. The arguments made here hold even when this qualification is taken into account.

20. Here I disagree with Charles and Peramatizis (2016, 110), who claim that "it is not part of the nature of being a friend—nor indeed of being a true, false, neutral, or just OK friend—that he or she involve an affirmation or a denial bearing certain relations to external things." While it may not be part of the nature of a friend, it is part of the nature of a true or false friend that she or he involve affirmations and denials bearing certain relations to certain things.

21. De Rijk (2002, volume 2, 127) claims that this first sense of ψεῦδος serves as the "focal meaning" for Aristotle. Crivelli also take the objectual sense of "true" and "false" to be the most fundamental in Aristotle's system, in terms of which the others ought to be defined. Whitaker, *Contradiction*, also claims that this sense of truth and falsehood is "secondary" in the sense that the truth and falsehood of "thoughts and assertions depends on the truth and falsehood, or combination or separation of the things in the world." This is surely true, but it is important to see that the sort of dependence in question here is different from the sort Crivelli asserts. Aubenque (1962) thinks the two senses are on a par. Rangos (2009) argues that Aristotle presents the kinds of falsehood in Δ 29 in an order that reflects "decreasing causal power."

22. CDHT does *not* entail that the relation of core-dependent homonymy is transitive. However, CDHT does not entail that the relation is intransitive either. So, in a given case, transitivity may obtain.

23. See *Categories* 12.

24. The exceptions will be cases where the act of assertion and the relation of real predicative belonging are essentially tied.

Chapter 6

1. De Rijk (2002, volume 2, 135ff.) raises the interesting question: Why doesn't Aristotle contrast the "substantivated" neuter adjective "τὸ ἀληθές" with

the similar (but apparently never used) form for "ψεῦδος," which would be "τὸ ψευδές"? Or, why doesn't Aristotle pair "τὸ ψεῦδος" with "τὸ ἀλήθεια"?

2. Whitaker (1996, 27) thinks the definitions in *Met*. Γ 7 are more superficial and less helpful than Aristotle's account of truth and falsehood in *Met*. E 4. He claims that "these definitions introduce the idea of a true assertion matching the way things are and a false one failing to match, without making clear what feature or aspect of the world it is that an assertion either succeeds in matching or fails to match." He thinks E 4 settles the latter issue.

3. Here taking "περὶ" to mean the same as "about."

4. My reading of 1027b18–19 differs from that in Charles and Peramatzis (2016, 104ff), who argue that in E 4 Aristotle conceives of a kind of disjunctive being—a way of being-true-or-false-as-a-whole—which is different from the being true of an assertion and the being false of an assertion considered independently and defined in Δ 7. Although I am sympathetic with the general approach to E 4 defended by Charles and Peramatzis, according to which propositional items are identified by Aristotle as the primary sort of truth bearers, I do not think Aristotle countenances their proposed disjunctive sort of being-true-or-false-as-a-whole.

5. Rangos (2009) notes that Aristotle's claim—in E 4—the true and the false are not in things, contradicts the claim—in Δ 29—that they are. He also notes that Aristotle "omits from his discussion in Δ 29 the sense of false as false *belief*, which is an attribute of a discursive mind and is clearly distinguishable from a false proposition." The appropriate responses are, first, that Aristotle works with different uses of "truth" and "falsehood," and so he is not contradicting himself—only employing the terms differently. Second, as Rangos himself suggests, the discussion in Δ 29, of false accounts is as much about false mental assertions (i.e., beliefs and the like) as it is about false linguistic assertions. Rangos is right to dismiss the idea that in Δ 29 Aristotle is concerned with mental combinations and separations, as *opposed* to real combinations and separations.

6. According to Pearson (2005), being-as-truth in E 4 is a kind of activity. Pearson treats the English phrase "being-as-truth" as an "equation" with two sides, an objectual side corresponding to the term "being" and a semantic side corresponding to the term "truth," so that the phrase "being-as-truth" has the sense of "being = truth." Pearson's general approach to the phrase "being-as-truth" is misguided. Pearson is correct to claim that the phrase "being-as-truth" really does express a kind of "equation." Aristotle is discussing a sense of "being" that he defines in terms of truth. The two terms do not differ in essential ways. One need not look further than the phrase itself to determine the sense of "being" that Aristotle has in mind—it is the sense of "being" taken to signify the same as "truth." On the reading defended here, the phrase "being-as-truth" has the same sense as "the use of 'is' that is identical with the semantic use of 'truth.'" A benefit of this reading is that it allows one to treat the phrase "being-as-truth" on a par with the other phrases Aristotle introduces in order to distinguish other senses of "being."

7. Charles (2000) has argued that these mental images are better understood as "likenings" and not as likenesses.

8. For recent discussion of these passages, see Polansky (2009) and Shields (2016).

9. For a more complete discussion of these issues, see Charles (2000) and Modrak (2001).

10. I ignore here the difficult issue of erroneous mental images and images of nonexistent objects. Caston (1998) considers the issue of erroneous mental images in a way directly relevant to the present concern.

11. Owens (1978) claims that according to the introductory treatment of being-as-truth in E 4—to be filled out in Θ 10—it is "a combination or separation in the intellect and not in things." This suggests that being-as-truth just is such a combination or separation. Owens would seem to agree with the reading defended here that being-as-truth in E 4 just is truth as defined in Γ 7 and discussed in Δ 7.

12. One way of describing this is in terms of the sort of bi-conditionals Pearson (2005) presents in presenting the truth conditions for contradictory pairs of simple assertions.

13. Pearson (2005) considers and rejects a thesis according to which "is" and "is not"—used in the senses of being-as-truth and being-as-falsehood in statements of the form "x is y" and "x is not y"—function in these different ways. Although Pearson rejects this thesis, it will be instructive to consider his reasons for doing so.

14. It is another question whether or not Aristotle acknowledged a purely copulative sense of "is" and "is not," or if he works with a "fused" sense incorporating copulative and existential functions. That issue is left aside here.

15. Bäck (2000) has proposed an interpretation of being-as-truth in *Met.* E 4 which appears similar to the one defended here but is importantly different. On Bäck's reading, "is" in the sense of being-as-truth means "it is true that," and "is not" in the sense of not-being-as-falsehood means "it is false that." However, Bäck assumes that being-as-truth only functions in the context of affirmations, whereas not-being-as-falsehood only functions in the context of denials. (In fact Bäck argues that Aristotle introduces two different kinds of being-as-truth. The first is introduced in E 4, and the second is discussed in *Met.* Δ 29 and Θ 10.) Bäck states that:

> In all cases, the schema is the same: in the alethic sense, "S is P" means "it is true (to say) that S is P"; "S is not P" means "it is not true, but false, (to say) that S is P." Here in the analysis "S is P" is to be taken as indicating the predication relation, that P is attributed to S. Given that being as truth indicates only the relation of subject to predicate, any affirmation of being *per accidens* or *per se*, as Aristotle has described them will make an assertion of truth. Likewise, any denial will make an assertion of falsity.

Thus, Bäck cannot explain the function of being-as-truth in the case of a true denial, nor can he explain how not-being-as-falsehood functions in the case of a false affirmation. These seem to be fatal problems with his approach.

Bäck notes that, in discussing the veridical use of "being" in E 4, "Aristotle identifies another sort of being here: being in thought." He considers whether or not this sense of being is identical with the later notion of existence *in intellectu*, and rejects the identification. Being-in-thought, for Bäck, is apparently a different sort of being than being-as-truth, but according to Bäck "being as truth has being in thought, because it deals with the combination or division of affects of the mind, or concepts, in statements in the mental language." No doubt Aristotle acknowledged that certain things have being in thought. However, if in E 4 Aristotle does distinguish a use of "being" that denotes being in thought, he does not distinguish this use of "being" in any of the lists of uses for "being" anywhere in the treatises. More likely, in E 4, Aristotle is not introducing a new use of "being" but is, rather, exploiting what he takes to be an obvious fact—that certain things exist in the mind, such as percepts, concepts and assertions constituted of concepts—in order to explain what is not so obvious, namely the relation between being-as-truth and the fundamental use of "being."

16. Aristotle discusses the nature of a coincident in *Metaphysics* Δ 30, and he addresses coincidental being in *Met.* E 2–3.

Chapter 7

1. Owen (1984) notes, for example, that E 4 "introduces being as truth and falsehood, with a reference forward to the discussion of simples and the τί ἐστιν in Θ 10."

2. See also *De Anima* III 6, 430b26–31 where Aristotle claims that thoughts about the "what it is'"are true without involving either combination or separation of the sort involved in discursive thought.

3. For examples, see Crivelli (2004) and Owens (1978). Whitaker (1996) thinks Θ 10 develops the theory in *De Interpretatione* and E 4, and that semantic truth and falsehood are defined in terms of combination and division. He also thinks that Aristotle introduces a new sense of truth in addressing the truth of simple thoughts.

4. Against this way of interpreting 1027b28–29, Halper (1989, 217) takes the phrase at 1027b29 to mean "what 'is' in the sense of being true which is appropriate to simple items and essences and what 'is not' in the sense of being false which is appropriate to simple items and essences." While a possible reading, it faces the problem that in Θ 10 Aristotle discusses being true in relation to both simple and composite things.

5. Crivelli (2004) is correct that Aristotle is claiming that here "to be" ("εἶναι") is to be combined and one and "not to be" ("μὴ εἶναι") is not to be combined and to be many. He is however incorrect in thinking that Aristotle here uses "to be" in the sense of "being in the strictest sense true." Rather, following Makin (2006), Aristotle is using "to be" here in the sense of "the figures of the categories" ("τὰ σχήματα τῶν κατηγριῶν").

6. Caston (1998, 205) cites 1051b3–5 in support of the claim that combination and division "are meant to stand for something like *asserting* or *denying* one term or another."

7. Caston (1998) cites 1051b6–8 in support of the claim that the world makes interwoven thoughts true.

8. Owen (1984) claims that truth and falsehood are "treated as properties of thought or speech, not of their objective correlates." The objective correlates have being or not being, not truth or falsehood. On the other hand, combination and separation "are treated as properties of pragmata not explicitly of their spoken/thought correlates." Pearson (2005) takes the second half of Θ 10 to be about being-as-truth for simples, as promised in E 4 at 1027b28–29.

9. Here following Makin (2006, 253ff.), in thinking that Aristotle is distinguishing between the pair "to be" ["εἶναι"] and "not to be" ["μὴ εἶναι"], on the one hand, and the pair "truth" and "falsehood," on the other. On Crivelli's (2004) view, apparently, Aristotle is distinguishing between "being in the strictest sense true" and "being in the strictest sense false," on the one hand, and less strict senses of "being true" and "being false"—those introduced in E 4. It is at least odd that Aristotle doesn't highlight the fact that he is concerned with different kinds of truth and falsehood here, were this his intention.

10. Here disagreeing with Makin (2006) who thinks that this sort of falsehood is a kind of quasi-falsehood. Rather, Aristotle is positing a robust falsehood for the case of incomposites. As such, if this is not the same as the view in *DA* III 8, then Aristotle has changed his mind. In fact, I think the correct reading of *DA* III 8 allows for the sort of falsehood Aristotle introduces here.

11. Here I am agreeing with Crivelli's reading of the text as against that offered by Charles and Peramatizis (2016). Charles and Peramatzis base their reading on the important recent work done by Primavesi. Were I to adopt their reading instead, none of my substantial claims would be undermined.

12. Crivelli's main interpretive argument for thinking that the strictest sense is the objectual sense may be reconstructed as follows. According to Crivelli (2004), at *Met.* E 4.1027b25–27, Aristotle claims that the common philosophical sense of "being true" does not hold of objects, but holds only of thoughts. At 1051b1–3, "being true" in the strictest sense holds only of objects. Thus, the strictest sense of "being true" at 1051b1–3 differs from the common philosophical sense of "being true" at 1027b25–27. In Θ 10, Aristotle defines the common philosophical sense of

"being true" in terms of the strictest sense of "being true." Hence, Θ 10 develops the ideas in E 4. Crivelli's main interpretive argument is similar to an argument he attributes to Heidegger, according to which, at 1027b31, "being true" denotes an attribute of thoughts, while at 1051b1–2, "being true" denotes an attribute of objects. Crivelli claims that Aristotle would not use the same phrase "being true" to express both an attribute of thoughts and an attribute of objects.

The claim that Aristotle would not use the same term or phrase to express different ideas is weak. He regularly does so, even in the same passage. One would need a more compelling argument to think that he would not do so in the different contexts of E 4 and Θ 10. Crivelli's proposal would have Aristotle using the same phrase "being true" in both passages, only qualifying one with "in the strictest sense." This hardly shows that he would not use the same phrase to express different senses. At 1024b17–26 and at 1051b1, he is discussing "being" in the sense of "being true." Contrary to Crivelli's proposal, he does not indicate that he has two distinct senses of "being," both of which are senses of "being true."

13. This is not to say that Aristotle doesn't work with a sense of "being true" that applies to objects. He does. It is obvious from *Met.* Δ 29.1024b17–26 that he does. The questions here—the answer to which is negative—is whether or not Aristotle has this objectual sense of "being true" in mind at 1051b1–2 and whether, by implication, he takes the objectual sense to be fundamental.

14. Here I agree with the general approach to the passage in Charles and Peramatizis (2016).

15. In addition, although I cannot demonstrate it here, Aristotle offers a robust compositional account of the semantics of assertions such that the truth values of all compound assertions are ultimately a function of the truth values of the simple assertions out of which they are composed.

16. This claim holds whether or not one thinks that Aristotle's account of primary substances changes between the *Categories* and the *Metaphysics*. For a careful discussion of the difficulties here, see Graham (1990).

17. A note on terminology: I translate "δύναμις" by "power," "potentiality," "capacity," or "possibility," as the context and charity dictate. I translate "ἐνέργεια" by "activity" or "actuality" as context and charity require. I translate "ἐντελέχεια" by "fulfillment." Here I follow Frede against Ross in thinking that Aristotle is concerned with potential and actual being throughout Θ.

18. It would be helpful here to compare what Aristotle says in book Θ with his remarks about potentiality in Δ 12, but this would lengthen an already long discussion of Θ.

19. See Beere (2009); Makin (2006, xii); Witt (1989, 130n16 and 132n17).

20. Owen (1984) thought that "to try and link Θ.10 as a whole to the theme of potentiality and actuality was implausible." Pritzl (1998) claims the chapter develops "the idea about combinations and divisions in things to which combinations and divisions in thought are related, the heart of Aristotle's so-called

correspondence theory of truth." Crivelli (2004) claims that Θ 10 is the most extensive discussion of truth in the corpus. He is surely correct when he writes that 1051a34–b23 "contains a rather complex theory" of truth and falsehood."

21. As reported by Owen (1984).

22. See Shute (1888) and Grayeff (1974) on the relation between the history of the text and its contents.

23. I follow Makin (2006) in translating both "κίνησις" and "μεταβάλλω" by "change."

24. In Θ 1, after marking the transition from the preceding discussion of categorical being and substance in books Z and H, Aristotle offers a focal analysis of the notion of potentiality, echoing a similar treatment in Δ 12. He then addresses the relationship between the capacity to act and the capacity to be acted upon. He ends the chapter with a discussion of incapacity and privation, a discussion that should be read in light of Δ 12 and 22.

25. In Θ 6.1048a25–30, Aristotle reaffirms that he is not principally concerned with potentiality in the strictest sense but with an extension of this sense. As becomes clear from the rest Θ 6, Aristotle is principally concerned with the sense of potentiality which is defined relative to actuality, both incomplete and complete actuality, and which includes the actuality of movement as a special case.

26. The concepts and arguments in book Θ prepare us for the claims Aristotle will make about God in book Λ. I don't see why this latter fact is incompatible with the widely shared and, I think, plausible view that the arguments in book Θ develop further Aristotle's arguments in books Z and H about the definable unity of sensible substances in terms of form, matter, potentiality, and activity.

Chapter 8

1. Ross in his commentary rejects Alexander's thought that the distinction is meant to block the inference from the simplicity of the primary unmovable substance to its oneness in number. Ross thinks Aristotle wishes merely to explain what is meant by "simple." I disagree.

2. The manuscript variations in lines 1072a32–34 do not seem to yield different senses. The claim made—that the one and the simple are not the same, etc.—does not depend for its sense on the sense of the surrounding argument. The reverse is true.

3. If my reading is correct, then Aristotle is establishing the following additional claims with his remark: substance, which is first in the list of opposites, is what is one and signifies a measure, and what is simple and exists actually signifies how it is for something itself to be in a particular condition. Ross (1924, comm376) refers us to *Metaphysics* Δ 6.1016b18. He states that "'One' denotes that a thing is the measure *of something*, the unit used in counting an assemblage;

'simple' denotes that a thing is *itself* in a certain condition, i.e., unmixed." Ross (1924, comm376; italics in original).

4. Ross (1924, comm.II.281) refers us to the discussion in *Metaphysics* Δ 6 of "the classification of the sense of 'one'." He lists the senses presented there. He states that according to this classification "the essence of 'one' is ἀρχῆι τινὶ ἀριθμοῦ εἶναι." Elders thinks the reference is to D.6; Jaeger too in the OCT footnote, but with reservations about placement of, and the relation between, books I and Δ in the treatise.

5. Here I am basically agreeing with Elders (1961, 58–59). Aristotle's exposition and explanation of the various kinds of unity conforms to what we would expect him to present were he to have self-consciously employed the account of core-dependent homonymy attributed to him by Shields (1999) and Ward (2008).

6. Here I follow Ross (1924), as against Castelli (2008), in thinking that Aristotle is drawing a semantic distinction well tracked by the contemporary distinction between the extension and intension of a term. See Castelli (2008, 169–82), for a different reading.

7. I follow Ross against Alexander in thinking that τῇ δυνάμει δ' ἐκεῖνα at line 1052b7 has the sense of "while they are nearer to the force (or application) of the word" as opposed to Alexander's "the others are only potentially one." I think the context makes it clear that Aristotle is concerned with the semantics of the term "one" and not whether or not the things to which the term is applied are potentially or actually one. Ross refers us to Lysias 10. 7 and *Cratylus* 394B3 as precedents for the semantic sense of δύναμις.

8. I disagree with Elders (1961) that the disjunction at 1052a19 poses a difficulty. He says that because the second disjunct denotes a part of what is denoted by the first, "we cannot speak of a complete disjunction." This seems manifestly false if by "complete disjunction" we mean the same as "the disjunction of two different things," and this is all Aristotle requires of the disjunction here. Elders's suggested reading confirms my supposition. I take it that Elders means by "complete disjunction" something like "a disjunction the disjuncts of which denote completely different things." But why think Aristotle would have us speak about this sort of disjunction?

9. Elders is correct to note (1961, 61–62) that a crucial difference between the first kind of thing said to be one and the second kind is that members of the second kind have a definite form and shape whereas things in the first kind don't. I also agree with him that Aristotle is using the phrase "that which is a whole and has a definite form and shape" to denote things that are either natural objects or artifacts, as Aristotle conceives of these in the *Physics* and elsewhere. However, I take it that the salient difference between the first kind and the second kind in the context of explaining why things in each kind are called "one" has to do with the difference in their indivisible movement: the movement of things in the second kind is *one and indivisible in place and in time* and, therefore, more

indivisible and simpler than the indivisible movement of things in the first kind. Elders may have this in mind—I am unsure—when he says that "the whole he [Aristotle] has in mind is qualified by the fact that its movement is one and indivisible in respect of place and time" (1961, 62).

10. Cited by Caston (1998, 203) in support of the claim that what is indivisible in form is the measure or standard against which our knowledge is to be measured.

11. Ross in his commentary argues that only thoughts about infima species are thoughts about objects that are one in the sense required by the passage. Other genera are one by virtue of having "a single definite nature" but are not one in the sense of being "logically indivisible." I disagree. It is true that thoughts about infima species are thoughts about things that are indivisible in the sense of intelligibility and knowledge; Aristotle tells us that they are *primary* among such indivisible objects of thought. However, thoughts about other genera are also indivisible in the sense of intelligibility and knowledge, though they are less so when compared with the indivisibility of infima species. Aristotle has explained the unity of the higher genera in *Metaphysics* Δ 6.1016b31ff in terms of the scheme of the category that defines it. I discuss 1016b31ff below.

12. Ross in his 1924 commentary (volume 1, 301) notes the relation between Δ 6 and I 1 and *Physics* 185b7. He sees the following partial correspondence between passages in Δ 6 and those I 1: 1015b36–1016a17 = 1052a19–21; 1016a32–b6 = 1052a29–34; 1016b11–17 = 1052a22–28; and 1016b17–31 = 1052b15–1053b8. He notes that I 1 is principally focused on "the primary meaning of 'one,' viz., measure."

In his commentary on *Physics* A 2, Ross notes the relationship between the senses of "one" in *Phys.* A 2—the continuous, the indivisible, and the same in definition—with the senses listed in *Metaphysics* Δ 6, claiming that indivisibility is the essential *connotation* of "one" in *Metaphysics* Δ 6, whereas continuity, identity of form, and identity of definition are the three main *denotations* of "one" in *Metaphysics* Δ 6. Aristotle does not mention the sense of "one" in terms of measurement in *Phys.* A 2; nor does Ross mention it in his commentary on *Phys.* A.2.

Aquinas sees *Metaphysics* Δ 6 as the first of a series of chapters that clarify the senses of the terms that signify in some way the subject of the science of being qua being. This series of chapters constitutes the remainder of book Δ. Aquinas divides the series into those chapters that deal with terms signifying the subject of the science (6–10) and then those that deal with terms signifying the parts of the subject of the science (11–30).

13. Halper (2009) usefully compares and contrasts the structure and content of *Metaphysics* Δ 6 with that of *Metaphysics* Δ 7. Halper aims to defeat the claim that unity is the same as being (vol. 2, 83). On this question, see also White 1971.

14. In his note on line 1016a34, Ross in his commentary claims that τί ἦν εἶναι in the phrase τὸν δηλοῦντα [τί ἦν εἶναι] τὸ πρᾶγμα is suspect and should be considered a gloss. He bases this claim on the fact that the accusative is used

with τί ἦν εἶναι in only one other passage in Aristotle's manuscripts, at *Met.* Z, at 1029b14. Eliminating τί ἦν εἶναι at line 1016a34 does not affect the sense of the phrase. The gloss, if it is a gloss, captures the intended sense.

15. With regard to the phrase μάλιστα ταῦτα ἕν, καὶ τούτων ὅσα οὐσίαι, Ross (1924, 303) clams that Aristotle "no doubt means that since the other categories are dependent on substance, the unity of things in them depends on the unity of substance." I agree.

16. Ross, in his note to line 1016b5, interprets the claim in light of line 1016a31 and in terms of specific and generic unity—"E.g., if two things are indistinguishable *qua* man, they are one (kind of) man." I disagree. Aristotle's claim reads more naturally as a claim about the unity of an individual man insofar as he is a man, an individual animal insofar as it is an animal, et cetera. Coriscus, for example, is not divisible insofar as he is a man; hence he is one insofar as he is a man.

17. In his note on line 1016b6, Ross (1924, 303–04) records Alexander's examples for each of the different categories listed by Aristotle. Kirwan finds 1016b6ff puzzling, worrying over the distinction between being somehow related to what is one and having one substance. My sense is that this distinction informs every sense of unity other than the strict sense of oneness in terms of measurement.

18. Aristotle appears to *argue* that what it is to be one [τὸ δὲ ἑνὶ εἶναι] is to be a beginning of number [ἀρχῇ τινί ἐστιν ἀριθμοῦ εἶναι]. Aristotle's argument is difficult. It explicitly goes like this:

P1: That by which we first know each genus is the first measure of the genus.

C1: The first measure is the beginning.

C2: What it is to be one [τὸ δὲ ἑνὶ εἶναι] is to be a beginning of number [ἀρχῇ τινί ἐστιν ἀριθμοῦ εἶναι].

C3: The one, then, is the beginning of the knowable regarding each class.

19. Remarking on the meaning of δίεσις here, Ross (comm, 304) notes that it refers to the smallest interval in music and that Philolaus and Aristoxenus differed as to what it is.

20. Ross in his commentary connects the bifurcation at line 1016b23 to the earlier distinctions among kinds of unity. He thinks that indivisibility in quantity "answers to the unity of continuity (1015b36–1016a17)," and that indivisibility in species answers to "the other forms of unity discussed in 1016a17–b6." I disagree.

21. Regarding the definition of the unit in line 1016b25, Ross cites Proclus

(*in Eucl.* p. 95. 26) on the Pythagorean definition—μονὰς θέσιν ἔχουσα. Ross takes μοναχῇ to qualify an implicit διαιρετόν in line 1016b26. The same will hold for the subsequent διχῇ.

Chapter 9

1. Here I develop ideas suggested by Hestir 2016, 229. Although in the end I think we disagree about the nature of the truth relation posited by Aristotle, I have benefitted from conversations with Hestir about the importance of book I for Aristotle's account of truth.

2. 1053a35–b6 cited by Crivelli (2004) as evidence that Aristotle maintains a correspondence theory of truth according to which thought is proportionate to its object.

3. For a different take on Aristotle's measure doctrine and the dialectical bearing of I.1 on the Protagorean dimensions of Plato's *Theaetetus* and *Met.* Γ 3–8, see McCready-Flora 2015.

4. For a sustained recent discussion of Aristotle account of relatives, with useful references, see Hood (2004).

5. He repeats this formulation at *Cat.* 6b6–8: "All things then are relative which are called just what they are, of or than something else—or in some other way in relation to something else." [πρός τι οὖν ἐστὶν ὅσα αὐτὰ ἅπερ ἐστὶν ἑτέρων λέγεται, ἢ ὁπωσοῦν ἄλλως πρὸς ἕτερον.]

6. At 7a22–23 he issues the caveat that the proposed correlative must be properly given: πάντα οὖν τὰ πρός τι, ἐάνπερ οἰκείως ἀποδιδῶται, πρὸς ἀντιστρέφοντα λέγεται. Given his considered definition of relatives, what matters for our purposes is that the being of every relative involves being related to some correlative.

7. If Aristotle is correct, then we know we have a perception if, and only if, we know the correlative of that perception, and we know we have knowledge just in case we know the correlative of that knowledge. This has bearing on contemporary discussions of what it takes to know that you know.

8. We cannot simply assume that I 6.1056b32–1057a1 parallels exactly what Aristotle says in *Metaphysics* Δ 15.

9. Aristotle claims that some pairs of opposites are pairs of relatives, and that some pairs of opposed relatives are not contraries. Between opposed relatives of this latter sort, he tells us, there is no intermediate. The reason for this, he tells us, is that they are not in the same genus. He then gives an example of this sort of correlative pair in the form of a rhetorical question: For what intermediate could there be between knowledge and the knowable? The point is that there is no intermediate between knowledge and the knowable. I take it that the same thing is true about measures and what is measured—there is no intermediate

between a measure and what it measures.

10. The situation is different for Aristotle's God. God's knowledge is essentially knowledge of God's knowledge. What is knowable in this case just is God's knowledge: God's knowledge is knowledge of God's knowledge. God's knowledge would seem to be the perfect example of the measure being identical with the measurable.

11. None of the variations among the manuscripts noted by Ross yield significant differences in the sense of the passage.

12. In his note on 1087a2–3, Ross (1924, comm, II.472) disputes Alexander's understanding (799. 21) of how things are indivisible in kind and according to perception. Based on my reading of I and Δ, I am inclined to think instead that Aristotle is remarking on the two main kind of indivisibility that are relevant to his account of measurement.

In his note on N 1.1087a5, Ross refers us to his notes at Δ.1020a13 and Z.13, 1039a12. The passage in question is 1087a4–a8:

> And this is reasonable [or, alternatively, "and this is according to definition"]: for the one signifies the measure of some plurality, and number means a measured plurality and a plurality of measures. Thus it is natural that one is not a number; for the measure is not measures, but both the measure and the one are starting-points.

As I read this passage, Aristotle is reinforcing points he has secured in Books I and Δ: (i) "one" signifies the measure of some plurality, (ii) "number" signifies both a measured plurality and a plurality of measures, (iii) the one is not a number, (iv) the measure is not measures, and (v) the measure and the one are first principles.

13. None of the other variations among the manuscripts noted by Ross yield significant differences in the sense of the passage.

Conclusion

1. There is solid textual evidence that Aristotle believed in approximate truth and falsehood. See, for examples, *Int.* 23b17–21; *APr.* 43b6–11, 53b4–57b17; *Top.* 149b4–9, 157b26–31, 160a24–28; *Rhet.* 1355a14–19. For a discussion of the difficulties, which I cannot go into here, see Dougherty (2004).

Bibliography

Ackrill, J. L. (1981). "Aristotle's Theory of Definition: Some Questions on Posterior Analytics II, 8–10." In E. Berti (ed.), *Aristotle on Science: The Posterior Analytics* (pp. 359–88). Padua.

———. (1963). *Aristotle's "Categories" and "De Interpretatione," translated with notes.* Oxford: Clarendon Press.

Alexander of Aphrodisias. (1891). *In Aristotelis Metaphysica Commentaria.* Edited by M. Hayduck. Berlin.

Allen, J. (2001). *Inference from Signs.* Oxford: Clarendon.

Alston, W. P. (1996). *A Realist Conception of Truth.* Ithaca, NY: Cornell University Press.

Anagnostopoulos, G., ed. (2009). *A Companion to Aristotle.* West Sussex, UK: Blackwell Publishing Ltd.

Armstrong, D. (1997). *A World of States of Affairs.* Cambridge, UK: Cambridge University Press.

Aubenque, P. (1962). *Le problème de l'être chex Aristote.* Paris: Quadrige.

Bäck, A. (2000). *Aristotle's Theory of Predication.* Leiden; Boston; Koln: Brill.

Baltzy, D. (1999). "Aristotle and Platonic Dialectic in Metaphysics gamma 4." *Apeiron,* 23(4), 177–202.

Barnes, J. (1994). *Arsitotle: Posterior Analytics, translated with a commentary.* Oxford: Clarendon Press.

Bednarowski, W. F. (1956). "The Law of the Excluded Middle." *Proceedings of the Aristotelian Society, Supplementary Volumes,* 30, 74–90.

Ben-zeev, A. (1984). "Aristotle on Perceptual Truth and Falsehood." *Apeiron,* XVIII, 118–25.

———. (1984). "Aristotle on Perceptual Truth and Falsity." *Apeiron,* XVIII (2), 109–16.

Blackburn, S. (1984). *Spreading the Word.* Oxford: Oxford University Press.

Block, I. (1961). "Truth and Error in Aristotle's Theory of Sense Perception." *Philosophical Quarterly,* 11(42), 1–9.

Bonitz, H. (1960). *Aristotelis Metaphysica: Commentarius*. Hildesheim: G. Olms.
Brentano, F. (1975). *On the Several Senses of Being in Aristotle*. Edited and translated by R. George. Berkeley, CA: University of California Press.
Brentano, F. (1973). *Psychology from an Empirical Standpoint*. New York: Humanities Press.
Bronstein, David. (2016). *Aristotle on Knowledge and Learning*. Oxford: Oxford University Press.
Brown, L. (1994). The Verb "to be" in Greek Philosophy: Some Remarks. In S. Everson (ed.), *Language* (Vol. Companions to Ancient Thought: 3, pp. 212–36). Cambridge, England: Cambridge University Press.
Burnyeat, M. *Notes on Eta and Theta of Aristotle's Metaphysics* (Study Aids Monograph No. 4 ed.). Oxford: Sub-Faculty of Philosophy.
Büttgen, P., S. Diebler, and M. Rashed, eds. (1999). *Théories de la Phrase et de la Proposition de Platon à Averroès* (Études de Littérature Ancienne 10 ed.). Paris: Éditions Rue d'Ulm/Presses de l'École normale supérieure.
Carson, Donald Scott. (1996). *Being and Truth: Elements of Aristotle's Philosophy of Language*, Dissertation, Duke University.
Cassin, B., and M. Narcy. (1989). *La Decision du sens: Le Livre Gamma de la Metaphysique d'Aristote*. Paris.
Castelli, L. M. (2008). *Problems and Paradigms of Unity: Aristotle's Accounts of the One*. Sankt Augustin: Academia Verlag.
Caston, V. (1998). Aristotle on the Conditions of Thought. *Proceedings of the Boston Area Colloquium in Ancient Philosophy*, 14, 202–14.
Cavini, W. (1998). Arguing from a Definition: Aristotle on Truth and the Excluded Middle. In N. Avgelis and F. Peonidas (eds.), *Aristotle on Logic, Language and Science* (pp. 5–15). Thessaloniki: Sakkoulas Publications.
Charles, D. (2000). *Aristotle on Meaning and Essence*. Oxford: Oxford University Press.
Charles, D., and P. Crivelli. (2001). 'ΠΡΟΤΑΣΙΣ' in Aristotle's *Prior Analytics*. *Phronesis* 56, 193–203.
Charles, D., and M. Frede, eds. (2001). *Aristotle's Metaphysics Book Lambda: Symposium Aristotelicum*, Symposia Aristotelica. Oxford: Clarendon Press, 2001.
Charles, D., and M. Peramatzis. (2016). Aristotle on Truth Bearers. *Oxford Studies in Ancient Philosophy*, 50, 101–41.
Church, A. (1956). *Introduction to Mathematical Logic* (Vol. 1). Princeton, NJ: Princeton University Press.
———. (1928 йил Jan–Feb). On the Law of the Excluded Middle. 75–78.
Classen, C. J. (1989). Protagoras' ALETHEIA. In P. Huby and G. Neal (eds.), *The Criterion of Truth* (pp. 13–38). Liverpool: Liverpool University Press.
Crivelli, P. (2011). *Plato's Account of Falsehood: A Study of the Sophist*. Cambridge, UK: Cambridge University Press.

———. (2009). "Aristotle on Signification and Truth." In G. Anagnostopolous (ed.), *A companion to Aristotle* (pp. 81–100). West Sussex: Wiley-Blackwell.

———. (2004). *Aristotle on Truth*. Cambridge: Cambridge University Press.

Crubelier, M., and A. Laks, eds. (2009). *Aristotle: Metaphysics Beta, Symposium Aristotelicum*. Oxford: Oxford University Press.

Dancy, R. M. (1975). *Sense and Contradiction: A Study in Aristotle*. Dordrecht: D. Reidel Publishing Company.

David, M. (1994). *Correspondence and Disquotation*. New York: Oxford University Press.

Davidson, D. (2005). *Truth and Predication*. Cambridge, MA, and London, England: The Belknap Press of Harvard University Press.

———. (1996). The Folly of Trying to Define Truth. *Journal of Philosophy*, 263–78.

De Koninck, Thomas. (2012). Aristotle on God as Thought Thinking Itself. *Review of Metaphysics*, 47(3), 471–515.

Décarie, V. (1972). *L'Objet de la Métaphysique selon Aristote* (Seconde édition ed.). Montréal: Institut D'Études Médiévales.

Deninger, Johannes G. (1961). *'Wahres Sein' in der Philosophie des Aristoteles*. Meisenheim am Glan: Verlag Anton Hein.

Denniston, J. D. (1952). *Greek Prose Style*. Oxford: Oxford Univeristy Press.

Denyer, N. (1991). *Language, Thought and Falsehood in Ancient Greek Philosophy*. London and New York: Routledge.

Deslauriers, M. (2007). *Aristotle on Definition*. Leiden and Boston: Brill.

Duminil, M.-P., and A. Jaulin (trans., introduction, and commentary). (1991). *Aristote: Métaphysiques. Livres Delta*, trans. M.-P. Duminil and A. Jaulin. Toulouse: Presses universitaires du Mirail.

Dougherty, M. V. (2004). Aristotle's Four Truth Values. *British Journal for the History of Philosophy* 12(4) 585–609.

Ebert. (1983). Aristotle On What is Done in Perceiving. *Zaitschrift fur Philosophische Forschung*, 37, 181–98.

Elders, L. (1961). *Aristotle's Theory of the One. A Commentary on Book X of the Metaphysics*. Assen, The Netherlands: Van Gorcum and Co.

Elgin, C. Z. (2017). *True Enough*. Cambridge, MA: MIT Press.

Enders, M., and J. Szaif, eds. (2006). *Die Geschichte des philosophischen Begriffs der Wahrheit (de Gruyter Studienbuch)*. Berlin and Boston: Walter De Gruyter.

Evans, J. D. (1977). *Aristotle's Concept of Dialectic*. Cambridge and New York: Cambridge University Press.

Falcon, A. (2005). *Aristotle and the Science of Nature: Uunity without Uniformity*. Cambridge: Cambridge University Press.

Field, H. (1972). Tarski's Theory of Truth. *Journal of Philosophy*, 69, 347–75.

Fink, J. L., ed. (2012). *The Development of Dialectic from Plato to Aristotle*. Cambridge: Cambridge University Press.

Frede, D. (1970). *Aristoteles und die "Seeschlacht": Das Problem der Contingentia Futura in De Interpretatione 9*. Göttingen: Vandenhoeck & Ruprecht.
Frege, G. (1977). Thoughts. In G. Frege, and P. T. Geach (eds.), *Logical Investigations* (P. T. Geach, and R. H. Stoothoff, trans., pp. 1–30). New Haven, CT: Yale University Press.
Furley, D. (1989). Truth as What Survives the Elenchos: An Idea in Parmenides. In P. Huby and G. Neal (eds.), *The Criterion of Truth* (pp. 1–12). Liverpool: Liverpool University Press.
Gabriel, M. (2009). God's Transcendent Activity: Ontotheology in *Metaphysics* 12. *Review of Metaphysics*, 63(2), 385–414.
Gale, R. M. (1976). *Negation and Non-being* (Vol. 10). N. Rescher, ed. Oxford: Basil Blackwell.
Garcia-Carpintero, M. (2007). Bivalence and What is Said. *Dialectica*, 61(1), 167, 190.
Gaskin, R. (1995). Bradley's Regress, The Copula and the Unity of the Proposition. *The Philosophical Quarterly*, 45(179), 161–80.
Geach, P. T. (1980). *Logic Matters*. Berkeley and Los Angeles.
Geach, P. T., and W. F. Bednarowski. (1956). The Law of Excluded Middle. *Proceedings of the Aritotelian Society, Supplementary Volumes*, 30, 59–90.
Goldin, O. (2002). To Tell the Truth: Dissoi Logoi 4 and Arsitotle's Responses. In V. Caston, and D. W. Graham (eds.), *Presocratic Philosophy: Essays in Honour of Alexander Mourelatos* (pp. 233–47). Aldershot, Hants, England: Ashgate.
Goodwin, W. W. (1965). *Syntax of the Moods and Tenses of the Greek Verb* (Reprint ed.). New York: St. Martin's Press.
Graeser, A. (1986). Aristotle and Aquinas on Being as Being True. In C. Gagnebin (ed.), *Métaphysique, histoire de la philosophie. Recueil d'études offert à F. Brunner* (pp. 85–97). Neuchâtel.
Graham, D. (1990). *Aristotle's Two Systems*. Oxford: Oxford University Press.
Haaparanta, L. (1986). Frege on Existence. In L. Haaparanta, and J. Hintikka, *Frege Synthesized* (pp. 155–74). Dordrecht: D. Reidel Publishing Company.
———. (1986). On Frege's Concept of Being. In S. Knuuttila, and J. Hintikka (eds.), *The Logic of Being*. Dordrecht: D. Reidel.
Halper, E. C. (2009). *One and Many in Aristotle's Metaphysics, Books Alpha-Delta*. LasVegas: Parmenides Publishing.
———. (1989). *One and Many in Aristotle's Metaphysics: The Central Books*. Columbus, OH.
Harvey, Peter John. (1975). *Aristotle on Truth with Respect to Incomposites*, Dissertation, University of Michigan.
Hestir, B. (2016). *Plato on the Metaphysical Foundations of Meaning and Truth*. Cambridge, UK.
———. (2013). Aristotle's Conception of Truth: An Alternative View. *The Journal of the History of Philosophy*, 51(2), 193–222.

———. (2003). A Conception of Truth in Plato's *Sophist*. *Journal of the History of Philosophy*, 4, 1–24.
———. (2000). A Conception of Truth in *Republic* V. *History of Philosophy Quarterly* 17, 311–32.
Hood, Pamela Michelle. (2004). *Aristotle on the Category of Relation*. University Press of America.
Hope, R. (1952). *Aristotle's Metaphysics*. Translated by R. Hope. New York: Columbia University Press.
Horwich, P. (2008). Being and Truth. *Midwest Studies in Philosophy*, XXXII, 258–73.
———. (1998). *Truth* (Second ed.). Oxford: Oxford University Press.
Huby, P., and G. Neal, eds. (1989). *The Criterion of Truth*. Liverpool: Liverpool University Press.
Hutchinson, D. S., and Monte Ransome Johnson. n.d. *Protrepticus: A Reconstruction of Aristotle's Lost Dialogue*, a web resource. http://www.protrepticus.info/index.html
Iamblichus. (1996). *Protrepticus. Ad Fidem Codicis Florentini*. Ermenegildro Pistelli, ed. De Gruyter.
Irwin, T. (1988). *Aristotle's First Principles*. Oxford: The Clarendon Press.
———. (1981). Homonymy in Aristotle. *Review of Metaphysics*, 34, 523–44.
Jaeger, W. (1948). *Aristotle, Fundamentals of His Development*, 2nd ed. Oxford: Clarendon Press.
———. (1957). *Aristotelis Metaphysica*. Oxford: Oxford University Press.
———. (1912). *Studien zur Entstehungsgeschichte der Metaphysik des Aristoteles*, University of California Libraries.
Jones, R. E. (2010). Truth and Contradiction in Aristotle's De Interpretatione 6–9. *Phronesis*, 55(1), 26–67.
Kahn, C. H. (2004). A Return to the Theory of the Verb Be and the Concept of Being. *Ancient Philosophy*, 24(2), 381–405.
———. (2003). *The Verb 'Be' in Ancient Greek* (Reprint of the 1973 edition published by D. Reidel Publishing Company, with a new introduction). Indianapolis, IN: Hackett Publishing Company, Inc.
———. (1986). Retrospect on the Verb 'To Be' and the Concept of Being. In S. Knuuttila and J. Hintikka (eds.), *The Logic of Being*. Dordrecht: D. Reidel.
———. (1981). Some Philosophical Uses of to be in Plato. *Phronesis*, 26, 105–34.
———. (1966). The Greek Verb "To Be" and the Concept of Being. *Foundations of Language*, 2, 245–65.
Kant, I. (1974). *Logic*. Translated by R. S. Hartman, and W. Schwarz. New York: Dover Publications, Inc.
Keeler, L. (1932). Aristotle on the Problem of Error. *Gregorianum*, 13, 241–60.
Ketchum, R. J. (1998). Being and Existence in Greek Ontology. *Archiv fuer Geschichte der Philosophie*, 80, 321–32.

Kirkham, R. L. (1995). *Theories of Truth: A Critical Introduction.* Cambridge, MA: The MIT Press.
Kirwan, C. (1993). *Aristotle's Metaphysics Books Gamma, Delta, and Epsilon* (2nd ed.). New York: Oxford University Press.
Kleene, S. C. (1952). *Introduction to Metamathematics.* New York: North-Holland Publishing Company.
Kneale, M., and W. Kneale. (1962). *The Development of Logic.* Oxford: Oxford University Press.
Kotwick, M. E. (2016). *Alexander of Aphrodisias and the Text of Aristotle's Metaphysics.* Berkeley, CA: University of California Press.
Kripke, S. (1975). Outline of a Theory of Truth. *Journal of Philosophy*, 72(19), 690, 716.
Künne, W. (2005). *Conceptions of Truth.* Oxford: Oxford University Press.
Larkin, S. M. (1971). *Language in the Philosophy of Aristotle.* The Hague and Paris: Mouton.
Le Blond, J. M. (1996). *Logique et Méthode chez Aristote* (Quatrième édition ed.). Paris: J. Vrin.
Leal Carretero, Fernando Miguel. (1983). *Der Aristotelische Wahrheitsbegriff und die Aufgabe der Semantik*, Dissertation, Universität zu Köln.
Lear, J. (1980). *Aristotle and Logical Theory.* Cambridge and New York: Cambridge University Press.
Long, C. P. (2011). *Aristotle on the Nature of Truth.* Cambridge, MA: Cambridge University Press.
Lukasiewicz, J. (1971). On the Principle of Contradiction in Aristotle. *Review of Metaphysics*, 24(3), 485–509.
Makin, S. (2006). *Aristotle's Metaphysics Book Theta.* (S. Makin, Trans.) Oxford: Clarendon Press.
Mann, W.-R. (2000). *The Discovery of Things: Aristotle's Categories and Their Context.* Princeton, NJ: Princeton University Press.
Mansion, S. (1976). *Le jugement d'existence chez Aristote* (2nd ed., revised and augmented ed.). Louvain: Éditions de l'institut supérieur de philosophie.
Marconi, D. (2009). Being and Being Called: Paradigm Case Arguments and Natural Kind Words. *The Journal of Philosophy*, CVI (3), 113–36.
Marino, P. (2008). Toward a Modest Corresponence Theory of Truth: Predicates and Truth. *Dialogue*, XLVII (1), 81–102.
Marmodoro, A. (2014). *Aristotle on Perceiving Objects,* Oxford: Oxford University Press.
Matthen, M. (1984). Aristotle's Semantics and a Puzzle Concerning Change. (F. J. Pelletier, and J. King-Farlow, eds.) *Canadian Journal of Philosophy*, Supplementary Volume X (Summer), pp. 21–40.
———. (1983). Greek Ontology and the 'Is' of Truth. *Phronesis*, 28, 113–35.

McCabe, M. M. (2007). Looking Inside Charmides' Cloak: Seeing Others and Oneself in Plato's Charmides. In *Maieusis: Essays on Ancient Philosophy in Honour of Myles Burnyeat* (pp. 1–19). Oxford: Oxford University Press.

McDowell, J. (1978). Physicalism and Primitive Denotation: Field on Tarski. *Erkenntnis*, 13, 131–52.

McKirahan, R. D. (1992). *Principles and Proofs: Aristotle's Theory of Demonstrative Science*. Princeton, NJ: Princeton University Press.

McCready-Flora, I. C. (2015). Protagoras and Plato in Aristotle: Rereading the Measure Doctrine. *Oxford Studies in Ancient Philosophy*.

Menn, S. (ongoing online draft). *The Aim and the Argument of Aristotle's* Metaphysics. https://www.philosophie.hu-berlin.de/de/lehrbereiche/antike/mitarbeiter/menn/contents

———. (2008). Al-Farabi's Kitab Al-Huruf and his Analysis of the Senses of Being. *Arabic Sciences and Philosophy*, 18, 59–97.

———. (1992). Aristotle and Plato on God as Noûs and as the Good. *Review of Metaphysics*, 45(3), 543–73.

Mignucci, M. (1975). *L'argomentazione dimostrativa in Aristotele: Commento agli Analitici Secondi* (Vol. 1). Padova.

Miller, Fred Dycus. (1971). *Aristotle on Being and Truth*, Dissertation, University of Washington.

Modrak, D. K. (2010). "Nominal Definition in Aristotle." In C. David, *Definition in Greek Philosophy*. Oxford: Oxford University Press. 252–85.

———. (2001). *Aristotle's Theory of Language and Meaning*. Cambridge, UK: Cambridge University Press.

———. (1987). *Aristotle: The Power of Perception*. Chicago: Chicago University Press.

Mourelatos, A. (1970). *The Route of Parmenides*. New Haven, CT: Yale University Press.

Neale, S. (2001). *Facing Facts*. Oxford: Clarendon Press.

Nightingale, Andrea Wilson. (2009). *Spectacles of Truth in Classical Greek Philosophy: Theoria in its Cultural Context*. Cambridge, UK: Cambridge University Press.

Noriega-Olmos, S. (2013). *Aristotle's Psychology of Signification*. De Gruyter.

Nuchelmans, G. (1973). *Theories of the Proposition*. Amsterdam and London: North Holland Publishing Company.

Olson, K. (1987). *An Essay on Facts*. Stanford, CA: CSLI.

Owen, G. E (1986). "Aristotle on the Snares of Ontology." In G. E. Owen, and M. Nussbaum (ed.), *Logic, Science, and Dialectic: Collected Papers in Greek Philosophy*. Ithaca, NY: Cornell University Press.

———. (1986). "Logic and metaphysics in some earlier works of Aristotle." In G. E. Owen, and M. Nussbaum (eds.), *Logic, Science, and Dialectic: Collected Papers in Greek Philosophy* (pp. 180–99). Ithaca, NY: Cornell University Press.

———. (1984). Notes on Theta, Chapter X. In M. a. Burnyeat, *Notes on Eta and Theta of Aristotle's Metaphysics* (Study Aids Monograph No. 4 ed.). Oxford: Sub-Faculty of Philosophy.

Owens, J. (1978). *The Doctrine of Being in the Aristotelian Metaphysics: A Study in the Greek Background of Mediaeval Thought* (3rd rev. ed.). Toronto: Pontifical Institute of Mediaeval Studies.

Pangle, L. S. (2001). Friendship and Human Neediness in Plato's Lysis. *Ancient Philosophy*, 21, 305.

Pearson, G. (2005). Aristotle on Being-as-Truth. *Oxford Sudies in Ancient Philosophy*, 201–31.

Peramatzis, M. (2011). *Priority in Aristotle's Metaphysics*. Oxford and New York: Oxford University Press.

Peterson, S. L. (1969). *The Masker Paradox*. Dissertation, Princeton University.

Pitcher, G. (1964). Introduction. In G. Pitcher (ed.), *Truth* (pp. 1–15). Englewood Cliffs, NJ: Prentice-Hall, Inc.

Priest, G. (2006). *In Contradiction* (2nd ed.). Oxford and New York: Oxford University Press.

———. (1998). To Be and Not To Be—That is the Answer. On Aristotle on the Law of Non-Contradiction. *Philosophieheschechte und logische Analyse*, 1, 91–130.

Prior, A. N. (1976). *The Doctrine of Propositions and Terms*. Edited by P. T. Geach. London: Duckworth.

Pritzl, K., ed. (2010). *Truth: Studies of a Robust Presence*. Washington, DC: The Catholic University of America Press.

———. (1998). "Being True in Aristotle's Thinking." In J. J. Cleary, and G. M. Gurtler (eds.), *Proceedings of the Boston Area Colloquium in Ancient Philosophy. XIV*, pp. 177–201. Leiden: Koninklijke Brill NV.

Rangos, S. (2009). "Falsity and the False in Aristotle's Metaphysics Δ." *Rhizai*, 1 (1), 7–21.

Rayo, A. (2008). "On Specifying Truth-Conditions." *The Philosophical Review*, 117(3), 385–443.

Reale, Giovanni. (1980). *The Concept of First Philosophy and the Unity of the Metaphysics of Aristotle: With a translation of Theophrastus's Metaphysics*, edited and translated by John R. Catan, State University of New York Press.

Reeve, C. D. C. (2016). *Aristotle's Metaphysics*. Indianapolis, IN: Hackett Publishing Company.

Reeve, C. D. C. (2002). *Substantial Knowledge: Aristotle's Metaphysics*. Indianapolis, IN: Hackett Publishing Company.

Rijen, J. V. (1989). *Aspects of Aristotle's logic of modalities*. Dordrecht: Kluwer.

Rijk, L. M. (2002). *Aristotle: Semantics and Ontology*. Two volumes. Leiden, Boston, Koln: Brill.

Rijksbaron, A. (1989). *Aristotle, Verb Meaning and Functional Grammar*. Amsterdam: J. C. Gieben.
Ringbom, M. (1972). Thoughts and Facts—An Aristotelian Problem. *Ajatus*, 34, 7–25.
Robins, R. H. (1951). *Ancient and Medieval Grammatical Theory in Europe*. London: Bell.
Ross, W. D. (1995). *Aristotle* (6th ed., with introduction and new material by John L. Ackrill, ed.). London and New York: Routledge.
Ross, W. D. (1985). Metaphysics. In J. Barnes (ed.), *The Complete Works of Aristotle: The Revised Oxford Translation*, trans. D. W. Ross, Vol. 2, pp. 1552–728). Princeton, NJ: Princeton University Press.
Ross, W. D. (1949). *Aristotle's Prior and Posterior Analytics, A Revised Text with Introduction and Commentary*. Oxford: Clarendon Press.
Ross, W. D. (1924). *Aristotle's Metaphysics: A Revised Greek Text with Introduction and Commentary*. Edited by W. D. Ross. Oxford: Clarendon Press.
Schiappa, E. (1991). *Protagoras and Logos: A Study in Greek Philosophy and Rhetoric*. Columbia, SC: Univerity of South Carolina Press.
Seel, G. (2001). *Ammonius and the Seabattle: Texts, Commentary, and Essays*. (G. S.-P. Schulthess, ed.). Berlin and New York: Walter de Gruyter.
Shields, C. J. (2016). *Aristotle De Anima*. Translated with introduction and commentary. Oxford: Clarendon Press.
———. (2007). *Aristotle*. New York and Oxford: Routledge.
———. (1999). *Order in Multiplicity: Homonymy in the Philosophy of Aristotle*. Oxford: Oxford University Press.
Sim, M., ed. (1999). *From Puzzles to Principles?: Essays on Aristotle's Dialectic*. Lanham, MD: Lexington Books.
Simons, P. (1988). Aristotle's Concept of States of Affairs. In M. Fischer, and O. Gigon (eds.), *Antike Rechts-und Sozialphilosophie* (pp. 97–112). Frankfurt/M: Lang.
Smith, R. (1993). Aristotle on the Uses of Dialectic. *Synthese*, 96(3), 335–58.
———. (1989). *Aristotle: Prior Analytics*. Indianapolis, IN: Hackett Publishing Company.
Smyth, H. W. (1956). *Greek Grammar*. (G. M. Messing, ed.) Cambridge, MA: Harvard University Press.
Soames, S. (1999). *Understanding Truth*. New York: Oxford University Press.
Steele, C., ed. (2012). *Aristotle's Metaphysics Alpha: Symposium Aristotelicum*. Oxford Symposium Aristotelicum. Oxford: Oxford University Press.
Striker, G. (2009). *Aristotle: Prior Analytics, Book I*. Oxford: Clarendon Press.
Szaif, J. (1996). *Platons Degriff der Wahrheit*. Freiburg/München: Alber.
Tait, W. W. (2005). *The Provenance of Pure Reason: Essays in the Philosophy of Mathematics and its History*. New York: Oxford University Press.

Tarski, A. (1995). *Introduction to Logic and to the Methodology of the Deductive Sciences*. Mineola, NY: Dover Publications, Inc.

———. (1983). The Concept of Truth in Formalized Languages. In A. Tarski and J. Corcoran (eds.), *Logic, Semantics, Metamathematics*. 2nd ed. trans. J. H. Woodger, pp. 152–277. Indianapolis, IN: Hackett Publishing Company, Inc.

———. (1983). The Establishment of Scientific Semantics. In A. Tarski and J. Corcoran (eds.), *Logic, Semantics, Metamathematics*. 2nd ed. trans. J. H. Woodger, pp. 401–08. Indianapolis, IN: Hackett Publishing Company, Inc.

Thorp, J. (1982). Being as Truth. *Philosophia*, 3, 1–9.

Tredennick, H. (1933). *Aristotle, Metaphysics, Books I–IX* (Vol. XVII). Cambridge, MA and London, England: Harvard University Press.

Ward, J. K. (2008). *Aristotle on Homonymy*. Cambridge, UK: Cambridge University Press.

Waterfield, R. (1989). Truth and the Elenchus in Plato. In *The Criterion of Truth* (pp. 39–56). Liverpool: Liverpool University Press.

Waterlow, S. (1982). *Passage and Possibility: A Study of Aristotle's Modal Concepts*. Oxford: Oxford University Press.

Wedin, M. (2004). Aristotle on the Firmness of the Principle of Non-Contradiction. *Phronesis*, 49(3), 225–65.

———. (2004). On the Use and Abuse of Non-Contradiction: Aristotle's Critique ofProtagoras and Heraclitus in Metaphysics Gamma 5. *Oxford Studies in Ancient Philosophy*, XXVI, 213–39.

———. (2003). A Curious Turn in Metaphysics Gamma: Protagoras and Strong Denial of the Principle of Non-Contradiction. *Archiv für Gsechichte der Philosophie*, 85(2), 107–30.

———. (2000). Some Logical Problems in Metaphysics Gamma. *Oxford Studies in Ancient Philosophy*, XIX, 113–62.

———. (1999). The Scope of Non-Contradiction: A Note on Aristotle's "Elenctic" Proof in Metaphysics Gamma 4. *Apeiron*, 32(3), 231–42.

Wedin, M. V. (2000). *Aristotle's Theory of Substance: The Categories and Metaphysics Zeta*. Oxford: Oxford University Press.

Weston, T. (1992). Approximate Truth and Scientific Realism. https://philpapers.org/asearch.pl?pub=827"\t_blank. *Philosophy of Science*, 59(1), 53–74.

———. (1988). Approximate Truth and Lukasiewicz Logic, *Notre Dame Journal of Formal Logic*, 29(2), Spring.

Weston, T. (1987). https://philpapers.org/s/Thomas%20Weston\t "_blank"\o. View other works by Thomas Weston" Approximate Truth. https://philpapers.org/asearch.pl?pub=568\t_blank. *Journal of Philosophical Logic* 16(2), 203–27.

Wheeler, M. R. (2011). A Deflationary Reading of Aristotle's Definitions of Truth and falsehood at *Metaphysics* 1011b26–27. *Apeiron*, 44, 67–90.

Wheeler, M. R. (1999). "Semantics in Aristotle's *Organon*." *Journal of the History of Philosophy*, 37(2), 191–226.

———. (1995). *Real Universals in Aristotle's Organon*. Ph.D. Dissertation, University of Rochester.
Whitaker, C. W. (1996). *Aristotle's De Interpretatione: Contradiction and Dialectic*. Oxford: Oxford University Press.
Williams, B. (2004). *Truth and Truthfulness*. Princeton: Princeton University Press.
Witt, C. (1989). *Substance and Essence in Aristotle: An Interpretation of Metaphysics VII–IX*. Ithaca, NY, and London: Cornell University Press.
Wolenski, J. (2004). Aletheia in Greek Thought until Aristotle. *Annals of Pure and Applied Logic*, 127, 339–60.
Wright, C. (1992). *Truth and Objectivity*. Cambridge, MA: Harvard University Press.

Index

Aquinas, Thomas, 1, 4, 117
Aristotle
  and affirmation and denial, 128–29, 135–37, 139, 143–48, 174, 176, 180, 181–83, 188, 192, 197, 225–26, 284
  and the *Analytics*, 100, 103, 183, 184
  and assertions, 177–78, 183, 191–201, 203–12, 214–16, 219, 240, 243–45, 248, 249–50, 251, 254–56, 258–59, 270, 272–73, 279, 281–84
  and assertoric truth or falsehood, 250–51
  asymmetrical measurement relation of, 258–73
  and being true or false, 202–203
  and causality, 13, 30, 32–36
  and combinations and separation, 196–97, 217
  and comprehension, 43, 213, 250
  and conception of friendship, 269–70, 285–86
  and contradictions, 88–99, 107–108, 111, 173–74, 179
  and contradictory opposition theory, 128
  death of, 9, 10
  and definition, 12, 18–20, 43, 53–56, 57, 61–64, 68, 69–78, 79, 83, 85–86, 111, 115–16, 161, 167–70, 178, 183–89, 222, 225–26, 239, 249, 251–52, 258, 276–77, 279–84
  and demonstration, 19–20, 43, 45, 57–60, 62, 65–68, 85–86, 87, 111, 272, 284
  and demonstrative knowledge, 183, 184, 213
  dialectic reasoning of, 20, 58, 59, 60, 61, 65, 66–67, 68, 88, 91–93, 96, 104, 106, 109, 111, 116
  epistemology of, 2, 284
  and falsehood, 71–72, 79, 83, 115, 117, 118, 119–20, 154, 158–60, 178–83, 191, 192, 194, 284
  and Fatalism, 70–71
  and first principles, 43, 44–45, 46, 58, 68, 115, 183, 221, 232–33
  formulae of, 186
  and Hestir's work, 4, 283
  on imagination, 177, 258
  and indemonstrability, 43, 59
  and intension of "one," 231–37
  and linguistic and mental assertions, 43, 61, 68, 72, 89–93, 96, 99, 102–107, 109, 115, 117–18, 158, 174, 176–77, 182–83, 187, 192, 193, 209, 215, 220–21, 225–26, 243–44, 249, 280, 282–83

Aristotle *(continued)*
  and mathematical objects, 13, 177, 212, 219–20, 254
  and mathematics, 281, 284
  and meaning, 4, 250
  and measurement, 248–50, 254, 259–73, 284
  normative theory of, 282, 284
  and numbers, 259–64, 284
  and objectual notions of truth and falsehood, 124, 132–39, 153, 160, 161–62, 211–12
  opponents of, 68–71, 86, 87, 104, 109, 110, 111, 214, 216–17, 284
  and perception and knowledge, 248–52, 255, 256–58, 271
  and philosophical wisdom, 24, 115–16, 213, 221, 280–81, 284, 285
  on philosophy, 30, 44, 58, 104, 237, 271, 280, 281, 284
  and posits, 57, 58, 61, 67, 74, 110–11, 239
  and practical wisdom, 213, 284
  and Principle of Bivalence, 70–71, 77
  and rational powers, 212–16, 221
  semantic theory of, 4, 60–68, 120, 228, 283
  and states of affairs, 132–34
  and substance, 11, 12, 13, 77, 115, 207, 222, 232–33, 237, 240, 244, 246, 283
  and term "one," 226–35, 237–40, 242
  and theology, 13, 25–26, 281, 283–84
  theory of being of, 4, 7–8, 11, 13, 19, 63–64, 68, 74–79, 111–12, 115–16, 141–48, 202, 279
  and truth, 3, 17–18, 19, 20, 21–23, 26–30, 39, 43, 44–57, 62–63, 64, 77–78, 79, 83, 85–88, 115–16, 148–49, 152, 154, 167–73, 178–83, 191–208, 211–22, 237, 279–86
  and truth and falsehood, 1, 2–3, 4–7, 12, 19, 21, 25, 36–37, 38, 45–52, 53, 62, 68–78, 79, 86–89, 115, 124, 142, 152, 153, 158–60, 167–72, 173, 191–20, 225–26, 237, 243, 276–77, 279–81, 282
  and verb "to be," 152, 178–81, 199, 202–203
  works of, 43, 61, 282
  and writing dates of *Metaphysics*, 9–11
  See also God; knowledge; measurement; *Metaphysics* (Aristotle); *Nicomachean Ethics* (Aristotle); philosophical wisdom; truth
Aristotle on Meaning and Essence (Charles), 4
Aristotle on the Nature of Truth (Long), 3
Aristotle on Truth (Crivelli), 3
Aristotle: Semantics and Ontology (De Rijk), 4
Aristotle's Theory of Meaning and Language (Modrak), 4
Aubenque, Pierre, 2

being
  accounts of, 68, 112
  and acts of assertion, 8, 19, 115, 118, 146–52, 157, 173–74, 176, 245, 256
  and actuality, 218
  and affirmation and denial, 138, 143–48, 174, 176
  and Aristotle's ontology, 74–79, 112, 115–16, 202, 279
  and assertions, 282

and being actual, 195
and being one being, 227
causes of, 17, 30, 36
combinations and divisions of, 193, 194, 196–97, 203
and definitions, 63–64, 77–79, 111, 115–16
of eternal things, 36
and falsehood, 117, 119–20, 157, 174, 176, 179–81, 194–97, 203, 209, 214–15, 220
first measures of, 272–73
and God, 222, 283, 285
and homonymous nature, 13
and humans, 71, 271
kinds of, 19, 75, 110, 115–19, 124, 131, 149–52, 178, 181–83, 188, 189, 193, 194–97, 225, 232, 233–35, 237, 249–50, 279, 280, 281, 283
and knowledge, 272
and measurement, 237, 249–50, 251, 256
and the *necessary*, 102
and non-being, 118, 126, 127–28, 131, 135, 139, 173, 188, 194, 199, 203, 211
and not-being, 119–20, 139, 141, 173–74, 176, 197
and oneness, 233–35, 241
and perceptions, 256
and philosophical wisdom, 43, 44
potential and actual being, 209–10, 211, 213, 220, 221, 222
and the psyche, 272
and relatives, 252
and signification, 70, 111, 119, 141–42, 147, 188, 235
simple beings, 193
and substance, 176, 246
and truth, 7–8, 12, 30, 36, 75–77, 111, 112, 115–24, 135, 140–52, 153, 173–74, 176, 179–83, 188, 191, 194–99, 200, 202–203, 209, 211, 220, 221, 225, 243, 272–73, 279, 280
and truth and falsehood, 193–200, 211, 273
and verb "to be," 74–79, 95, 117, 119–23, 140–48, 180–81, 199, 202–203
and work of Owens, 11
See also measurement; oneness
Brentano, Franz, 1, 153

Categories (Aristotle)
and affirmation and negation, 122–23, 128
and equivocal terms, 161
and perception and knowledge, 252
priority in, 43, 140
and quantity, 236
relations of belonging in, 100, 130
and relatives, 251–52, 271
causality
and the *Analytics* (Aristotle), 32–34
and Aristotle, 13, 30, 32–36
and falsehood, 166–67
and truth, 32–35, 166–67, 171, 208
Charles, David, 4, 117, 266, 283
See also *Aristotle on Meaning and Essence* (Charles)
Crivelli, Paolo
and assertions, 283
and being, 117
and states of affairs, 132–34, 136–38
and truth and falsehood, 2–5, 127, 153, 194–95, 200, 202–203
See also *Aristotle on Truth* (Crivelli)

De Anima (Aristotle)
and being actual, 195
indivisibility in, 238

De Anima (Aristotle) *(continued)*
  knowledge in, 19
  and mental images, 176–77
  themes of, 43, 89
  truth in, 243
De Anima III (Aristotle), 191, 192, 193, 200, 258
De Interpretatione (Aristotle)
  and affirmations and denials, 144
  and assertions, 47, 57, 88–90, 104, 109, 128–29, 176, 191–92
  and false things, 130
  and oneness, 188
  and truth, 243
De Rijk, Lambertus, 4, 117, 153
  See also *Aristotle: Semantics and Ontology* (De Rijk)
Dewey, John, 3
Diogenes, 63

Eudemian Ethics (Aristotle), 22–23

falsehood
  activity of, 220–21
  and affirmation and denial, 188, 192, 197–201, 225–26
  and Aristotle's ontology, 117–20, 122–24, 193
  and assertions, 38, 57, 68, 80–82, 86, 96–97, 104–106, 107, 128–29, 151, 153, 154–58, 162–67, 170, 173–74, 176, 178–81, 189, 192, 193, 197, 200–201, 205, 208, 209–12, 215–16, 219, 226, 230–31, 237, 245, 258–59, 280
  assertoric falsehood, 160–72, 176, 178, 179, 181–83, 191, 193, 200, 201–209, 217, 220–21, 243, 248, 249, 250, 255, 276–77
  and being, 139, 157, 173, 193–96, 197–200, 203, 209, 211, 213, 220, 273
  and causality, 166–67
  and combinations and divisions, 194, 196–97, 216
  correspondence conception of, 80–83
  definitions of, 1, 5, 6, 12, 25, 45–57, 62, 65, 68–83, 86, 87, 88, 96–97, 104–107, 109, 110, 111, 112, 129, 142, 149, 154, 157–60, 161, 164, 179, 188, 201–208, 220–21, 225–26, 230, 249, 276–77, 284
  degrees of, 32
  and dialectic reasoning, 20, 88–89, 111
  different kinds of, 5–7, 153–54, 160–64, 167–72, 200, 204, 225
  essence of, 2, 5, 161, 209, 220, 243
  and false accounts, 154, 156
  and false denials, 134–35, 138
  and false persons, 153, 154–56, 160, 161–62, 164–67, 168, 171, 204
  and false things, 124–27, 130–31, 133–36, 138, 154, 158–60, 170–71, 175, 200–201
  genus of, 188
  homonymous kinds of, 153–54, 161–63, 167–68, 169, 170, 171–72, 200–202, 204, 206
  and impossibility, 214–15, 217
  and the intellect, 21, 175–78
  and Law of Non-Contradiction, 115
  and Law of the Excluded Middle (LEM), 109–12, 115
  and linguistic and mental assertions, 115, 158, 205–206, 216, 220, 277
  and logical axioms, 38, 66–67, 86, 96, 109–12, 115, 284
  and measurement, 280, 281
  nature of, 178, 211, 219, 220
  nominal definition of, 80–83, 86, 96, 104–107, 110, 111, 112, 115,

129, 142, 149, 157–58, 161, 173, 179, 188, 201–202, 204–208, 225, 279, 284
and non-being, 117, 135, 173, 188, 199–200, 211
as not-being, 119–20, 122–23, 174, 179, 180, 181
objectual notions of, 132–39, 153, 160, 161–62, 167–72, 195, 201, 204, 211, 212
and the psyche, 19, 182–83, 187, 188, 205, 220, 277, 280
and rational powers, 212–14
and real-world correlates, 226, 249–50
and relations of belonging, 225, 277
and signification, 62–63, 159, 182, 198, 205
and simples, 178, 193–94, 201, 277
and truth, 36–37, 153–72, 191–201, 276–77, 282
various theories of, 2–4, 71–72
and verb "to be," 139–48, 202–203
See also logical axioms; *Sophist, The* (Plato); truth
Frege, Gottlob, 3, 118, 281

God
and assertions, 221–22, 283–84
and being, 222, 283, 285
essence of, 25, 221–22, 283
as a first cause, 221, 222, 283
as first measure of genus, 283
gods, 274, 276
and human beings, 283
and measurement, 284
and philosophical wisdom, 24–26, 30, 116, 284, 285
and substance, 283
as thought thinking thought, 12–13, 25, 26, 221–22, 283

and truth, 12–13, 24, 25–26, 30, 116, 283, 285
as unmoved first mover, 283

Halper, Edward, 2, 11, 117
Heidegger, Martin, 3, 72
Homer, 76
Husserl, Edmond, 3, 72

Jaeger, Werner, 2, 10–11, 46–47, 48, 209, 228

Kant, Immanuel, 118
knowledge
and the *Analytics* (Aristotle), 19, 32–33
and assertions, 18–20, 256, 284
and being, 272
and the correlative pair, 268, 269
demonstrative knowledge, 19, 20, 21, 183–84, 213, 270
and first principles of argument, 19, 272
and measurement, 268–72, 284
and noetic comprehension, 18, 19, 20, 272
and numbers, 266–67
and oneness, 266–67
and perceptions, 248–52, 255, 271
and philosophical wisdom, 18, 19, 24, 29, 30, 31, 285
and relatives, 256, 263–71, 272
scientific knowledge, 263, 264–65, 267
and truth, 17–21, 23, 27–30, 31, 248, 251, 255, 284
types of, 17–21
See also measurement

Law of Non-Contradiction (LNC)
and assertions, 37, 50, 66, 89–103
and being, 94–96

Law of Non-Contradiction (LNC)
    (continued)
  and demonstration, 57, 66, 87
  and intermediate assertions, 94–103
  metaphysical LNC, 94, 96, 99
  and Principle of Bivalence, 70–71
  and truth and falsehood, 69, 86,
    96–99, 110–11, 115
Law of the Excluded Middle (LEM)
  and affirmation and denial, 38, 46,
    87–88, 90–93, 104, 106–107
  and contradictory assertions, 109, 110
  and definitions, 57, 68–69, 70, 78,
    109
  and demonstration, 66, 87, 103–
    104, 106–108
  and intermediate assertions, 47,
    49–50, 88, 90, 92–94, 101–103,
    109
  and linguistic and mental
    assertions, 89–93, 107–10
  metaphysical LEM, 94–95, 109
  and relations of belonging, 109
  and truth, 86–88, 109–12, 115
  and truth and falsehood, 45, 46, 48,
    51, 86–88, 109–12, 115
logical axioms
  and assertions, 45, 47, 57, 66,
    85–86, 89–103, 104, 109, 111
  and contradiction, 45, 47, 61, 96,
    103, 111
  defense of, 4, 5, 6, 12, 13, 46, 47,
    50, 51–52, 58, 59–60, 62, 67, 69,
    115, 153, 284
  and demonstration, 57–60, 65–67,
    85, 111
  and elenctic arguments, 284
  and falsehood, 66, 284
  and first principles of reasoning,
    44–45
  and intermediate assertions,
    100–103, 111

Law of Identity (LI), 86
Law of Non-Contradiction (LNC),
  50, 57, 66, 69, 70–71, 86–103,
  110–11, 115
Law of the Excluded Middle
  (LEM), 38, 47, 66, 86–95,
  101–104, 106–10, 115
  and philosophical wisdom, 30,
    44–45
  and truth, 45, 66, 67, 68, 85–88,
    96–99, 110–12, 284
  and truth and falsehood, 38, 66–69,
    86–89, 96–99, 111–12, 284
  vindication of, 39
  See also Law of Non-Contradiction
    (LNC); Law of the Excluded
    Middle (LEM)
Long, Christopher P., 2, 6

Matthen, Mohan, 120, 139–42
measurement
  and the active or passive, 254–55
  Aristotle's doctrine of, 248–50, 254
  and assertions, 7, 237, 251, 254
  and asymmetrical measurement
    relation, 258–73, 275–76
  and being, 237, 251, 256
  and correlates, 251–55, 268, 281
  and the correlative pair, 251–52,
    268
  and correspondence-as-congruence,
    248
  and epistemology, 284
  and exactness, 235–36, 243, 246,
    249–50, 276
  and falsehood, 280, 281
  and first measure of a genus,
    249–50, 259–60, 276
  and first principles, 273
  and God, 284
  and human beings, 71, 246, 274,
    275–76

and human perception, 246–51, 271
and indivisibility, 235–36, 243, 264, 274
and knowledge, 231, 235, 243, 248–50, 251, 263–72, 284
and mind and language, 245
and numbers, 236, 237, 252–54, 255, 259–64, 266–67, 274, 284
and objects of perception and knowledge, 271–72
and oneness, 226–28, 231–45, 251, 266–67, 273, 274–75, 284
and Protagoras's doctrine, 245, 246–48, 249, 265, 271
and quantity, 235, 236, 237, 243, 245–46, 253, 260–61, 273
and relatives, 251–59, 261–64, 265, 267–69, 271
and term "one," 273–75
and things measured, 273, 275, 276
and truth, 5–6, 8, 237, 245, 248, 250–51, 254–55, 258–59, 276, 280, 281, 282
See also oneness; truth
Menn, Stephen, 2, 11
Metaphysics (Aristotle)
and affirmation and denial, 72, 90–93, 117, 121–23, 136–39, 143–48, 151–52, 158, 174, 180–81, 188, 192, 197, 200, 216
and assertions, 6–7, 8, 31, 32, 38, 47–49, 50, 67, 70, 127–29, 140–58, 160–67, 173–74, 178–84, 186–89, 191–93, 197–201, 203–208, 211–12, 222, 243–44, 258–59, 273, 280–83
and being, 12, 13, 17, 36, 43, 44, 70, 77–79, 112, 115–24, 135, 138, 139, 141–54, 157, 173–74, 179–83, 188, 191, 193–200, 202–203, 221, 222, 225, 227, 243, 272–73, 274

book B of, 36–38
and definition, 61–62, 77–78, 83, 115–16, 174, 183–89, 204
and demonstration, 37–38, 59, 60–61, 85–86
different books of, 5, 6–12, 17, 25, 26, 28–32, 39, 44–45, 47, 51–54, 72, 77, 85, 94, 104, 112, 116–18, 124, 142, 152, 160, 172–76, 179–81, 183–89, 191, 193–94, 201–202, 208–209, 211, 214, 221–22, 225, 227–28, 231–32, 238, 240–41, 279
essences in, 183–89, 191, 208–209, 220–21, 222, 228, 232, 235, 237, 238–40, 268–69, 277, 279
and falsehood, 2, 4–7, 12, 25, 36–37, 45–46, 68, 77–78, 83, 86, 111, 112, 115, 117, 118–27, 139, 153–76, 191, 193–220, 225–26, 276–77, 280, 281
and first principles of argument, 11–12, 17, 21, 26, 31, 35–36, 44–46, 67, 68, 117, 183
and God, 12–13, 24–26, 30, 116, 221–22, 283–85
and human cognition, 18, 21, 218, 271–72
and knowledge, 24, 215, 246–48, 263–72, 285
Law of Non-Contradiction (LNC) in, 37, 50, 69, 89–103
and logical axioms, 12, 30, 38, 39, 44, 45, 46, 47, 50–51, 67, 68–69, 85–99, 109–11, 112, 153, 284
and mathematical activities, 254
measurement in, 226–28, 237–44, 245, 246–54, 259–73
and objects of perception and knowledge, 250–58, 271–72
oneness in, 111–12, 184, 188–89, 222, 226–46

Metaphysics (Aristotle) *(continued)*
  and philosophical wisdom, 17–31, 36, 38–39, 43, 116, 183, 213, 221, 225
  potentiality and actuality in, 209–21
  and relations of belonging, 100–103, 225
  relatives in, 250–59, 264–71
  and simples, 187, 191, 193–94, 204, 227, 235
  and substance, 7, 8, 11, 12, 13, 21, 24, 30, 37–39, 44, 176, 178, 183, 184–85, 188, 222, 227, 234–35
  themes of, 4, 11–13, 17, 26, 121, 210–11, 215, 242, 279
  and truth and falsehood, 96–97, 99, 111–12, 118–27, 129–32, 135, 136, 139, 140–49, 153–76, 178, 179–83, 191, 193–201, 209–20, 225–26, 237, 243, 258–59, 276–77, 279–81
  truth in, 1–2, 4–8, 9, 11–13, 17–18, 23, 24–39, 43–52, 68–78, 83, 85–88, 111–12, 115–24, 129, 139, 140–152, 153, 154–176, 191–220, 221, 222, 225–26, 243–44, 279–81
  as a unified work, 9–11, 279
  Wheeler's approach to, 8–13
  See also being; causality; Law of the Excluded Middle (LEM); logical axioms; Matthen, Mohan; philosophical wisdom
Modrak, Deborah, 3, 4, 153, 203, 283
  See also *Aristotle's Theory of Meaning and Language* (Modrak); *Power of Perception, The* (Modrak)

Nicomachean Ethics (Aristotle)
  book VI of, 19
  and human cognition, 18, 284
  and kinds of knowledge, 18–19
  and philosophical wisdom, 18–19, 43
  and rational powers, 212–13
  themes of, 43, 285
  truth in, 21, 22, 23, 284, 285

oneness
  and being, 235, 241
  essence of, 111, 112, 226, 228, 232, 235, 237, 238–40, 242
  as first measure of genus, 231, 232–34, 236, 237, 238, 240–41, 243, 275
  and the individual, 229, 230, 239
  and indivisibility, 229–32, 236, 237–40, 241, 242, 267, 274–75
  kinds of, 184, 188, 227–28, 241–42
  and knowledge, 232–33, 240
  and measurement, 226–28, 231–44, 245, 251, 267, 273–75, 284
  and the naturally continuous, 229–30, 237–38, 240, 241
  and numbers, 188, 189, 230, 232, 240, 241, 242, 259–62, 264, 266–67
  and quantity, 232, 233, 240, 241, 260–61, 274
  and relatives, 261–62
  and signification, 188, 227, 238, 274
  and simplicity, 227
  and substance, 232–35, 237, 240, 274
  and term "one," 226–35, 237–40, 242, 243, 261, 264, 267, 273–75
  and truth, 116, 222, 226
  and the universal, 229, 230
  and wholeness, 229–30, 240
Organon (Aristotle), 43, 47, 61, 282
Owens, Joseph, 2, 6, 11

Peramatzis, Michail, 4, 117
philosophical wisdom
  and acts of assertion, 18–21, 25, 31, 280, 281

and being, 43
and causes of eternal things, 31, 36
defense of, 4
definitions of, 19–21, 24, 31, 36, 43
and demonstrative knowledge, 21, 24–25, 36, 43
and first principles, 11–12, 20–21, 24, 31, 36, 37, 38, 39, 43–45, 183, 221
goal of, 31, 36
and God, 12–13, 24–26, 116, 284, 285
and knowledge, 18–21, 24, 31
nature of, 225, 285
and noetic comprehension, 21, 24–25, 30, 36
and theology, 24
and truth, 2, 7, 11–12, 17–36, 43, 115, 213, 225, 280–81, 285
Physics (Aristotle), 43, 214, 227

Plato
Academy of, 9
as Aristotle's precursor, 50, 71, 142
cave analogy of, 28
Euthyphro of, 257, 258
followers of, 70, 79
and linguistic and mental assertions, 68, 109
and meaning, 4
and truth and falsehood, 71–72, 142, 171
See also *Plato on the Metaphysical Foundations of Meaning and Truth* (Hestir)
Plato on the Metaphysical Foundations of Meaning and Truth (Hestir), 4
Posterior Analytics (Aristotle)
and binary relations of belonging, 100
and causality, 32–34
and common axioms, 57, 103

and contradictions, 91–92
and demonstration, 57, 58, 270
and first principles of argument, 183
and kinds of definition, 54–57, 63, 183, 184
and knowledge, 19, 32–33, 270
and stages view of inquiry, 2, 279
Power of Perception, The (Modrak), 4
practical wisdom, 2, 18, 22–23, 28, 31, 282
Prior Analytics (Aristotle), 91, 120, 121, 139
Pritzl, Kurt, 4
Protagoras, 71, 245–49, 265, 271

Randall, John, 3
Reale, Giovanni, 2, 10, 11
Reeve, C. D. C., 1, 2
Ross, W. D.
and being, 79, 117, 145, 146
and categories, 241
and false things, 134, 200
and mathematical activities, 254
and measurement, 236–37, 275, 276
and oneness, 228, 238–39
and perception and knowledge, 249
and theory of truth, 2, 46–48, 52, 53, 77, 200
Russell, Bertrand, 3, 281

Santayana, George, 3
Socrates
and assertions, 33, 104–105, 245
and being, 117, 196
and substance, 244
and truth and falsehood, 71, 133, 134, 136, 137, 140–50 *passim*, 156, 175
Sophistical Refutations (Aristotle), 58, 59, 282
Sophist, The (Plato), 71, 142

Topics (Aristotle)
  and assertions, 54, 88–89
  and binary relations of belonging, 100
  and circular definitions, 258
  and dialectic reasoning, 58, 59, 88–89
  and first principles of argument, 20
  and kinds of definition, 53–54
  and truth, 282
truth
  activity of, 208–10, 212, 213, 220–21
  and affirmation and denial, 179–80, 182, 183, 188, 197, 200, 213, 225–26, 284
  and "Aristotle on Truth Bearers" (Charles and Peramatzis), 4
  and Aristotle's ontology, 4, 80, 112, 115–24, 176, 193
  and assertions, 5–8, 18–21, 28, 31, 32, 34, 57, 66, 68, 76, 80–82, 85–106, 107, 111, 116, 118, 122, 128–29, 140–58, 162–67, 169–74, 176, 178–81, 188, 191–93, 197–201, 205, 208, 209–13, 215–16, 219, 221–22, 225, 226, 230–31, 237, 243–45, 258–59, 279, 280, 281, 282, 283
  assertoric truth, 160–72, 173, 176, 178, 179, 181–83, 186–88, 191, 193, 197, 199, 200–209, 216, 218–21, 243, 248, 249, 250, 255, 276–77
  canonical definition of, 45–52
  and causality, 32–36, 166–67, 171, 208
  and combinations and divisions, 194, 196–97, 216
  correspondence conception of, 80–83, 226
  and definition of essence, 188–89
  definitions of, 1, 2, 5, 6, 7, 8, 12, 24, 25, 44, 45–57, 62, 63, 64, 65, 68–88, 96–97, 104–107, 109, 110, 111, 112, 115–16, 129, 142, 148–49, 153, 154, 157–61, 164, 167–71, 173, 179, 188, 191–92, 201–208, 220–22, 225–26, 230, 243, 249, 276–77, 279–84
  degrees of, 31, 32, 34, 35
  and demonstrative knowledge, 213
  and dialectic reasoning, 20, 88–89, 106, 111
  different kinds of, 5–7, 31–32, 35, 152–54, 160–64, 167–72, 191, 202, 204, 206, 225, 279, 282, 284
  essence of, 1, 2, 5, 6–9, 12, 43–44, 85, 112, 115, 116, 161, 173, 191, 209, 221, 222, 225, 243, 248, 279
  and first measure of a genus, 244, 280, 281, 283
  and first principles of argument, 28, 31, 32, 115
  and friendship, 285–86
  fundamental truths, 31, 35–36
  genus of, 173–83, 188, 191, 222, 225
  and God, 12–13, 24–26, 30, 221–22, 283–84
  and Hestir's work, 4
  homonymous kinds of, 153–54, 161–63, 167–72, 200–202, 204, 206, 208
  and the intellect, 21–23, 175–78, 250–51, 284, 285
  and knowledge, 17–18, 20–21, 23, 27, 29–30, 215, 245, 251, 255
  and language and thought, 282
  and Law of Non-Contradiction, 115
  and Law of the Excluded Middle (LEM), 86–88, 109–12, 115
  and linguistic and mental assertions, 115, 158, 192, 205, 206, 216, 221, 277, 280, 282–83

and logical axioms, 38, 45, 66–67, 85–88, 96–99, 109–12, 115
and measurement, 5–8, 245, 254–55, 276, 280, 281, 282
nature of, 2, 3, 6, 11–13, 17, 27–30, 39, 43, 44, 116, 178, 211, 219, 220, 279
nominal definition of, 80–83, 85–88, 96, 104–107, 110, 111, 112, 115, 116, 129, 142, 148–49, 153, 157–58, 161, 173, 179, 188, 191, 201–202, 204–208, 222, 225, 279, 284
objectual notions of, 132–39, 153, 154, 160–62, 167–72, 191, 193, 195, 197, 201, 204, 211, 212
and oneness, 6, 8, 116, 222, 226
and philosophical wisdom, 7, 17–36, 43–44, 115, 213, 225, 280–81, 285
and possibility, 214–15
practical truth, 282
and the psyche, 182–83, 187, 188, 206, 243, 250, 271, 277, 280, 284
and rational powers, 212–14, 219
and real-world correlates, 226, 250–51, 280
and relationship with being, 1–2, 7–8, 12, 36, 78–79, 115–24, 135, 138–54, 173, 174, 179–83, 188, 191, 193–96, 199–200, 202–203, 209, 211, 213, 220, 221, 225, 243, 249–50, 273, 279, 281
and relations of belonging, 225, 276–77
and signification, 62–63, 116, 182, 186–87, 197–98, 202, 220, 276, 280, 281
and simples, 178, 191, 193–94, 201, 216
and substance, 8, 21
and true accounts, 156
and true persons, 153–56, 160–62, 164–68, 171, 204
and true things, 125–27, 130–33, 136, 158–60, 171, 175, 200–201
various theories of, 2–4, 8–9, 71–72, 118, 158, 202–203, 280
and verb "to be," 80, 117, 139–48, 195–96, 198–99, 202–203
See also *Metaphysics* (Aristotle); Protagoras

Wedin, Michael, 2, 11
Wheeler, Mark, 8–13, 283

Index Locorum

Aristotle

Categories
2a4–10, 2n2
4a23–b10, 2n2
6a36–37, 251–52
6b2–6, 252
6b6–8, 9n5
6b28–7b14, 252
7a22–23, 9n6
7b22–8a12, 252
8a28–37, 251–52
8a37–b4, 252
11b23, 122, 4n3
12b5–16, 122–23, 128, 130
12b15–16, 4n3
13a37–b35, 2n2
14b11–23, 2n2
14b14–23, 140

De Anima
412b8–9, 195
418a5, 1n2
421a20, 1n2
424a20, 1n2
426b20, 1n2
427a20, 1n2
427b2–17, 2n2
427b7, 1n2

427b8–20, 2n2
428a1–2, 177
428a5, 1n2
428a11–18, 2n2
428b10–429a2, 2n2
428b30–429a4, 176–77
430a26–b6, 2n2
430a27–b5, 4n5
430b6, 238
430b26–30, 182
430b26–31, 7n2
430b27–33, 4n5
431b2, 177
431b10–18, 2n2
431b26–432a6, 177
432a7–14, 177
432a10–14, 2n2, 4n5
449b20, 1n2

De Interpretatione
16a6–8, 176
16a8–13, 4n5
16a9–19, 2n2
16a32–b5, 2n2
16b26–17a7, 2n2
16b33–17a26, 4n5
17a1–7, 191–92
17a2–3, 20, 4n27
17a23–34, 128–30

Aristotle, *De Interpretatione* (continued)
17a25–26, 20, 4n27
17a31–37, 90–91
17a38–18a7. 2n2
17b27–28, 4n27
18a12–27, 2n2
18a28–19b4, 2n2
21b18–19, 2n2
23a27–24b9, 2n2
23b17–21, Cn1

Eudemean Ethics
1215a35–b5, 22
1221b27–30, 22–23

Metaphysics
980a22, 17
982a1–3, 17
982a4–6, 23–24
982a6–19, 1n6
982a19–b8, 24
982b11–28, 24
982b30–983a3, 24
983a21–23, 26
983a4–11, 24
993a30–31, 29
993a30–b19, 26
993a30–b7, 27
993b4–6, 29
993b7–11, 27–28
993b19–20, 31
993b19–31, 26
993b23–31, 31–36
995a24–25, 37
995a27–36, 1
995b5–8, 37
996b26–33, 37–38
997a12–15, 38
1003a33–b15, 4n16
1003b22–1004a2, 2n34
1005a33–b8, 44
1005b5–8, 44

1005b19–20, 94
1005b23–24, 95–96
1005b26–27, 97–99, 111–12, 115
1005b32–34, 110
1005b35–1006a2, 111
1006a3–4, 94–95, 110
1006a11, 2n29
1006a11–27, 59–60, 65
1006a13–15, 2n36
1006a15, 58
1006a15–16, 2n29
1006a18–21, 60–61, 65
1006a22–24, 2n36
1006a24–25, 61
1006a26–28, 2n33
1006a31–b18, 2n34
1006a32–34, 64
1006b1–4, 64
1006b10–11, 64
1006b11–13, 64
1006b11–18, 64
1006b12–13, 63
1006b18–22, 95
1006b25–28, 63
1006b32–35, 102
1007b18, 94
1009a6–15, 140
1009a16–1011a13, 3n3
1011b13–22, 96–97
1011b23–24, 90, 92–93, 3n12
1011b23–28, 57
1011b23–29, 46–53, 68–71, 77, 87–88, 103–111, 2n6, 3n5, 3n19
1011b25, 2n16, 2n20, 2n64
1011b25–27, 129
1011b26–27, 1, 5–7, 12, 45–46, 60, 62, 70–71, 71–83, 86–87, 97, 142, 148–52, 153, 158, 161, 173–75, 179, 188, 191, 2n5, 2n19, 2n41, 2n54, 2n57, 2n58, 2n62, 3n15, 4n31, 5n15
1011b28, 3n23
1011b29, 3n13

Index Locorum

1012a3, 51
1012a5, 3n13
1012a9, 3n13
1012a21–24, 51, 61, 69
1012a22–25, 2n21
1012b21, 3n13
1012b5–8, 62, 69
1012b7–11, 51–52
1015a33–36, 102
1015b16, 240
1015b16–1015b34, 237
1015b16–1017a2, 238, 242
1015b35–1016a17, 237–38
1015b36–1016a17, 8n20
1016a17–b6, 8n20
1016a17–1017a17, 238
1016a21–1017a3, 242
1016a31, 8n16
1016a32–b3, 238–39
1016a32–b6, 8n12
1016a34, 8n14
1016b3–6, 239
1016b5, 8n16
1016b6, 8n17
1016b6–11, 239–40
1016b11–17, 240, 8n12
1016b17–21, 240–41
1016b17–31, 8n12
1016b18, 8n3
1016b21–23, 241
1016b23, 8n20
1016b23–31, 241
1016b25–26 8n21
1016b31, 8n11
1016b31–1017a6, 241–42
1017a7, 119
1017a18–22, 118
1017a22–30, 118
1017a31–32, 120–24
1017a31–33, 146, 180–81
1017a31–35, 117–19, 139–48, 152, 173, 188, 4n2, 4n3, 4n8, 4n13, 4n29

1017a32–33, 135–36
1017a33–35, 124, 126–27, 131, 133–39
1017a35–b9, 118
1019b21–32, 211
1019b21–35, 213
1020a13, 9n12
1020b26–32, 252, 255
1020b32–1021a14, 252
1021a12–14, 252–53
1021a14–1021a26, 253–54
1021a26–29, 255
1021a26–30, 263
1021a26–b3, 255
1021a29–30, 255–56, 258
1021a30–b3, 256–58
1024b17–20, 5n3
1024b17–26, 124–27, 129–32, 136–39, 154, 158–59, 200, 4n3, 4n8, 7n12, 7n13
1024b18–20, 159–60
1024b26–1025a1, 154, 156–58, 160–71, 5n8
1025a1–13, 154–56
1026a19, 24
1027b18–19, 6n4
1027b18–25, 173–4, 178–82
1027b25–27, 7n12
1027b25–28, 175
1027b25–29, 193
1027b27–28, 194
1027b28–29, 178, 195–96, 7n4, 7n8
1027b29, 191
1027b29–31, 178
1027b29–33, 175–76, 194–96
1027b31, 202–3, 7n12
1027b34–1028a1, 176
1028a1–3, 173
1028a10–31, 4n16
1029b3–13, 28–29, 35
1029b14, 8n14
1029b29, 183–84
1030a2–1031a13, 2n21

Aristotle, *Metaphysics* (continued)
1030b3, 184
1030b4–23, 183
1031a12, 184
1031b18–22, 183
1034a31, 184
1034b20, 184, 186
1034b20–1038a36, 2n21
1037a17–20, 183
1037b8–27, 183
1038a5, 186
1038a19, 186
1038a25, 186
1038a28–30, 183
1038b6–16, 183
1039a12, 9n12
1039a15–23, 184–85
1040b16–27, 183
1042a16–23, 2n21
1042a20, 186
1043a12–1044a14, 2n21
1043b27, 188
1045a15, 187–88
1045a7–20, 2n21
1045b26–28, 213–214
1046a4–9, 211, 213
1048a25–30, 7n25
1048b18–36, 217–18
1050a34–1051b6, 203–4
1051a34–b13, 127–28
1051a34–b2, 194–96, 211
1051a34–b2, 211
1051a34–b23, 7n20
1051b1–2, 202–3, 7n12, 7n13
1051b2–17, 196–97, 211, 216
1051b3–5, 7n6
1051b5–6, 200
1051b9–15, 199
1051b17–1052a4, 193–94
1051b17–25, 198–99
1051b17–33, 211, 217

1051b21–25, 200
1051b33–35, 199–201
1051b33–1052a1, 125–27, 136–39
1051b33–1052a4, 211, 219
1052a4–14, 211, 219
1052a15–16, 227, 228
1052a15–b1, 229
1052a19, 8n8
1052a19–21, 8n12
1052a19–29, 229–30
1052a22–28, 8n12
1052a29–34, 230, 8n12
1052a36–b1, 230
1052b1–1053a14, 231
1052b1–1053b8, 228
1052b3–5, 229
1052b15–1053b8, 8n12
1052b15–19, 231
1052b20–24, 231
1052b24–31, 232
1052b31–34, 235
1052b34–36, 235
1052b36–1053a14, 236
1052b7, 8n7
1052b7–15, 228
1053a14–20, 233–34, 236, 246
1053a1–b3, 265
1053a5–8, 245–46
1053a20–24, 236
1053a24–25, 233–34, 236–37
1053a31–35, 247–48
1053a31–b3, 251, 271
1053a31–b8, 246–47
1053a35–36, 9n2
1053a35–b3, 246–47
1053b25–28, 233–34
1053b28–1054a5, 233–34
1054a5–9, 234
1054a9–19, 235
1055b8–10, 3n2
1056b16–20, 262

1056b16–32, 259
1056b20–1057a17, 259
1056b20–22, 260–61
1056b32–1057a1, 9n8
1056b32–33, 261–63
1056b33–1057a1, 262–64
1057a4–17, 264–67
1060b31–1061a10, 4n16
1064b3, 24
1069b27, 4n2
1072a32–34, 226–27, 273, 8n2
1072b2–4, 283
1072b10–11, 283
1072b24–30, 283
1072b26–27, 283
1074b34–35, 283
1087a2–3, 9n12
1087a4–8, 9n12
1087b33–1088a14, 273–76
1089b26–28, 4n2
1051b1–5, 200

Nicomachean Ethics
1055a3–6, 285
1096a14–17, 285
1108a19–23, 5n4
1111b31–34, 2n2
1124b6, 2n2
1127a13–32, 5n4
1127b2, 2n2
1139a27–31, 22
1139b12–13, 22
1139b15, 1n14, 212–13
1139b15–18, 18, 284, 2n2
1139b31, 191141a3–8, 2n2
1140a20–23, 213
1140b31, 19
1141a8, 19
1141a18–20, 19
1141b1, 1n7
1141b2–3, 19

1142b10–11, 2n2
1169b7–10, 285

Physics
185b7, 8n12

Posterior Analytics
71b9–17, 34
71b19–22, 34
71b33–72a6, 35
71a14, 103
71b17–26, 20
71b25–26, 58
72a7, 58
72a8–9, 57–58
72a8–14, 91–92
72a11–13, 57
72a14–16, 57
72a20, 57
72a21–24, 57
76a41, 3n2
76b14–15, 58
77a22–23, 3n6
77a30, 3n6
81b18–29, 2n2
88b1, 3n6
89b24–25, 55
90a14–15, 55
93a27–29, 2n25
93b29–30, 55
93b29–37, 54, 56
93b35, 184
93b39–40, 54
94a7–9, 54
94a20–24, 33

Prior Analytics
24a10–b17, 20
24a17, 91, 3n11
43b6–11, Cn1
47a8–9, 2n2

Aristotle, *Prior Analytics* (continued)
48b1–3, 120–21, 139
49a6–10, 120–21, 139
52a24–38, 121, 2n2, 4n17
53b4–57b17, 2n2, Cn1
64b9–10, 2n2

Rhetoric
1355a14–19, 2n2, Cn1

Sophistical Refutations
164b25, 58
170a39, 58
171a1, 58
174b19, 58
178b24–29, 2n2
174b36, 58

Topics
100a27–30, 20
101b3–6, 53
101b19, 53
111a14–20, 2n2
130b25–26, 53
139a37–b3, 2n2

149b4–9, 2n2, Cn1
Topics 157b26–31, 2n2, Cn1
Topics 160a24–28, 2n2, Cn1

Lysias
10.7, 8n7

Plato

Cratylus
385b2–11, 71
394b3, 8n7

Euthyphro
10b–c, 257

Hippias Minor
365–75, 171

Sophist
240d1–241a1, 71
263a11–16, 71–72

Protagoras
DK 81 B1, 71

www.ingramcontent.com/pod-product-compliance
Lightning Source LLC
Chambersburg PA
CBHW030127240426
43672CB00005B/45